Lecture Notes in Computer Science

Commenced Publication in 1973
Founding and Former Series Editors:
Gerhard Goos, Juris Hartmanis, and Jan van Leeuwen

T0238159

Mike Hazas   John Krumm
Thomas Strang (Eds.)

Location- and Context-Awareness

Second International Workshop, LoCA 2006
Dublin, Ireland, May 10-11, 2006
Proceedings

Volume Editors

Mike Hazas
Lancaster University
Computing Department, Infolab
South Drive, Lancaster, LA1 4WA, UK
E-mail: hazas@comp.lancs.ac.uk

John Krumm
Microsoft Corporation
One Microsoft Way, Redmond, WA 98052, USA
E-mail: jckrumm@microsoft.com

Thomas Strang
Deutsches Zentrum für Luft- und Raumfahrt
P.O. Box 1116, 82234 Wessling/Oberpfaffenhofen, Germany
E-mail: Thomas.Strang@dlr.de

Library of Congress Control Number: 2006924878

CR Subject Classification (1998): H.3, H.4, C.2, H.5, K.8

LNCS Sublibrary: SL 3 – Information Systems and Application, incl. Internet/Web
and HCI

ISSN   0302-9743
ISBN-10   3-540-34150-1 Springer Berlin Heidelberg New York
ISBN-13   978-3-540-34150-5 Springer Berlin Heidelberg New York

Springer is a part of Springer Science+Business Media

springer.com

© Springer-Verlag Berlin Heidelberg 2006
Printed in Germany

Typesetting: Camera-ready by author, data conversion by Scientific Publishing Services, Chennai, India
Printed on acid-free paper   SPIN: 11752967   06/3142   5 4 3 2 1 0

Preface

These proceedings contain the papers presented at the 2nd International Workshop on Location- and Context-Awareness in May of 2006. As computing moves increasingly into the everyday world, the importance of location and context knowledge grows. The range of contexts encountered while sitting at a desk working on a computer is very limited compared to the large variety of situations experienced away from the desktop. For computing to be relevant and useful in these situations, the computers must have knowledge of the user's activity, resources, state of mind, and goals, i.e., the user's context, of which location is an important indicator. This workshop was intended to present research aimed at sensing, inferring, and using location and context data in ways that help the user.

Our call for papers resulted in 74 submissions, each of which was assigned to members of our Program Committee. After reviews and email discussion, we selected 18 papers for publication in these proceedings. Most of the accepted papers underwent a shepherding process by a reviewer or a member of the Program Committee to ensure that the reviewers' comments were accounted for in the published version. We feel our selective review process and shepherding phase have resulted in a high-quality set of published papers.

We extend a sincere "thank you" to all the authors who submitted papers, to our hard-working Program Committee, our thoughtful reviewers, and our conscientious shepherds.

May 2006 Mike Hazas and John Krumm, Program Co-chairs
Thomas Strang, Workshop Chair

Organization

Program Committee

Gaetano Borriello	University of Washington and Intel Research Seattle
Anind Dey	Carnegie Mellon University
William Griswold	University of California, San Diego
Robert Harle	University of Cambridge
Jeffrey Hightower	Intel Research Seattle
Minkyong Kim	Dartmouth College
Gabriele Kotsis	Johannes Kepler University of Linz
Marc Langheinrich	ETH Zurich
Claudia Linnhoff-Popien	Ludwig Maximilian University Munich
Henk Muller	University of Bristol
Chandrasekhar Narayanaswami	IBM T.J. Watson Research Center
Harlan Onsrud	University of Maine
Donald Patterson	University of California, Irvine
Thorsten Prante	Fraunhofer IPSI
Aaron Quigley	University College Dublin
Bernt Schiele	Darmstadt University of Technology
Chris Schmandt	MIT Media Lab
Flavia Sparacino	Sensing Places and MIT
Thomas Strang	German Aerospace Center and University of Innsbruck
Yasuyuki Sumi	Kyoto University
Hiroyuki Tarumi	Kagawa University
Daniel Wilson	Author

Reviewers

Ian Anderson	University of Bristol
Michael Beigl	University of Karlsruhe
Alastair Beresford	University of Cambridge
David Cottingham	University of Cambridge
Florian Fuchs	Siemens and Ludwig Maximilian University Munich
Caroline Funk	Ludwig Maximilian University Munich
Thomas Grill	Johannes Kepler University of Linz
Tom Gross	Bauhaus University Weimar
Sinem Guven	Columbia University
Ismail Ibrahim	Johannes Kepler University of Linz
Axel Küpper	Ludwig Maximilian University Munich
David Molyneaux	Lancaster University
Mandayam Raghunath	IBM T.J. Watson Research Center

Anand Ranganathan	IBM T.J. Watson Research Center
Wieland Schwinger	Johannes Kepler University of Linz
Peter Tandler	Fraunhofer IPSI
Georg Treu	Ludwig Maximilian University Munich
Diana Weiss	Ludwig Maximilian University Munich

Shepherds

Alastair Beresford	University of Cambridge
Gaetano Borriello	University of Washington and Intel Research Seattle
Sinem Guven	Columbia University
Robert Harle	University of Cambridge
Mike Hazas	Lancaster University
Jeffrey Hightower	Intel Research Seattle
Minkyong Kim	Dartmouth College
Marc Langheinrich	ETH Zurich
Henk Muller	University of Bristol
Aaron Quigley	University College Dublin
Flavia Sparacino	Sensing Places and MIT
Daniel Wilson	Author

Table of Contents

Context Sensing

Social Context

Representation and Programming

Particle Filters for Position Sensing with Asynchronous Ultrasonic Beacons*

Henk L. Muller, Michael McCarthy, and Cliff Randell

Department of Computer Science, University of Bristol, UK
http://www.cs.bris.ac.uk/

Abstract. In this paper we present a user-centric position sensing system that is based on asynchronous, independent ultrasonic beacons. These stationary transmitter units are small, cheap to manufacture, and have power requirements low enough to run each from a small solar cell and a nearby light source. Each beacon is programmed to emit a short, 40 kHz ultrasonic signal with a unique transmission period. The mobile receiver unit first associates a received signal with a beacon based on the observed periodicity, then measures the Doppler shift in the periodicity that results from movements of the receiver. Using Doppler shifts from a number of different beacons, the receiver is able to estimate both its position and velocity by employing a particle filter. In this paper, we describe our positioning algorithm, the hardware, and proof-of-concept results.

1 Introduction

There are many design decisions involved in building a positioning system. Traditionally, accuracy and system costs are the two most important factors. Other factors include the weight and power consumption of the mobile unit, the refresh rate, whether the system is user-based or infrastructure-based, the positioning coverage, the ease of setup and maintenance, and aesthetic impact.

We present a system which has been designed to optimise aesthetics and component costs. The system is based around small, low power beacons that are fixed within a room. The beacons are also wireless and independent, making it possible to minimise their visual impact. We do not use RF or any other synchronising technology, which helps to minimise power consumption and bring component numbers down. The power consumption of the beacons is sufficiently low to enable them to be powered by a small solar cell, illuminated by a nearby domestic or office light source.

The beacons produce only minimal information: they transmit ultrasonic signals (or 'chirps') with a regular periodicity, usually around 500 ms. The receiver unit consists of an ultrasonic transducer and a medium-power processing device. It approximates its position with an accuracy of, at present, 25 cm by measuring the Doppler shift in the transmission periods. This accuracy may seem low, but we expect it to be adequate for use in coarse-grained location-based applications such as automated museum guides or indoor navigation aids. Also, we believe that the accuracy can be improved by fine tuning the system.

---

* Funding for this work is received from the U.K. Engineering and Physical Sciences Research Council as part of the Equator IRC, GR-N-15986.

M. Hazas, J. Krumm, and T. Strang (Eds.): LoCA 2006, LNCS 3987, pp. 1–13, 2006.

In the design space, we have made a trade-off between costs and aesthetics on the one hand, and accuracy on the other hand. Our accuracy is better than that obtained with some RF based systems such as those using WiFi [1] but not as accurate as other ultrasound-based positioning systems [2, 3, 4]. Our system is similar to the Cricket [5] in that wireless beacons are used to infer position. However, we believe that our design provides a new contribution by minimising the size and power consumption of the devices in the infrastructure. By setting this as our main design constraint we have been forced to come up with novel methods for inferring position.

In the rest of this paper, we first introduce the problem domain in Section 2, then present our algorithms in Sections 3, 4 and 5. Section 6 details the hardware that we used for the initial results, which are shown in Section 7. We discuss improvements that we believe can be made to our algorithms in Section 8.

2   The Problem

Our positioning system comprises a number of beacons scattered around a room (mostly along the ceiling and walls) and one or more mobile receivers that can position themselves using the signals received.

The beacon units (described in detail in Section 6) have been designed to be simple, low power, and require no wiring. In order to reduce complexity, they only transmit ultrasound. The mobile receivers are untethered, and comprise an ultrasonic microphone, amplifier, and a processing unit to estimate position and velocity.

The principle mode of operation of our system is to estimate the position by measuring the Doppler shift in the periodicity of each of the beacons. We assume that the receiver knows that there are N beacons in a room (around eight), and that the receiver knows the position T_i of each beacon i ($0 \leq i < N$). Furthermore, the receiver has knowledge of the transmission periods P_i, which are around 500 ms.

The receiving unit will ideally receive a pulse train as shown in Figure 1. The horizontal axis is time in seconds, the vertical bars denote the arrival of a chirp from a beacon. Because of the different periodicities of, for example, Beacons 6 and 0, their reception times shift relative to each other. A real chirp train that has been recorded using our hardware is shown in Figure 2. Some signals have gone missing altogether (such as the signal from Beacon 6), some signals collide (chirps from Beacons 2 and 3 arrive simultaneously at time 1006), and there are reflections and noise (signified by shorter bars) which muddle the picture.

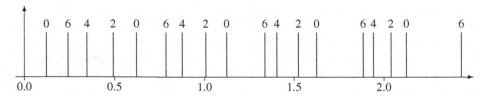

Fig. 1. Ideal chirp trace received from four beacons

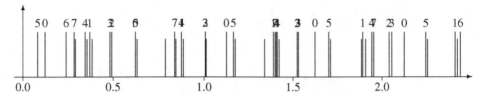

Fig. 2. Actual chirp trace received from eight beacons. Note that the labelling is added for clarification only, no identification is received.

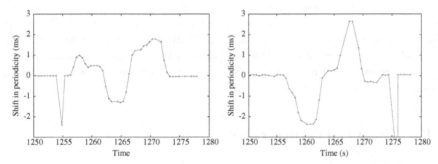

Fig. 3. Deviations from mean periods for two receivers over a period of time. The time (X-axis) is measured in seconds, the deviation (Y-axis) is measured in milliseconds.

When the receiver is static, the reception time of the pulses from each beacon are spaced by their periods P_i. This is a method for determining the correspondence between pulses and beacons; a series of chirps separated by P_i is likely to come from Beacon i. Measurements from a static receiver also enable us to measure transmission periods P_i to a high precision. This may be necessary as clock crystals used in the beacons and the receiver will have slightly different frequencies (up to 500 ppm). This difference may cause drifting of the position when not corrected for.

When the receiver is moving, the transmission periods will appear to vary. As it moves through the tracking area, the receiver's distance to each beacon will change. This will affect the time that it takes for the signals to travel, causing the separation between chirps to vary. The changes in separation observed by the receiver is, essentially, a Doppler shift in the periodicity of each beacon. If the receiver moves towards a beacon, the pulses will be brought closer together; if the receiver moves away, the pulses will be pushed further apart. To illustrate, some measured Doppler shifts are provided in Figure 3. Note that the outlying downward spikes are caused by missing chirps, all other deviations are caused by the receiver's movement.

The amount the pulses shift is proportional to the distance moved over the period:

$$\Delta d = v_s \Delta P_i$$

Here, Δd is the movement of the receiver relative to the beacon and v_s is the speed of sound, 343 ms^{-1}. This distance is equal to the distance travelled in the direction of the beacon over the time period $P_i + \Delta P_i$ [6]:

$$\Delta d = \frac{(X_0 - T_i)}{|X_0 - T_i|} \cdot (X_0 - X_{P_i + \Delta P_i})$$

Hence,

$$v_s \Delta P_i = \frac{(X_0 - T_i)}{|X_0 - T_i|} \cdot (X_0 - X_{P_i + \Delta P_i}) \tag{1}$$

Equation 1 formulates a relationship between two expressions: one containing the speed of sound v_s and the shift in periodicity ΔP_i on the left-hand side; and the other containing the previous position of the mobile receiver X_0, the location T_i of transmitter i and the current position $X_{P_i + \Delta P_i}$ (the current time is $P_i + \Delta P_i$, where P_i is the periodicity of transmitter i) on the right-hand side. With a sufficient number of readings, it is possible to iteratively estimate the receiver position using this equation. We have found that a particle filter is capable of performing this estimation, even in the presence of noise.

3   Background on Particle Filters

In order to estimate position, we use *particle filters* in two different parts of our algorithm. In this section, we provide a brief background on this type of estimator.

Particle filters [7] are a method to approximate random variables. This is similar to a Kalman filter [8, 9], except that a particle filter can cope with arbitrary error distributions and, in particular, with multi-modal distributions.

A particle filter requires two sets of equations to operate. One set of equations models state progression. This is similar to the state transition of a Kalman filter, except that random noise is added to the state on every iteration. This noise should be distributed according to the variation that is expected in the system over that period of time.

The second set of equations should compute the likelihood of a measured observation, given a particular state of the system. This likelihood function models the error distribution of the measurements.

A particle filter operates by maintaining a number of states in parallel, called *particles*. Each particle is progressed using the state equations, after which the likelihood of each particle is computed. The probability distribution function (PDF) of the state space is modelled by the particles, and can have any shape, as long as there are enough particles to sample this shape.

In order to prevent the filter from deteriorating, the filter can be periodically *resampled*. Resampling is performed by first translating the set of likelihoods into a cumulative distribution function (CDF). The CDF can be sampled using a uniform random number, duplicating particles in areas of the state space that have a high probability, and removing particles in the areas of the state space that have a low probability.

The final stage of a particle filter is to distill a single state from the particles. In many cases the *mean* state of all particles is useful, especially on single-modal distributions. In multi-modal state spaces one can compute the *mode* of the distribution, which can be problematic as the mode of the state can change dramatically from one iteration to the next.

In comparison with a Kalman filter, a particle filter is advantageous if it is expensive to compute the Jacobian of the measurement equation, if the state space errors are multimodal, or if one intends to use low precision arithmetic.

Particle filters have been used in the estimation of location successfully before. They have been used both for low level filtering of data, and in order to fuse sensor information at a high level (see for example [10, 11]).

4 Associating Chirps with Beacons

The first problem is that of associating each chirp in Figure 2 with a beacon, or classifying it as a reflection or noise. The only information that is available to the receiver is an estimate of the periodicity of each beacon. It is an estimate in that the clock crystals on each beacon are only cut with a limited precision, and their frequency varies with temperature. The typical variation is in the order of 50 ppm, or 25 μs in a 500 ms period. In addition, movement of the receiver will cause further variation. Assuming a maximum movement of the receiver of 2 ms^{-1}, we expect this to be on the order of $2/v_s = 2/343 = 0.58\%$, or 2.9 ms in a 500 ms period.

Our strategy to solve the measurement association problem is to use a particle filter to model each beacon. The particle filter modelling beacon i estimates the time that this beacon produced its first chirp, a value that we call the *Epoch* and represent using the variable E (a number between 0 and P_i). Hence, the state of the filter is just a one-dimensional variable that tracks E. The state progression function adds noise to the state with a standard deviation of 50 μs.

When a chirp is received at time t, the likelihood function is applied to the particle filter. For a particle j with value E_j, the likelihood of $t - E_j$ is computed using the sawtooth curve in Figure 4. If the chirp corroborates the epoch time of the particle, then the probability will fall on one of the peaks of the sawtooth. If it is off by, say, half a period, then the particle will be unsupported. If the signal is slightly late, then the probably function shows intermediate support (the diagonal of the sawtooth) as the chirp may be a reflection of the original signal. The closer to the peak a measurement is, the more likely that it is a reflection. Particles will converge first on all sequences of signals that are P apart, including systematic reflections. The groups of particles

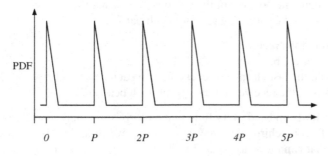

Fig. 4. Likelihood for a particle to associate with a beacon

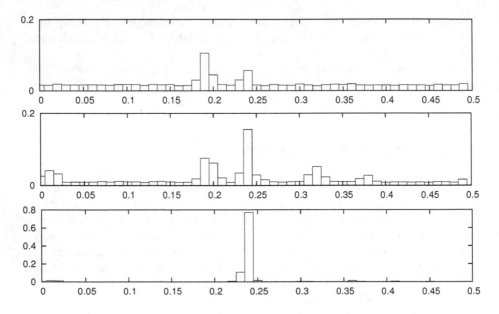

Fig. 5. Distribution of the particle filter after 0.5, 1 and 2 seconds

tracking reflections will climb up the slope and merge with the main group, latching on to the actual chirps from the beacon.

The evolution of the distribution of particles is visualised in Figure 5, which shows the probability distribution functions of the particles for Beacon 0. The graphs are 0.5, 1, and 2 seconds into the run, showing that the particles latch onto Beacon 0 after 2 seconds (equivalent to four chirps).

It is possible for the particle filter to latch onto noise that is roughly separated by P_i. In order to avoid this, we keep refreshing a fraction of the particles if we have not yet observed a consistent signal. Using this method, we usually latch onto all beacons within a 10 second period.

5   Estimating the Position of the Receiver

In order to estimate the position of the receiver we use another particle filter. This position filter maintains the following state for each particle:

X the position of the receiver
V the velocity of the receiver
R_i the time that the last chirp was received from each beacon i $(0 \leq i < N)$
O_i the position of the receiver at time R_i for each beacon i

The particle filter is updated every time that a chirp is uniquely associated with one of the beacons. That is, chirps that may have come from multiple beacons are ignored, as are chirps that cannot be associated with any beacons. A chirp is associated with a beacon if it falls within a 4 ms window around the expected arrival time of that beacon.

This window size excludes most reflected signals. A better method for dealing with reflections, occlusions and collisions is under investigation and is discussed in Section 8.

5.1 State Progression

State progression comprises two parts. The first part integrates the velocity into position and updates the velocity:

$$X = X + \Delta t V \tag{2}$$

$$V = V + \Delta t A \tag{3}$$

where A is a noise term representing the acceleration. We assume that the acceleration is normally distributed with a mean of 2 ms^{-2} in the X and Y directions and a mean of 0.1 ms^{-2} in the Z direction. This models a receiver which is mounted on a person, where we expect little movement in the Z direction.

The second part of the state progression deals with the update of R_i and O_i, where i is the number of the beacon from which we have just received a chirp. R_i is set to the current time and O_i is set to the value of X.

5.2 Likelihood

The likelihood function of the particle filter gives us the probability of the state being supported by a measurement. A measurement comprises the difference in the periodicity of the signal ΔP_i from Beacon i. The two sides of Equation 1 calculate the distance that the receiver has travelled relative to Beacon i. The left-hand side computes this distance in terms of ΔP_i, whereas the right-hand side computes it in terms of the past and current position of the receiver. The difference between these values is a metric for the particle's error:

$$\epsilon = v_s \Delta P_i - \frac{(O_i - T_i)}{|O_i - T_i|} \cdot (O_i - X)$$

We translate the error ϵ into a support measure by using the following formula:

$$p_i = \frac{c}{c + \epsilon^2}$$

where c is a constant that controls how sharp the distribution is. At $\epsilon = 0$, the likelihood will be 1, whereas at a distance of $\epsilon = \sqrt{c}$, the likelihood will be $\frac{1}{2}$. We use a c value of 0.1, equivalent to a distance of 31 cm.

The likelihood function presented above gives us the likelihood given one measurement only. The state-space is six-dimensional, and this measurement only constrains one degree of freedom. A successive series of measurements provides a series of constraints, eventually forcing the particles to converge on the solution.

6 Prototype Hardware

We have constructed two hardware prototypes: one that we have used for measurement and testing, and one that we are developing for future deployment. The rig that we have used for measurement is wired, but is programmed to behave as an asynchronous system.

Fig. 6. Light-powered beacon, top view and bottom view. The solar panel measures 23 by 20 mm, the unit is mounted by means of Blue-tac.

6.1 Hardware Used for Measurement

The hardware that we have used for the tests and measurements in this paper is a re-programmed configuration that we have used for other experiments. It consists of eight beacons that are placed on the ceiling and walls. Each beacon is wired to a control unit that controls the transmission activity. The control unit is programmed to generate a 10 cycle chirp for each beacon, with unique periodicities of 500, 508, ..., 556 ms.

The main difference between this setup and the prototype under-development is that even though the beacons appear to be asynchronous in the wired system, all eight are actually guaranteed to collide once every 13 millenia. On the other hand, the hardware in development uses beacons with independent clock crystals, meaning that collisions in this system happen randomly with a low probability.

6.2 Prototype for Deployment

The prototype hardware that we intend to use with the system is shown in Figure 6. It is composed of eight components:

- an open face ultrasonic transducer
- a radial inductor
- a PIC micro-controller
- a ceramic resonator
- 3 capacitors
- a solar panel of 3x4 cm (less than 2 square inch)

Optionally, the system can be powered by a 3V battery, obviating the need for the solar cell and one of the capacitors.

The periodic chirps are entirely generated in software. In order to create a 40 KHz signal, the PIC pulls two of its output pins up and down in a complementary fashion. For example, when pin 1 is up, pin 2 is down and vice versa. This generates a 6V ptp swing from a 3V supply. The ferrite cored inductor is tuned to resonate with the piezoelectric transducer resulting in a signal of over 12V ptp at 40 KHz. The consequent sound pressure level (SPL) is in excess of 105 dBm for a period of 250 μs. The transducer is selected for a wide beam angle of 140 deg at -12 dB.

Fig. 7. Beacon mounted in a standard office light

Flipping beacon output pins into one state and back again in this fashion takes two instructions. Given that each instruction consumes four clock cycles, we need to run the PIC at at least (or multiples of) 320 KHz to generate a 40 KHz signal. The system also needs to sleep for around 500 ms before transmitting the next chirp. The "official" method for implementing a low-power suspend mode is to use the PIC's on-chip RC watchdog timer. However, this method is temperature sensitive and can cause timing to degrade. Instead, our program sits in a tight loop performing NOP instructions and uses the interrupt timer to break out for the next chirp.

In order to run the system from a solar panel, it is essential that we take power consumption down to less than 100 μA. We do this by running the PIC with a 640 KHz ceramic resonator. We were unable to find a suitable 320 KHz resonator, however if one was available, the size of the solar panel could be further reduced.

The range of the beacon unit is over 7m, and needs to be mounted close to a light source; preferably fixed to the inside of a shade or reflector, such as shown in Figure 7. The range of the signal can be extended by using a solar panel that produces 6V rather than 3V. Although this is just a matter of a change in wiring, manufacturers have no interest in building small panels that are high voltage with low ampage.

7 Results

Our test environment consists of eight beacons on the ceiling and walls, and one receiver. The eight beacons are actually wired up to one controller (because at present we only have one light powered beacon), but the controller is programmed to fire the beacons independently. The minimum number of beacons that our system requires is six, because of the six degrees of freedom in the solution: speed and velocity in three dimensions. Six is however not sufficient because occlusions and collisions between signals reduce the effective use of the beacons. If we use more than eight beacons, it is necessary to reduce the transmission periods so as to prevent saturation of the 40 KHz frequency band.

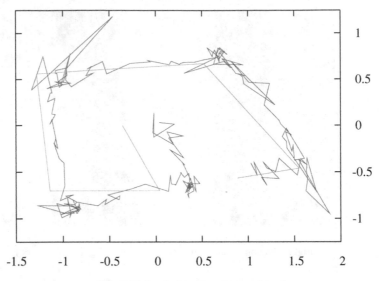

Fig. 8. Estimated track and moved track

Our test track consists of a more or less rectangular track, 2.5 by 1.4 metres, 60cm off the floor (2m below the receivers). It starts near the origin, and moves around the rectangle clockwise once. We move with varying speeds, stopping at the corners for a few seconds in order to test our filter. In the nature of using Doppler effects, we expect the receiver to be tracked best when it is moving.

The receiver is left stationary for two minutes in order for the algorithm to lock onto the beacons. The rectagular track is then completed in 20 seconds, of which 2-3 seconds is spent in each corner. The receiver is moved at 1-2 ms^{-1} between the corner points. We initialise the filter with particles scattered around the space with the mean centred at the origin; around 30 cm from the receiver's starting point.

The results are shown in Figure 8. The green line is the track that we followed, the red line is the track that the particle filter recovered. We make a couple of observations. First, along the straight lines, where the receiver moves relatively fast, the particle filter appears to track the direction of movement quite well. In the corners, where the receiver stops moving for a couple of seconds, the particle filter deviates. This is observed in the top left-hand corner where the deviation is around 70 cm.

7.1 Errors

The average error is 20-30 cm, while the maximum error is 70 cm. The results may seem poor, but the errors are small in absolute terms. When the system is deployed in a bigger room, we expect the errors to stay roughly the same in absolute terms, becoming smaller in relative terms. We note also, that this is an untuned first version of the system.

The errors can be attributed to two causes. The first source of error is caused by beacons "dropping out" due to occlusions and collisions. A second source of error is caused by the nature of the particle filter; random movements of particles will cause fluctuations in the measurements.

It appears that, in general, the system is better at recovering velocity than it is at recovering position. If we re-run the particle filter on the measured track data, seeded with different random values, then we get different deviations in the position. However, in all cases, the movements seem to be precisely in the right direction. We are at present investigating the cause of this.

7.2 Failure Modes

The worst failure mode occurs when the receiver does not lock onto the beacons successfully. In this case, the receiver is not able to position itself until it does get a lock. This results from the fact that the algorithm requires at least six beacons to operate. Accounting for echoes and collisions, we need to be locked onto at least seven beacons; using eight improves the precision. We have overcome this failure mode by re-seeding a particular beacon-tracking filter if it hasn't seen a beacon for four seconds.

A second failure mode occurs when the receiver is stationary and the measured Doppler shifts begin to approach zero. When the receiver stops moving for short periods of time, the algorithm will usually deviate only slightly. However, when the receiver is stationary for a prolonged period of time, the algorithm will diverge. This is the natural progression of the filter as it continues to iterate using measurements containing little or no position information (ie. Doppler shifts of zero).

8   Discussion

We believe that the current version of our system is over-engineered and we see it as a step towards a better solution. Using particle filters to find the association between chirps and beacons is a surprisingly robust method, but not necessarily very accurate when moving the receiver over longer distances. A better method may be to integrate the position and velocity filter with the periodicity tracking filters to form a single filter. With position and velocity information, we can infer when the next chirp from each beacon will arrive, allowing us to associate a more representative likelihood to each beacon. By folding all nine particle filters into one particle filter, where each particle has a memory of past beacons, we can determine the likelihood using that past information.

We have implemented this unified particle filter, and find that it works well with simulated data, but we have yet to produce robust results on real data. Interestingly, the single particle filter will create multi-modal solutions when chirps collide. For example, one mode will follow the hypothesis that the most recent chirp came from beacon A, and the other mode will follow the hypothesis that it came from beacon B. These different modes are then unravelled a few chirps later, when it becomes clear which beacon the chirp belonged to. The method also extends to the case where chirps are occluded or go missing. This is simply a matter of allocating particles to account for this possibility.

A second observation is that, at present, our filter only works when the receiver is moving. When the receiver stops moving, particles begin to disperse randomly in all directions. After a 10 second period, the particles have dispersed so far that the position starts to diverge. We are planning to identify situations where there are no observed shifts on any of the beacon transmission periods, and to suspend our main particle filter over the corresponding time frame.

We would like to scale our system up to be able to cover larger areas. We believe that this is feasible as long as we find an appropriate density of beacons. With too many beacons we will saturate the 40 KHz ultrasonic channel; with too few beacons there will not be enough measurements to constrain the solution and solve for position.

9   Conclusions

In this paper we have presented a method for positioning that uses Doppler shifts in transmission periods of signals. It employs a number of particle filters to associate measurements with beacons as well as recover the position and velocity of the mobile receiver. In comparison with existing solutions, our recovered position is rather crude (20-30 cm on average). However, the infrastructure that we employ is minimal and unobtrusive. Our system is similar to the Cricket, but without RF synchronisation and powered by a small solar panel near a domestic light source.

The present system works as a prototype, but has several shortcomings that need further research. We think that the two different types of particle filter can be integrated in a single particle filter (this works in simulation, but is yet to be shown effective on real data). We also plan to improve the stability of the system when there is little movement and, therefore, little information provided in the measurements. It may be interesting to design an experiment to measure how common it is for people to remain stationary, and to establish how well a system like this would perform as, for example, a positioning system for a museum guide.

We note also that the present system is confined to working in one area or in a single room setting. However, we believe that by uniquely grouping and distributing beacons based on their unique periods, it will be possible to identify the room that the receiver is in by observing audible beacons. A simple method such as this should allow us to deploy the system on a larger-than-room scale.

References

1. LaMarca, A., Chawathe, Y., Consolvo, S., Hightower, J., Smith, I.E., Scott, J., Sohn, T., Howard, J., Hughes, J., Potter, F., Tabert, J., Powledge, P., Borriello, G., Schilit, B.N.: Place Lab device positioning using radio beacons in the wild. In Gellersen, H.W., Want, R., Schmidt, A., eds.: Pervasive. Volume 3468 of Lecture Notes in Computer Science., Springer (2005) 116–133
2. Ward, A., Jones, A., Hopper, A.: A New Location Technique for the Active Office. In: IEEE Personnel Communications, volume 4 no.5. (1997) 42–47
3. Hazas, M., Ward, A.: A Novel Broadband Ultrasonic Location System. In Borriello, G., Holmquist, L.E., eds.: Proceedings of UbiComp 2002: Ubiquitous Computing, Göteborg, Sweden, Springer-Verlag (2002) 264–280
4. McCarthy, M., Muller, H.L.: RF Free Ultrasonic Positioning. In: Seventh International Symposium on Wearable Computers, IEEE Computer Society (2003) 79–85
5. Smith, A., Balakrishnan, H., Goraczko, M., Priyantha, N.: Tracking Moving Devices with the Cricket Location System. In: Proceedings of the 2nd international conference on Mobile systems, applications, and services, ACM Press (2004) 190–202

6. McCarthy, M., Muller, H.L.: Positioning with independent ultrasonic beacons. Technical Report CSTR-05-005, Department of Computer Science, University of Bristol (2005)
7. Arulampalam, M.S., Maskell, S., Gordon, N., Clapp, T.: A tutorial on particle filters for on-line non-linear/non-gaussian bayesian tracking (2002)
8. Kalman, R.E.: A New Approach to Linear Filtering and Prediction. In: Journal of Basic Engineering (ASME). (1960) 82(D):35–45
9. Welch, G., Bishop, G.: An Introduction to the Kalman Filter. In: Technical Report TR95-041, Department of Computer Science, University of North Carolina - Chapel Hill. (1995)
10. Hightower, J., Borriello, G.: Particle filters for location estimation in ubiquitous computing: A case study. In Davies, N., Mynatt, E., Siio, I., eds.: Proceedings of the Sixth International Conference on Ubiquitous Computing (Ubicomp 2004). Volume 3205 of Lecture Notes in Computer Science., Springer-Verlag (2004) 88–106
11. Cheng, Y.C., Chawathe, Y., LaMarca, A., Krumm, J.: Accuracy characterization for metropolitan-scale Wi-Fi localization. In: MobiSys. (2005) 233–245

Cluster Tagging: Robust Fiducial Tracking for Smart Environments

Robert Harle and Andy Hopper

Computer Laboratory, University of Cambridge,
Cambridge, UK
{rkh23, ah12}@cl.cam.ac.uk

Abstract. Fiducial scene markers provide inexpensive vision-based location systems that are of increasing interest to the Pervasive Computing community. Already established in the Augmented Reality (AR) field, markers are cheap to print and straightforward to locate in three dimensions. When used as a component of a smart environment, however, there are issues of obscuration, insufficient camera resolution and limited numbers of unique markers.

This paper looks at the advantages of clustering multiple markers together to gain resilience to these real world problems. It treats the visual channel as an erasure channel and relevant coding schemes are applied to decode data that is distributed *across* the marker cluster using an algorithm that does not require each tag to be individually numbered. The advantages of clustering are determined to be a resilience to obscuration, more robust position and pose determination, better performance when attached to inconvenient shapes, and an ability to encode more than a database key into the environment. A real world example comparing the positioning capabilities of a cluster of tags with that of a single tag is presented. It is apparent that clustering provides a position estimate that is more robust, without requiring external definition of a co-ordinate frame using a database.

1 Introduction

Recent Computer Science research has seen an explosion of interest in location-aware systems. Such systems seek to robustly determine the position and pose of a variety of objects. The process is typically separated into three stages; determine the identity of an object; measure a quantity related to distance to one or more sensors; compute a location.

Many physical mediums have been harnessed by previous research efforts designed to locate objects, including infra-red, visible light, sound (both audible and inaudible to humans) and radio (using signals from wireless LAN, bluetooth, UWB and GSM networks, to name a few) [7]. The majority tag the objects in some manner and semantically associate the object with the tag. Active tags (with a local power source) are common since they allow greater tag-sensor distances and smarter operation. However, passive tags (which draw no local power) are preferred for their low cost and minimal maintenance. Unfortunately, present day tracking systems based on passive tags can be unreliable—the increasingly pervasive RFID [16] systems are a good example. Those tracking systems that use computer vision for tracking passive 'fiducial' tags are, however, more robust and reliable. The use of fiducials simplifies the general problem of tracking objects in moving images, which is notoriously complex.

M. Hazas, J. Krumm, and T. Strang (Eds.): LoCA 2006, LNCS 3987, pp. 14–29, 2006.

Fig. 1. A variety of tag designs that combine a recognisable shape with a unique payload

A fiducial tag is essentially a visual barcode designed to be easily recognisable to a machine. Systems based on them are well established in the postal and shipping industries (where they are used primarily for identification rather than high accuracy spatial tracking) and in Augmented Reality systems. The latter exploits the reliable identification, location and pose estimation properties of fiducial tags. Many implementations exist: the ARtoolkit [4, 3] software is widely used, but there are a growing number of competitors [10, 15, 6]. In addition, the TRIP project at Cambridge [5] used the concept for tracking objects in an office environment. The evaluation framework presented within this paper makes use of Cantag, an open source competitor to these systems, developed in-house, that is more flexible and extensible [1].

The advantages of fiducial systems are manyfold: markers can be printed quickly and cheaply, using commodity items available in every office. Even the sensor hardware amounts to off-the-shelf cameras and, when properly calibrated, it gives accurate orientation estimates (something often lacking in fine-grained location systems).

The basic operation of a fiducial system is straightforward. A camera captures an image of one or more fiducial tags. Each tag has two components: at least one recognisable geometric shape and a payload (Figure 1). The shape acts as a-priori knowledge about the tag and by searching the image for valid perspective projections of this shape we can identify where tags are in the image and calculate the position and pose that would give rise to that perspective shape. For example, ARtoolkit uses squares (becoming quadrilaterals under projection) and TRIP uses circles (becoming ellipses). Once all the tags in a scene have been determined they must be identified; this is achieved through the payload which is a per-tag symbol or code that is unique. ARtoolkit uses monochrome shapes as an identifying payload and pattern matching for recognition, although herein we adopt the binary coding found in the other systems since it lends itself to analysis. For such encoding, the payload size (in bits) is determined by the size of the tag and the size of a single bit element (the *feature size*).

In this paper we develop the idea of tagging objects with multiple tags in a manner we term 'cluster tagging', where:

1. Tags are used for both data communication and location information,
2. Multiple tags are used to increase resilience to obscuration,
3. Tags are arranged in a known spatial configuration,
4. Data is encoded redundantly *across* the tags,
5. Tags are *not* uniquely indexed.

The use of multiple tags in fiducial tracking systems is not in itself novel. Both ARtoolkit and ARtag support the use of multiple tags in labelling objects. A database maps arrays of tags to known positions. When a subset of the array is observed, the system is able to compute where the other tags in the array are, providing a degree of robustness in tracking. These systems also permit the computation of camera position and pose given one or more sighted tags in an array [14]. Cluster tagging is distinguished from these systems through criteria 1, 4, and 5 above. It allows for arrays of tags to distribute information between them. In addition, we use this opportunity to more completely map out the general advantages of multiple tagging.

The remainder of this paper looks at the motivations for cluster tagging, considers how to achieve it practically (including spatial arrangements, coding schemes, and multiple independent clusters) and gives results from a real world implementation. The solution uses coding techniques from established information theory, but is unusual in its demand for small data packets, discouraging the standard solutions.

2 Motivating Cluster Tagging

Most applications of fiducial systems require the tag-camera distance to be relatively small (one or two metres). Expanding them into larger-scale pervasive systems poses interesting problems: using today's systems we require a greater number of unique tags (i.e. more payload bits) and larger feature sizes to capture images further away with sufficient resolution. Unfortunately, a bigger feature size and payload equates to bigger tags, which increases the likelihood of obscuration. Cluster tagging addresses this problem and others:

Smaller tag sizes. Distributing data across multiple tags has the potential to allow a smaller per-tag payload size. When using pure index-based tag labelling, the payload is determined by the number of unique tags required, and any error correcting coding used. When the tags are not explicitly indexed, the payload can be chosen to be smaller, permitting a greater feature size.

Redundancy. By distributing the data *redundantly* across tags, the system can cope with a proportion being obscured (Figure 2).

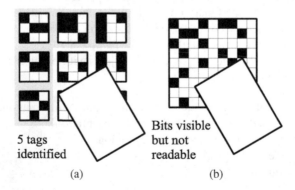

(a)   (b)

Fig. 2. Clustering advantages (a) A singly-tagged object has visible bits, but the lack of a full shape border (a square) prevents them being read. (b) Clustering small tags allows some data to be read and potentially 20 corner correspondences to be identified for more accurate pose and position determination.

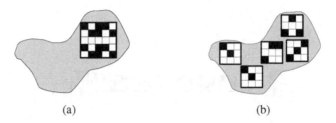

(a)   (b)

Fig. 3. Cluster tagging allows for irregular shapes. (a) Tag limited to 25 bits. (b) Clustering allows at least 45 bits.

Geometric arrangements. Geometric arrangements and patterns of tags can convey extra information, including where other tags *should* be. This can assist the image processing algorithms.

Better Fitting. Multiple small tags can better cover an irregular object (Figure 3).

Robust pose estimation. Each tag provides independent estimates of location and orientation for the attached object (Figure 2).

More data. Multiple tags can be used to convey more information overall. Data could be encoded about the object it is attached to (spatial bounds, composition, owner, etc). This may be sufficient to remove the dependency on a local database.

The latter idea of 'imprinting' data onto the environment for direct interpretation has an number of additional advantages. Data dissemination is intrinsically location private since a sensor must be physically present to read the information. This is useful to ensure physical presence rather than remote spoofing. For example, a computer may display a tag (or tags) alongside a standard login box which encodes a key that changes regularly. As a user approaches the machine, a wearable camera could decode the key and use it in conjunction with a standard password to prove both identity and physical proximity. There is also an advantage in heterogeneous deployments: tagged

Fig. 4. Cluster tagging for document tracking

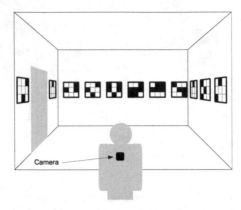

(a) Inside-out Positioning. Tags at known positions, camera unknown. The camera estimates its position using as many tags as possible and may use the data encoded across them to derive more information such as room name.

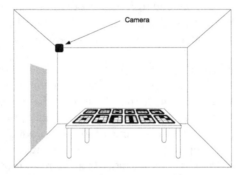

(b) Outside-in Positioning. Camera at known position, tags estimate table position and pose. The tags may encode details about the object as well as provide multiple estimates of position and pose and dealing with obscuration.

Fig. 5. Cluster tagging for positioning

objects can be moved from proprietary system to proprietary system without requiring export/import of data. This is particularly important for a highly mobile user.

Disadvantages include a limit on the size of data and an inability to edit dynamic data (such as object owner). In these cases, hybrid approaches seem reasonable, where static data is encoded on tag clusters alongside a key that allows access to dynamic data.

2.1 Applications of Cluster Tagging

Applications for visual tagging that can provide identity, data and accurate location/pose information are varied. Here we present a few sample applications to clarify the contribution cluster tagging can have.

Augmented Reality. Many augmented reality systems already make use of the identity and location capabilities of single tags [8, 2, 9]. Tag sizes are typically of the
order of $0.1m \times 0.1m$ and attached to stiff card to minimise warping. This size is
convenient for human handling and suits the current resolution capabilities of commodity video cameras. However, uninitiated users show a tendency to obscure parts
of the symbols with their hands. This problem is only compounded if the symbol is
invisible to the naked eye through the use of ink pigments outside the visible range.
Cluster tagging allows for this obscuration through redundancy.

Document Tracking. A complete document tracking system which can reliably and
inexpensively track individual sheets of paper is the holy grail of many adminis-
terial departments. Fiducial tagging is one option for such a system: in a world of
visual sensors, a system can log a timestamped location of specific documents. The
inherent obscuration (Figure 4) favours small clusters of tags over larger single tags.

Wide Area Positioning System. Fiducial tags offer the possibility of a simple positioning system: tags could be placed within an environment, acting as landmarks
that a camera could compute its relative location and pose from. Cluster tagging
would allow smaller tags, greater resilience to obscuration, more independent location estimates, and the possibility of imprinting room bounds and details. This
concept can also be inverted, with a static camera at a known location and mobile objects cluster tagged. Such a system would be ideal for monitoring the current location and pose of large scale objects such as tables and chairs, thereby
autonomously maintaining an up-to-date world model. Figure 5 illustrates the two
concepts.

3   Cluster Tagging Specifics

The ideal cluster tagging scheme should aim for three major goals:

Maximal spatial coverage. The cluster should aim to maximise coverage of the associated object to increase robustness in tracking it from a variety of angles.

Minimise redundancy cost. The clustering scheme should maximise the size of the
true data being encoded.

Allow cluster identification. When multiple clusters are in view it is important to be
able to identify separate clusters so data does not get irretrievably mixed. The solution should avoid requiring each packet to be labelled with a unique cluster ID.

3.1   Coding Schemes

Present tag systems tend to use forward error correction (FEC) coding on a per-tag
basis to ensure a valid read of the ID. This 'inner code' is assumed to guarantee that a
given tag is decoded correctly or not at all. With the payload encoded across multiple
tags, each tag carries a 'packet' of data and the processing of an image can be viewed
as a transmission of the payload over a channel. The properties of the inner code as
described characterise this channel as a packet erasure channel, where a packet is either
reliably read or lost (Figure 6). Encoding data across packets such that it can be decoded
over such a channel requires an effective 'outer code'.

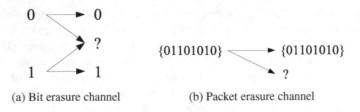

(a) Bit erasure channel   (b) Packet erasure channel

Fig. 6. Erasure channels

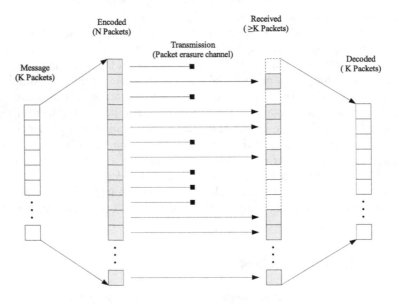

Fig. 7. Adding redundancy to deal with erasure channels

The outer code must introduce sufficient redundancy to cope with obscuration within images (leading to erasures). This is achieved by encoding a K-packet message to N>K packets (Figure 7). Established coding schemes for erasure channels (linear codes, convolutional codes, fountain codes, etc) make one fundamental assumption: the erasures are known at the receiver. i.e. an arbitrarily chosen packet can be labelled as lost or received. This is usually achieved by indexing each packet and amortising this cost over large packet sizes. In cluster tagging, packet sizes are necessarily small and the cost of numbering each one is too high. A typical tag may only offer a payload of 25 bits (some of which are reserved to ensure a packet erasure channel)—a cluster of 20 tags would require at least 5 bits for a per tag index, significantly affecting the size of the data encoded.

Without per-packet indexing, decoding the information from a random cluster of tags would require that every possible permutation of packets and erasures be considered, each one being decoded and tested for validity (this is achievable if a CRC or similar check is included in the original data). If the coding scheme encodes to N packets, this could require N! invocations of the decoding algorithm. It is thus very important

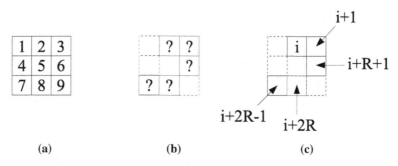

Fig. 8. Relative indexing. (a) A correctly indexed pattern as deployed (b) Five observed tags of unknown indexes (c) Indexing the first tag allows remaining tags to be relatively indexed in terms of the row width, R=3.

to reduce the possible permutations by exploiting the geometry of the cluster (for this reason regular tag arrangements are preferable over irregular ones since rigid structure significantly limits available permutations).

3.2   Inferring Erasures from Structure: Relative Indexing

A cluster of tags arranged in a known configuration effectively indexes them since the configuration can provide the necessary ordering information without having to encode it explicitly in the tag payloads. However, erasures complicate this picture—when unindexed tags are missing it may not be possible to uniquely number those that remain. In these situations we select a reference tag and index the remaining tags *relative* to it. The a-priori configuration of tags should be chosen such that, given a set of tags and a reference tag, the remaining tags can be given a unique relative index. For example, consider a 3×3 array of tags that encodes 5 packets of data. The arrangement is such that the true indexes of the tags is as in Figure 8(a). Given that the tag spacing and layout is known beforehand, observing a subset of the tags (Figure 8(b)) will allow indexing relative to a member of the subset. In Figure 8(c) the reference tag is given an arbitrary *shift index*, denoted i, and the remaining four tags can then be indexed relative to it and the row width, R.

In this way relative indexing allows the definition of a set of possible receives/ erasures (one set for each valid value of i). The difference between the largest relative-index and the reference then defines the *span*—i.e. the number of true indexes between the first and last packet decoded. For a given span, s, there may be up to (N-s) possible channel candidates, one for each of the (N-s) possibilities for the shift index, i. As a specific example, consider Figure 8 where the received vector spans 6 original indexes. This means the shift index, i, can only take one of three (=9-6) values (i=1,2, or 3) as illustrated in Figure 9. In fact, this result only applies if the layout was a row of 9 elements. The 3×3 layout can be used to further limit the possible shift indexes—since there are only three columns and there is one sighted tag either side of the first (albeit in different rows), the first tag must be in the second column; by a similar analysis we find it must be in the first row and thus this scenario is not ambiguous at all: the shift index is known instantly despite a lack of indexing within the tag payload.

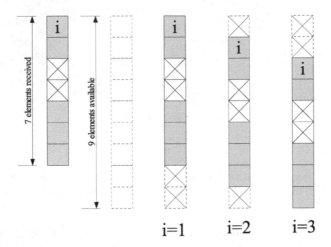

Fig. 9. Possible shifts for Figure 8

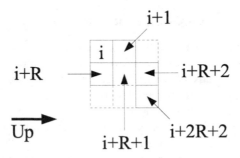

Fig. 10. Rotational invariance masks the lowest-indexed element

In general,the worst case scenario occurs when the layout pattern is a simple row, when s=K and when the correct value of the shift index is the last one trialled. This requires (N-K) attempted decodes before the correct decode occurs. In practice, however, this is an unlikely situation, and significant computational savings will be made by considering the layout pattern carefully as described.

3.3 Determining the First Tag: Rotational Invariance

An important issue is the determination of the reference first tag. A regular arrangement of tags introduces rotational invariance which can complicate this identification—a 90° rotation of the image in Figure 8(c) results in a very different relative indexing (Figure 10). Tags, then, need to incorporate directionality; a problem not unique to cluster tagging. In fact the solutions proposed for the inner coding for individual tags are equally applicable here [11]. The essential principle is to use a rotationally-invariant inner code, with specific bits used to indicate direction.

4   Dealing with Multiple Clusters

If each tag within a cluster does not carry a label identifying its parent cluster, problems can clearly arise when tags from multiple clusters are in view—not only does a viewing system need to determine the indexing of tags within a cluster, but also the clusters present. Regular geometric arrangements can also help here. Once a tag within in a cluster is sighted, the arrangement allows determination of where other tags in the same cluster may be and what their orientations should be, based on an arrangement template (Figure 11). In most cases, this alone should be sufficient to group tags by cluster.

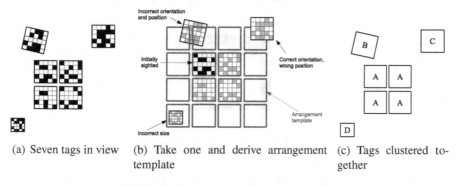

(a) Seven tags in view   (b) Take one and derive arrangement template   (c) Tags clustered together

Fig. 11. Coping with multiple clusters in view

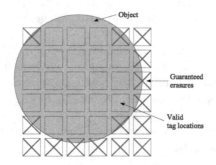

Fig. 12. Applying a standard 6×6 tag array to a non-square object with guaranteed erasures

A further problem may be that different geometric arrangements may suit different surface shapes, and hence multiple arrangement templates would be required. Similarly, different sizes of arrangement may also be favoured (e.g. the row width may change from cluster to cluster). These problems are very difficult to cope with robustly, so instead it is favourable to set the arrangement and its row width. This in turn allows the values of N and K to be set, simplifying decodes. The overall scale of the arrangement can, however, be varied. Thus it is possible to set an arrangement (for example, a square tessellation) and expand it to suit the object. Where whole tags do no fit on an object, they may be excluded, taken as guaranteed erasures (Figure 12).

5   Real World Results

We have implemented cluster tagging within the open-source fiducial tracking software library Cantag [1], developed in-house and freely available. Cantag supports arbitrary tag shapes, data encodings and interpretation algorithms and is well suited to both production and development of novel fiducial systems.

In the example provided here, we use a 7×7 cluster of 5-element square tags (Figure 13) to encode a global co-ordinate system by defining the position and pose of the cluster itself in that frame. A camera then decodes this information and can compute its pose in that global co-ordinate frame without an external database.

Fig. 13. A sample tag used in evaluation

The choice of a square tag allowed for ease of tessellation. Each tag carried 24 bits of data split into four blocks of 6 bits. Each block was encoded on the tag such as to readable in any orientation. One bit per block was reserved for orientation information, three bits for data and the remaining two bits formed parity check bits. This allowed each tag to represent 12 bits of data and to have sufficient resilience to produce the necessary erasure channel.

The data encoded across the tags defined three points in 3D. The first defined the position of the first tag in the cluster, the remaining two defined the direction of the x- and y- axes in the same frame. 32 bit floating point values were used for each of the nine co-ordinates, making a total data length of 288 bits. To this a 32-bit CRC was added to assist in decoding the cluster, making 310 bits to encode. This data size requires at least 26 tags (312 bits) and hence K=26, whilst N=49. Thus the cluster can cope with any 23 tags being obscured without effect.

5.1   The Outer Code

For the outer code a linear BCH code was implemented, similar to that of Rizzo [13]. The premise of such a code is that a $K \times N$ generator matrix, $\mathbf{G}$, acts on an input vector, $\mathbf{x}$, of size K to produce an encoded vector of size N,

$$\mathbf{y} = \mathbf{G}\mathbf{x}. \tag{1}$$

The received data vector, $\mathbf{y}'$, is then a subset of $\mathbf{y}$ and must have a size of at least K for decode. A decode matrix can be created by first constructing a $K \times K$ matrix $\mathbf{G}'$ and then inverting it.

$$\mathbf{x} = \mathbf{G}'^{-1}\mathbf{y}'. \tag{2}$$

From this relation is should be apparent that $\mathbf{G}'$ is constructed from the rows of $\mathbf{G}$ corresponding to any K elements of $\mathbf{y}'$. The remaining question is how to form the matrix $\mathbf{G}$. For this implementation, a systematic code was chosen, whereby the first K rows are the identity matrix. The remaining rows must be linearly independent, and this can be assured by the use of a Vandermonde matrix, making $G_{ij} = \alpha^{(i-1)(j-1)}$ for $j > K$ and α the generator element for a Galois Field of the chosen size (see [13] for more details).

5.2 Positioning

Positioning of square tags in Cantag is generally based on the identification of the corners within the image. These form correspondences between the image and the real world and are sufficient to locate a tag within the reference frame of the camera. Cantag implements a variety of algorithms that have been evaluated elsewhere [12]. The key point regarding the localisation of a particular tag is that the algorithms trade-off between accuracy and computational complexity. The fastest algorithm in Cantag is presently the *Linear Projective* algorithm, based on a linearisation of the localisation problem, whilst the most accurate algorithm, *Space Search*, uses a minimisation algorithm to iteratively find the most likely tag position and pose ([12]).

In implementing cluster tagging, we use the fast linear algorithm to identify and decode as many tags as possible in the frame. The decoded data is then used to create correspondences between image pixels and the global reference frame (four correspondences per square). A minimisation algorithm is then used to find the optimal camera position, effectively inverting the Space Search algorithm.Essentially, there are six parameters necessary to define the 3D position and pose of the camera. With each iteration of the algorithm, the location of each tag corner is computed, assuming the camera to be at the present estimate. This location is then projected to an image frame, and the error distance to the corresponding projections in the true image are calculated. By minimising this error, the camera position and pose is determined. The source code for this process is contained within the present Cantag distribution as the *EstimateTransform* algorithm.

5.3 Results

The cluster was printed on A4 paper using a standard laser printer. Each tag measured 2.15cm×2.15cm and the layout used row and column gaps of 0.5cm. To aid comparisons a single tag with the dimensions of the entire cluster was printed onto a second piece of paper.

In each experiment the relevant sheet was affixed to a desk and a camera mounted above it, pointing towards it. Care was taken to level the camera to point perpendicular to the desk surface. The camera position was measured to within an estimated error of 1cm in each dimension, and was not moved throughout the experiments. 100 image frames were captured with the cluster sheet in place and 100 further with the single tag sheet in the same place, suitably aligned. Using Cantag the camera position was estimated for each image. The positions were calculated in up to three different ways:

1. Using all observed tags from the cluster sheet,
2. Using each individual tag observed from the cluster sheet,
3. Using the single large tag from the single tag sheet.

The position distributions are shown in Figure 14. The estimated camera position is shown in each, although it should be noted that the experimental error in measuring this quantity is significant on this scale. For clarity, Figure 15 shows the CDFs for each of these results. Given the relatively large estimated error of the true position, we find little difference between using a cluster and a single large tag of equivalent dimensions, both of which exhibit an error consistent with today's fiducial systems.

Whilst the small position distribution for the single large tag appears to imply a better localisation than the other methods, this is not necessarily the case. Because its four corners lie away from the centre of the image, towards the bounds, they are more affected by lens distortion. Whilst we have corrected for this distortion using a standard radial model within Cantag, this is only a generic lens model and less trust can be placed in points further from the principal point in the image. The (slightly) larger spread of positions when using the entire cluster is indicative of the fact that the location algorithm has many points extracted from across the image upon which to base its estimate. The error distribution thus better reflects the true state of affairs.

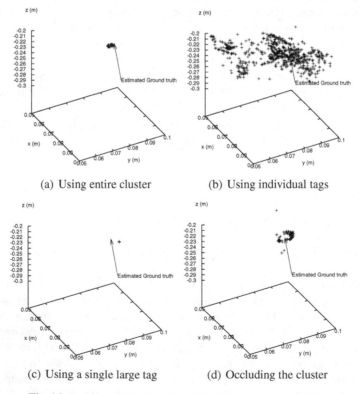

(a) Using entire cluster   (b) Using individual tags

(c) Using a single large tag   (d) Occluding the cluster

Fig. 14. Position distributions for different processing and setups

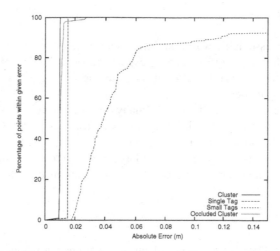

Fig. 15. Cumulative density functions of results in Figure 14

Figure 14(d) shows the results of repeating the cluster experiment with approximately one third of the cluster occluded. The data remains decodable and the position distribution changes little, as evidenced by the CDF in Figure 15. When a similar occlusion was applied to the single large tag, no positions were possible since no tags were identifiable. We conclude from this that cluster tagging has the potential to locate a camera to at least a comparable precision to that when using a single large tag. This is true even with occlusion present, increasing the robustness of the position measurement over the latter approach.

These results reflect our general findings with clustering: position estimates can be significantly improved over tags of similar size, whilst resilience is inherent in the redundancy. Beyond the example given here, the code for camera position and pose estimation has been shown to be robust and reliable and many empirical experiments using different arrays of tags have demonstrated the strengths of the approach over single tags.

6 Advantages and Disadvantages

The ideal positioning solution depends heavily on the application envisaged. Our experiences have found cluster tagging to be particularly useful for ubiquitous computing. Lighting conditions can be a particular problem with single tag systems in a general environment, and cluster tagging assists by increasing the chance that a useful proportion of encoded data can be retrieved by using smaller tags.

In terms of disadvantages, there is a clear problem with how to 'print' the information to a space. Traditional inks will fade and the initial deployment is complex unless the tags are incorporated a the time of manufacture (for example into wallpaper). The difficulty in accurately placing tags both in a global reference frame and within a local geometric template during a very large and ubiquitous deployment may counteract the location accuracy advantages on offer. Nonetheless, we expect cluster tagging to perform as well or better than single tagging in almost every respect in the general case.

7 Future Work

Cluster tagging has associated with it similar questions to single tagging: what is the best tag shape? What bit error rate can be expected? How does resolution affect the result? These questions are difficult to answer, but the Cantag platform provides the flexibility to investigate them.

As regards cluster tagging itself, there are many open questions regarding the optimal coding scheme, the best way to optimise the decode process and the best way to combine all the redundant information to produce the best estimates of position and pose; we hope to investigate the many options available and also to move the symbols from the visible spectrum into the near infrared spectrum to minimise aesthetic disturbance.

8 Conclusions

This paper has introduced the concept of cluster tagging with fiducial tags. Cluster tagging uses multiple small tags to encode data redundantly across a space, such that observing any subset is sufficient to recover the data fully. The advantages to doing this over a traditional single-tag deployment have been determined as a reduced need for a database, inherent location privacy, greater robustness for tracking, the capability to cope with partial view occlusion, and to make better use of the available tagging space. We have implemented and analyzed the technique in the real world and hope to develop and deploy the idea in the future.

Acknowledgements

The authors would like to thank the reviewers who have helped to improve the work presented in this paper, and to recognise the contributions of the other Cantag authors.

References

1. R. K. Harle A. Rice, A. R. Beresford. "cantag:. In *Proceedings of the Fourth Annual IEEE International Conference on Pervasive Computer and Communications (PerCom), Pisa, Italy, 13-17 Mar*, 2006.
2. M. Billinghurst, H.Kato, and I. Poupyrev. The MagicBook: Moving seamlessly between reality and virtuality. *IEEE Computer Graphics and Applications*, pages 2–4, May 2001.
3. Mark Billinghurst, Hirkazu Kato, and Ivan Poupyrev. The MagicBook—moving seamlessly between reality and virtuality. *IEEE Computer Graphics and Applications*, 21(3):6–8, 2001.
4. Mark Billinghurst and Hirokazu Kato. Collaborative mixed reality. In *Proceedings of the First International Symposium on Mixed Reality*, pages 261–284, 1999.
5. Diego López de Ipiña, Paulo R. S. Mendoną, and Andy Hopper. TRIP: a low-cost vision-based location system for ubiquitous computing. *Personal and Ubiquitous Computing*, 6(3):206–219, May 2002.
6. Mark Fiala. ARTag revision 1, a fiducial marker system using digital techniques. Technical report, National Research Council Canada, 2004.
7. J. Hightower and G. Borriello. Location sensing techniques. *IEEE Computer*, August 2001.

8. H.Kato, M. Billinghurst, I. Poupyrev, K. Imamoto, and K. Tachibana. Virtual object manipulation on a table-top AR environment. In *Proceedings of ISAR 2000*, October 2000.
9. Hideki Koike, Yoichi Sato, and Yoshinori Kobayashi. Integrating paper and digital information on enhanceddesk: a method for realtime finger tracking on an augmented desk system. *ACM Transactions on Computer-Human Interaction (TOCHI)*, 8(4):307–322, December 2001.
10. Jun Rekimoto. Matrix: A realtime object identification and registration method for augmented reality. In *Proceedings of Asia Pacific Computer Human Interaction*, pages 63–68, July 1998.
11. Andrew Rice, Christopher Cain, and John Fawcett. Dependable coding for fiducial tags. In *Proceedings of the 2nd Ubiquitous Computing Symposium*, pages 155–163, 2004.
12. Andrew Rice and Robert Harle. Evaluating lateration-based positioning algorithms for fine-grained tracking. In *Proceedings of the Joint Workshop on Foundations of Mobile Computing (DIAL-M-POMC) 2005*. ACM Press, 2005.
13. L. Rizzo. Effective Erasure Codes for Reliable Computer Communication Protocols. *ACM Computer Communications*, 27(2):24–36, April 1997.
14. U. Neumann and S. You and Y. Cho and Lee and J. Park. Augmented Reality Tracking in Natural Environments. In Y. Ohta and H. Tamura, editor, *Mixed Reality - Merging Real and Virtual Worlds*, pages 101–130. Ohmsha and Springer-Verlag, 1999.
15. Daniel Wagner, Thomas Pintaric, Florian Ledermann, and Dieter Schmalstieg. Towards massively multi-user augmented reality on handheld devices. In *Third International Conference on Pervasive Computing*, 2005.
16. Roy Want. RFID: A key to automating everything. *Scientific American*, pages 56–65, January 2003.

Automatic Mitigation of Sensor Variations for Signal Strength Based Location Systems

Mikkel Baun Kjærgaard

Department of Computer Science, University of Aarhus,
IT-parken, Aabogade 34, DK-8200 Aarhus N, Denmark
mikkelbk@daimi.au.dk

Abstract. In the area of pervasive computing a key concept is context-awareness. One type of context information is location information of wireless network clients. Research in indoor localization of wireless network clients based on signal strength is receiving a lot of attention. However, not much of this research is directed towards handling the issue of adapting a signal strength based indoor localization system to the hardware and software of a specific wireless network client, be it a tag, PDA or laptop. Therefore current indoor localization systems need to be manually adapted to work optimally with specific hardware and software. A second problem is that for a specific hardware there will be more than one driver available and they will have different properties when used for localization. Therefore the contribution of this paper is twofold. First, an automatic system for evaluating the fitness of a specific combination of hardware and software is proposed. Second, an automatic system for adapting an indoor localization system based on signal strength to the specific hardware and software of a wireless network client is proposed. The two contributions can then be used together to either classify a specific hardware and software as unusable for localization or to classify them as usable and then adapt them to the signal strength based indoor localization system.

1 Introduction

In the area of pervasive computing a key concept is context-awareness. One type of context information is location information of wireless network clients. Such information can be used to implement a long range of location based services. Examples of applications are speedier assistance for security personnel, healthcare professionals or others in emergency situations and adaptive applications that align themselves to the context of the user. The implementation of speedier assistance could, for example, come in the form of a tag with an alarm button that, when pressed, alerts nearby persons to come to assistance. The alarm delivered to the people nearby would contain information on where in the physical environment the alarm was raised and by whom. Applications that adapt themselves to the context they are in are receiving a lot of attention in the area of pervasive computing, where they can solve a number of problems. One type of context information is location which can be used in its simplest form to implement new services optimized based on the location information.

M. Hazas, J. Krumm, and T. Strang (Eds.): LoCA 2006, LNCS 3987, pp. 30–47, 2006.

Table 1. Signal strength variations

	Spatial	Temporal	Sensor
Small-scale	Movement around one wavelength	Transient effects	Different examples of the same WRC combination
Large-scale	Normal movement	Prolonging effects	Different WRC combinations

One type of indoor location system, which can be used to support the above scenarios, is systems based on signal strength measurements from an off-the-shelf 802.11 wideband radio client (WRC). The WRC can be in the form of either a tag, phone, PDA or laptop. Such systems need to address several ways in which the signal strength can vary. The variations can be grouped into *large* and *small-scale spatial*, *temporal*, and *sensor* variations as shown in Table 1. The spatial variations can be observed when a WRC is moved. Large-scale spatial variations are what makes localization possible, because the signal strength depends on how the signals propagate. The small-scale spatial variations are the variations that can be observed when moving a WRC as little as one wave length. The temporal variations are the variations that can be observed over time when a WRC is kept at a static position. The large-scale temporal variations are the prolonged effects observed over larger periods of time; an example is the difference between day and night where during daytime the signal strength is more affected by people moving around and the use of different WRCs. The small-scale temporal variations are the variations implied by quick transient effects such as a person walking close to a WRC. The sensor variations are the variations between different WRCs. Large-scale variations are the variations between radios, antennas, firmware, and software drivers from different manufactures. Small-scale variations are the variations between examples of the same radio, antenna, firmware, and software drivers from the same manufacture. The chosen groupings are based on the results in [1, 2].

Most systems based on signal strength measurements from off-the-shelf 802.11 wideband radio clients do not address the above variations explicitly, with [1] and [2] as exceptions. Especially the handling of sensor variations has not been given much attention. Therefore current location systems have to be manually adapted by the provider of the location system for each new type of WRC to work at its best. This is not optimal considering the great number of combinations of antennas, firmware, and software drivers for each radio. To the users the large-scale sensor variation poses another problem, because the different implementations of firmware and software drivers have different properties with respect to localization. To the users it would therefore be of help if the system could automatically evaluate if the firmware and software drivers installed could be used for localization.

The contribution of this paper is twofold. To solve the problem of large-scale sensor variations, an automatic system is proposed for adapting an indoor localization system based on signal strength to the specific antenna, radio, firmware, and software driver of a WRC. To solve the problem of evaluating different sensors, an automatic system for evaluating the fitness of a specific combination of antenna, radio, firmware, and software driver is proposed. The two contributions can then be used together to either classify a combination of antenna, radio, firmware, and software drivers as unusable for localization or to classify them as usable and then adapt them to the signal strength based indoor localization system.

The methods proposed for providing automatic classification and adaptation are presented in Section 2. The results of applying these methods to 14 combinations of antennas, radios, firmware, and software are given in Section 3. Afterwards the results are discussed in Section 4 and finally conclusions are given in Section 5.

1.1   Related Work

Research in the area of indoor location systems, as surveyed in [3, 4], spans a wide range of technologies (wideband radio, ultra-wideband radio, infrared,...), protocols (IEEE 802.11,802.15.1,...), and algorithm types (least squares, bayesian, hidden markov models, ...). Using these elements the systems estimate the location of wireless entities based on different types of measurements such as time, signal strength, and angles. Systems based on off-the-shelf 802.11 wideband radio clients using signal strength measurements have received a lot of attention. One of the first systems was RADAR [5], that applied different deterministic mathematical models to calculate the position in coordinates of a WRC. The mathematical models used had to be calibrated for each site where the systems had to be used. In comparison to RADAR, later systems have used probabilistic models instead of mathematical models. This is because a good mathematical model which can model the volatile radio environment has not been found. As in the case of the mathematical models in RADAR, the probabilistic models should also be calibrated for each site. Examples of such systems determining the coordinates of a WRC are published in [2, 6, 7, 8] and systems determining the logical position or cell of a WRC are published in [1, 9, 10][1]. Commercial positioning systems also exist such as Ekahau [11] and PanGo [12]. In the following, related work is presented with respect to how the systems address the signal strength variations introduced above.

Small-scale spatial variations are addressed by most systems using a method to constrain how the location estimate can evolve from estimate to estimate. The method used for the system in [7] is to average the newest estimate with previous estimates. In [1, 6, 8, 13] more advanced methods based on constraining the estimates using physical properties are proposed. The constraints include both the layout of the physical environment and the likely speed by which a WRC can move. One way these constraints can be incorporated in a probabilistic model is to use a Hidden Markov Model to encode the constraints with. In [2] another method is proposed which in the case of movement triggers a perturbation technique that addresses the small-scale variations. In [14] a graph-inspired

---

[1] The system in [9] uses the signal to noise ratio instead of the signal strength.

solution is presented which weights measurements based on the physical distance between location estimates. Large-scale spatial variations are, as stated in the introduction, the variation which makes indoor location system using signal strength possible. The different methods for inferring the location are a too extensive area to cover here in detail. Some examples of different types of systems were given above.

Small-scale temporal variations can be addressed using several techniques. The first concerns how the probabilistic model is build from the calibration measurements. Here several options exist: the histogram method [6, 7, 8], the Gaussian kernel method [7], and the single Gaussian distribution [1]. The second technique is to include several continuous measurements in the set of measurements used for estimating the location. By including more measurements quick transient effects can be overcome. This can be done as in [1, 7], where the measurements are used as independent measurements or as in [2], where a time-averaging technique is used together with a technique which addresses the correlation of the measurements. Large-scale temporal variations have been addressed in [14] based on extra measurements between base stations, which were used to determine the most appropriate radio map. In [1] a method is proposed were a linear mapping between the WRC measurements and the radio map is used. The parameters of this mapping can then be fitted to the characteristics of the current environment which addresses the large-scale temporal variations.

Small-scale sensor variations have not been explicitly addressed in earlier research. One reason for this is that the small variations between examples often are difficult to measure, because of the other variations overshadowing it. Therefore there exist no general techniques, but possibly the techniques for the large-scale sensor variations could be applied. For large-scale sensor variations [1] proposed applying the same linear approximation as in the case of large-scale temporal variations. They propose three different methods for finding the two parameters in the linear approximation. The first method is a manual one, where a WRC has to be taken to a couple of known locations to collect measurements. For finding the parameters they propose to use the method of least squares. The second method is a quasi-automatic one where a WRC has to be taken to a couple of locations to collect measurements. For finding the parameters they propose using the confidence value produced when doing Markov localization on the data and then find the parameters that maximize this value. The third is an automatic one requiring no user intervention. Here they propose using an expectation-maximization algorithm combined with a window of recent measurements. For the manual method they have published results which show a gain in accuracy for three cards; for the quasi-automatic method it is stated that the performance is comparable to that of the manual method, and for the automatic one it is stated that it does not work as well as the two other techniques.

The methods proposed in this paper to solve the problem of large-scale sensor variations are a more elegant and complete solution than the method proposed in [1]. It is more elegant, because it uses the same type of estimation technique for both the manual, quasi-automatic, and automatic case. It is more complete, because it can recognize WRCs that cannot be used for localization. Also it has been shown to work on a larger set of WRC combinations with different radios, antennas, firmware, and software drivers.

2   Methods for Classification and Normalization

A cell based indoor localization system, such as the ones proposed in [1, 9, 10], should estimate the probability of a WRC being in each of the cells which the system covers. A cell is here normally a room or part of a room in larger rooms or a section of a hallway. Formally a set $S = \{s_1,...,s_n\}$ is a finite set of states where each state corresponds to a cell. The state s^* is the state of the WRC that should be located. The location estimate of the WRC can then be denoted by a probability vector $\boldsymbol{\pi}$ with each entry of the vector denoting the probability that the WRC is in this particular state $\pi_i = P(s^* = s_i)$.

To solve the localization problem the vector $\boldsymbol{\pi}$ has to be estimated, which is addressed by infrastructure-based localization using two types of measurements. First, there are the measurements $M = \{m_1,...,m_s\}$ reported by the WRC, which is to be located. Second, there is a set $C = \{c_1,...,c_t\}$ of calibration measurements collected prior to the launch of the location service. Each measurement is defined as $M = V \times B$ where $B = \{b_1,...,b_k\}$ is the set of base stations and $V = \{0,...,255\}$ is the set of signal strength values for 802.11 WRCs. The calibration measurements are collected to overcome the difficulties in localizing clients in the volatile indoor radio environment.

The estimation of the vector $\boldsymbol{\pi}$ based on the two types of measurements can be divided into three sub-problems. The first problem is the normalization problem, which adresses how WRC-dependent measurements are transformed into normalized measurements. The reason the measurements need to be normalized is that otherwise they cannot be combined with the calibration measurements which have most often not been collected by the same WRC. The next problem, state estimation, is how the normalized measurements are transformed into a location estimate. The last problem, tracking, is how the physical layout of the site and prior estimates can be used to enrich the location estimate. In respect to these problems, it is the problem of normalization made in an automatic fashion that this paper addresses. For evaluating the proposed methods in the context of a localization system an implementation based on the ideas in [1] without tracking is used.

In the following sections methods are proposed for solving the problem of automatic normalization (Section 2.3-2.6) and the problem of classifying the fitness of a WRC for localization automatically (Section 2.2). The solutions are stated in the context of indoor localization system using signal strength measurements from off-the-shelf 802.11 wideband radio clients. However, the solutions could be applied to other types of radio clients which can measure signal strength values.

2.1   Automatic Still Period Analyzer

In the proposed methods an analyzer, called an automatic still period analyzer, is used to divide measurements into groups of measurements from single locations. The idea behind the analyzer is that, if we can estimate if a WRC is still or moving, we can place a group of still measurements in one location. One thing to note here is that localization cannot be used to infer this information, because the parameters for adapting the WRC to the localization system have not yet been found. The still versus moving estimator applied is based on the idea in [6] of using the variations in the signal strength to infer moving versus still situations. To do this, the sample variation is calculated for the signal strength measurements in a window of 20 seconds. The estimation is then based on having training data from which distributions of the likelihood of the WRC being still or moving at different levels of variations is constructed. To make a stable estimate from the calculated variations and likelihood distributions a Hidden Markov Model (HMM) is applied as estimator with the parameters proposed in [6]. To evaluate the implemented estimator two walks were collected with the lengths of 44 minutes and 27 minutes, respectively, where the person collecting the walks marked in the data when he was still or moving. These two walks were then used in a simulation, where one was used as training data to construct the likelihood distributions and the other as test data. The results were that 91% of the time the estimator made the correct inference and with a small number of wrong transitions between still and moving because of the HMM as experienced in [6]. However, the estimator performs even better when only looking at still periods, because the errors experienced are often that the estimator infers moving when the person is actually still.

The estimator used here differs in two ways with respect to the method proposed in [6]. First, weighted sample variations for all base stations in range are used instead of the sample variation for the strongest base station. This was chosen because our experiments showed this to be more stable. Second, the Gaussian kernel method is used instead of the histogram method to construct the likelihood distributions. One thing to note is that the estimator does not work as well with WRC combinations, which cache measurements or have a low update frequency.

2.2   Fitness Classifier

Methods for classifying the fitness of a single combination of antenna, radio, firmware, and software drivers for localization are presented. To make such a classifier, it first has to be defined what makes a combination fit or unfit. A good combination has some of the following characteristics: the radio has high sensitivity so that it can see many bases, has no artificial limits in the signal strength values, does not cache the signal strength values, and has a high update frequency.[2] On the other hand, a bad combination has low sensitivity, limits the

---

[2] Pure technical constraints, such as cards that can not return signal strength values, are not addressed in this paper.

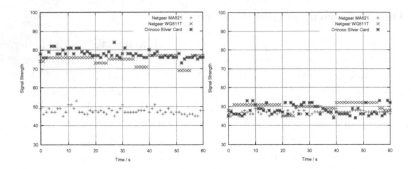

Fig. 1. Plots of signal strength measurements from different cards and base stations at the same location

signal strength values, the signal strength values reported do not represent the signal strength but some other measurements, such as the link quality, caches the measurements, and has a low update frequency.

To illustrate the effects of good and bad combinations on data collected from several WRCs, Figure 1 shows signal strength measurements for different WRCs taken at the same location and at the same time, but for two different 802.11 base stations. On the first graph the effect of caching or low update rate for the Netgear WG511T card can be seen, because the signal strength only changes every five seconds. By comparing the two graphs, the effect of signal strength values not corresponding to the actual signal strength can be seen for the Netgear MA521 card. This is evident form the fact that the signal strength values for the Netgear MA521 card does not change when the values reported by the other cards change for specific base stations.

In the following it is assumed that, for evaluating the fitness of a WRC combination, five minutes of measurements are available. The measurements should be taken in an area where at least three base stations are in range at all times. The measurements should be taken over five minutes and the WRC combination should be placed at four different locations for around 30-60 seconds. Of course, the techniques could be applied without these requirements. The system could, for instance, collect measurements until it had inferred that the WRC combination had been placed at four locations. Then it would of course depend on the use of the WRC combination when enough measurements have been collected.

To automatically evaluate the fitness of a specific combination, methods for finding the individual faults are proposed. For caching or low update frequency a method using a naive Bayesian estimator [15] based on the autocorrelation coefficient is proposed. For measurements that do not correspond to the signal strength a method using a naive Bayesian estimator based on the variations between measurements to different base stations at the same place is proposed. For artificial limits a min/max test can be applied, but it is difficult to apply in the five minutes scenario, because data for a longer period of time is needed. For sensitivity a test based on the maximum number of bases can be used, but requires data for a longer period of time. The evaluation of the two last methods has not been carried out and is therefore left as future work.

Caching or low update frequency. To evaluate if a combination is caching or has a low update frequency the signal strength measurements for each base station are treated as time series. Formally, let $m_{t,j}$ be the signal strength measurement of time t and for base station b_j. The autocorrelation coefficient[16] $r_{k,j}$ is then for base station b_j with lag k where $\overline{m_j}$ is the mean of the signal strength measurements for base station b_j:

$$r_{k,j} = \frac{\sum_{t=1}^{N-k}(m_{t,j} - \overline{m_j})(m_{t+k,j} - \overline{m_j})}{\sum_{t=1}^{N}(m_{t,j} - \overline{m_j})^2} \tag{1}$$

$r_{k,j}$ is close to 1.0 when the measurements are in perfect correlation and close to -1.0 when in perfect anticorrelation. This can be used to detect WRC combinations that are caching or has a low update frequency because the autocorrelation coefficient will in these cases be close to 1.0. The autocorrelation coefficient is then calculated from signal strength measurements for different base stations and different lags. Based on initial experiments lag 1 and 2 were used in the evaluations. These coefficients are then used with a naive Bayesian estimator to calculate the probability of the WRC combination is caching or having a low update frequency. To construct the likelihood function for the naive Bayesian estimator, a training set of known good and bad combinations with respect to caching or low update frequency are used. The examples in the training set were classified by the author. A likelihood function constructed from the training data used in one of the evaluations is plotted in Figure 2. The Figure shows the likelihood for different autocorrelation coefficients that the WRC combination is good or bad.

Measurements do not correspond to signal strength values. The best test to determine if measurements do not correspond to signal strength measurements is to calculate if the measurements at a known location correlate with

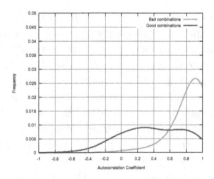

Fig. 2. Plot of the likelihood for different autocorrelation coefficients that the WRC combination is good or bad

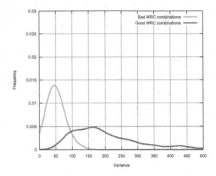

Fig. 3. Plot of the likelihood for different average sample variations that the WRC combination is good or bad

measurements from a known good combination. However, this can not be used in an automatic solution. Another way to automatically test this is to calculate the average sample variation for measurements to different base stations. It is here assumed that if the measurements do not correspond to signal strength values they will be more equal for different base stations. One example of this is the Netgear MA521 as shown in the plot in Figure 1.

The calculated average sample variation is used as input to a naive Bayesian estimator. The estimator calculates the probability that a combination's measurements do not correspond to the signal strength. It is assumed in the evaluation that measurements are collected for at least three base stations at each location. To construct the likelihood function for the naive Bayesian estimator, a training set of known good and bad combinations with respect to correspondence to signal strength is used. A likelihood function constructed from the training data used in one of the evaluations is plotted in Figure 3. The Figure shows the likelihood for different average sample variations that the WRC combination is good or bad.

2.3   Normalization

In the following sections the methods proposed for normalizing the measurements reported by WRC combinations are presented. The measurements are normalized with respect to the measurements reported by the WRC combination that was used for calibrating the deployment site of the localization system. The first method is a manual method in which a user has to take a WRC to a number of known locations and collect measurements. The second is a quasi-automatic method where the user has to take the WRC to some unknown locations and collect measurements. The third is an automatic solution where there is no need for initial data collection, the user can just go to locations and use the WRC. The formulation of these three types of methods is the same as in [1], however, this work applies other techniques to solve the problems. As done in [1], it is assumed that a linear model can be used to relate measurements from one combination to another. The reason this is a reasonable assumption is that most WRC combinations use a linearized scale for the reported signal strength values. Formally, $c(i) = c1 * i + c2$, where $c1$ and $c2$ are two constants, i is the normalized signal strength that can be compared with the calibration observations, and $c(i)$ is the signal strength of the combination.

2.4   Manual Normalization

To solve the problem of manual normalization, the method of linear least squares [17] is used. In stead of applying this method to the individual signal strength measurements, the mean $\mu_{o_{i,j}}$ and the standard deviation $\sigma_{o_{i,j}}$ of the measurements for some state s_i and base station b_j are used. For the calibration measurements also the the mean $\mu_{c_{i,j}}$ and the standard deviation $\sigma_{c_{i,j}}$ of the measurements for some state s_i and base station b_j are used. Formally, a linear observation model is assumed, where x is the true state, $\widetilde{y}$ is the measurement vector and v the measurement error:

$$\widetilde{y} = Hx + v \tag{2}$$

To make an estimate of $c1$ and $c2$ denoted by $\widehat{x}$, the following definitions are used for $\widehat{x}$, $\widetilde{y}$ and H. It is assumed that a set of observations for some subset of S denoted by 1 to r and some subset of base stations for each location denoted by 1 to s are given.

$$\widehat{x} = [c1, c2] \quad \widetilde{y} = \begin{bmatrix} \mu_{o_{1,1}} \\ \sigma_{o_{1,1}} \\ \vdots \\ \mu_{o_{1,s}} \\ \sigma_{o_{1,s}} \\ \vdots \\ \mu_{o_{r,1}} \\ \sigma_{o_{r,1}} \\ \vdots \\ \mu_{o_{r,s}} \\ \sigma_{o_{r,s}} \end{bmatrix} \quad H = \begin{bmatrix} \mu_{c_{1,1}} & 1.0 \\ \sigma_{c_{1,1}} & 0.0 \\ \vdots & \vdots \\ \mu_{c_{1,s}} & 1.0 \\ \sigma_{c_{1,s}} & 0.0 \\ \vdots & \vdots \\ \mu_{c_{r,1}} & 1.0 \\ \sigma_{c_{r,1}} & 0.0 \\ \vdots & \vdots \\ \mu_{c_{r,s}} & 1.0 \\ \sigma_{c_{r,s}} & 0.0 \end{bmatrix} \tag{3}$$

The relations between c_1 and c_2 and the mean and deviations comes from the following two equations [18].

$$\mu_{o_{i,j}} = c_1 * \mu_{c_{i,j}} + c_2 \tag{4}$$

$$\sigma_{o_{i,j}} = c_1 * \sigma_{c_{i,j}} \tag{5}$$

By using linear least squares an estimate of $\widehat{x}$ is found using:

$$\widehat{x} = (H^T H)^{-1} H^T \widetilde{y} \tag{6}$$

2.5   Quasi-automatic Normalization

To solve the problem of quasi-automatic normalization, the method of weighted least squares [17] is used. Since the locations of the measurements are unknown they have to be compared to all possible locations. But some locations are more likely than others and therefore weights are use to incorporate this knowledge. It is assumed that a set of observations for some unknown subset of S denoted by 1 to r and some subset of base stations for each unknown location denoted by 1 to s are given.

First $\widetilde{y}_i$ and H_i are defined as:

$$\widetilde{y}_i = \begin{bmatrix} \mu_{o_{i,1}} \\ \sigma_{o_{i,1}} \\ \vdots \\ \mu_{o_{i,1}} \\ \sigma_{o_{i,1}} \\ \vdots \\ \mu_{o_{i,s}} \\ \sigma_{o_{i,s}} \\ \vdots \\ \mu_{o_{i,s}} \\ \sigma_{o_{i,s}} \end{bmatrix} \quad H_i = \begin{bmatrix} \mu_{c_{1,1}} & 1.0 \\ \sigma_{c_{1,1}} & 0.0 \\ \vdots & \vdots \\ \mu_{c_{n,1}} & 1.0 \\ \sigma_{c_{n,1}} & 0.0 \\ \vdots & \vdots \\ \mu_{c_{1,s}} & 1.0 \\ \sigma_{c_{1,s}} & 0.0 \\ \vdots & \vdots \\ \mu_{c_{n,s}} & 1.0 \\ \sigma_{c_{n,s}} & 0.0 \end{bmatrix} \tag{7}$$

With these definitions $\widehat{x}$, $\widetilde{y}$ and H can be defined as:

$$\widehat{x} = [c1, c2] \quad \widetilde{y} = \begin{bmatrix} \widetilde{y}_1 \\ \vdots \\ \widetilde{y}_r \end{bmatrix} \quad H = \begin{bmatrix} H_1 \\ \vdots \\ H_r \end{bmatrix} \tag{8}$$

The weight matrix W is then defined as:

$$W = diag(w_{1,1}, ..., w_{1,n}, ..., w_{r,1}, ..., w_{r,n}) \tag{9}$$

Two methods are proposed for the definition of $w_{i,j}$, where i is an observation set from an unknown location and j denotes a known location. The first method is to attempt to apply bayesian localization with the ith observation set from an unknown location and to define $w_{i,j} = \pi_j$. The second method is a comparison method which tries to match the means and standard deviations of the observations and calibration observations using the following definition, where $O_{i,k} \sim \mathcal{N}(\mu_{o_{i,k}}, \sigma_{o_{i,k}})$ and $C_{j,k} \sim \mathcal{N}(\mu_{c_{j,k}}, \sigma_{c_{j,k}})$, where $w_{i,j}$ can be defined as:

$$w_{i,j} = \frac{1}{s} \sum_{k=1}^{s} \sum_{v=0}^{255} \min(P(v - 0.5 < O_{i,k} < v + 0.5), P(v - 0.5 < C_{j,k} < v + 0.5)) \tag{10}$$

By using weighted least squares an estimate of $\hat{x}$ is then found using:

$$\hat{x} = (H^T W H)^{-1} H^T W \tilde{y} \tag{11}$$

2.6   Automatic Normalization

To solve the problem of automatic normalization, the automatic still period analyzer is used. Given signal strength measurements from five minutes, the analyzer is used to divide the data into parts which come from the same location. These data are then used with the solution for quasi-automatic normalization. If, however, the automatic still period analyzer is unable to make such a division the complete set of measurements from the five minutes is used.

3   Results

In this section evaluation results are presented for the proposed methods based on collected measurements. The measurements used in the evaluation were collected in an 802.11 infrastructure installed at the Department of Computer Science, University of Aarhus. Two types of measurements were collected, and for both types the signal strength to all base stations in range was measured every second. The first type was a set of calibration measurements collected using WRC combination number 11 from Table 2. The calibration set covers 18 cells spread out over a single floor in a office building as shown on Figure 4. The second type of measurements were walks collected by walking a known route on the same floor where the calibration set was collected. Each walk lasted for around 5 minutes and went through 8 of the cells; in four cells the WRC combination was placed at a single spot, each shown as a dot in Figure 4, for around a minute. Two walks were collected for each of the WRC combinations listed in Table 2 on different days. For collecting the measurements on devices running Windows XP, Mac OS X or Windows Mobile 2003 SE, the Framework developed as part of the Placelab[19] project was used. For the single WRC combination installed on a device running Linux a shell script was used to collect the measurements.

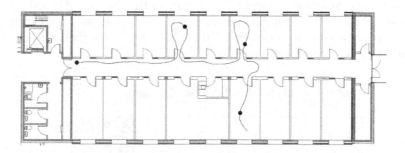

Fig. 4. Floor layout with walking path

Table 2. WRC combinations with classification, where *Not SS* means that the reported values do not correspond to signal strength values

Product name	Antenna	Firmware/Driver	OS	Classification
1. AirPort Extreme (54 Mbps)	In laptop	OS provided	Mac OS X (10.4)	Good
2. D-Link Air DWL-660	In card	D-Link 7.44.46.450	Windows XP	Good
3. Fujitsu Siemens Pocket Loox 720	In PDA	OS provided	Windows Mobile 2003	Caching/Low Freq
4. Intel Centrino 2100 3B	In laptop	Intel 1.2.4.35	Windows XP	Caching/Low Freq
5. Intel Centrino 2200BG	In laptop	Intel 9.0.2.31	Windows XP	Caching/Low Freq
6. Intel Centrino 2200BG	In laptop	Kernel provided(ipw2200)	Debian (2.6.14)	Caching/Low Freq
7. Netgear MA521	In card	Netgear 5.148.724.2003	Windows XP	Not SS
8. Netgear WG511T	In card	Netgear 3.3.0.156	Windows XP	Caching/Low Freq
9. Netgear WG511T (g disabled)	In card	Netgear 3.3.0.156	Windows XP	Caching/Low Freq
10. NorthQ-9000	In dongle	ZyDAS ZD1201	Windows XP	Good
11. Orinoco Silver	In card	OS provided (7.43.0.9)	Windows XP	Good
12. Ralink RT2500	In dongle	Ralink 2.1.10.0	Windows XP	Good
13. TRENDnet TEW-226PC	In card	OEM 5.140.521.2003	Windows XP	Not SS
14. Zcom XI-326HP+	In card	Zcom 4.0.7	Windows XP	Good

3.1 Classifier

To evaluate the proposed classifiers for evaluating the fitness of a WRC combination for localization, the walks collected as explained above were used. In Table 2 the different classifications for the WRC combinations are shown. These classifications were made by the author by inspecting the measured data from the WRC combinations.

Two evaluations were made to test if the proposed method can predict if a WRC combination caches measurements or has a long scanning time. For the first evaluation for each of the WRC combinations, one of the walks was used as training data and the other as test data. This tests if the methods can make correct predictions regardless of the influence of small and large-scale temporal variations. The results from this evaluation are given in Table 3 and show that the method was able to classify all WRC combinations correctly.

In the second evaluation it was tested if the method worked without being trained with a specific WRC combination. This was done by holding out a single WRC combination from the training set and then using this to test the method. The results are given in Table 3 and the method were in this case also able to classify all the WRC combinations correctly.

To test the method for predicting if a WRC combination is not returning values corresponding to signal strength values, the same two types of evaluations were made. The results given in Table 3 and in this case the method was able to classify all the WRC combinations correctly in the time case. For the holdout evaluations there were, however, two WRC which were wrongly classified as not returning signal strength measurements.

Table 3. Classification results

	Correct	Wrong
Caching/Low Freq (Time)	24	0
Caching/Low Freq (Holdout)	24	0
Correspond to Signal Strength (Time)	28	0
Correspond to Signal Strength (Holdout)	26	2

3.2   Normalization

To evaluate the performance of the proposed methods for normalization, the walks and calibration set collected as explained above were used. In the evaluation of a specific WRC combination one of the walks was used to find the normalization parameters and the other was used to test how well the WRC combination could predict the route of the walk with normalized measurements. In the test the location accuracy in terms of correctly estimated cells and the average likelihood of the measurements with respect to the probabilistic model of the localization system were collected. The probabilistic model used was constructed from the calibration set. The average likelihood was collected to show how close the actual measured values come to the calibration measurements after they have been normalized. The average likelihoood is calculated by averaging the likelihood for each measurement looked up in the probabilistic model. The higher these values are the more equal the normalized measurements are to the measurements that was used to construct the probabilistic model. The

Table 4. Results for evaluating the normalization methods with respect to localization accuracy and average likelihood. The location accuracy given are the correct localizations in percent and the likelihoods are given in the parentheses.

	All	Good	Caching/Low frequency
Original	32.6% (1.83%)	41.7% (2.08%)	24.5% (1.87%)
Manual	52.1% (2.80%)	73.6% (3.40%)	38.8% (2.66%)
Quasi-Automatic(Compare)	41.0% (2.13%)	56.1% (2.67%)	32.2% (1.93%)
Automatic(Bayesian)	45.7% (2.52%)	64.3% (2.81%)	33.6% (2.61%)
Automatic(Compare)	43.4% (2.20%)	55.1% (2.47%)	39.8% (2.29%)

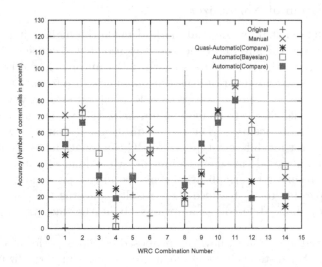

Fig. 5. Results of the localization accuracy with correct localization in percent for the different WRC combinations

localization results and the average likelihood results are given in Table 4. For single WRC combinations localization results are given in Figure 5.

The results show that the manual normalization method gives the highest gain in localization accuracy. Among the automatic methods, the Bayesian method gives the highest gain for all and the good WRC combinations. However, for the caching/low frequency WRC combinations the method based on comparison gives the best results. One reason for this is that the Bayesian method does not work well with highly correlated measurements. The likelihood results show that there is some correspondence between the gain in localization accuracy and the average likelihood. However there are also exceptions as for the Caching/Low Frequency WRC combinations, where the automatic Bayesian method gives the highest average likelihood but has a lower accuracy than the automatic comparison method which has a lower average likelihood. The results in Figure 5 also highlight that the accuracy a indoor location system can achieve is highly dependent on the WRC combination used.

4   Discussion

4.1   Application of Classifiers

The method for classifying if a WRC combination is caching or has a low update frequency were, as presented in the result section, able to classify all combinations correctly. The method for classifying if a WRC combination is not returning values corresponding to signal strength value were, however, not able to classify all correctly. One method for improving the last method is maybe to use another estimator as for example a linear classifier[15].

4.2   Application of Normalizer

The results showed that the manual method made the highest improvement in accuracy. However, the automatic method was also able to considerably improve the accuracy. A method for addressing that the automatic method for some cases did not give as good a result as the manual is to integrate the two. This could for instance be done so a user of a localization system with automatic normalization could choose to do manual normalization if the automatic method failed to improve the accuracy. The results also showed that the two automatic methods were best for different types of WRC combinations. A solution to this was to use the proposed classifiers to find out what kind of automatic method to apply. The results for normalization reported in this paper are, however, not directly comparable to [1] because their results concerns temporal variations. Therefore they make different assumptions about the data they use in their evaluation.

An interesting question is, how the proposed methods perform over a longer period of time. For instance if a location system could run normalization several times and then try to learn the parameters over a longer period of time, some improvement in accuracy might be observed. To do this some sequential technique has to be designed that makes it possible to include prior estimates. Such a technique could also be used to address large-scale temporal variations.

4.3   The Still Period Analyzer

The use of the still period analyzer solved the problem of dividing measurements into groups from different locations. This actually made the automatic normalizer perform better than the quasi-automatic normalizer because noisy measurements were filtered off. However, the still period analyzer also had problems with some of the WRC combinations such as WRC combination 1 for which signal strength values did not vary as much as for WRC combination 11, which the still period analyzer was trained with. Also generally the caching/low frequency WRC combinations made the period analyzer return too many measurements. This was because the variations were too low due to the low update rate at all times making the still period analyzer unable to divide the measurements into different parts. A solution to these problems might be to include some iterative step in the method so that the automatic normalization is run several times on the measurements. This would also normalize the variations so they would be comparable to the variations for which the still period analyzer was trained for.

4.4   The Linear Approximation

The use of a linear approximation for normalization gave good results in most cases. However, for WRC combinations that do not report signal strength values which are linearized, the linear approximation does not give as good results. One example of this is WRC combination 14 which was classified as good but only reached a location accuracy of 32% with manual normalization. The reason is that the signal strength values reported by WRC combination 14 are not linear as can be seen on Figure 6 (Because the manufacture did not implement a linearization step of the signal strength values in either the firmware or software driver). To illustrate the linearity of the measurements reported by other WRC combinations, results from WRC combination 1 have also been included

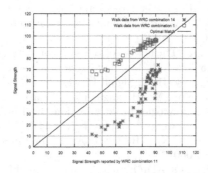

Fig. 6. Plots of signal strength values reported by different WRC combinations relative to the values reported by WRC combination 11 which was used for calibration

in the Figure. The optimal match line in the Figure shows what the measurements should be normalized to. To address this issue an option is to include a linearization step in the methods for WRC combinations that do not return linearized signal strength values, such as WRC combination number 14.

5   Conclusion

In this paper methods for classifying a WRC combination in terms of fitness for localization and methods for automatic normalization were presented. It was shown that the proposed classifiers were able to classify WRC combinations correctly in 102 out of 104 cases. The proposed methods for normalization were evaluated on 14 different WRC combinations and it was shown that manual normalization performed best with a gain of 19.2% over all WRC combinations. The method of automatically normalization was shown also able to improve the accuracy with 13.1% over all WRC combinations. The applicability of the methods for different WRC combinations and scenarios of use was also discussed. Possible future extensions to the methods include: extending the fitness classification to the last two cases of artificial limits and sensitivity, adding a linearization step to the normalization methods, and make normalization iterative to address some of the issues of applying the automatic still period analyzer.

Acknowledgements

The research reported in this paper was partially funded by the software part of the ISIS Katrinebjerg competency centre http://www.isis.alexandra.dk/ software/. Carsten Valdemar Munk helped collecting signal strength measurements and implementing the facilities for collecting these.

References

1. Haeberlen, A., Flannery, E., Ladd, A.M., Rudys, A., Wallach, D.S., Kavraki, L.E.: Practical robust localization over large-scale 802.11 wireless networks. In: Proceedings of the Tenth ACM International Conference on Mobile Computing and Networking (MOBICOM). (2004)
2. Youssef, M., Agrawala, A.: The horus WLAN location determination system (2005)
3. Sun, G., Chen, J., Guo, W., K.J., Liu, R.: Signal processing techniques in network-aided positioning: A survey. IEEE Signal Processing Magazine (2005)
4. Muthukrishnan, K., Lijding, M., Havinga, P.: Towards smart surroundings: Enabling techniques and technologies for localization. In: International Workshop on Location- and Context-Awareness. Volume LNCS 3479. (2005) 350–362
5. Bahl, P., Padmanabhan, V.N.: "RADAR: An in-building rf-based user location and tracking system" (2000)
6. Krumm, J., Horvitz, E.: LOCADIO: Inferring motion and location from wi-fi signal strengths. In: First Annual International Conference on Mobile and Ubiquitous Systems: Networking and Services (Mobiquitous 2004). (2004)

7. T.Roos, P.Myllymäki, H.Tirri, P.Misikangas, J.Sievänen: A probabilistic approach to WLAN user location estimation. Int. Journal of Wireless Information Networks **9**(3) (2002) 155–164
8. Ladd, A.M., Bekris, K.E., Rudys, A., Marceau, G., Kavraki, L.E., Wallach, D.S.: Robotics-based location sensing using wireless ethernet. In: Eight ACM International Conference on Mobile Computing and Networking (MOBICOM 2002), ACM Press (2002) 227238
9. Castro, P., Chiu, P., Kremenek, T., Muntz, R.: A probabilistic room location service for wireless networked environments (2001)
10. Locher, T., Wattenhofer, R., Zollinger, A.: Received-signal-strength-based logical positioning resilient to signal fluctuation (2005)
11. Ekahau. (http://www.ekahau.com)
12. PanGo. (http://www.pangonetworks.com)
13. P.Kontkanen, P.Myllymäki, T.Roos, H.Tirri, K.Valtonen, H.Wettig: Topics in probabilistic location estimation in wireless networks. In: Invited talk at the 15th IEEE Symposium on Personal, Indoor and Mobile Radio Communications. (2004)
14. Bahl, P., Padmanabhan, V.N., , Balachandran, A.: "a software system for locating mobile users: Design, evaluation, and lessons". Microsoft Research Technical Report MSR-TR-2000-12, Microsoft (2000)
15. Witten, I.H., Frank, E.: Data Mining: Practical machine learning tools and techniques. 2nd edn. Morgan Kaufmann, San Francisco (2005)
16. Wikipedia. (http://en.wikipedia.org/wiki/Autocorrelation)
17. Crassidis, J., Junkins, J.: Optimal Estimation of Dynamic Systems. Chapman & Hall/CRC Press, Boca Raton, FL (2004)
18. Berry, D.A., Lindgren, B.W.: Statistics: Theory and Methods. 2nd edn. Duxbury/Wadsworth, Belmont, CA (1996)
19. Placelab. (http://www.placelab.org)

KOTOHIRAGU NAVIGATOR: An Open Experiment of Location-Aware Service for Popular Mobile Phones

Hiroyuki Tarumi[1,2], Yuko Tsurumi[1], Kazuya Matsubara[1],
Yusuke Hayashi[1], Yuki Mizukubo[1], Makoto Yoshida[1], and Fusako Kusunoki[3]

[1] Faculty of Engineering, Kagawa University,
2217-20 Hayashi, Takamatsu, Kagawa 761-0396, Japan
`tarumi@eng.kagawa-u.ac.jp`
[2] SpaceTag, Inc.,
2217-15 Hayashi, Takamatsu, Kagawa 760-0301, Japan
[3] Tama Art University,
2-1723 Yarimizu, Hachioji, Tokyo 192-0394, Japan

Abstract. We have developed a location-aware sightseeing support system for visitors to KOTOHIRAGU Shrine, using only popular mobile phones employing the gpsOne system. Its design is not a map-based navigation system, but a shared virtual world system like multi-player online role-playing games. We conducted an experiment recruiting 29 subjects from *real* tourists visiting the shrine, who had their own compatible GPS-phones. From the survey, we have found that location-aware sightseeing support system using mobile phones can be accepted by young people, but the generation gap is wider than expected.

1 Introduction

As many of the readers know, Japan is in a special situation in the deployment of mobile phones. GSM is not available but the third generation phones are widely used. Au[1], one of the three major mobile phone companies in Japan, employs CDMA 1X or CDMA WIN system and many of its terminals are equipped with the GPS function based on the gpsOne system[2] by Qualcomm. More than 15 million GPS phones have already been shipped out in Japan.

Au also provides some flat-rate packages for data packet communication. This means that many Japanese people can enjoy GPS-based applications without paying extra costs. Au is actually offering some pedestrian navigation systems and location tracking services for parents and their children.

On the other hand, there are some research projects developing virtual world model for mobile users [1-8]. However, they adopted PDA (with an attached GPS antenna) or larger terminals that are not appropriate for real business. Since they are relatively costly and heavy, it is difficult to expect many consumers to buy such terminals and

---

[1] A brand name provided by KDDI. (http://au.kddi.com/)
[2] As well known, gpsOne uses location information of cellular base stations, as well as GPS. However, we do not pay attention to this issue in this paper.

M. Hazas, J. Krumm, and T. Strang (Eds.): LoCA 2006, LNCS 3987, pp. 48–63, 2006.

walk with them. PDA is rather popular but we cannot expect that it has a GPS antenna.

The difference between PDA and phones are not only in the hardware resources such as CPU or memory. There are more restrictions on user interfaces of phones, including the size of display. Application programming interfaces (API) and peripheral devices for phones also put restrictions on programming. For example, location values from GPS cannot be obtained as frequently as in the cases of PDA or laptop PCs. Hence we needed to develop and evaluate a system with mobile phones, though there have already been several evaluation results using PDA or laptop PCs by other researchers.

Recently some techniques using GPS (or GSM) and other sensing technologies like WiFi are actively researched (e.g., [9]). However, we avoid it because WiFi is not available everywhere, especially in many tourists' destinations.

For such reasons, we started to develop a virtual world service for popular mobile phones in Japan, so that Japanese users can enjoy virtual world service without buying extra devices or paying extra costs if they already have any GPS-phone.

According to this design policy, we have succeeded to develop a location-aware virtual world system "KOTOHIRAGU NAVIGATOR" to guide tourist visiting the KOTOHIRAGU Shrine. We have asked real tourists (not a priori recruited subjects) who have their own GPS-phones to use the system and collected their reaction. In this paper, we will describe the system outline and the evaluation by real tourists.

2 Virtual World System Based on SpaceTag

The outdoor shared virtual world developed by us is based on our concept of SpaceTag [10-13]. Our goal is to develop and deploy a system with which people can experience virtual worlds using their mobile phones. Each virtual world has the same geographical structure (with respect to latitude and longitude) with the real world. In other words, we can create various virtual worlds that have same geographical structure, and they can be overlaid onto the real world. We call it the overlaid virtual model (Fig. 1 [10]). A user can select and visit one (or even more) virtual worlds with his/her mobile terminal.

A virtual world consists of virtual architectural objects and virtual creatures. Virtual architectural objects are static objects like buildings, houses, and bridges. Virtual creatures are dynamic objects that can move or interact with other objects, or with users visiting the virtual world. In other words, a virtual creature is an active agent that can react to stimuli from the environment and dynamically execute methods like giving messages to the user. They can also exchange messages with other agents. Sometimes we call virtual creatures just agents.

From a user with a mobile phone, a virtual world can be seen with a perspective view. A far object is drawn as a small image, whereas a closer object is shown as a larger image. If a face of a virtual creature can be seen from the north side of the virtual animal, its back can be seen from its south side. Location of a user can be detected by the GPS embedded on the mobile phone. Hence a user can walk in the virtual world while he/she walks in the real world. The correspondence between the two worlds is based on location.

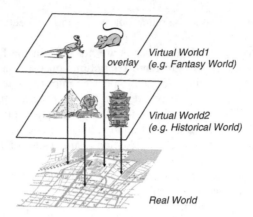

Fig. 1. Overlaid Virtual Model

We have two versions of the virtual world system: a *browser-based* version and a *Brew-based* version.

The browser-based version does not need any special software on a mobile phone. Only a built-in browser is used. All the necessary processing for the virtual world system is performed at the server side. However, it is a *pull* information system, so a user should manually send a request to the server whenever he/she has moved to a new location, to download a new description or an image of the virtual world,.

On the other hand, the Brew-based version needs special software based on Brew, at the terminal side. Brew (http://brew.qualcomm.com/brew/) is a software platform for mobile terminals designed by Qualcomm, Inc. With the Brew-based version, the graphics is dynamically redrawn [11]. It gives more satisfying user interfaces than the browser-based version. However, since it needs an electronic compass that is not popular among phones on the current market, we used the browser-based version.

Fig. 2 shows the configuration of our virtual city system prototype. It is basically a client-server system. Clients are mobile phones on the Japanese market with a GPS function and internet accessibility.

In Fig. 2, the server is drawn as one block, but it consists of two computers. Because the graphics processing needs computer power, one machine is used only for drawing.

The server's main function is to generate a static image of virtual world for each user. When a user accesses to the server, location parameters are attached to the request message by the gpsOne location server. The virtual city server can then detect the location of user by latitude and longitude values ("Convert (Lat, Lon) to Internal Parameters" module). These location parameters are converted to the internal coordinates, and the distance and direction of virtual objects are computed ("Compute Distance and Direction" module).

The "Compute Distance and Direction" module gives a default direction to the "Image Generation" module. A default direction is defined as the direction in which the closest object exists. The user can look into another direction by selecting from a direction list (its flow is shown as broken arrows). In this case, a user is asked by the server about the direction he/she wants to see.

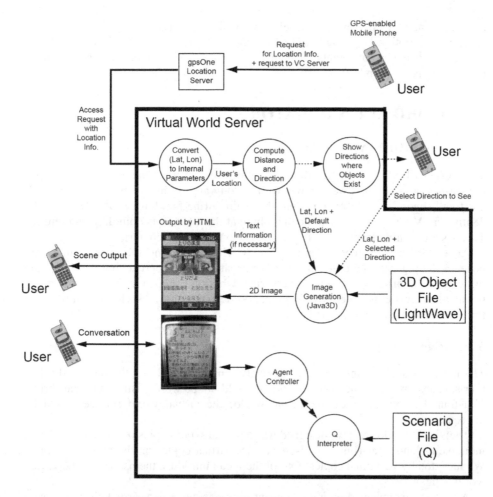

Fig. 2. System Configuration (Browser-based Version)

Data of virtual objects are stored as LightWave 3D data files on the server. A LightWave file is loaded to an image generation module written by Java using Java3D package, and is converted to a 2D image. An image generation process is invoked by the servlet mechanism triggered by the user's request. By adopting a popular tool like LightWave, many people will have chances to take part in the activities of authoring virtual city objects. However, we cannot take full advantage of LightWave, because complex objects with many polygons or fine textures cannot be handled by Java3D and phone terminals.

In Fig. 2, two images are shown. The upper image is an example of the viewing mode. In this case, the generated page in HTML format containing an image of scenery is just sent to the user's terminal.

The lower image in Fig. 2 is an example of the conversation mode. A user is in this mode when talking with an agent. Conversation by an agent is controlled by the "Agent Controller" module. This module uses the Q interpreter to control the conversation. Q is a language developed by the Q consortium [14], which is a scenario-description language based on the Scheme language. With Q, we can easily define the behavior of agents. A more detailed description of the agent control mechanism is given in [12].

3   KOTOHIRAGU NAVIGATOR

3.1   The KOTOHIRAGU Shrine

The KOTOHIRAGU Shrine (in Kagawa Prefecture, Japan) is one of the most famous old shrines in Japan. It is well known with its long approaching way of stone steps. It has totally more than 1300 steps, but the main shrine building (HONGU) is at the 785th step. Many of the tourists stop climbing at the main shrine building and returns. Tourists are coming from all over Japan and also from other countries.

At the 365th step, there is a big gate (OOMON). Along the approaching way beneath the big gate there are many souvenir shops. The approaching way after the big gate is the official territory of the shrine, where no shops are allowed and many points of interest exist. We have developed to design a virtual world system between the big gate and the main shrine building.

3.2   Design Concept

The most important point is the balance between the virtual and the real world. If a tourist is absorbed into the virtual world, it would not be worth visiting the real shrine. If a tourist rarely accesses the virtual world, the virtual world service would be unnecessary.

The virtual world we have designed was a partial set of copies of the real buildings, monuments, and trees (Fig. 3.). Users can see virtual copies on the phone's display. We have totally 22 virtual copies; four of them can introduce themselves in the virtual world. (Fig. 4.)

A user is accompanied by a guide agent. A guide agent is a virtual character, who gives a short message to the user whenever the user requests. We have defined three areas within the total experiment space and ten to eleven prepared sentences for each area. Each sentence is an area-dependent description of the shrine, or sometimes just an encouraging comment to the user climbing the mountain. One of the sentences is randomly selected and shown as the guide agent's message.

On the other hand, there are eleven location-dependent guide agents that look like SAMURAI (Japanese old soldiers) as shown in Fig. 5. They give (narrow) location-dependent comments to tourists. For example, a SAMURAI agent gives a description of the nearest building.

To encourage users, some of the location-dependent comments given by virtual monuments and SAMURAI agents include the number of steps to the main shrine building. Since they should climb up a large number of stone steps, they are strongly interested in the number of steps. By giving the number of remaining steps to the user, we expect frequent accesses to the server (Fig. 4, right.).

With these agents and messages, we expect balanced interest of users to the real and virtual worlds.

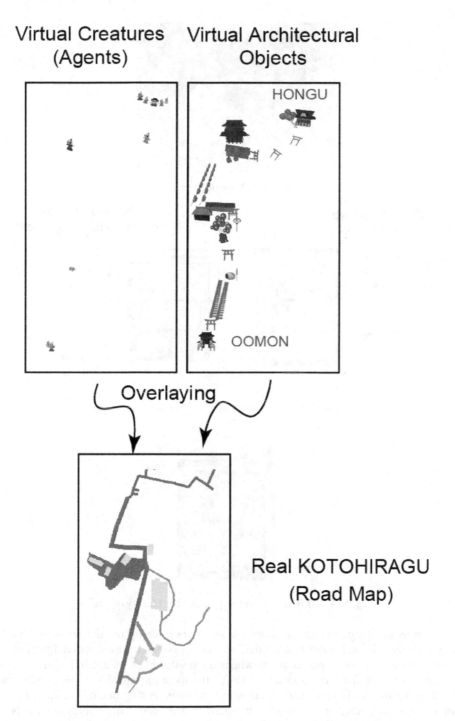

Fig. 3. Real KOTOHIRAGU Map and Overlaid Virtual Objects

A Real Monument

Virtual Counterpart
of the Monument

Self Introduction
by the Virtual Monument

User Avatar

A Guide Agent

Number of
Stone Steps

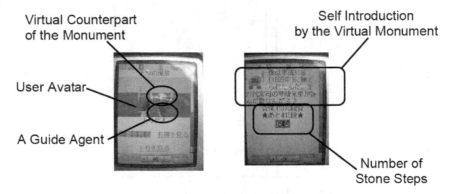

Fig. 4. A Real Monument and Its Virtual Counterpart

Fig. 5. A SAMURAI Agent Explaining the History of Shrine

Another challenge for us was to encourage users to enjoy the shared virtual world among users. To accomplish this goal, we have designed a *generation* function. A user can generate one special agent whenever he/she likes. A special agent can be given a message from the user and stays at the location where it is born. This can be done easily by clicking "leave comment" button, selecting one of the appearances of the special agent, and typing a comment to leave. We designed nine kinds of appearances for them, each of which is an animal in the sea, like an octopus, a turtle,

Generated Character
by a Former Visitor
(Special Agent)

Message by
the Former Visitor

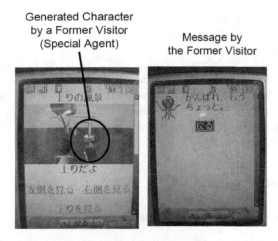

Fig. 6. A Generated Character and Its Message

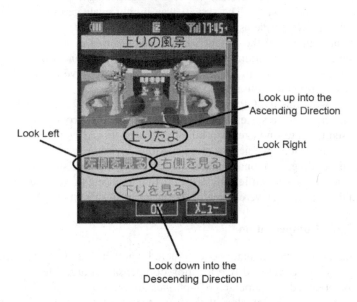

Look up into the
Ascending Direction

Look Left

Look Right

Look down into the
Descending Direction

Fig. 7. User Interface for Directions

etc. This is just because KOTOHIRAGU enshrines the God of marine transportation. A special agent will give the comment from its creator to other guests it encounters. Hence tourists can see how other people feel at the place by the shared comment given from a special agent. In Fig.6 (left), a user is finding a octopus that is a special agent; in Fig. 6 (right), the octopus is showing a message given by a former visitor.

3.3 Interface Design

The most difficult problem for the interface is how to represent orientation and how to make users to input it. If a phone has an electronic compass that can be sensed by our software, we can use it. However, only a few types of GPS-phones have compasses. As shown in Fig. 2, a user has to select a direction in order to change the virtual view to another direction.

On past systems [11-13], "north", "east", "west", etc. (eight or four directions) were used to indicate directions on the user interface[3]. On KOTOHIRAGU Navigator, however, we employed another set of expression, up, down, left, and right. "Up" means, of course, the climbing-up direction; other directions can be naturally understood (Fig. 7). This design is possible since all users are always climbing up. (This system is only for the climbing up situation.)

4 Development Process

4.1 The Previous Experiment at Takamatsu Port

In January 2005, we had another experiment that recruited 20 student subjects for evaluation [13]. The evaluated system was also a sightseeing-support system using the same concept of virtual world. The system was highly evaluated as an entertainment system, but we had two problems left.

One was the balance of the virtual and the real worlds. The system rather gave story-following type of experiences like role-playing games, and was mostly focused on the virtual world. In order to challenge this problem, we have designed the current system as we described in section 3.2.

Another problem was the GPS inaccuracies. As we just used the raw location data obtained from the gpsOne system, we sometimes had GPS errors of more than 10m, which confused users to find agents or buildings in the virtual world.

On the current system, we need a more accurate location system because we have copies of real buildings or monuments in the virtual world that should be at the same location of the real ones, while only truly virtual buildings (we mean non-existing buildings in the real world) were given in the experiment in January.

4.2 GPS Error Compensation

After the January's experiment, we conducted another experiment recruiting ten student subjects. We developed five location compensation algorithms and input real location data obtained by popular GPS-phones to each algorithm. Using modified location data output from each algorithm, simulated virtual scenes were computed and shown to the subjects. The algorithms were map-matching, moving-average, avoiding big jumps, etc. We have found that we need the strongest algorithm, map-matching, for our purpose of virtual world navigation.

Fortunately, as the walking path of visitors to the KOTOHIRAGU Shrine is limited to the stone steps, map-matching can be easily implemented to the KOTOHIRAGU Navigator. There is only one path from the start to the goal, except the square in the middle and some very short branches. Thick lines in Fig. 8 are possible walking paths defined in the system. This data is given in the system by a bitmap image. Raw

---

[3] We had permitted to select one of eight directions in an earlier version, but we re-designed it since users preferred a simpler interface.

location data are also mapped on the same surface and modified to the nearest black dot in the bitmap image of possible paths.

At the places where the path is straight, near OOMON for example, we are free from the location error in the orthogonal direction against the path, with this method. However, we still have an inaccuracy of five to ten meters in the direction of the path.

There is a square in the middle of OOMON and HONGU. In the square, the walking path is less restricted, but not perfectly free due to some monuments and trees. Of course in this square and near the square, the compensation effect is weak. Also, if the path has a corner, the compensation result is sometimes confusing near the corner. We also have some places of bad condition. Fig. 9 is the worst place at the 652nd step, where leafy trees block off radio waves from satellites and we could not give correct location data.

Despite the imperfectness of compensation, we can still say that the service quality has been much improved compared to the January's system.

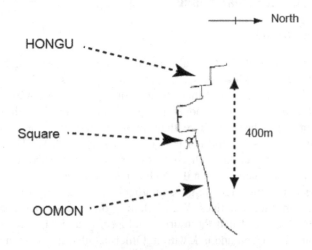

Fig. 8. A Map for GPS Error Compensation

Fig. 9. The Worst Place for GPS

4.3 Development of Information Contents

3D graphics and messages to users were developed by three of the co-authors for about two months[4]. They were novice users of LightWave 3D, but could successfully create fantastic objects. In order to use Java 3D, we needed to limit the number of polygons for each 3D object: to 5000 or less.

For the development, we also needed to visit KOTOHIRAGU several times, to measure location values, to check GPS condition, to find interesting monuments to deal with in the KOTOHIRAGU Navigator, to find tourists' typical walking paths, and to confirm that our system would not cause any troubles to the souvenir shops or other visitors. In order to develop high-quality location-oriented services, we should also take into account such investigation cost.

5 Experiment with Real Tourists

5.1 Evaluation Method

From November 9th to 15th, 2005, totally seven days, we were staying at the entrance of the approaching way, which was below the first stone step. We caught tourists walking along the way and asked them to join our experiment. We offered them a book coupon of 500 yen for their cooperation. It was a hard task to find tourists who could accept our offer, because more than 70% of them did not have compatible phones and many tourists just did not like to cooperate. As KOTOHIRAGU visitors are mostly in senior generation, such visitors often had never used the GPS function nor the Internet access function, even if they had a GPS-phone.

If a tourist accepted our offer, we gave him/her a card that only shows the URL for the service and some legal notices. We explained that the service area is between OOMON and HONGU and that the tourist could enjoy a sightseeing-guide service, take an accompanying agent, and talk with it. Other detailed description of the system was given by the system itself. Receiving little information before using the system is a natural situation if the service is really intended for the public. Also we needed to avoid taking long time for explanation before the experiment, in order to make the tourist agree with our sudden offer.

Scenes in the trial sessions are shown in Fig. 10. In these photographs, models are not real tourists but recruited students who were asked to try this system during the same period of experiment. We avoided neither taking photographs of real tourists nor following them in order to let them use it in a natural situation. One difference between real tourists' usage and Fig. 10 would be that real tourists were often in a group of two to five people and only one of them had a compatible phone to use our system.

After 90 minutes or so, the tourists came back to us. We asked them to fill a survey form (two pages). We gave a book coupon to each tourist and also obtained a sequence of access log for each user.

---

[4] We are not trying to evaluate the human power for the development. Their time was not 100% devoted to the task.

Fig. 10. Scenes in the Trials. (left: beneath OOMON, right: in front of HONGU).

5.2 Results

During the seven days experiment, totally 29 tourists (21 men and 8 women) agreed to participate. Twelve of them were between 25 and 30 years old, which was the most frequent age. Thirteen of them visited KOTOHIRAGU for the first time.

They accessed the system 24.2 times in average, including 5.8 times of location acquisition. They talked with agents 7.7 times in average.

Analysis by Age. Table 1 shows some results of survey in a four-grade scale, where 1 is the worst and 4 is the best score. The most highly evaluated function was the indication of remaining steps to HONGU (question (6)). This is because there are no real signboards along the steps showing the number of remaining steps, although most climbers would like to know it.

Location-aware description of monuments (question (1)) scored 3.18, which is not very good. However, its S.D. is rather large and some subjects appreciate it in their free comments, explicitly. This evaluation of the system varies by generation. If we observe only young tourists under 30 years old (17 subjects), the score is much better, 3.56. On the other hand, tourists over 30 years old gave average score of 2.67. Surprisingly, the difference between generations is much wider than other evaluations, for example, usage understandability (question (3)). The difference is proved to be statistically significant by a t-test ($p < 0.01$). On the other hand, answers to questions (2) to (6) did not show statistically significant difference between generations. Question (7) was given to obtain the total evaluation of the system. Answers to this question is also different between generations (statistically significant, $p < 0.01$).

The comments-sharing function was not used by all subjects because we did not have enough time for explanation of this function. This function was only described in the function description message that was shown to the user at the beginning, and also in the help file. Only six subjects left their comment using this function. However, this function was fairly well evaluated among users who experienced it. Example comments they left were "I have been exhausted by climbing," and "You can find a stamp at the rest house." These types of messages are what we expected.

Table 1. Results from the Survey Sheets (by Age)

Question or Evaluation Target	Total Average (N=29)	Young Users' Average (age <=30, N=17)	Senior Users' Average (age >30, N=12)	Total S.D. (N=29)
(1) Location-aware description of monuments	3.18	3.56	2.67	0.86
(2) Is it better than guidebooks or brochures?	2.86	3.00	2.64	0.66
(3) Did you understand how to use it?	3.17	3.29	3.00	0.85
(4) To leave shared comments	3.10	3.21	2.86	0.62
(5) To read shared comments	3.19	3.21	3.14	0.51
(6) Indication of the number of remaining steps	3.59	3.69	3.44	0.59
(7) Do you like to use a similar system again at other sightseeing destinations?	3.28	3.47	3.00	0.53

Score range: 1-4, 1 is worst, 4 is best.

Look at the results of questions (4) and (5). The average evaluations were not so different, but the generation gap was wider in question (4) than question (5). The gap in question (4) was not statistically significant, but we can assume that younger people are more willing to actively communicate with others in a shared virtual world.

Analysis by Visitor's Experience. Table 2 shows the evaluation by visitors who visited KOTOHIRAGU for the first time and for the second or more times, based on the same data as Table 1. We could not find any statistically significant differences between the two groups. However, there are some interesting suggestions.

Question (6) is supported by both groups. The number of stone steps is important information for visitors. From question (1), we can assume that the first-time visitors need more descriptions of monuments than the repeaters. On the other hand, from questions (4) and (5), we can assume that communication with other visitors was more accepted by the repeaters than the first-time visitors. These assumptions can be naturally understood. We can consider that repeaters need another kind of entertainment other than just to know the shrine itself. We assume that the repeaters evaluated questions (2) and (7) better than the first-time visitors, because the system provides a communication function. However, it is still an assumption that should be confirmed by using much bigger number of visitors, though it is difficult to conduct such a large-scale survey.

We believe that different service designs for first-time visitors and for repeaters should be considered.

Table 2. Results from the Survey Sheets (by Experience)

Question or Evaluation Target	Total Average (N=29)	Average of First-Time Visitors (N=13)	Average of Repeaters (N=16)	Total S.D. (N=29)
(1) Location-aware description of monuments	3.18	3.33	3.06	0.86
(2) Is it better than guidebooks or brochures?	2.86	2.75	2.94	0.66
(4) To leave shared comments	3.10	3.00	3.15	0.62
(5) To read shared comments	3.19	3.00	3.31	0.51
(6) Indication of the number of remaining steps	3.59	3.56	3.62	0.59
(7) Do you like to use a similar system again at other sightseeing destinations?	3.28	3.15	3.37	0.53

Score range: 1-4, 1 is worst, 4 is best.

GPS Accuracy. Subjective evaluation of GPS accuracy was 2.37 in total average, which had not been improved from the January's experiment, although it became much better in our own evaluation. We consider that this is because the subjects did not know the former system and it was no comparative evaluation between the two experiments. Subjects are always requiring more accurate location-based system.

In order to understand the bad effects of GPS inaccuracy on the service, we have calculated correlation coefficients of the evaluation data. All absolute values of coefficients are less than 0.4. This shows that subjects recognized the GPS inaccuracy as an independent problem from the system's value.

Free Comments. In the free description on the survey sheet, they also gave negative comments. A popular comment was on the battery, as the GPS-related functions consumed energy.

Another popular comment was that they preferred a map on the display. In our case, we avoided using a map to focus on the virtual world model, and also due to the copyright problem. This problem should simply be solved by adopting map interfaces in the future system.

Some people pointed out that they felt it dangerous to use this system when they were on the stairways, especially when they were going down (though this system was just for the situation of climbing up). One of the subjects claimed that when he was using this system he was almost left alone from his friends. These facts suggested that the service was attractive enough.

The function of showing the number of stone steps was also appreciated in their free comments. Some subjects appreciated that this system gave some information that they did not know. From these comments, we can conclude that one of the most important functions is to provide information that is not on the guidebooks, brochures, or signboards. It seems to be a paradox, because this system would become of no value if such real information sources were very rich. However, handy guidebooks cannot be too thick. Many signboards cannot be set up, because they would spoil the scenery. As a conclusion, we should design the service to well balance the real and virtual information sources.

6 Conclusion

In this paper, we have introduced our location-aware system with the virtual world metaphor, and one of its applications, the KOTOHIRAGU Navigator. The most important feature of our system is that it employs only popular mobile GPS-phones on the market. Due to this fact, we succeeded to recruit 29 real tourists, whose motivation was not the evaluation of our system but sightseeing, to participate in the evaluation sessions.

According to the survey, we have found that the location-aware sightseeing support service was accepted and appreciated by young people, in particular. The generation gap between senior and young people was wider than other evaluation points like usability.

Virtual world functions like comments-sharing were not fully enjoyed by visitors because of the nature of this experiment with real tourists, i.e. very novice users, but were accepted by at least some of the subjects, especially visitors who visited there for a second or more times.

Although our GPS error compensation mechanism was successful, the remaining GPS inaccuracy was still a problem. However, tourists could recognize it as a different problem from the information service quality.

We have also described the development experience of ours. It should be noted that deep investigation of the site was necessary to develop such kind of location-aware information service, in order to adjust location parameters and error compensation functions, to find a better representation to fit the visitors' requirements, etc. An appropriate balance between the real and the virtual information sources is the most important point in the information service design.

Acknowledgments

Part of this research was supported by Kagawa Industry Support Foundation (Grant for Industry-Academia-Government Liaison for Research and Development). We very much appreciate the kind support by Professor Tohru Ishida's laboratory for Q language. Finally we very much appreciate the kind support by the KOTOHIRA town office and the KOTOHIRAGU Shrine. We thank Prof. Gancho Vachikov for his kind help in proofreading.

References

1. Cheok, A. D., et al: Game-City: A Ubiquitous Large Area Multi-Interface Mixed Reality Game Space for Wearable Computers, Proceedings of the 6th International Symposium on Wearable Computers (ISWC'02), IEEE (2002)
2. Flintham, M., et al.: Where On-Line Meets On-The-Streets: Experiences With Mobile Mixed Reality Games, Proceedings of CHI 2003, ACM (2003) 569-576
3. Tenmoku, R. Kanbara, M., and Yokoya, M.: A Wearable Augmented Reality System Using Positioning Infrastructures and a Pedometer, Proceedings of the Seventh IEEE International Symposium on Wearable Computers (ISWC'03), IEEE (2003)
4. Vlahakis, V., et al.: Personalized Augmented Reality Touring of Archaeological Sites with Wearable and Mobile Computers, Proceedings of the 6th International Symposium on Wearable Computers (ISWC'02), IEEE (2002)
5. Schnadelbach, H., et al.: The Augurscope: A Mixed Reality Interface for Outdoors, Proceedings of CHI 2002, ACM (2002) 9-16
6. Izadi, S. et al.: Citywide: Supporting Interactive Digital Experiences across Physical Space, Personal and Ubiquitous Computing, Springer-Verlag, Vol. 6 (2002) 290-298
7. Björk, S., Falk, J., Hansson, R., and Ljungstrand, P.: Pirates! – Using the Physical World as a Game Board, Proceedings of Interact 2001, IFIP TC. 13 Conference on Human-Computer Interaction (2001) 423-430
8. Cheverst, K., Davies, N., Mitchell, K., Friday, A., and Efstratiou, C.: Developing a Context-aware Electronic Tourist Guide: Some Issues and Experiences, Proceedings of CHI 2000, ACM (2000) 17-24
9. Welbourne, E., Lester, J., LaMarca, A., and Borriello, G.: Mobile Context Interface Using Low-Cost Sensors, Proceedings of LoCA 2005, Springer (2005), 254-263
10. Tarumi, H., Morishita, K., Nakao, M., and Kambayashi, Y.: SpaceTag: An Overlaid Virtual System and its Application, Proceedings of International Conference on Multimedia Computing and Systems (ICMCS'99), IEEE, Vol.1 (1999) 207-212
11. Tarumi, H., Tokuda, S., Yasui, T., Matsubara, K., Kusunoki, F.: Design and Evaluation of a Location-Based Virtual City System for Mobile Phones, Proc. of 2005 Symposium on Applications and the Internet (SAINT 2005), IEEE (2005) 222-228
12. Matsubara, K., Mizukubo, Y., Morita, T., Tarumi, H., and Kusunoki, F.: An Agent Control Mechanism in Virtual Worlds for Mobile Users, Proceedings of the 2005 International Conference on Active Media Technology, IEEE (2005) 475-480
13. Tarumi, H., Nishihara, K., Matsubara, K., Mizukubo, Y., Nishimoto, S., and Kusunoki, F.: Experiments of Entertainment Applications of a Virtual World System for Mobile Phones, Proceedings of International Conference on Entertainment Computing 2005 (ICEC 2005), Lecture Notes in Computer Science, Vol. 3711, Kishino, F. et al. (Eds), Springer, (2005) 377-388
14. Ishida, T.: Q: A Scenario Description Language for Interactive Agents. IEEE Computer, Vol.35, No. 11 (2002) 42-47

A Wearable Interface for Topological Mapping and Localization in Indoor Environments

Grant Schindler[1], Christian Metzger[2], and Thad Starner[1]

[1] Georgia Institute of Technology, College of Computing, Atlanta, GA, USA
{schindler, thad}@cc.gatech.edu
[2] ETH-Swiss Federal Institute of Technology, Information Management, Zurich, Switzerland
cmetzger@ethz.ch

Abstract. We present a novel method for mapping and localization in indoor environments using a wearable gesture interface. The ear-mounted FreeDigiter device consists of an infrared proximity sensor and a dual axis accelerometer. A user builds a topological map of a new environment by walking through the environment wearing our device. The accelerometer is used to identify footsteps while the proximity sensor detects doorways. While mapping an environment, finger gestures are used to label detected doorways. Once a map is constructed, a particle filter is employed to track a user walking through the mapped environment while wearing the device. In this tracking mode, the device can be used as a context-aware gesture interface by responding to finger gestures differently according to which room the user occupies. We present experimental results for both mapping and localization in a home environment.

1 Introduction

We are interested in quickly and automatically mapping indoor environments to facilitate context-aware wearable computing interfaces. When brought into an unknown environment, an ideal wearable device would map the environment with little user intervention and then continue to track the user's movements throughout the constructed map. Though the mobile robotics community has studied this same problem for decades, many of their solutions involve sensors (e.g. laser range finders) which are either too large, too heavy, or too expensive to be built into a wearable computer. Instead, for this task we propose a cheap, lightweight device requiring minimal user intervention.

The device we use for this task, the FreeDigiter, was conceived as a contact-free finger-gesture interface for mobile devices [7]. It is equipped with a dual axis accelerometer and uses an infrared proximity sensor to detect numerical finger gestures. We extend the capabilities of this interface to detect when the user has walked through a doorway, thus enabling the construction of topological maps of new environments and the subsequent localization of users within these environments.

The contribution of our approach is in solving the mapping and localization problems for the case of extremely sparse sensor data from inexpensive wearable hardware – a situation which necessitates the development of a unique map representation to make these tasks possible. The implications of a cheap, wearable mapping and

M. Hazas, J. Krumm, and T. Strang (Eds.): LoCA 2006, LNCS 3987, pp. 64–73, 2006.

Fig. 1. The FreeDigiter device is equipped with a dual axis accelerometer, an infrared proximity sensor, and a Bluetooth radio for wireless communication. The entire device is worn like a pair of headphones with the sensors positioned over one of the ears.

localization device go beyond domestic applications, extending to fire, rescue, and other dangerous situations involving unknown indoor environments.

2   Related Work

In their location-recognition work, Lee and Mase [5, 4] have used wearable accelerometers and other sensors to recognize when users perform specific activities and transition between known indoor locations. They use a dead reckoning approach, integrating accelerometer data over time to build a metric map of a user's path through an environment. While we similarly count a user's steps, we take an otherwise different approach by building and tracking in topological maps which capture the connectivity of an indoor environment composed of multiple rooms.

Much work has also been done in the field of robotics on the dual problems of mapping and localization. Simmons and Koenig did work on mobile robot navigation in partially observable environments in which they integrated topological maps with metric information for localization purposes [10]. The augmented topological maps they use are constructed by hand and the intended movements of the robot are known. In contrast, we must infer the movements of the user through the environment from sensor information and automatically construct maps of the environment.

A large portion of the robotics literature focuses on Simultaneous Localization And Mapping (SLAM). For example, Howie Choset discusses the use of the Generalized Voronoi Graph [2, 3], a specific topological map, for mapping and navigating in unknown environments. This work has recently been applied to the problem of person tracking [6] by placing sensors throughout a known environment and employing a particle filter to track multiple individuals. For tracking, we also take an approach based on particle filtering, but we have only one sensor module, our sensors are mobile, and we know nothing about our environment.

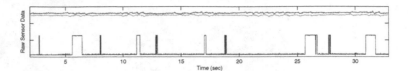

Fig. 2. Raw sensor data. The three data streams include dual axis accelerometer data (top) and proximity sensor data (bottom). The top (red) signal indicates side-to-side motion, the middle (green) signal shows front-to-back motion, and spikes in the bottom (blue) signal indicate finger or door detection events by the proximity sensor. All mapping and localization is performed utilizing only these sensor readings.

3   Sensors

The FreeDigiter is equipped with a dual axis accelerometer and an infrared proximity sensor. By processing the signals returned by each of these sensors (see Figure 2), we are able to detect footsteps, doorways, and finger gestures.

3.1   Proximity Sensor

The proximity sensor emits infrared light and detects reflected light from objects within a range of 10cm to 60cm. The output from the sensor is binary, indicating whether there is or is not an object within range. Originally intended as a method for input of numerical finger gestures, the FreeDigiter counts the number of peaks in the proximity detector signal as a user sweeps some number of fingers past the sensor. We extend the functionality of the proximity sensor by also detecting when a wearer has passed through a doorway. To the sensor, the difference between a finger and a doorway is the length of the pulse generated when each object passes (see Figure 3). Due to the high temporal resolution of the proximity sensor (160 Hz), even differently-shaped doorways will generate unique pulse-lengths.

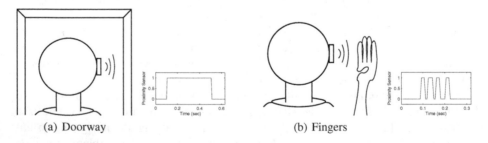

(a) Doorway   (b) Fingers

Fig. 3. The proximity sensor worn over the ear detects both a) when the user passes through a narrow space such as a doorway and b) when the user waves any number of fingers past the sensor. The two cases are reliably distinguished by the durations of spikes in the respective signals.

3.2 Accelerometer

We are particularly interested in detecting when a person wearing our device has taken a step forward. There is a large body of work in wearable computing that makes use of accelerometers for motion analysis[1, 8]. In many cases, accelerometers are placed on the feet or legs to extract walking data. Our device is head-mounted, and we found the most dependable footstep information comes from the x-axis accelerometer measuring motion perpendicular to the direction of walking (i.e. left-to-right motion). Though the raw data is rather noisy, it has a consistent sinusoidal motion during walking that can be examined with a low-pass filter (see Figure 4). Each peak and trough of this signal is a step with the left and right foot, respectively. Thus, we can define a footstep as a zero-crossing of the first derivative of the low-pass-filtered accelerometer data. The reliability of footstep detection provided by this method is suitable for our purposes.

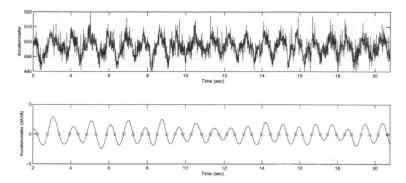

Fig. 4. The raw accelerometer data (top) for left-right motion is quite noisy. We can accurately and reliably detect footsteps (red circles in the bottom figure) as zero-crossings of the first derivative of the signal convolved with a Gaussian.

4 Mapping and Localization

We are interested in not only mapping an unknown indoor environment, but also in using the constructed map to track a user moving through the rooms of that environment. Thus, we need a representation that is easy to construct from our limited stream of data and that also has enough descriptive power to allow us to discriminate between features of the environment. For this purpose, we make use of an augmented topological map, similar to the maps used by Simmons and Koenig [10].

A map is represented as a set of edges E and vertices V defining a graph $G = \{E, V\}$. Each edge is augmented with a length l (in footsteps) and an edge-specific probability distribution over proximity sensor readings (the mean μ and variance σ of a Gaussian). By this definition, each edge corresponds to a constant part of the environment – i.e. the world looks the same to the sensors at every point on an edge. We define two types of edges:

1. **undirected edges** - Any edge $E_{i,j}$ between two different doorways with vertices V_i and V_j represents an undirected path across a room, where $l_{E_{i,j}}$ is the length of the

edge in footsteps. For undirected edges, we specify a probability distribution over proximity sensor readings with $\{\mu_{E_{i,j}} = 0, \sigma_{E_{i,j}} = 1\}$ since no doorways will be detected while traversing undirected edges inside of a room.

2. **directed edges** - We represent every doorway as a pair of vertices V_k and V_{-k} connected by two oppositely directed edges (an entrance $E_{k,-k}$ and an exit $E_{-k,k}$), each having its own distribution over sensor readings parameterized by $\{\mu_{E_{k,-k}}, \sigma_{E_{k,-k}}\}$ and $\{\mu_{E_{-k,k}}, \sigma_{E_{-k,k}}\}$. By convention, doorway edges are one footstep long ($l_{E_{k,-k}} = l_{E_{-k,k}} = 1$).

Given this representation, it follows that any clique of nodes in the graph G connected solely by directed edges represents a doorway, while a room is defined as a clique of nodes connected by undirected edges in the graph. Rooms that are "dead ends" consist of a single edge looping back to the same vertex.

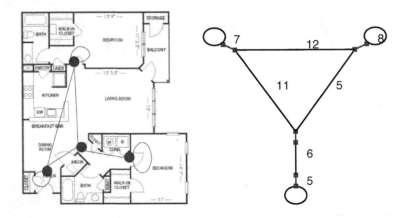

Fig. 5. Left: Topological map constructed by hand and overlaid on a metric map of our indoor environment. Right: Augmented topological map constructed automatically by walking through the physical environment. Each undirected black edge is labeled with edge length in footsteps. Each blue edge is really a pair of oppositely directed edges that correspond to the two ways of passing through a doorway, each of which is associated with its own probability distribution over proximity sensor readings.

4.1 Mapping

To map an unknown environment, a user wearing our device walks through the environment, passing through doorways and moving between rooms that should be connected in the graph. In building these maps, we will rely on a proximity sensor to detect and measure doorways and use an accelerometer to determine the distance between doorways, as outlined in Section 3, but this is not enough. When building a topological map, there is ambiguity in knowing when one has come back to the same place – e.g. traveling in a loop, or simply exiting through a door one had entered through previously in the opposite direction. Also note that the proximity sensor only sits on one side of the head. Thus, it will not have seen both sides of the doorway on the way into a room, and

---

Algorithm 1. Building an Augmented Topological Map

$E = \{\}, V = \{\}$ //empty graph

$while\,(BuildingMap)$

  $if\,(ProximitySensor.DoorDetected$ &&

     $ProximitySensor.FingerGesture)$ //detected and labeled door

    $k = ProximitySensor.Label$ //numerical label from finger gesture

    $if\,(V_k \cap V = \{\})$ //new doorway

      $V = V \cup \{V_k, V_{-k}\}$ //create vertices for new doorway

      $new = k$

    $else\,if\,(V_{-k} \cap V = \{\})$ //known doorway from different direction

      $new = -k$

    $endif$

    $E = E \cup \{E_{new,-new}\}$ //add directed edge through doorway

    $\mu_{E_{new,-new}} = ProximitySensor.Measurement$ //augment edge with sensor reading

    $l_{E_{new,-new}} = 1$ //augment edge with footstep length

    $if\,(E = \{\})\,old = new$ //first doorway

    $E = E \cup \{E_{old,new}\}$ //add undirected edge

    $l_{E_{old,new}} = Accelerometer.Footsteps$ //augment edge with footstep length

    $Accelerometer.Footsteps = 0$

    $old = new$

  $endif$

  $if\,(Accelerometer.Step)\,Accelerometer.Footsteps + +$

$end\,while$

---

the two sides of a doorway can look vastly different to the proximity sensor. Though there are methods for inferring topology from unlabeled landmarks [9], we choose to avoid this problem by letting the user indicate, through numerical finger gestures, labels for each doorway after s/he passes through it. Thus, if a user waves four fingers past the sensor after entering through the front door of a building, then when the user later exits through that front door, s/he should also signal with four fingers, providing a unique identifier for each doorway. Note that this user interaction is only needed during the initial mapping phase, and not during tracking.

The underlying algorithm for building the map is described in detail by Algorithm 1. To summarize, when the the proximity sensor indicates that the user has encountered a new doorway, we add two vertices, one directed edge, and one undirected edge to the graph. The directed edge is augmented with the current proximity sensor reading for the doorway, while the undirected edge is augmented with the counted number of footsteps since the previous doorway. The only other case involves passing through a previously mapped doorway in a different direction, in which case the algorithm proceeds in the same manner, except that the two vertices representing the doorway already exist and do not need to be added to the graph. In this way, the graph can be constructed incrementally in real time.

Note that Algorithm 1 deals only with the case where each doorway is visited twice with exactly one trip in each direction, i.e. tree-structured environments with allowances for simple loops. Relaxing this assumption leads to the possibility of doorway ambiguities that require additional doorway-identifying input from the user (or a non-deterministic map-building approach). Note also that learning a true distribution

$\{\mu_E, \sigma_E\}$ over proximity sensor readings for each doorway requires walking through the map more than once to have multiple instances of training data for each doorway.

4.2 Localization

Once we have constructed this map, we use a particle filter [11] to track the user's movements across the edges of the graph. Bayesian filtering is a traditional approach to the localization problem in which, at time t, we recursively estimate the posterior distribution $P(X_t|Z_{1:t}, U_{1:t-1})$ of some state X_t (the location of the user) conditioned on all measurements $Z_{1:t}$ (door detections from proximity sensor readings) and control data $U_{1:t-1}$ (footstep estimates from accelerometer data) up to times t and $t-1$ respectively as:

$$P(X_t|Z_{1:t}, U_{1:t-1}) = kP(Z_t|X_t) \int_{X_{t-1}} P(X_t|X_{t-1}, U_{t-1})P(X_{t-1}|Z_{1:t-1}, U_{1:t-2})$$

We call $P(Z_t|X_t)$ the *measurement model* and $P(X_t|X_{t-1}, U_{t-1})$ the *motion model*.

In a particle filter formulation we maintain a number of samples, each of which is a hypothesis about where the user is in the environment. Taken together, this set of samples approximates the probability distribution $P(X_t|Z_{1:t}, U_{1:t-1})$ over the user's current state. Each sample $x^{(i)} = \{e^{(i)}, r^{(i)}, d^{(i)}\}$ indicates a position on the map in terms of the current edge $e\epsilon E$, a distance r along that edge, and a direction of motion $d\epsilon\{-1, 1\}$. To implement tracking with the particle filter, we iteratively update each sample's state with the motion model, weight each sample according to the measurement model, and resample a new set of particles according to these weights.

Motion Model. The motion model $P(X_t|X_{t-1}, U_{t-1})$ is used to predict where the user will be in the next time step, given the previous state X_{t-1} and our accelerometer readings U_{t-1}. In sampling from the motion model we move each particle $x_{t-1}^{(i)}$ by adjusting the value of $r_{t-1}^{(i)}$ according to a Normal distribution $\mathcal{N}(\mu = d_{t-1}^{(i)} * u_{t-1}, \sigma = 0.1)$, where u_{t-1} is the number of footsteps sensed since the last time step and $d_{t-1}^{(i)}$ is the current direction of the particle. If $r_t^{(i)} > r_{e_{t-1}^{(i)}}$ or $r_t^{(i)} < 0$ then the particle has moved off of the previous edge $e_{t-1}^{(i)}$ and a new edge $e_t^{(i)}$ is assigned by sampling uniformly from all edges adjacent to the vertex which the particle overstepped. Finally, if the sample is on an undirected edge, we reverse its direction with some small probability according to $P(d_t^{(i)} = -d_{t-1}^{(i)}) = 0.1$.

Measurement Model. The map we have constructed makes the measurement model $P(Z_t|X_t)$ particularly simple. At each time step we get a measurement Z_t which is the pulse length of the proximity sensor's currently observed doorway, or zero if there is no doorway present. We simply evaluate the current doorway reading with respect to the probability distribution that lives on each sample's current edge, i.e. $P(Z_t|x_t^{(i)}) = \mathcal{N}(\mu_{e_t^{(i)}}, \sigma_{e_t^{(i)}})$ and weight each sample by this amount. Intuitively, if the motion model propagates a particle onto a directed doorway edge, it will only survive the resampling process if the sensor's current reading truly indicates passage through that doorway at the current time step. Thus, particles are kept from escaping through doorways too early, but are free to roam from edge to edge within the same room.

5 Results

To determine the feasibility of solving the tracking task with our limited sensor data, we first evaluated the performance of each sensor individually. Note that rather than doing computation on the wearable device, in these experiments the device communicated wirelessly through BlueTooth to a stationary PC within range.

We tested the accuracy of the footstep detector in a home environment. Over several minutes of data totaling 418 footsteps, the system correctly identified 407 footsteps for an accuracy of 97.4%. In these tests, no effort was made to alter walking patterns in any way to improve accuracy.

In an office setting, we designed an obtacle course involving a mixture of walking through doorways and performing finger gestures. Each run of the course involved 5 doorways and 7 distinct finger gestures (the gestures themselves were the numbers 1 through 7). The system recognized 58 out of 60 events correctly, including identifying the correct number of fingers used in gesturing, for a total of 96.7% accuracy, with one false positive due to a human walking too closely past the user, a clear weakness of the current system. Out of the 5 runs, the final 4 had 100% accuracy, suggesting that a user can learn to correct his or her errors over time while using the device.

Given that the sensors were sufficiently accurate for our tasks, we tested both mapping and localization in a home environment. An apartment consisting of five rooms with four doorways was chosen for testing. As expected, the results improved as a user became more experienced with the sytem. Thus, to illustrate the results of our tests, we present a representative mapping and tracking result for a single experienced user. For the mapping task, the user was able to traverse all the rooms in under 35 seconds at a normal walking pace and by pausing only to label each doorway with a finger gesture before moving through the next doorway. The data from the device was sent wirelessly via BlueTooth in realtime to a desktop computer in the same apartment. Through this process, a topologically-correct augmented map with accurate footstep measurements was successfully constructed (see Figure 5).

Finally, using this map just after it was constructed, the user was successfully tracked walking around all five rooms, going through doorways on eight separate occasions. 500 particles were used during tracking. Figure 6 shows the distribution of particles at six time slices in the tracking sequence. When no doors are observed, the distribution grows uncertain, and the particles spread out. When a door is sensed, the distribution becomes sharply peaked in one or two locations, and the particles are more tightly bunched. The weighted mean location of particles amounts to a hypothesis about which room on the map is being occupied. Accordingly, the tracking accuracy was 100% for the results shown here from an experienced user of the system.

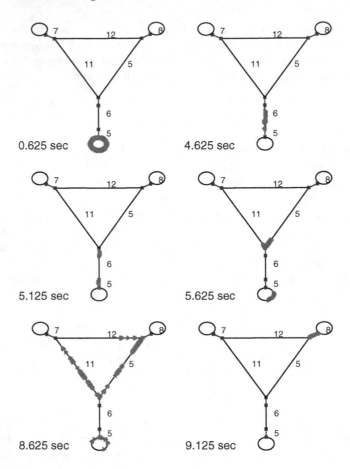

Fig. 6. Tracking results. As the subject passes through three doorways in succession, the motion model propagates particles along edges according to detected footsteps, and each particle is weighted by comparing observed and expected sensor readings.

6   Future Work and Conclusions

Weaknesses of our method include the reliance on significant differences between doorway sensor readings and the effective inability to recover from a tracking failure at any time when a doorway is not being sensed. These problems can be addressed by replacing the binary proximity sensor with one or more analog proximity sensors to obtain more detailed doorway measurements. In addition, since the sensors are worn on the body, the performance of the system depends upon the behavior and skill of the user. For example, at present, the size of a doorway is dependent upon the speed with which it is passed through. A user who is unable to maintain a constant speed across multiple runs will not be tracked as well as a more consistent walker. It is our hope that using additional accelerometer data can alleviate this problem.

The significance of our contribution here is two-fold. First, we have shown that an inexpensive wearable device using small amounts of sensor data can be used for quick and easy topological *mapping* of completely unknown environments. Second, we have demonstrated success in *tracking* users across these automatically constructed maps. Most importantly, we have illustrated the feasibility of cheap, lightweight, wearable mapping and localization devices.

References

1. I. Choi and C. Ricci. Foot-mounted gesture detection and its application in virtual environments. In *IEEE International Conference on Systems, Man and Cybernetics*, 1997.
2. H. Choset. *Sensor based motion planning: The hierarchical generalized voronoi graph*. PhD thesis, California Institute of Technology, 1996.
3. H. Choset and K Nagatani. Topological simultaneous localization and mapping (SLAM): toward exact localization without explicit localization. *IEEE Trans. on Robotics and Automation*, 17(2), April 2001.
4. S-W. Lee and K. Mase. Incremental motion-based location recognition. In *ISWC*, 2001.
5. S-W. Lee and K. Mase. Activity and location recognition using wearable sensors. *Pervasive Computing*, 1(3), July-Sept 2002.
6. L.Liao, D.Fox, J.Hightower, H.Kautz, and D.Schulz. Voronoi tracking: Location estimation using sparse and noisy sensor data. In *IROS*, 2003.
7. C. Metzger, M. Anderson, and T. Starner. Freedigiter: A contact-free device for gesture control. In *ISWC*, 2004.
8. C. Randell and H. Muller. Context awareness by analysing accelerometer data. In *ISWC*, 2000.
9. A. Ranganathan and F. Dellaert. Inference in the space of topological maps: An mcmc-based approach. In *IROS*, 2004.
10. R. Simmons and S. Koenig. Probabilistic robot navigation in partially observable environments. In *IJCAI*, 1995.
11. S. Thrun, D. Fox, F. Dellaert, and W. Burgard. Particle filters for mobile robot localization. In Arnaud Doucet, Nando de Freitas, and Neil Gordon, editors, *Sequential Monte Carlo Methods in Practice*. Springer-Verlag, New York, January 2001.

Taking Location Modelling to New Levels: A Map Modelling Toolkit for Intelligent Environments

Christoph Stahl and Jens Haupert

Saarland University,
66123 Saarbrücken, Germany
stahl@cs.uni-sb.de

Abstract. We present a map modelling toolkit that meets the special requirements of pedestrian navigation in intelligent environments. Its central component is a graphical editor, which supports geometric modelling of architectural ground plans through polygon meshes. Multiple levels and their interconnections, such as ramps and staircases, can be represented through the aid of layers. In order to support a full range of activities, from travelling to interacting with pervasive user interfaces, coarse models on an outdoor scale can be hierarchically refined by submodels on building and room scales. The XML-encoded models can be useful for positioning systems, referencing spatial context and for route finding through multi-story buildings. Besides the editor, the toolkit provides a routing module for pedestrian navigation.

Keywords: geometric location modelling, pedestrian navigation, intelligent environment.

1 Introduction

Modelling the physical environment is a basic requirement for the development of a mobile pedestrian assistance system, especially if navigational aid has to be conveyed to the user. Furthermore, any intelligent environment may benefit from the ability to relate the location of their users and devices to features of their surrounding space. Due to the diversity of research conducted in the field of mobile and pervasive computing, current off-the-shelf products are however unlikely to meet all potential requirements for location modelling. During the past five years of pedestrian navigation system development, our own research group has indeed faced many limitations of existing models like CAD drawings and commercial street map data. Primary shortcomings exist in the form of conversion and maintenance of geographical data through proprietary tools and data structures. Our contribution was to ease the whole modelling process through the development of a new editor and XML-style file format, dedicated to the specific requirements of pedestrian navigation in indoor environments.

The situation of a pedestrian differs from driving, since the user is not bound to follow paths or streets. Instead users typically cross open spaces, directly following their line of sight. The model has to particularly reflect this and represent places as polygonal objects, in contrast to commercial street map databases, which usually

M. Hazas, J. Krumm, and T. Strang (Eds.): LoCA 2006, LNCS 3987, pp. 74–85, 2006.

consist only of line segments. As pedestrians spend most of their time inside buildings, indoor environments have to be modelled. Sophisticated architectural designs, such as the spiral ramp inside of the Guggenheim museum in New York, pose a challenge to their modelling through 2D levels, and require a solution somewhere in between the simplicity and complexity of two and three dimensional space.

In order to represent the situational context of places, such as room temperature and inhabitants, we need to relate a symbolic model to the geometric model. Therefore the modelling tool should allow one to reference places through symbolic names.

Finally, we assume that we can not base our modelling activity on a single source of information. For some outdoor areas, highly detailed aerial photographs may be available. For other areas, CAD drawings with features such as the outlines of paths and buildings may be used. Indoors however, typically only large-scale printouts of architectural drawings exist. Thus the editor should allow for a partial mapping of the environment through multiple views at arbitrary scales and granularities, and support their arrangement to form a hierarchic tree-like structure. Such a 'divide-and-conquer' strategy would also ensure scalability and maintainability.

In the following sections, we will give a brief summary of related work on location modelling before we motivate and introduce our toolkit. We describe how to use the editor and explain our routing algorithm. We close with application examples and conclusions.

2 Related Work

A survey on the state of the art of location modelling can be found in [2], which distinguishes five basic model types. The traditional models include *physical locations* in the form of geographic (latitude, longitude) coordinates, and *geographical locations*, which denote natural objects like countries, cities, and also post codes. For our domain, we are interested in the more abstract models: In a *geometric model*, locations and located objects are represented accurately by sets of coordinate tuples in one or more reference systems. However, for human interaction it is more convenient to refer to a location by name: A *symbolic model* is a location directory that delivers meaningful information about places and their relations. Finally, the combination of a geometric and symbolic model is called a *semi-symbolic* or *hybrid* model. Our editor primarily supports the creation of geometric models that optionally include geographic coordinates, and in [7] we have outlined how to build a hybrid location model.

The *Geography Markup Language GML* [3] can be used to represent abstractions of real-world phenomena, such as rivers, roads and buildings, as a collection of geographical features. Each feature might have simple properties, such as a name and classification, as well as geometry-valued properties, such as centreline coordinates.

Recently toolkits for the prototyping and development of location-aware applications have been published, which also include geometric location modelling support. The *FLAME* Framework [1] for location aware modelling provides the graphical WorldBuilder tool to map polygonal regions. A region manager calculates overlaps between static and dynamic regions around objects, and a spatial relation manager creates events to notify the applications about changes, such as a person moving from one room into another. The *Topiary* Tool [3] is focused on the prototyping and testing of location-enhanced applications. The designer uses the *Active Map* workspace to create a model of people, places and things. A background image helps the user to draw paths, which are used for wayfinding, and to model the boundaries of places. Location-dependent behaviours can be specified through scenarios and tested with application mockups.

3 Motivation

Our research aims towards a system that provides ubiquitous navigational aid for its users, with an emphasis on indoor environments, but which also covers outdoor places and routes on a large scale. This vision of a seamless indoor-outdoor navigation system has already been implemented as a research prototype, the *BMW Personal Navigator* (BPN) [5]. In this scenario a user can plan a route at home and then be instructed by the system in different situations, driving the car, walking in the street and inside the destination building. Whereas the *BPN* prototype has been quite successful in demonstrating the overall concept, we have learned several lessons about location modelling. The *BPN* system is based on a commercial street database, which has been imported into the free GIS system *OpenGIS* and manually extended by indoor route segments. This approach lacks the scalability that would be required for a truly ubiquitous location model, as too many buildings need to be represented and maintained in a single database. Since the environment model is solely based on a path network (which is represented as a graph) it has severe limitations for the pedestrian navigation domain. The suggested routes will often direct the user on a detour that strictly follows the modelled paths, even if it would be possible for a pedestrian to abbreviate the route across large places. An actual example is shown in Figure 1, where the dotted lines indicate the path network and the thick line shows the abbreviated route. Furthermore, since the GIS system's routing module operates with two-dimensional geographic coordinates, it takes several workarounds to denote destinations in the upper floors of buildings. Inside the building, no GPS data can be received, so the *BPN* system used infrared beacons, and the position of the user was looked up from a database, that returns the geometric coordinates of the received beacon IDs (16 bit of information). The installation of the beacon infrastructure took several days, since no tools were available at this time to graphically model the position, range and orientation of the beacons. Other difficulties arose from the fact, that three different location models were required. Start and destination addresses are usually given as geographic locations (postal addresses), and have to be mapped to physical locations in the *WGS84*[1] coordinate system (longitude, latitude) used by GPS. The physical locations have to be mapped to screen coordinates (x, y) in the map's texture bitmap reference system, in order to visualize the position of the user. Indoors, no *WGS84* coordinates are known, and the paths and beacons have been entirely modelled in bitmap coordinates instead. The alignment of the indoor space with the outdoor space has been done manually and hence was error prone. Besides map visualization, the *BPN* system has been designed to convey automatically

---

[1] World Geodetic System 1984, Website: http://www.wgs84.com, visited 23.9.2005.

generated verbose instructions to the user, such as "turn right after 10 meters". As the underlying location model consisted of a set of two-dimensional floor maps without height information, additional annotation workarounds were required to guide the user through the staircase ("please go *up* the stairs to the 2nd floor").

In summary, we conclude the following research issues for pedestrian navigation in mixed indoor/outdoor environments from our previous experiences with the *BPN*:

- scalability and maintainability of the underlying location model
- polygonal representation instead of abstract line segments
- mapping of beacons for indoor positioning
- hybrid geographic (symbolic) and physical (geometric) location modelling
- modelling height information

4   A Web-Based Approach Towards Ubiquitous Location Modelling

We will now describe the approach that we are currently pursuing in order to cope with the issues mentioned in the previous section, which has been published in [7]. We have decided to utilize the Web for the storage of environmental models in arbitrary scales and levels of detail, encoded in a XML-based language. The relationships between models and sub-models, for example a city quarter model and a building model, can be expressed through hyperlinks, so that the models form a hierarchic tree-like structure. The Web-based approach will ensure the scalability, maintainability (everyone can update his model any time), and accessibility required for ubiquitous pedestrian navigation.

As we have stated before, a simple path-network is not sufficient for pedestrian navigation (see Figure 1), instead we have to explicitly model the outlines of entities such as streets, buildings, rooms or corridors through polygonal objects, using vertices and edges. In order to represent the slope of terrain, ramps and stairs, each vertex represents a coordinate in three-dimensional space. Furthermore, each face may be assigned to a layer. In order to maximize consistency and avoid intersections or overlapping areas, we choose a mesh structure, where polygons share their adjacent edges and vertices. For route finding purposes, each edge between two adjacent polygons is attributed by their passability to distinguish between walls and doors. An example is shown in Figure 2, where dots represent vertices, lines represent walls and dotted lines represent doors (passable edges).

In addition to polygon objects, sometimes the mapping of navigational fixpoints, such as beacons or landmarks, is desired. For this reason we allow additional geometric primitives, such as points, spheres and sections.

The proposed model requires a sophisticated editing tool, which allows the graphical manipulation of polygons and primitives in three dimensions and multiple layers. Furthermore, the editor has to support the creation of hyperlinks between models and sub-models, and to allow for the visual alignment of refinement nodes in the hierarchy. We also have to adapt a shortest path algorithm to exploit our polygonal data structure and return typical pedestrian paths, as shown in Figure 1.

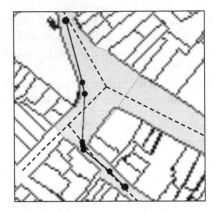
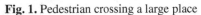

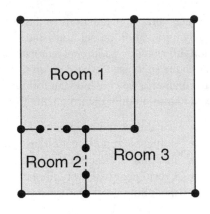

Fig. 1. Pedestrian crossing a large place   **Fig. 2.** Modelling rooms as polygons

5   The Map Modelling Toolkit

The central component of our map modelling toolkit is a graphical editor, that has been implemented in the *C#* language on Microsoft's *.NET* platform. A current release can be downloaded from [9]. The editor allows the user to trace the silhouettes of geographical or architectural features depicted in a backdrop bitmap image and thereby to create a mesh of polygonal objects. The user interface is based on the *OpenGL* 3D-graphics architecture, which enables top-down projections as well as perspective views, free rotation and zoom. The modelling of multi-story buildings is assisted through multiple layers.

As a file format, we have chosen the XML standard to encode the model in a human-readable, yet easily machine-processable manner. We have written parsers in the C#, C++ and Java programming languages.

Since the complexity of a model is inevitably limited by its file size, we adopt a 'divide-and-conquer' strategy. Consider for example a city model A, which represents the outlines of some buildings, and a refinement model B, which represents the rooms inside one of A's buildings. The editor allows one to graphically assign B to it's outline in A by direct manipulation. The link information is stored in the header of model B, together with the necessary transformations (translation, scale and rotation) of B's local coordinate system. Thus higher-level models may be refined, even if the user has no permissions to modify them directly. Browsing through nested models is supported through a tree window.

As the toolkit has been designed with pedestrian navigation in mind, it includes a route finding module. It is able to generate routes between any two points in a model, which follow the line-of-sight whenever possible instead of a restrictive path network. Since even multi-story buildings can be represented as a single mesh, the pedestrians will be routed through staircases, if needed. During the modelling process, the results of the route finding module can be tested at any time within the editor. For the developers of mobile applications, the routing module's *C++* code is also available.

6 Using the Editor

We will now describe step by step how the editor, as shown in Figure 3, can be used to model complex environments comprising outdoor areas and the interior of multi-story buildings. The process begins with the selection of an image source that partially depicts the geographical or architectural features of the environment in an appropriate scale. In the next step, the editor allows the user to model the outlines of these features as a mesh of polygon objects by tracing the backdrop template. Additionally, navigational fixpoints can be marked using geometric primitives such as points or circles. If multiple levels have to be modelled, the user can create new layers. Finally, models of different scale can be linked together. The resulting models are encoded in XML.

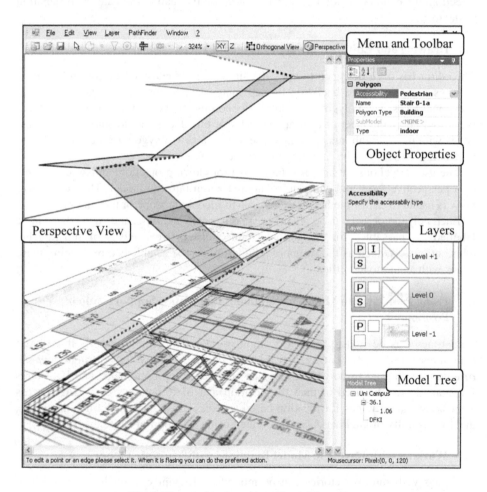

Fig. 3. The graphical user interface of the editor

6.1 Creating and Georeferencing a New Model

The creation of a new model begins with the selection of a backdrop bitmap image, which should be quadratic and may have a resolution up to 2048x2048 pixels due to current restrictions of *OpenGL* textures. The image may be an aerial or satellite photograph, as provided by *Google Maps*[2], or a scanned architectural plan. Once the image is loaded and displayed, the user is asked to place three reference points for a geographic coordinate system such as the *WGS84* geodetic system used by GPS receivers. These points allow the transformation of model coordinates measured in pixels, into geographic coordinates measured in longitude and latitude, and vice versa. Additionally, a scale vector can be specified to convert between model distances (pixels) and real-world units (meters). If the image is not aligned to the north-south direction, the points of a compass can be placed on the map to indicate the orientation of the map.

6.2 Drawing and Editing a Mesh of Polygonal Faces

The editor has been designed to trace the silhouettes of geographical or architectural features depicted in the backdrop bitmap image and to model their shape through polygonal faces. The polygons should ideally completely cover the modelled area as a mesh, but never intersect or overlap. To achieve this, faces should share vertices and edges with their neighbours. When the user draws a new polygon, the cursor will snap to existing vertices nearby in order to reuse them.

The user can choose at any time between a top-down projection, an isometric view or a perspective view and can pan, rotate and zoom into the model. The perspective view is useful to adjust the height of vertices to model the slope of terrain or stairs.

Each polygon object can be given a symbolic name and type, and each edge can be labelled as "passable" for navigation. Connections between edges of separate but adjacent models, such as the wings of a building, can be established by naming these edges with a unique identifier.

6.3 Using Primitives to Model Navigational Fixpoints – Support Indoor Positioning

Sometimes it is desired to mark a position or spot. The editor supports three basic primitives: *Point (x, y)*, *Circle (x, y, radius)*, and *Section (x, y, radius, angle, orientation)*. Similar to polygons, they can be given a symbolic name and ID. Points for example can be used to map the position and MAC address of WLAN access points. Activation zones for location-based services can be easily defined as circles, and the visibility of landmarks can be defined using a section of a circle.

6.4 Working with Layers to Model Buildings with Multiple Floors

Buildings with multiple stories can be modelled efficiently through the concept of layers. These layers define new workspaces above the ground plane, which use their

---

[2] Google Maps Beta Website: http://www.maps.google.com, visited 23.9.2005.

own backdrop images, and they can be selectively shown or hidden. To avoid confusion, all polygon selection and manipulation operations are restricted to a single 'active' layer. It is possible to add, duplicate or remove layers at any time. When new polygons are drawn, it is possible to snap and connect to vertices on other layers or to clone them by projecting their coordinates into the active layer.

6.5 Hierarchical Modelling at Multiple Scales

The refinement of some polygonal object, such as the outline of a building through a more detailed model of this area, e.g. an interior model, can be a done in three simple steps. First the user has to select the polygon and a refinement model. The editor now tries to automatically scale and rotate the refinement model according to its georeference points or alternatively its scale and orientation information. It is displayed within the larger model, and the user can now manually align the building model to match its outline, if necessary, as shown in Figure 4. The resulting correction factor can either be applied to the interior model or the refinement model, or stored together with the link information. The hierarchical model structure can be explored through a tree view window, as seen in the lower right section of Figure 3.

Fig. 4. Refining a building object by its interior model

7 The Route Finding Algorithm

The route finding algorithm has been designed to return a path between any two points in a mesh of adjacent polygons. The route is only allowed to cross edges if they are annotated to be passable and should directly follow the line-of-sight unless turning points are caused by obstacles like walls. We make the assumption that the turning points are most likely determined by corners, where two walls include an angle greater than 180 degrees. Thus in the first step a set of relevant points P is automatically created from all these corners. We also include the endpoints of passable edges (such as doors) in P. The points are moved slightly from the walls to keep a safety distance. In the second step, a graph $G(P,E)$ is constructed. An edge $e(p,q)$ exists in E if (and only if) both p and q lie inside adjacent polygons and the edge e intersects only 'passable' polygon borders. Now an $A*$ search [4] for the shortest path in $G(P,E)$ is conducted where the set of edges E is build 'on-the-fly' during their visit by the algorithm to avoid an exponential growth. Due to the construction of P, the result might not be the 'true' shortest path, so we have to optimize it. In the third step, we try to straighten the path to follow the line-of-sight wherever it is possible. An example path through multiple levels is depicted in a perspective view in Figure 5.

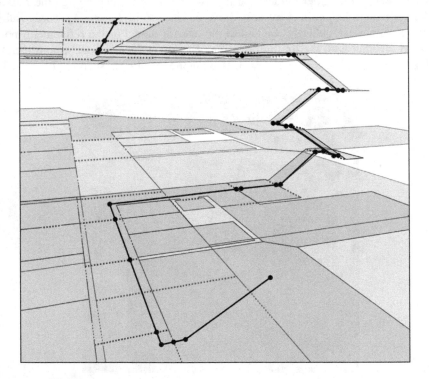

Fig. 5. This is an example of a planned route that includes staircases

8   Application Examples

In this section we will report on our experiences with the toolkit in three different application examples. We have modelled a three-story building and we use the system to represent navigational beacons. We also use it for a mobile audio guide.

8.1 Modelling a Three-Story Research Institute with Two Staircases

In order to evaluate the usability of the rather complex three-dimensional user interface of the editor in a real-life example, we have completely modelled one wing of a three-story building, the DFKI research institute. We have scanned the original architectural drawings, and then the modelling of the rooms in the ground floor took a few hours. We spent less time on the upper floors, since a snap-on feature allows copying existing points from below. Finally, connecting the floors through staircases requires only three new polygons each. This task has been done best in the perspective view. The DFKI model includes approx. 120 rooms and two staircases, see Figures 3, 5, and 6. It has also been linked as a refinement to a larger scale outdoor model of the university's campus, where the building is represented by its outline.

   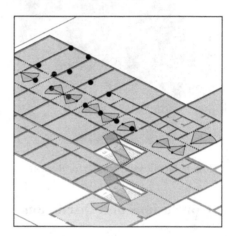

Fig. 6. Close-up of the DFKI building model   **Fig. 7.** Modelling infrared and RFID beacons

8.2 Indoor Positioning in Intelligent Environments

We are also using the editor in the RENA research project for a geometric model of an instrumented environment, as published in [8]. The model comprises two floors of the computer science department, and represents the boundaries of the offices and the positions of beacons within, which are used for our indoor positioning system. We have modelled both the location and identifier of RFID tags and the perception range of infrared beacons, as depicted in Figure 7. As the user receives these signals by their mobile device, the positioning service looks up their locations from the model and estimates the device's position accordingly. The position is described geometrically as a coordinate tuple, and symbolically as the name of the room containing the position.

8.3 Developing a Mobile Audio Guide for the Zoo

We have recently used the toolkit to aid the development of a mobile GPS-based audio guide for a zoo. As the visitor reaches an activation zone around a nearby animal enclosure, the animal will be briefly announced by pre-recorded speech. Upon reaching the animal, a detailed description is played. The zoo guide application has been implemented and successfully tested as shown in Figure 8. A bitmap of the zoo area has been provided by the land registry office, together with the required longitude and latitude information. We have used the editor to represent the animal enclosures and associated explanatory sound files with them, as shown in Figure 9. Support for wayfinding and indoor navigation will be integrated in the next phase.

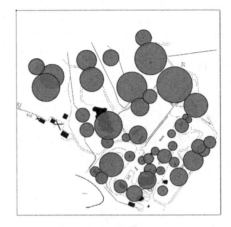

Fig. 8. Mobile audio guide for the zoo   **Fig. 9.** Mapping sound activation zones

9   Conclusions and Discussion

We have presented a map modelling toolkit that supports the geometric modelling of architectural spaces as a mesh of polygonal objects with symbolic names, using a backdrop image as the template. The resulting data structure allows one to relate positions to places through their containment relation. The editor allows for the representation of multiple floors as well as for a 'divide and conquer' strategy through hierarchical modelling. This approach allows one to refine objects that are modelled at a large scale, through more detailed models at a smaller scale. The benefits are scalability and maintainability of such a distributed world model, and indoor models can inherit geographical coordinates from their parent outdoor maps. The toolkit also provides a route finding module, which can be used for pedestrian navigation.

Regarding the visual presentation of navigational aid to the user, we propose to use separate models, since the requirements for a meaningful internal representation differ substantially from an appealing appearance on the screen. However, one could write an export module for the toolkit to convert the model e.g. into X3D[3], and enhance it using a regular editor for 3D scenes. The toolkit has passed through many development cycles, but the overall concept has been stable from the beginning and proven to be useful in many situations.

---

[3] X3D Website: http://www.web3d.org/x3d/overview.html, visited 30.9.05.

References

[1] Coulouris, G., Naguib, H. and Samugaling, K. FLAME: An Open Framework for Location-Aware Systems. Technical Note, Laboratory for Communications Engineering, Cambridge, UK (2002).Document URL: http://www-lce.eng.cam.ac.uk/qosdream/Publications/flame.pdf

[2] Domnitcheva, S. Location modeling: State of the Art and Challenges. In *Workshop on Location Modeling for Ubiquitous Computing* (Atlanta, September 30th, 2001). Held as part of the Ubicomp 2001 Conference.

[3] Geography Markup Language (GML) 2.0, OpenGIS Implementation Specification, OGC Document Number: 01-029, 20 February 2001. Document URL: http://www.opengis.net/gml/01-029/GML2.html

[4] Hart, P., Nilsson, N. and Raphael, B. A Formal Basis for the Heuristic Determination of Minimum Cost Paths. In *EEE Trans. on Systems Science and Cybernetics*, vol. 4, no. 2, pages 100-107, 1968.

[5] Krüger, A., Butz, A., Müller, C., Stahl, C., Wasinger, R., Steinberg, K.-E., Dirschl, A. The Connected User Interface: Realizing a Personal Situated Navigation Service. *In Proceedings of the 9th International Conference on Intelligent User Interfaces* (IUI 2004), ACM Press, 2004, pp. 161-168.

[6] Li, Y., Hong, J. I., and Landay, J. A. 2004. Topiary: a tool for prototyping location-enhanced applications. In *Proceedings of the 17th Annual ACM Symposium on User interface Software and Technology* (Santa Fe, NM, USA, October 24 - 27, 2004). UIST '04. ACM Press, New York, NY, 217-226.

[7] Stahl, C. and Heckmann, D. Using Semantic Web Technology for Ubiquitous Location and Situation Modeling. In *The Journal of Geographic Information Sciences*, CPGIS: Berkeley, Vol. 10, No. 2., December 2004, pages 157-165.

[8] Stahl, C., Baus, B., Brandherm, B., Schmitz, M. and Schwarz, T. Navigational – and Shopping Assistance on the Basis of User Interactions in Intelligent Environments. In *The IEE International Workshop on Intelligent Environments* (June 29, 2005, Colchester, UK), IEE, UK, pages 182-191.

[9] Yamamoto Project Website, 2006. URL: http://w5.cs.uni-sb.de/~stahl/yamamoto/

Harvesting of Location-Specific Information Through WiFi Networks

Jong Hee Kang[1] and Gaetano Borriello[1,2]

[1] Department of Computer Science and Engineering,
University of Washington,
Seattle, WA, USA
[2] Intel Research Seattle,
Seattle, WA, USA
{jhkang, gaetano}@cs.washington.edu

Abstract. Ubiquitous computing requires ready access to information that is relevant to users' context – especially information relevant to their current location. Applications on our personal devices should be able to autonomously and continuously harvest the information provided at that location and interrupt us only when it is important to do so. Currently, client devices are designed for explicit querying for information rather than continuous background harvesting of relevant information. To enable ubiquitous access to location-specific information, we can take advantage of the widespread deployment of WiFi networks. There is a wealth of location-specific information that network providers are willing to make publicly available to any users. However, today's models for accessing wireless networks do not easily support this due primarily to concerns over security and bandwidth utilization. In this paper, we present and compare the different methods that can be applied to solve the problem of continuous background access to location-specific information. Specifically, we compare client-pull and server-push models and show how tradeoffs can be made involving privacy, power consumption on devices, and utilization of wireless bandwidth. We also present three applications and discuss how the tradeoffs affect their design.

1 Introduction

WiFi networks are rapidly proliferating and are already available almost everywhere in large metropolitan areas. WiFi access points are being installed for many reasons: by enterprises to support their workers, by service providers selling access to private subscribers, by businesses such as cafés to attract customers, and by individuals expanding the uses of computing devices in their own homes. People are becoming more and more accustomed to having the ability to access information from wherever they are and more of us are carrying WiFi enabled devices such as laptops and PDAs to let us access and view that information. Having access to relevant information can be quite empowering and can help us in innumerable ways. For example, by giving us the ability to access information about the locations we visit.

M. Hazas, J. Krumm, and T. Strang (Eds.): LoCA 2006, LNCS 3987, pp. 86–102, 2006.
© Springer-Verlag Berlin Heidelberg 2006

As client devices that can use these WiFi networks proliferate, it is unlikely that we will want to attend to each one individually. Explicit user interaction has been the norm for humans using computing devices for several decades. However, in the future it is highly likely that we will want to delegate many tasks to our devices and will want to have to pay attention to them only when something interesting is discovered or requires a decision [14]. Each device will be running applications that will need access to location or context-specific data (that may be quite dynamic) to take care of a background task. They will provide users with alerts, prompts, and peripheral displays when it is important to do so. At the very least, they will just make it easier to get to relevant data by pre-fetching it rather than waiting for explicit actions by the user. Examples of this usage model include: information about transportation options (such as evolving traffic conditions between where I am and where I am going or when the next bus will arrive); special offers from stores in the mall I am visiting; and the services available in the building I am in.

There are some issues with this model, however. Do we really want our devices to autonomously connect over whatever networks they find? Do we trust that they will not compromise our privacy? How much power will they use in doing all this? How much will our devices' actions cost us in usage fees? Managing all of this may have a large impact on our cognitive load (our ability to deal with decisions and parallel tasks) than the hoped for savings from the proactive devices and applications.

WiFi networks are the natural choice as they are nearly ubiquitous already and have an infrastructure model already geared towards serving large numbers of users. However, WiFi has its own challenges. Currently deployed networks require prior registration or payment before allowing a connection can be made. We would have to develop policies to guide our devices, for example, to only connect when a particular service provider's network is available. Another approach is for wireless service providers to limit access to only the data associated with the location of their access points, thereby limiting use of available bandwidth while still providing access to dynamic location-specific information. However, this may allow these providers to track our presence and interests and potentially violate our privacy. In crowded situations, so many users may be making requests for the same data (e.g., airports or sporting events) that the available wireless bandwidth may be saturated and more infrastructure required to keep customers happy. Finally, data could just be broadcast in the immediate area and used by any device that can hear it. Unfortunately, this last approach may require lots of data to be broadcast to users who may or may not need it and their devices will need to expend power as they need to filter it. Of course, the broadcasting approach is also limited in that it only moves data in one direction: from provider to client.

This paper makes three contributions:

1. expand the range of location-specific information dissemination solutions available to ubiquitous information systems designers by presenting methods using existing WiFi network infrastructure,
2. an analysis of each approach that clarifies how each uses available bandwidth and the implications it has for privacy and power consumption in client devices, and
3. guidelines for system designers to use when building systems to provide such location-specific information dissemination services.

We use three applications we have prototyped to illustrate our points and show how we apply our guidelines. It is important to remember that what we are interested in is location-specific dynamic data and we are not interested in arbitrary network access. We would expect that arbitrary network access will be available as it is today. Our model is one of background applications that continuously and autonomously monitor certain conditions for their users rather than foreground applications requiring explicit interactions. An example of the former is keeping tabs on traffic conditions to get a more timely warning when it is time to leave for a next appointment. An example of the latter is user-initiated web browsing.

2 Implementation Approaches

WiFi network owners are in a good position to provide location-specific information to users because they know the physical area within which those users are highly likely to be. This information can be provided either as a public service to help streamline visits by customers or in exchange for advertising. This parallels closely the signage, kiosks, and displays that are already used by many organizations on their premises to help visitors or attract the attention of passers-by.

However, there are important concerns related to security and privacy that hinder this model from being used. On the one hand, network owners are concerned about the security of their network and how much bandwidth is utilized by non-paying customers. On the other, client devices acting autonomously of their human owners may compromise their owner's privacy, increase usage fees, or use too much power.

In this section, we describe the approaches that enable WiFi networks to provide general-purpose location-specific information to users (even to unregistered users) without compromising their network security. First, we describe the client-pull approach where clients initiate the communication by asking for information. This is the dominant model today. Then, we describe a complementary approach, based on server-push, where the location-specific information services continuously broadcast potentially useful information without being asked to so explicitly by clients. Finally, we discuss what techniques we can apply to these approaches to enhance their performance as well as the user experience.

2.1 Client-Pull Approach

Client-pull approach is also known as the client-server approach. Clients initiate the communication. When a client device comes under the coverage area of a WiFi network, it associates itself with an access point (AP) of the network and obtains an IP address from the DHCP server of that network. Applications running on the client device can connect to the location-specific information services that they are interested in and send requests for data.

However, network owners would not want to allow unregistered users or visitors to use their network without restriction. The captive portal technique [8, 9] can be used to restrict anonymous users' access to only location-specific information services. A registered user can use the network to its full extent. However, anonymous devices whose MAC addresses are not registered with the system are only allowed to access the limited set of location-specific information services. All other requests from unregistered devices to other services are redirected to the network's authentication service.

The implementation of this approach is simple and straightforward because the client-pull communication model is the most widely used communication model and many programming primitives and tools are available including web service creation tools. Location-specific information services can be implemented as web services. And, as mentioned earlier, captive portal implementations can be used to restrict anonymous users' network access.

2.2 Server-Push Approach

A complementary approach is to have the location-specific information services periodically broadcast their information over the WiFi network while client devices listen to the information silently – without even associating with access points. Location-specific information services broadcast their information using the standard UDP broadcast mechanism. Client devices set their WiFi network interfaces to monitor mode and listen for packets broadcast by the access points. In monitor mode, the WiFi network interface captures all the packets in the air. Among the captured packets, the client device has the burden of selecting those that carry the location-specific information that its running applications are interested in, filtering out and ignoring all the other packets.

Broadcasting is inherently unreliable because it does not provide guaranteed delivery of packets through acknowledgement and retransmission. However, periodic broadcasting can be considered eventually reliable because data is periodically retransmitted and clients can receive the missed packets in the next broadcast. To understand whether the broadcast approach is reliable enough to be used for disseminating information in WiFi networks, we performed an experiment with the WiFi network in our department's building. The WiFi network covers the entire six story building (plus basement) with 71 access points, and is actively used by a community of 1000 people. We set up a service that periodically broadcasts its data and measured the packet losses. During the experiment, we did not ask people to suppress the use of WiFi network because we wanted to understand the broadcast packet loss rate during normal use of the network. The packet loss rate was less than 2 %, and in most these cases the client received the missed packet in the very next broadcast cycle.

To make it easy to write services and client applications using this approach, we have developed a toolkit. The toolkit is composed of two parts: one for the server side and one for the client side. There is one server toolkit running on each broadcast-enabled WiFi network and all the location-specific information services share the same server toolkit by sending it the data they want to disseminate.

Each client device runs one instance of the client toolkit which is shared by all the applications in that device. The client toolkit receives all the captured packets from the WiFi network interface and checks the signature of the packets. If a packet is a broadcast packet and contains location-specific information, the toolkit parses the packet into an XML element and forwards it to the applications interested in the information. All the other packets are dropped right away. Applications express an interest in the information by registering their interest with the toolkit much as they would in querying a discovery service.

2.3 Variations of the Two Approaches

We can enhance these two basic approaches (client-pull and server-push) by applying some well-known variations. Here, we discuss only two of these, one for the client-pull approach and the other for the server-push approach.

2.3.1 Better Privacy with Disposable MAC Address

One of the concerns for the users in the client-pull approach is privacy. While communicating with a service in the network, a client device reveals its network interface's MAC address – assigned by its manufacturer. Because the MAC address generally remains fixed, it is relatively easy for attackers to trace the communication history of a client device and possibly obtain valuable private information through data mining and linking. To address this concern, we can use disposable MAC addresses to make it much harder for attackers to trace each device's communication history [3]. An issue with this approach is the appropriate rate of change for the MAC address (based on time, number of requests, session duration, etc.) and the overhead that the change incurs in securing a new IP address and re-establishing connections.

2.3.2 Saving Power with Index Information

In the server-push approach, a client device sets its network interface to monitor mode, captures all the packets in the air, and checks the signature (and also contents, in some cases) of each packet. The heavier the wireless traffic is, the more power is consumed in processing the packets -- only to find that most of them are not of interest to the applications on the client.

The ideal would be to process only the broadcast packets that are of real interest to the applications. The indexing techniques used in Broadcast Disks [4] can be applied to help client devices selectively listen to the broadcast packets. In this technique, in addition to the location-specific information, an index is also periodically broadcast. The index information contains the timetable of the broadcast (when each location-specific information service will broadcast its information). From the timetable, client devices can appropriately schedule their listening for when useful information is actually being broadcast and save power by not listening the rest of the time.

Our broadcast toolkit supports broadcasting index information. Location-specific services first let the server toolkit know what kind of location-specific information they have and how often they want to broadcast it. The server toolkit automatically generates the timetable information and broadcasts it periodically to inform clients of what types of information is available and when. On the client side, the client toolkit determines when to listen for broadcast packets from the timetable information. It can decide when the device can sleep and save power while ignoring packets that contain no data of interest and how often it should wake up and listen for updated information. Considering the jitter in delivery of packets in the WiFi network, the client toolkit needs to wake up little earlier than the scheduled arrival time of the packet. According to our experiment, the jitter was less than 200 ms in our WiFi network. We adjusted the toolkit to wake up 200 ms before the scheduled time and listen for the packet for 400 ms.

It also decides when it needs to obtain new timetable information based on the period of the time schedule broadcast or movement to a new location (determined via

PlaceLab [11]). This approach lets the client device individually control its power usage rather than being on a fixed schedule that may prove to be wasteful given its user's interests.

3 Analysis

In this section, we analyze and compare the two approaches both from the client's perspective and from the network owner's perspective, discussing which approach is better in different situations. This discussion can be used as a guideline for system designers in building their location-specific information systems.

3.1 From the Client's Perspective

From the client's point of view, the two approaches are quite different in three important aspects: 1) privacy, 2) CPU usage, and 3) power consumption. We analyze the two approaches in each of the three aspects.

3.1.1 Privacy

As users move from place to place and communicate with location-specific information services through potentially untrusted networks, privacy becomes a crucial issue. Thus, it is important to understand the privacy implications of the two approaches. To compare the two approaches, we borrow the notion of degree of anonymity [12] or degree of privacy. The degree of a client's privacy against an attacker can be viewed as a continuum. On one end of the spectrum is *absolute privacy*, which means that the attacker cannot even observe that the client is receiving any information (*unobservability*). On the other end of the spectrum is *no privacy* meaning that the attacker has complete knowledge of the user and the user's communication. In this case, the attacker knows the identity of the client device's user (*no pseudonymity*). And, the attacker can observe all the packets that clients receive from services (*observable*). Also, the attacker can link the packets that a client has received (*linkable*).

Absolute privacy is ensured in the server-push approach, where client devices are silently listening to the broadcast without associating with access points. Clients do not emit any packet or signal, and an attacker would not even know whether there is anyone actually listening to the broadcasts.

In the client-pull approach, client devices associate with access points and send requests to the services using their addresses. So, attackers can observe the communication (observable). And, if a client device uses the same MAC address for its communication, attackers can trace all the packets the device has received (linkable). However, client devices do not reveal the owner's identity because location-specific information services are for anonymous users and do not require authentication (pseudonymity). Thus, the client's privacy in the client-pull approach is a bit better than no privacy. However, should attackers obtain the user's identity (breaking pseudomymity), they can then have ready access to a significant amount of private information. For example, attackers can know the user's current location, trace of locations, what the user is interested in, how often the user asks for particular information, etc.

The disposable MAC address technique [3] enhances the privacy of the client-pull approach by limiting or eliminating linkability. Although client devices constantly change their MAC addresses, attackers can still observe the communication making it possible to link requests using the contents of the packets (addressed to the same service) or exploiting that there may be just a few users in the same coverage area. Table 1 summarizes this section.

Table 1. Level of privacy for each approach

Degree of privacy	Privacy properties			Approach
	Unobservability	Unlinkability	Pseudonymity	
Absolute Privacy	Yes	Yes	Yes	Server-push approach
	No	Yes	Yes	Client-pull approach with disposable MAC address
	No	No	Yes	Client-pull approach (for anonymous access)
No Privacy	No	No	No	Client-pull approach (in authenticated networks)

3.1.2 CPU Usage

CPU usage is important because it can affect the power consumption and also the number of applications that can run on a client device at any one time. We can expect that the server-push approach requires more CPU cycles than the client-pull approach because client devices have to process all the broadcast packets even if only a subset of them are actually of use to the client's applications. We present our experimental results that show how many more CPU cycles are used by the server-push approach. The experiment was performed on a tablet PC (Intel Pentium M 1 GHz, 512 MB RAM) running Windows XP.

Table 2. CPU usage of a client device when non-broadcast traffic increases

Non-broadcast traffic	0 Mbps	1 Mbps	2 Mbps	3 Mbps	4 Mbps	5 Mbps
CPU usage	0 %	1 %	2 %	3 %	4 %	5 %

In the server-push approach, the CPU usage of a client device is affected by the to-tal wireless traffic because client devices are set to monitor mode and capture all the packets in the air and process them to find out the packets containing relevant loca-tion-specific information. However, they only need to parse the broadcast packets that contain location-specific information, dropping all the other packets by just checking the signature of the packets. Therefore, the packets that do not contain location-specific information should not significantly affect the CPU usage of a client device. To see that, we measured CPU usage of a client device while increasing non-broadcast traffic (non location-specific information traffic) from 0 Mbps to 5 Mbps. As seen in Table 2, non-broadcast traffic does not have a significant effect on the CPU usage of a client device. When non-broadcast traffic increases from 0 Mbps to 5 Mbps (about 50 % network utilization in 802.11b), the CPU usage increases by only 5 %.

However, as more location-specific information services are broadcasting their information in a network, the CPU usage of a client device in server-push approach will increase regardless of the amount of information that is actually used by the applications in the device because the client device needs to parse all the location-specific information packets to determine whether to use or not. To mitigate that effect, client devices can schedule their WiFi interface based on the index (time table) information. To see how many more CPU cycles are used by the server-push approach compared to the client-pull approach and how effective the WiFi interface scheduling is, we measured the CPU usages of a client device in client-pull mode and server-push mode while increasing the location-specific information broadcast traffic. In the client-pull approach, when there was only one client application in the client device consuming 1 kbps location-specific information, the CPU usage was 1 %. When there were four applications consuming total 4 kbps of information (1 kbps each), the CPU usage went up to 2 %. The CPU usages for the server-push approach are shown in the graph in Figure 1. If the client device does not schedule its WiFi interface, the CPU usage increases linearly as the broadcast traffic increases regardless of the amount of information consumed by the applications in the device. The CPU usage for one application consuming 1 kbps information ('no-idx-1' in the graph) and that for four applications consuming total 4 kbps information ('no-idx-4') are not significantly different. When the WiFi interface is not scheduled, the CPU usage of the server-push is much higher compared to the client-pull approach. However, when the client device schedules its WiFi interface based on the index information, the CPU usage drops

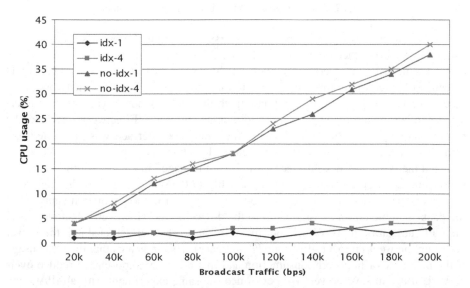

Fig. 1. CPU usage of a client device in server-push approach. In the label, 'idx' means that the client device schedules its WiFi interface based on index information, and 'no-idx' means that there is no scheduling of WiFi interface. The number in the label means the number of client applications running on the client device (each application is consuming 1 kbps information).

significantly and becomes comparable to that of client-pull approach. The CPU usage in the server-push mode is higher than that in the client-pull mode by only 1 or 2 % (see 'idx-1' (1 kbps) and 'idx-4' (4 kbps) in the graph).

3.1.3 Power Consumption

As client devices are always on and powered by batteries, power consumption is becoming a crucial factor in the design of a complete system and it is important to understand the major factors that affect power consumption on client devices and how the two approaches differ in power consumption.

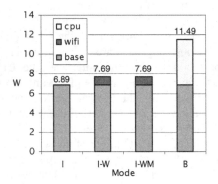

I: idle with no WiFi card
I-W: idle with WiFi card on
I-WM: idle with WiFi monitor mode
B: busy with no WiFi card

Fig. 2. Power consumption in different operation modes

For both approaches we first need to understand how much power is consumed by using the WiFi interface continuously. Figure 2 shows the power consumption of our tablet PC in different operation modes. In this measurement, the tablet PC's LCD screen was turned off so that we could determine the effect of the WiFi network interface more accurately (also we don't anticipate the background activities we are interested in requiring a screen to be on). In idle mode with no WiFi network interface, the power consumption is 6.89 W. When a WiFi network interface was connected and turned on, the power consumption increased by about 12% to 7.69 W. When we changed the WiFi network interface setting from managed mode to monitor mode, the power consumption did not change appreciably (7.69 W). This shows that the WiFi network interface does not spend more power in monitor mode although it captures all the packets in the air and passes them to the device driver. However, when we raised the CPU utilization to 100% without the WiFi network interface enabled, the power consumption went up to 11.49 W (a 67% increase). This indicates that the CPU usage is the major factor in power consumption and that it is very important to reduce overall CPU usage to save power. We performed the same experiment with an iPAQ and got a similar result. Our conclusion is that power consumption is more dependent on CPU usage than on the network interface. Thus, the server-push approach is comparable to the client-pull approach in terms of power consumption when their CPU usage is similar.

3.2 From the Network Owners' Perspective

From the network owners' point of view, bandwidth usage and ease of deployment are the main concerns. We discuss these two issues here.

3.2.1 Bandwidth Usage

Network owners naturally prefer the approach that uses less bandwidth as it allows them to provide services to more clients. Intuitively, the client-pull approach is better when there are fewer clients, and the server-push approach is better when there are more clients. Now, we formally analyze both approaches in terms of bandwidth usage and calculate the tradeoff point.

We analyze the bandwidth consumption of one service here. It can easily be extrapolated to the case where multiple services are sharing the wireless bandwidth. Usually, a service has multiple data items, and a client needs only one of them. For example, consider a bus information service that provides bus arrival information at a particular bus stop. The service has the arrival information for all the buses serving the stop. However, a user at the bus stop is usually only interested in the one specific bus that she is waiting for.

The bandwidth consumption of a service in the client-pull approach (B_C) and in the server-push approach (B_S) can be described as follows:

$$B_C = (B_D + O_C) \times R_C \tag{1}$$

$$B_S = B_D \times N_D \times R_S \tag{2}$$

In the above equations, B_D is the average size of each data item, O_C is the TCP connection overhead in the client-pull approach (which is approximately 300 bytes from our experiment), N_D is the number of different data items in the service, R_C is the data request rate in the client-pull approach, and R_S is the broadcast rate in the server-push approach. In the client-pull approach, when a client wants to receive a data item, it establishes a TCP connection (O_C) to a service and requests the data item. The service then sends back only the data item (B_D) specified by the request. Whereas, in the server-push approach, each broadcast packet includes all the data items ($B_D \times N_D$) in the service. The overhead is negligible because no connection is required to broadcast packets. In the bus information service example, a client in the client-pull approach asks for the bus arrival information for only that one bus that the user is waiting for. However, in the server-push approach, the service broadcasts multiple (N_D) bus arrival data for all the buses serving that bus stop.

The request rate (R_C) and the broadcast rate (R_S) are dependent on how often data changes (T_D), how long a user stays in the location on average (T_U), and the arrival rate of users (R_U, how many users are entering the location in a unit time). The ideal request rate (R_C) and broadcast rate (R_S) can be described as follows:

$$R_C = \begin{cases} R_U & \text{(when } T_U < T_D) \\ R_U \times (T_U / T_D) & \text{(when } T_U \geq T_D) \end{cases} \tag{3}$$

$$R_S = \begin{cases} 1/T_U & \text{(when } T_U < T_D) \\ 1/T_D & \text{(when } T_U \geq T_D) \end{cases} \tag{4}$$

When the average time that a user stays in the location is shorter than the time interval that the information changes ($T_U < T_D$), a user has to receive the information only once while they are at that location. In the client-pull approach, each user requests the information only once at that location, and R_C is equal to the arrival rate R_U. In the server-push approach, for each user to receive the information once, the information must be broadcast periodically every T_U.

In the case where the information changes once or more while a user stays in that location ($T_U \geq T_D$), the user must receive updated information at a useful frequency appropriate for their application (e.g., every 15 seconds for bus arrivals, every 5 minutes for flight departures). In the client-pull approach, each user requests the information T_U / T_D times while she is in the location, and R_C becomes $R_U \times (T_U / T_D)$. In the server-push approach, the information is broadcast every time the information is updated, and R_S becomes $1 / T_D$.

From the above equations, we can determine which approach is better in terms of bandwidth usage. The client-pull approach is better if $B_C < B_S$. If we substitute equations (3) and (4) into equations (1) and (2), we can conclude that the client-pull approach is better if $(B_D + 300\ bytes) \times (R_U \times T_U) < B_D \times N_D$ both when $T_U < T_D$ and when $T_U \geq T_D$. The expression $R_U \times T_U$ is basically the average number of people in the location at a single moment. Thus, the client-pull approach is better when the number of people in the location is small and the number of different data items that are provided by the service is large. On the other hand, if the number of people is large and the number of data items is small, the server-push approach is better. This is basically what we expected from our intuition that server-push is better when there are a lot of listeners and they find the information useful. This analysis provides us an idea of where the break even point is for the two approaches.

3.2.2 Ease of Deployment

Both of the approaches can be deployed in the existing WiFi network infrastructures without additional hardware costs. The only additional software component is the captive portal for the client-pull approach which may need to be installed on each AP. The server-push approach does not require any other software component. However, in WiFi networks with more than one AP, the server-push approach may need the ability to have each AP broadcast different data to get better location resolution.

In environments without existing wireless infrastructure, the server-push approach can be deployed more easily. The client-pull approach requires an access point that clients can associate themselves with and a DHCP server that can assign IP addresses to the clients. On the contrary, the server-push approach does not require these services. At a minimum, all it requires is a computer equipped with a WiFi network interface that can emit broadcast packets without even requiring an access point. Because clients use monitor mode, they can receive the packets without an AP or a DHCP server. Of course, in the client-pull approach, we could also use the same computer to deploy all the required service components. In that case, the WiFi network interface is set to master mode and functions as an access point with a DHCP server running on the same machine. However, it is more cumbersome than using the machine for the server-push and has inherent security concerns.

4 Applications

In this section, we describe some applications that we have prototyped and discuss how we can apply the results outlined above in designing them.

4.1 Bus Stop Information Service

We have prototyped a system to disseminate bus schedule information near bus stops. Some bus stops in our city already provide bus arrival information using scrolling LED display. However, the LED display can display only a minimal amount of information and its cost is prohibitive, limiting deployment to only the busiest bus stops. Moreover, vandalism has already claimed at least two of the dozen displays installed so far.

Our bus information service provides real-time bus information, gathered by our local bus service agency, to riders at or near a bus stop over a local wireless network. As a user approaches a bus stop, the bus information client application running on the user's device starts receiving the real-time bus status information from the bus stop information service through a WiFi access point near the bus stop. The client application checks the status of the bus that the user is likely to be interested in (from preferences set earlier or from inference as to where they may be heading [10]) and alerts the user when the bus is coming near or simply provides a display of estimated time of arrival (Figure 3). This application allows the user to read her book or newspaper inside a shelter or get a cup of coffee without constantly checking if the bus is coming. The client application can also show the list of all the buses coming to the bus stop with their estimated arrival times and destinations.

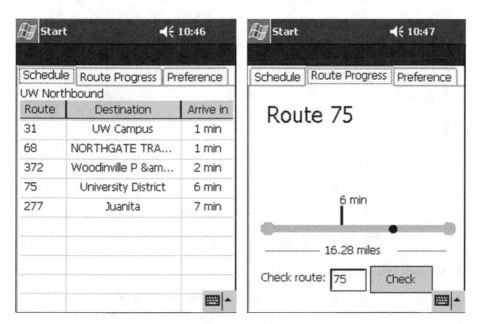

Fig. 3. Screenshot of the bus stop information application

In designing this service, the bandwidth usage was the main issue. So, we applied the analysis result from section 3.2.1 to the design of the service. The bandwidth usage of the service depends on how many different buses are serving the bus stop and how popular the bus stop is. The bus stop where we installed and tested the service has 8 different bus lines, and the size of the bus arrival information for each bus is about 100 bytes. If we substitute these numbers into the equation from section 3.2.1, the number of different data items (N_D) is 8, and the average size of each data item (B_D) is 100 bytes. Thus, the client-pull approach is better when $(R_U \times T_U) < 2$. In other words, the client-pull approach consumes less bandwidth when the number of people in the bus stop at a single moment is less than two. Otherwise, the server-push approach is better in terms of bandwidth usage.

To verify the result we obtained from the equation, we performed an experiment and measured the bandwidth usage while varying the number of users. Figure 4 shows the experiment result. The bus information changes every 15 seconds. So, in the client-pull approach, clients request information every 15 seconds. And, in the server-push approach, the service broadcasts the bus arrival information every 15 seconds. The bandwidth usage of the server-push approach remains the same regardless of the number of users. In the client-pull approach, the bandwidth usage increases with the number of users. And, as predicted by the equation, when there are more than two users in the bus stop, the server-push approach uses less bandwidth. As the bus stop has about 5 people waiting at any one time on average and up to 45 people during peak hours, the server-push approach is a better choice for this application.

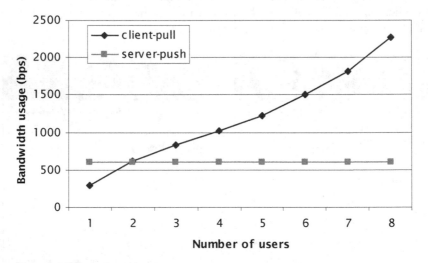

Fig. 4. Bandwidth usage of the bus stop information service

4.2 On-Bus Trip Assistant

In addition to the bus stop information service, we are working with our city bus administration to create an application to guide handicapped users along a pre-planned route. A typical bus rider has the goal of getting from a start location to a destination by riding one or more buses. Sometimes this goal takes the form of a routine daily commute while other trips might be one's first attempt to negotiate the bus system. In any of these cases, bus riders are interested in knowing the status of the remaining trip segments along one's route. Schedule information and planned route may be pre-loaded on the user's device. However, riders want to know real-time information such as when they will be getting to the stop at which they need to disembark and how long they can expect to wait for the next bus to arrive. These needs are even greater for bus riders with sight impairment or limited mobility.

We have built a prototype system for guiding a rider through a pre-planned bus trip. Our initial target users are special needs individuals who require assistance using the bus system. Users or their caregivers plan their bus trip at home using an online web tool and download the trip information into a PDA. The trip assistant application running on the PDA guides them through each bus they need to take sequentially. Users can either look at an overview of all the buses they need to take and their current status or find out about their next bus transfer. The real-time information that the client application needs is provided by a service running on the bus's on-board computer. The information includes what bus stops the bus will be reaching in the next few minutes, what transfer opportunities are available at those stops, and how long it will be before those buses arrive to pick up the user (Figure 5).

The main concern in developing this system is the deployment of the real-time information service inside each bus (as discussed in section 3.2.2). Inside a bus, we do not have enough computing and communication resources. In our case, each bus has a computer equipped with a WiFi network interface and a GPRS modem. The GRPS modem is for connecting to a central server at the bus service agency that provides the real-time status information. The WiFi network interface is for communicating

Fig. 5. Screenshot of on-bus trip assistant application

with client devices inside the bus. We chose the server-push approach because this approach works better than the client-pull approach with this limited resource. We configured the computer to be a peer-to-peer node so that the service can broadcast the information without requiring an access point or a DHCP server. Client devices can listen to the broadcast information in monitor mode without the requirement to associate with an AP or obtain an IP address from a DHCP server. Furthermore, the bus does not track or authenticate the user thereby not compromising the person's privacy.

4.3 Room-Level Location Sensing System

We have recently developed a room-level location sensing infrastructure that uses WiFi and ultrasound together to help client devices determine the particular room they are in rather than a coordinate [1]. The system works as follows. A packet is broadcast to the local area announcing that a particular room (which includes specific resources such as URL, room number, floor, owner, phone number, etc.) will soon generate a short ultrasound pulse. We use a PC with standard speakers to generate this ultrasound chirp within the room (bounded by its walls). The client device first hears the WiFi broadcast packet and then checks if it also hears the ultrasound chirp within the specific window of time allocated to that room that was broadcast as part of the schedule. If it does, then it must be in the same room. If it doesn't, then it must be in another room within WiFi range.

We have used the server-push approach in designing this system for two main reasons. First, we wanted to provide the location information without infringing on users' privacy (as discussed in section 3.1.1). Second, the server-push approach is much better than the client-pull approach in terms of bandwidth usage. All the clients need to receive the location announcement packets (N_D equals 1) and the broadcast approach saves bandwidth if there is more than one user in the area (a common situation). In our building, one AP covers about 10 rooms and broadcasts announcement packets every 5 seconds. And, the size of an announcement packet is about 10 kbit (1 kbit for each room) ($B_D = 10$kbit). Thus, the bandwidth usage (B_S) is 2 kbps. If we used the client-pull approach, the bandwidth usage (B_C) would be 2.48 kbps (=2kbps + 0.48kbps (O_C)) multiplied by the number of users under one AP's coverage area.

5   Related Work

There are many systems that implement the idea of ubiquitous access to location-specific information. In such systems, as a user moves around, the user's applications obtain information relevant to their context, especially to their location, from various types of nearby wireless base stations. WiFi is the most commonly used wireless medium with Lancaster's Guide [2] as one of the earliest examples. This system was designed to provide visitors to the city with tour guide information by using WiFi access points to broadcast mostly static web pages that were frequently accessed by users in the coverage area.

Cooltown [5] uses infrared beacons to implement location (or object) specific information access. However, the infrared beacons attached to objects emit only URLs for the actual information, and the information itself has to be accessed through other networks.

Wristwatch devices such as Microsoft's SPOT (Smart Personal Object Technology) [13] receives data such as news stories, local weather forecasts, and traffic updates broadcast over the sidebands of FM radio stations. Their approach is an excellent example of the server-push approach in that they are using the existing wireless infrastructure to transmit data that could be interesting to many people. However, their location resolution is quite coarse because they use FM radio. Thus, it is difficult to provide finer grain information to users [6].

Similar to SPOT is the cell broadcasting in cellular network. Cell broadcasting allows text messages to be broadcast to all cell phones in a specified geographical area. Different types of information (emergency alert, weather, etc.) can be broadcast on different channels, and subscribers can listen to the only channels that they are interested.

6 Conclusion and Future Work

In this paper, we presented two methods – client-pull and server-push – that allow WiFi network owners to provide location-specific information to any users through their networks without compromising the security of their networks. We also analyzed the two methods from various aspects including privacy, power consumption on client devices, and wireless bandwidth usage. The server-push approach is a better choice when privacy is the main concern. In terms of power consumption, both approaches are comparable. The server-push approach uses less bandwidth when there many users with the same interests gathered in the same area. The three applications we described shows how this analysis can be applied to designing location-specific information dissemination systems with existing WiFi networks.

We are now working on the client toolkit that can switch between client-pull mode and server-push mode autonomously without affecting the applications. Different network owners may provide the same type of information using different approaches and as the user moves about, their client will need to dynamically adapt. We are also developing other interesting applications that require an access to location or context-specific information with existing WiFi networks. One class of application is about automatically associating a user's client device with the object that the user is currently operating. For specific example, in a fitness center, each treadmill is equipped with an acceleration sensor. And, a service running inside the WiFi network of the fitness center can provide the current acceleration data of each treadmill to client applications. While a user is exercising on a treadmill, the user's exercise application determines which treadmill is best correlated to the user's sensors records the detailed settings of the treadmill for the user's exercise history [7].

References

1. Gaetano Borriello, Alan Liu, Tony Offer, Christopher Palistrant, and Richard Sharp. WALRUS: Wireless Acoustic Location with Room-Level Resolution using Ultrasound. 3rd International Conference on Mobile Systems, Applications, and Services, Seattle, WA, June 2005.
2. Keith Cheverst, et al. Developing a Context-aware Electronic Tourist Guide: Some Issues and Experiences. CHI 2000, April 2000.

3. Marco Gruteser, Dirk Grunwald. Enhancing Location Privacy in Wireless LAN Through Disposable Interface Identifiers: A Quantitative Analysis. WMASH '03, September 2003.
4. T. Imielinski, S. Viswanathan, B. R. Badrinath. Data on Air: Organization and Access. IEEE Transactions on Knowledge and Data Engineering, Volume 9, Issue 3, May 1997.
5. T. Kindberg, et al. People, Places, Things: Web Presence for the Real World. WMCSA 2000, December 2000.
6. John Krumm, Gerry Cermak, Eric Horvitz. RightSPOT: A Novel Sense of Location for a Smart Personal Object. Ubicomp 2003, October 2003.
7. Jonathan Lester, Blake Hannaford, and Gaetano Borriello. "Are You With Me?" – Using Accelerometers to Determine if Two Devices are Carried by the Same Person. 2nd International Conference on Pervasive Computing, Linz, Austria, pp. 33-50, April 2004.
8. NoCatAuth. http://nocat.net.
9. OpenSplash. http://www.opensplash.org.
10. Donald J. Patterson. et al. Opportunity Knocks: a System to Provide Cognitive Assistance with Transportation Services. Ubicomp 2004, September 2004.
11. PlaceLab. http://www.placelab.org.
12. Michael K. Reiter and Aviel D. Rubin. Crowds: Anonymity for Web Transactions. ACM Transactions on Information and System Security. Volume 1, Issue 1, Nov. 1998.
13. SPOT. http://direct.msn.com
14. David Tennenhouse. Proactive Computing. CACM, Vol. 43, No. 5, May 2000.

Re-identifying Anonymous Nodes

Stefan Schlott, Frank Kargl, and Michael Weber

University of Ulm, Dept. of Media Informatics
{stefan.schlott, frank.kargl, michael.weber}@uni-ulm.de

Abstract. In mobile scenarios, privacy is an aspect of growing importance. In order to avoid the creation of movement profiles, participating nodes change their identifying properties on a regular basis in order to hide their identities and stay anonymous. The drawback of this action is that nodes which previously had a connection have no means to recognise this fact. A complete re-authentication would be necessary – if possible at all.

This paper discusses this new problem and proposes two possible solutions for re-identification of anonymous nodes, one based on symmetric encryption and one based on secure hashes.

1 Introduction

Information on a device's context – especially its location – offers a huge variety of interesting new applications. As a drawback, the same information in the wrong hands poses a threat to the users' privacy: It enables a malicious observer to track a user's movements; more detailed context information allows an attacker to infer additional personal data like personal habits.

As a consequence, privacy aspects have been addressed in several publications; naturally, location privacy has been the main issue. In order to defeat an attacker trying to track someone, most of these proposals suggest anonymisation of electronic device identity, i.e. make a device indistinguishable from others. A drawback of this measure is that the devices lose (probably very interesting) context information: The devices can no longer distinguish between nodes in their neighbourhood that they have met before and foreign ones. Our goal is to mitigate this disadvantage in order to allow scenarios analogous to the one described in the next section.

1.1 In the Real World...

In an environment without electronic surveillance, everybody is able to act with a reasonable amount of privacy. Imagine yourself walking through a crowded mall. You can stop at shops, browse through the goods for sale, and buy whatever you like. If you pay in cash, you will leave no trace of your transaction, and if the mall is visited by enough people, the shop owners (as well as the other customers in the hallways) won't remember you.

On the other hand, when you walk through the hallway, you might suddenly recognise a known face - just like "isn't that the guy I met on the party last

M. Hazas, J. Krumm, and T. Strang (Eds.): LoCA 2006, LNCS 3987, pp. 103–115, 2006.

week?". To everyone else, he is just another visitor of the mall; but you can single him out of the mass.

A digital representation of scenarios like the one described above can prove very useful in ubiquitous computing scenarios (e.g. allowing your colleague's PDA to re-identify your PDA for data exchange). But due to the possibility of automatic mass-surveillance, care has to be taken not to violate the individuals' privacy.

1.2   ...and Its Electronic Companion

The users' privacy is an important aspect in almost all distributed systems. In a ubiquitous scenario, privacy becomes even more important: As the miniature computers blend with everyday items, the users are no longer aware of potential threats to their privacy [1]. Some of these items will be carried around all day.

This rises the question of location privacy: How can users interact with (probably location-based) services while denying them the chance to create movement profiles? A first step toward the circumvention of movement profiles is to constantly change one's identifying attributes [2, 3].

In some cases however, this behaviour bears several disadvantages: Connecting to a known node requires knowledge of its current pseudonym. Solutions which have been discussed include a trusted relay [4], similar to the home location register of mobile IP [5].

There may be several reasons why other solutions would be preferable. First, in scenarios without any infrastructure or reliable Internet connection, this approach is unusable for obvious reasons. Further, it requires a service provider which the user is obliged to trust. Depending on the scenario, a local solution (i.e. without the involvement of a third party) may be more efficient. Finally, a protocol which does not rely on a third party may be employed in a wide variety of different contexts, e.g. in anonymous peer-to-peer overlay networks.

2   Scenario

In our scenario, we allow for nodes with different processing capabilities. Some nodes may be battery-powered and be equipped with very little CPU power. A very popular example are the MICA Motes [6], which are powered by 4 – 8 MHz 8-bit microcontrollers.

Regarding the limited capacity of memory and processing power, the use of public key cryptography becomes next to impractical: Even in an optimised implementation [7], a single RSA decryption operation takes up to 22 seconds. Therefore, costly algorithms like RSA should be substituted by less demanding public key schemes (like elliptic curves) and should be used sparsely.

2.1   Prerequisites and Goals

The goal is to design a protocol which represents a digital equivalent of the scenario depicted in the motivation section. The protocol should enable nodes to re-identify each other when meeting again. We assume that they met before and had the chance to communicate over a secure channel. Note that this does not imply that the nodes needed to authenticate each other: There is no need to exchange names or other identifiers during this first step. It is possible to re-identify another subject and only know that it is the same entity that you met at an earlier time.

As mentioned above, privacy is of great concern. Thus the protocol has to cope with the fact that an entity has no clue who its counterpart is (and vice versa). No part of the protocol must reveal any clue on the identity of the nodes. In case of a successful negotiation, both nodes should re-identify each other; otherwise, neither should gain information on the other node.

2.2 Anonymity

The definition of the term "anonymity" tends to differ depending on the literature. Since the year 2000, Pfitzmann et. al. are trying to fix a precise definition [8]. In their ongoing work [9], they define anonymity as "the state of being not identifiable within a set of subjects (the anonymity set)". This is sometimes referred as k-anonymity (with k being the size of the set of subjects).

We assume that nodes change their identifying attributes on a regular basis, either after a given time or after a completed communication with another node [10]. In the following, we call the union of these identifying attributes the node's pseudonym.

The pseudonyms chosen by the nodes are supposed to be random. This results in unlinkable IDs, i.e. a pseudonym gives an observer no clue on the future pseudonym.

2.3 The Attacker

In the following considerations, we assume an attacker according to the classic Dolev-Yao model [11]. This adversary has full control over the network, i.e. he can generate, modify, or delete messages. Side channels (like timing, etc.) are more difficult to deal with. Side channel attacks are a threat with a wide variety of possibilities, making a formal evaluation impossible. Some possible side channels will be discussed informally later in the paper.

3 Related Work

The fundamental privacy problem from a non-technological point of view is discussed in [1]. In [8], the authors define a terminology for privacy-related facts. Several works on security in ubiquitous computing also point out specific privacy issues [12, 13].

Classic identification schemes cope with the problem of certifying the identity of a communication partner; neither the observed communication nor the data obtained when being part of the protocol may be usable for impersonation [14, p. 283].

Well-known algorithms like Schnorr's scheme [15] fulfil these requirements. Since anonymity is a new requirement, these protocols do not regard this fact, requiring the participants to disclose their identity (which later will be verified) in the course of the protocol.

In the context of location-based services, privacy issues are being discussed. Most approaches rely on some kind of mix net; the concept of mix nets was first introduced by David Chaum in [16]. The Mist routing infrastructure [4] employs such a network in order to allow untraceable use of location-based services. In [17], Kölsch et. al. suggest a single trusted intermediary for anonymising requests to services. To further increase the amount of privacy, several authors (e.g. [18]) suggest controlling the granularity and precision of the data given to a service. In the context described in the introduction, these approaches suffer from several drawbacks: First, they require a given infrastructure, which provides anonymity. Second, the resolution of the pseudonyms of nodes in the neighbourhood could be integrated in these designs, but this would require a single trusted entity knowing all node positions.

The usage of zero-knowledge protocols [19] is an obvious thought. However, most zero-knowledge protocols are interactive protocols using several rounds; many involve complex computing operations making them an inappropriate means on resource-limited devices. In [20], Goldreich notes the existence of non-interactive zero-knowledge protocols. They too are rather demanding for devices with limited computing resources. Further, these protocols also assume that both parties have a common understanding of precisely what secret should be verified. In case of a re-encounter of two anonymous nodes, neither of these two nodes knows the identity of the other node and hence the nodes have no idea what secret the other node wants to prove.

Balfanz et. al. presented in [21] a protocol addressing the problem of authentication while not revealing any information to observers or unknown communication partners. The scenario described here was the effort to prove one's group membership by performing a "secret handshake". Only members of a group should be able to perform the appropriate authentication steps; non-members and observers should gain no information on the outcome of the protocol. For our scenario, this protocol has several drawbacks: It requires a trusted entity issuing certificates, and it employs large number operations. Both makes it inappropriate for many ubiquitous scenarios. Finally, our scenario requires no group authentication, but merely a 1:1 authentication.

Abadi discusses a private authentication protocol for two participants in [22]. According to the publication, the protocol does not require the participants to have met before. Both protocol variants introduced in the paper employ public key cryptography, making its frequent use on small devices very costly. Further, in both protocols, the first message is encrypted with the public key of the communication counterpart. This poses two unsolved problems: First, the identity of the communication partner is unknown, which means that either the identity has to be exchanged in advance, or all known keys have to be tested. Second, in contrast to the initial claim, the public keys of the communication partners must be known (at least in the first step).

The emerging RFID technology has several properties which are very similar to mobile and ubiquitous computing, e.g. portability, wireless communication, limited resources, and invisibility for most users. As industry deploys more and more RFID tags in end user products, the question for privacy has risen, too [23]. In consequence, researchers addressed that problem. Molnar et. al. propose in [24] a means for RFID chips to retain their anonymity unless they are contacted by an authenticated RFID reader. The protocol deals with the special circumstances of RFID technology, namely very limited memory and processing power. However, the protocol assumes that the RFID reader(s) reveal their identities.

In contrast to that, the two protocols that we present in the next sections protect the privacy of both communication partners.

4   Identification Using Symmetric Ciphers

In the following sections, these symbols are used:

- $E_k(v)$ denotes a symmetric encryption with key k of the value v.
- $H(v)$ is the cryptographic hash of the value v.
- n represents a nonce. These values should be used only once. Additionally, we require values of n to be randomly chosen.
- T is a token – an initially randomly chosen, fixed value which serves as unique identifier.
- *decoy* stands for random data.
- A is the node initiating the protocol
- B denotes the second communication partner. The identity of this node is initially unknown to A (and vice versa).
- The table storing old session data has s entries.

We specify neither specific algorithms nor bit lengths. These should be chosen with reasonable sizes but with regard to hardware limitations. The size of the values should be chosen in a way that brute-force enumeration is not possible within an acceptable time span.

4.1   Naive Approach

The naive approach shown below is a description of the basic approach without any optimisations. It should serve to describe the rough idea and to point out the problems.

When two nodes meet for the first time, they exchange a session key k_{ab} and an identifier for this session, T_{ab}, over the secure channel.

The re-identification protocol is initiated by A. Since A does not know who B is, A simply tries all keys stored in its session storage:

$$A \longrightarrow B : \forall b : E_{k_{ab}}(T_{ab}, n_1) \tag{1.1}$$

For each message, B tries to decrypt the payload with all stored session keys k_{ba}. B can verify the successful decryption by comparing the decrypted value with the stored T_{ba}. If T_{ba} matches, B replies with message 1.2:

$$B \longrightarrow A : E_{k_{ab}}(n_1, n_2) \tag{1.2}$$

Otherwise, B sends the decoy message 1.3 with identical length:

$$B \longrightarrow A : decoy \tag{1.3}$$

A in turn can check for a successful identification by decrypting the data received from B. If A yields the nonce n_1 (which was never transmitted in plain and thus is known to nobody except the correct recipient), the re-identification is successful. A and B may then continue to communicate encrypted using the session key k_{ab}. The first message sent by A should contain n_2 in order to guarantee freshness of the protocol run.

If every participant stores s entries in his session list, the complexity may be estimated as followed: $O(s)$ messages are sent, A has to perform $O(s)$, B $O(s^2)$ symmetric crypto operations.

The protocol allows an anonymous re-identification of nodes which already exchanged their credentials. The names A and B may sound a bit misleading, since they imply a known, fixed identity; in common protocol descriptions, this is (hopefully) true – the communication partners know whom they are talking to (or, at least, think that they know; there still might be a man in the middle). In our case, A and B represent just some node. Since in the beginning, both A and B are anonymous, neither knows who he is talking to.

As a natural consequence, when using a broadcast medium for message transmission, there might be a node C within range, which also exchanged a session key with A earlier. C will be able to identify A, too. This is analogous to the scenario of the introduction: All passers-by in the mall can see you, and if someone knows you, he will recognise you.

If this side effect is unwanted, A and B have to make sure that no one else is listening - either by using a direct link for transmission, or by establishing an encrypted communication. The setup of such an encrypted channel is out of the focus of this paper, see [25, 26, 27] for possible approaches.

4.2   Enhancing Performance with Indexes

Although this simple approach fulfils the goal of anonymous re-identification, it causes high traffic and high processing load, especially for B. This section shows a variation of the protocol that enhances the performance at the cost of a slightly increased chance that an adversary can successfully identify the communication partners.

In order to reduce the amount of decryption operations for B, A and B store an additional index identifier i_{ab} during their first meeting. i is chosen randomly. The purpose of the index is to narrow down the amount of possible session keys. This index should not be unique, since this would provide a simple way for an attacker to identify a node. The domain of i should be small enough to have enough collisions to maintain privacy. In many applications, a small number of bits will be sufficient; for example, a node with 1000 stored session keys can reduce the number of possible keys to an average of approximately 60 keys with a four bit index.

A sends packets as depicted in message 2.1:

$$A \longrightarrow B : \forall b : i_{ab}, E_{k_{ab}}(T_{ab}, n_1) \tag{2.1}$$

Similar to the naive approach, B tries to decrypt the received packets – but only with keys which have a matching i_{ab}. The theoretical complexity remains the same; in practise, with proper values for s and the domain of i, the amount of computations can be reduced to a certain degree.

The rest of the protocol is identical to the naive approach: On success, B replies with message 2.2, otherwise with a decoy message of identical length.

$$B \longrightarrow A : E_{k_{ab}}(n_1, new i_{ab}) \tag{2.2}$$

In message 2.2, B sends a new (random) i_{ab} to A. A replaces the old value with the new one, which will be used during the next authentication.

4.3   Problems with the Index

The introduction of the index is a trade-off between performance and privacy preservation: Even though the index is changed during every successful handshake, most index entries remain unchanged. That means that the sequence of indexes forms a characteristic string, which may be used by an adversary for identification. For the sake of simplicity, we assume in this section that all nodes store the same number of sessions.

Two unsuccessful protocol runs would result in identical index sequences. The degree of anonymity can be amounted to the probability that two different nodes bear the same characteristic string. In this case, the probability is $1 : 2^{s \cdot l}$, with s being the number of indexes an l the length of the index (in bits). Obviously, this does not provide adequate privacy.

Randomly changing the sequence of keys during each run of the protocol reduces the information which can be gathered by an observer. A drawback of this procedure is the requirement of more randomness, which may be difficult to gain.

The information exploitable by an adversary is the frequency of the index values. Assuming that the index values are equally distributed, the probability of two nodes having the same frequency of index values[1] is $1 : \binom{2^l + s - 1}{s}$, which equals $1 : \frac{(2^l + s - 1)!}{s! \cdot (2^l - 1)!}$. This results in an adequate amount of privacy only for small numbers of s.

---

[1] Combination with repetition (order does not matter, objects can be chosen more than once), under the assumption that the hints are equally distributed.

Alternatively, A could suggest a new index to B (instead of receiving a newly chosen index generated by B in message 2.2). This enables A to pick the new index value in a way that balances the differences in the occurrences of the index values in A's session list. The key sequences sent by A should be sorted by the index values. That results in very homogeneous (and indistinguishable) sequences.

The only information left for the adversary is the difference from the average count ("one less than the average" or "average"). This results in a probability of $1 : 2^l$, which can be considered an adequate result.

5   Identification Using Hashes

A further reduction of messages and computation steps can be achieved by the following protocol while retaining all the positive properties of the naive approach. Now all nodes possess an identity token T. On their first meeting, A and B exchange their identity tokens T_a and T_b together with a session key k_{ab}.

A initiates the protocol by sending a nonce in message 3.1:

$$A \longrightarrow B : n_1 \tag{3.1}$$

B calculates the hash of the nonce and its identity token T. An additional nonce n_2 is inserted to defeat identification via message replay.

$$B \longrightarrow A : n_2, H(T_b, n_1, n_2) \tag{3.2}$$

After receiving message 3.2, A calculates the hash of n_1, n_2 and all stored T_b; if the result matches the data received, A has successfully identified its communication partner. To allow B to identify A, A sends the respective message 3.3.

A includes an additional challenge in form of an encrypted nonce. This is necessary because all associated nodes know the identities T of other nodes. This challenge proves that neither party is lying about the identity T employed during the protocol, because session keys are only used pairwise.

$$A \longrightarrow B : H(T_a, n_1, n_2), E_{k_{ab}}(n_3) \tag{3.3}$$

B can now determine the identity of A, and proves the possession of the correct session key by replying with message 3.4:

$$B \longrightarrow A : E_{k_{ab}}(n_3 + 1, n_4) \tag{3.4}$$

Message 3.5 concludes the handshake with A's session key possession proof.

$$A \longrightarrow B : E_{k_{ab}}(n_4 + 1) \tag{3.5}$$

This protocol reduces the complexity to a fixed number of messages and $O(s)$ cryptographic operations on both sides.

6   Verification

In this section we will prove the correctness of our two approaches, namely the naive and the hash-based alternative. We assume a Dolev-Yao style attacker that can eavesdrop and even modify all packets.

6.1   Assumptions

Let A be the originator of the communication, B the recipient. From a previous session, A and B share a common cryptographic secret $k_{ab} = k_{ba}$ of reasonable length that is unknown to any other party. They have also exchanged a pair-wise token $T_{ab} = T_{ba}$ for the symmetric cipher case, and per-node tokens T_a and T_b for the identification with hashes. E_k is a symmetric cipher that is assumed to be secure, i.e. it cannot be broken faster than by brute-forcing the key space and produces output that cannot be distinguished from random noise. H is a cryptographically perfect hash-function, which means it generates uniformly and completely random output, and is strong collision resistant. Finally, we assume that A and B are able to generate true random numbers for generating nonces n_i.

6.2   Identification Using Symmetric Ciphers

In the naive case, A knows n keys $k_{ax_i} \forall i = 1 \ldots n$ and has no knowledge about the identity of its communication partner B. $\forall i = 1 \ldots n$, A sends a message $E_{k_{ax_i}}(T_{ab}, n_1)$ resulting in a total of n messages (message 1.1). As assumed above, any attacker E eavesdropping these messages and not knowing the correct key will see only random noise and cannot derive any information from the message, besides that one party with a random address sends a message to another party with a random address. The nonce n_1 ensures that A will never send the same message twice, so E cannot correlate the current message to any messages sent earlier in order to gain some information.

Next, B will try to decrypt the received messages with all known keys $k_{by_j} \forall j = 1 \ldots m$. If $y_j \neq a$ (i.e. the selected key is not k_{ba}), the result of this process will again be randomly distributed data, so B learns nothing about A's relationship to other nodes. Only if $y_j = a$, B will recognise the common token T_{ab} and learn the nonce n_1.

For each message received, B will send back either a message containing random noise (message 1.3) or $E_{k_{ab}}(n_1, n_2)$ (message 1.2). In both cases, the eavesdropper E will see only a random string from which he cannot derive any additional information. In order to prevent a side-channel attack, B will send all answers at the same, fixed time intervals, e.g. strictly 100 ms after receiving the incoming message. Again the nonce n_2 prevents E from correlating the response message to any response sent earlier, and defeats a possible identification by replaying a captured packet 1.1.

When A receives the response Res_i from B, it will try to decrypt it with the corresponding key used in the request Req_i. If it detects i it now knows the identity of B and can reuse k_{ab} for further communication. If the keys do not match, the result of the decryption operation will be random noise from which A gains no additional knowledge.

Finally, we will look at the effects of an active attacker M. When M inserts a request Req into the communication from A to B, eventually replacing original requests from A, B will only decrypt random noise or the identity of M, if they share a common key k_{bm} and token T_{bm} from a previous session and if M constructs conforming requests. In the first case B will answer with random noise and A and B will not recognise each other which is an Denial of Service attack on the protocol. In the second case M will recognise the communication with B which is equivalent to M running the protocol instead of A, which is perfectly legal in our scenario. Again this leads to a Denial of Service for A, as A might not recognise B.

When M replaces response messages, A will not be able to decrypt messages containing the nonce n_1 so it will not recognise B. This is again a Denial of Service attack.

If M shares both a key with A and with B it might capture all the request from A to B, replacing them with requests from M to B. It can do the same with all responses from B to A. In this case, both A and B will recognise the communication with M, so this is no Man-in-the-Middle attack, as the Man-in-the-Middle cannot impersonate A or B.

So for the naive approach the best attack possible against identification using symmetric ciphers is a Denial of Service.

6.3   Identification Using Hashes

When using hashes, A first sends a nonce n_1 for initiating the communication (message 3.1). Therefore an eavesdropper E will learn the nonce whereas a malicious intruder M may also modify the nonce. As a result, A will refuse message 3.2 which results in a Denial of Service attack.

In the next step (message 3.2), B replies with a message containing a nonce n_2 and a hash value calculated for the values T_b, n_1, and n_2. A will now calculate hash values for all T_x that it has stored from earlier authenticated communications with hosts x. When it knows T_b, it will find a match and discovers the identity of its communication partner. Likewise, an eavesdropper E that had earlier communicated with B and knows T_b, is able to discover the identity of B. As this is equivalent to running the protocol between E and B, this is not considered an attack.

If a malicious attacker M intercepts and changes message 3.2, it can change the nonce n_2 which leads to a corrupted message that will be rejected by A. This is again a Denial of Service attack. Alternatively, M can try to forge a hash value $H(T_x, n_1, n_2)$ using any token T_x that it possesses. This is why in later steps (messages 3.3 to 3.5) a symmetric encryption using a shared secret key k_{ab} is used to verify the authenticity of the communication partner.

Message 3.3 sends another hash $H(T_a, n_1, n_2)$ from which B can learn the identity of A. Again, an eavesdropper E that already knows T_a can learn this identity too and again this is not considered an attack, as it is equivalent to a correct protocol run. As stated earlier, the encryption of nonces n_3 and $n_3 + 1$ (and n_4 and $n_4 + 1$ accordingly) in steps 3.3 to 3.5 using a shared secret key negotiated in earlier communication prevents an attacker M from impersonating other nodes X for which the token T_x is known.

Like in the previous section on identification using symmetric cipher, M may try to act as Man-in-the-Middle by inserting its T_m instead of T_a and T_b. It then also needs shared keys k_{am} and k_{mb}; A and B will recognise that they are communicating with M. This is again no valid Man-in-the-Middle attack.

So the worst attack possible is again a Denial of Service.

7   Discussion

In practise, some optimisations can be made. To reduce the number of transmissions, the network datagrams may be filled with several guesses/replies.

Further, implementors can exploit the broadcast nature of the wireless media: Since the first step(s) of the described protocols are independent of the addressee, they can be sent via broadcast to all neighbouring nodes.

An intrinsic problem are observing nodes which have an association with the protocol initiator (A in the first, B in the second protocol), too. They will be able to reveal the initiator's identity. Due to the fact that the initiator does not know who is addressing when starting the communication, this is inevitable.

The revocation of an association to a node may be an issue, too. In case of the first protocol variant, it is sufficient to delete the respective entry from the session table. The second protocol variant allows to abort an unwanted communication only by A; in message 3.2, B has no idea who he is talking to. The only means of revocation of B would be to change T_b, revoking all associations simultaneously. Alternatively, a node may chose to have several T's for different roles.

The second protocol reduces the number of messages, but uses a single identifier T for each node. Depending on the attack model, this can be a problem: Malicious communication partners who exchange collected data can easily identify the communications made by the same node. In contrast, when using the first protocol, this is not possible since every node uses a different identifier in each communication.

Especially on resource-limited nodes, the session data cannot be stored indefinitely. After a given amount of memory has been filled, the node will have to purge some data. This could be done according to a timeout or a least recently used policy. Purging an association results in "forgetting" a node.

8   Summary and Outlook

We have introduced two protocols for re-identifying anonymous nodes, allowing all communication partners to maintain their anonymity. Both protocols do not use public key cryptography. Due to the assumption that the nodes had prior contact over a secure channel, no third party is necessary.

Both protocol variants have their advantages and disadvantages. It depends on the scenario which variant should be used.

Future efforts will focus on the time-privacy trade-off when using indexes. Further we plan to do timing evaluations using a protocol implementation on small devices (e.g. MICAz motes).

A very interesting problem is the hinting problem: In this paper, we described a method using an index value. Using other techniques, probably from the field of steganography, could further improve efficiency of the protocol.

References

1. Langheinrich, M.: Privacy by design - principles of privacy-aware ubiquitous systems. In Abowd, G.D., Brumitt, B., Shafer, S.A., eds.: Ubicomp. Volume 2201 of Lecture Notes in Computer Science., Springer (2001) 273–291
2. Beresford, A.R., Stajano, F.: Location privacy in pervasive computing. IEEE Pervasive Computing **2** (2003) 46–55
3. Görlach, A., Heinemann, A., Terpstra, W.W.: Survey on location privacy in pervasive computing. In Robinson, P., Vogt, H., Wagealla, W., eds.: Privacy, Security and Trust within the Context of Pervasive Computing. The Kluwer International Series in Engineering and Computer Science. Kluwer Academic Publishers (2005) 23–34
4. Al-Muhtadi, J., Campbell, R., Kapadia, A., Mickunas, M.D., Yi, S.: Routing through the mist: Privacy preserving communication in ubiquitous computing environments. In: ICDCS '02: Proceedings of the 22 nd International Conference on Distributed Computing Systems (ICDCS'02), IEEE Computer Society (2002) 74
5. Perkins, C.: IP Mobility Support for IPv4. Internet Engineering Task Force: RFC 3220 (2002)
6. Crossbow: Mica motes. http://www.xbow.com/ (2005)
7. Gupta, V., Millard, M., Fung, S., Zhu, Y., Gura, N., Eberle, H., Shantz, S.C.: Sizzle: A standards-based end-to-end security architecture for the embedded internet (best paper). In: PerCom, IEEE Computer Society (2005) 247–256
8. Pfitzmann, A., Köhntopp, M.: Anonymity, unobservability, and pseudonymity - a proposal for terminology. In Federrath, H., ed.: Workshop on Design Issues in Anonymity and Unobservability. Volume 2009 of Lecture Notes in Computer Science., Springer (2000) 1–9
9. Pfitzmann, A., Köhntopp, M.: Anonymity, unlinkability, unobservability, pseudonymity, and identity management - a consolidated proposal for terminology. http://dud.inf.tu-dresden.de/Anon_Terminology.shtml (2005)
10. Schlott, S., Kargl, F., Weber, M.: Random IDs for preserving location privacy. In: SecureComm. (2005) 415 – 417
11. Dolev, D., Yao, A.C.C.: On the security of public key protocols. IEEE Transactions on Information Theory **29** (1983) 198–207
12. Stajano, F.: Security for ubiquitous computing. Wiley (2002)
13. Stajano, F.: Security for whom? the shifting security assumptions of pervasive computing. In Okada, M., Pierce, B.C., Scedrov, A., Tokuda, H., Yonezawa, A., eds.: Software Security – Theories and Systems, Mext-NSF-JSPS International Symposium, ISSS 2002, Tokyo, Japan, November 8-10, 2002, Revised Papers. Volume 2609 of Lecture Notes in Computer Science., Springer (2003) 16–27

14. Stinson, D.R.: Cryptography: Theory and Practice. CRC Press, Inc., Boca Raton, FL, USA (1995)
15. Schnorr, C.P.: Efficient signature generation by smart cards. J. Cryptology **4** (1991) 161–174
16. Chaum, D.: Untraceable electronic mail, return addresses, and digital pseudonyms. **24** (1981) 84–88
17. Kölsch, T., Fritsch, L., Kohlweiss, M., Kesdogan, D.: Privacy for profitable location based services. [28] 164–178
18. Wishart, R., Henricksen, K., Indulska, J.: Context obfuscation for privacy via ontological descriptions. In Strang, T., Linnhoff-Popien, C., eds.: LoCA. Volume 3479 of Lecture Notes in Computer Science., Springer (2005) 276–288
19. Goldwasser, S., Micali, S., Rackoff, C.: The knowledge complexity of interactive proof systems. SIAM J. Comput. **18** (1989) 186–208
20. Goldreich, O.: Zero-knowledge twenty years after its invention. Technical report, Weizmann Institute of Science, Israel (2002) updated 2004.
21. Balfanz, D., Durfee, G., Shankar, N., Smetters, D., Staddon, J., Wong, H.C.: Secret handshakes from pairing-based key agreements. In: SP '03: Proceedings of the 2003 IEEE Symposium on Security and Privacy, Washington, DC, USA, IEEE Computer Society (2003) 180
22. Abadi, M., Fournet, C.: Private authentication. Theor. Comput. Sci. **322** (2004) 427–476
23. Sarma, S., Weis, S., Engels, D.: RFID systems and security and privacy implications. In Kaliski, B., Kaya ço, c., Paar, C., eds.: Cryptographic Hardware and Embedded Systems – CHES 2002. Volume 2523 of Lecture Notes in Computer Science., Redwood Shores, CA, USA, Springer-Verlag (2002) 454–469 Knapper Überblick über technische Funktionsweise von RFID. Eine der ersten Publikationen zum Thema RFID und Privacy.
24. Molnar, D., Wagner, D.: Privacy and security in library RFID: Issues, practices, and architectures. In Pfitzmann, B., Liu, P., eds.: Conference on Computer and Communications Security – ACM CCS, Washington, DC, USA, ACM, ACM Press (2004) 210–219
25. Diffie, W., Hellman, M.E.: New directions in cryptography. IEEE Transactions on Information Theory **IT-22** (1976) 644–654
26. Stajano, F., Anderson, R.: The resurrecting duckling: Security issues for ad-hoc wireless networks. In Christianson, B., Crispo, B., Roe, M., eds.: Security Protocols, 7th International Workshop Proceedings. (1999) 172–194
27. Hoepman, J.H.: Ephemeral pairing on anonymous networks. [28] 101–116
28. Hutter, D., Ullmann, M., eds.: Security in Pervasive Computing, Second International Conference, SPC 2005, Boppard, Germany, April 6-8, 2005, Proceedings. In Hutter, D., Ullmann, M., eds.: SPC. Volume 3450 of Lecture Notes in Computer Science., Springer (2005)

Anonymous User Tracking for Location-Based Community Services

Peter Ruppel, Georg Treu, Axel Küpper, and Claudia Linnhoff-Popien

Mobile and Distributed Systems Group, Institute for Informatics,
Ludwig-Maximilian University Munich, Germany
{peter.ruppel, georg.treu, axel.kuepper, linnhoff}@ifi.lmu.de

Abstract. In *location-based community services (LBCSs)*, the positions of several targets are interrelated. Users can be notified when targets approach or separate from each other. Typical application areas are instant messaging, mobile gaming, dating, fleet management and logistics, as well as child tracking. Finding appropriate anonymization techniques for LBCSs is a hard problem since (i) the targets are continuously monitored and (ii) identifiers of the targets must not change in order to maintain coherence within a community. LBCSs are inherently stateful. Therefore, existing anonymization techniques for *location-based services* are not suited for LBCSs. In this paper, we present an anonymization technique for LBCSs, which employs distance-preserving coordinate transformations in conjunction with pseudonyms. It is based on the idea that for determining the distance between targets only relative positions are needed. It supports target anonymity, either with respect to the location provider, which collects the position fixes, or the LBS provider. The paper also presents the results of simulations, which we have performed in order to evaluate the proposed mechanism.

1 Introduction

Location-based Services (LBSs) take into account the geographic positions of one or several individuals, which are referred to as *targets* in the following, in order to create, compile, filter, or select information that is presented to their users, see for example [Küp05]. Today, cellular operators offer them as a complement to existing data or voice services, e.g., in order to show their users restaurants or ATMs in their close proximity. This type of LBS can be characterized as *reactive* and *self-referencing*, i.e., location-based information is only passed on demand to the user and refers only to the user's own position.

Unfortunately, support for advanced functions is still rudimentary. They are needed for realizing *proactive* LBSs that are automatically initialized in dependence on the target's position, *cross-referencing* LBSs that correlate or exchange the positions of several targets, or a combination of both of them. The reasons for the lack of these functions are manifold. Besides regulatory and economic issues there are a number of limitations that need to be overcome, one of the most important being privacy concerns of the tracked targets.

M. Hazas, J. Krumm, and T. Strang (Eds.): LoCA 2006, LNCS 3987, pp. 116–133, 2006.

This paper describes an anonymity mechanism for the advanced LBS functions *proximity* and *separation detection*, which are necessary for realizing a special type of LBS referred to as *location-based community services (LBCSs)*. We define proximity detection as the capability to determine if two targets are closer than a pre-defined *proximity distance*. Analogously, separation detection refers to the capability to determine if two targets are apart from each other by more than a pre-defined *separation distance*. The two functions support reactive as well as proactive LBCSs. An example for the latter ones are members of a community, which are automatically alerted when others approach, depart, or both. Typical application areas are instant messaging, mobile gaming, dating, fleet management and logistics, as well as child tracking.

The proposed anonymity mechanism employs coordinate transformations for protecting target pseudonyms. While this general idea has been brought up in [TKR05], this paper contains the details of an actual anonymization technique based on transformations together with an in-depth evaluation.

The remainder of this paper is structured as follows: in Section 2 we examine existing privacy mechanisms for LBSs and discuss if they are applicable to LBCSs. After that, in Section 3, we formally state the problem of detecting proximity, respectively separation, between two targets and give an overview about related position reporting strategies, which are a prerequisite for understanding our anonymization technique for LBCSs. In Section 4, we present the mechanism in detail together with associated role and trust models. After evaluating the approach in Section 5, we conclude and give an outlook to further work.

2   Related Work

The following gives an overview about related work concerned with privacy protection in LBSs, see also [GHT04].

With *privacy policies*, targets can specify how their location data has to be processed by an LBS [MFD03]. The associated problem is that after data has been handed out in the first place, it depends on the trustworthiness of the participating organizations if policies are respected.

In contrast to the policy-based approach, *anonymization* mechanisms aim to technically hide a target's true identity with respect to emitted location information. We can distinguish between techniques of data or identifier abstraction.

In the data abstraction approach, anonymization is achieved by cloaking location data, e.g., by reducing temporal and/or spatial accuracy, so that location information of different individuals cannot be distinguished. In [GG03], this is achieved based on the formal model of k-anonymity [Swe02]. k-anonymity is given if the location data of a person cannot be distinguished from that of at least $k - 1$ other individuals. The drawback of k-anonymity as presented in [GG03] is that data accuracy is reduced, especially in sparsely populated areas. For the temporal version, service response time may significantly rise due to the introduced delay. This conflicts with high quality-of-service requirements of LBCSs like mobile gaming. Furthermore, the model is only applicable to single position fixes of targets and not to longer traces, which disqualifies it for LBCSs and proactive LBSs in general.

In identifier abstraction, pseudonyms are associated with the location information to protect target identity. The problem is that pseudonyms can be uncovered by statistical attacks. Locations known to be highly frequented by a given person, like living- or workplaces, can be related with sampled, pseudonym-associated location data so that the mapping to a target's identity can be done. For this reason, in [BS03], the usage of LBSs is restricted to *application zones*, which exclude typical whereabouts of a target. Unfortunately, with this restriction the service cannot be used most of the time, which may be unacceptable. Additionally, in [BS03], pseudonyms are dynamically changed in *mix zones* in order to avoid linking different pseudonyms of a target together. However, for LBCSs, frequently changing pseudonyms are not an option, since consistent target identifiers are needed to maintain community memberships. In general, changing pseudonyms is critical for any kind of LBS that requires persistent information like a user profile to be maintained for a target. With the help of such information an attacker may link different target pseudonyms together, which makes the mechanism ineffective.

In Section 5, we explain in more detail how [BS03] and [GG03] prevent an obvious attack scenario (compare *Known Whereabouts Attack*) and why these procedures are not suited for LBCSs.

To which extent an anonymization mechanism is useful strongly depends on the type of LBS. Cloaking of location data is sufficient for reactive self-referencing LBSs with low or medium requirements on data accuracy such as, e.g., a restaurant finder service. On the other hand, using mix-zones for changing pseudonyms can be suitable for proactive self-referencing LBSs with high accuracy requirements and associated with a bounded application area. An example is a tourist guide, which alerts visitors of a foreign city when they approach important monuments.

A model concerned with tracking of targets is *path privacy* [GBG04]. The authors propose path segmentation and minutiae suppression to allow anonymous tracking of targets. That way, longer movement paths are split up into several smaller paths and – from the LBS provider's point of view – within each path segment a target appears as a new target. Minutiae suppression requires targets not to reveal their location if they are staying in a sensitive area that is highly typical for them.

In [DK05], a formal model for *obfuscating* location information is given. In contrast to anonymization techniques, which have the objective of hiding targets' identities, in this approach the identity is supposed to be known. Instead, position accuracy is reduced as far as application requirements can still be adhered to. Though this provides some privacy, in many situations it may not be sufficient. If, e.g., an employer wants to track the location of his employee to check whether she is at work or not, the accuracy of the transmitted position does not really matter. If the employee is not at work, but at home, the employer will know.

In [FJ04], a mechanism is described that allows a party X to determine if two pre-calculated routes get within a given proximity distance to each other without the actual route information being revealed to X. Though in a way similar to our assumption of preserved relative distances, the approach is not suited for LBCSs as our objective is to dynamically monitor targets' positions that are *not* known in advance.

3 Proximity and Separation Detection

In our approach, we assume terminal-based positioning, i.e., targets are equipped with *GPS-capable mobile terminals (MTs)*, which report their position to a *location server (LS)* in the fixed Internet.

At an abstract level the LS manages the positions of a set of targets $E = \{e_1, e_2, ..., e_n\}, 1 < i \leq n$, which form a community. For each pair of targets $i, j \in E$ with (unknown) Euclidean distance $dist(i, j)$ and a given proximity distance $d_p > 0$ the problem of detecting proximity is defined as follows:

1. if $dist(i, j) <   d_p$ proximity *must be* detected.
2. if $d_p \leq   dist(i, j) \leq   d_p + b$ proximity *may be* detected.
3. if $dist(i, j) >   d_p + b$ proximity *must not be* detected.

The introduced borderline tolerance b is a quality parameter. As shown later, by varying b service quality can be traded off against the protection level provided by our approach.

The problem of detecting separation between i and j, given separation distance $d_s > 0$, is defined analogously:

1. if $dist(i, j) >   d_s + b$ separation *must be* detected.
2. if $d_s \leq   dist(i, j) \leq   d_s + b$ separation *may be* detected.
3. if $dist(i, j) <   d_s$ separation *must not be* detected.

Thus, we distinguish two types of queries: $prox(i, j) : E \times E \rightarrow Boolean$ tells if i and j are within proximity distance, while $sep(i, j) : E \times E \rightarrow Boolean$ does the same for separation. Reactive as well as proactive services are supported. While a reactive proximity query can be immediately answered by telling if a target is located within proximity radius of another target, a proactive query blocks until a target has approached another one. Queries for separation detection work analogous.

In any case, for answering the queries the positions of targets have to be controlled somehow. For this purpose *position updates (PUs)* are reported from the targets' MTs to the LS, which can be done according to one of the following *PU methods* [LR02] [KT05]:

- **Polling.** In the polling method, the MT delivers the derived position on request.
- **Immediate updating.** The MT sends an immediate PU to the LS each time the position changes with regard to the last reported position.

- **Periodic updating.** A periodic update is triggered if a pre-defined time interval has elapsed since the last PU.
- **Distance-based updating.** A distance-based PU is triggered if the distance between the current and the last reported position exceeds a pre-defined threshold.
- **Zone-based updating.** A PU is initialized if the target enters or leaves a pre-defined zone, where a zone can be fixed as a single point, a circle or ellipse, or a polygon.
- **Piggybacking.** Position data is included in a service request that is passed from the MT to the LBS application server.

Obviously, reactive queries can be handled by polling the MTs of the respective targets. However, for implementing proactive queries the MTs need to be continously monitored. Naively, for this purpose immediate updating could be employed. However, more efficient strategies for (proactive) proximity and separation detection have been devised. Their objective is to reduce the number of messages exchanged between LS and MT in order to save valuable bandwidth and reduce the energy consumption of the MTs. To this end, the PU methods of an MT can be dynamically configured. So far, there are strategies based on *distance-based updating* [TK05] as well as *zone-based updating* [AEM+04].

Apart from efficiency benefits, reducing the amount of position data collected about a target is also preferable in terms of privacy. As we will see later, one particular premise for the robustness of the presented approach is to guarantee that the *minimum sampling distance* d_{sample} does not fall below a given value, that is, two subsequent PUs collected about one target are spaced apart at least by d_{sample}. In general, it can be said that the higher d_{sample} is, the better the protection. Therefore, the following sections discuss which lower bound for d_{sample} can be safely assumed.

Figure 1 illustrates the point of view of the LS with respect to the positions of two targets i and j that are tracked with sampling distance d_{sample}. Given the last reported PUs, $lastPU(i)$ and $lastPU(j)$, both targets can have moved within a circle of radius d_{sample} without notice by the LS. According to the figure, for every possible value of the proximity distance d_p, one of the following cases

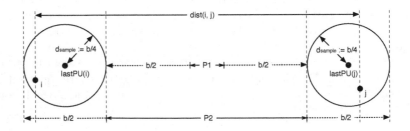

Fig. 1. Targets i and j with actual distance $dist(i, j)$, tracked with a *minimum sampling distance* of d_{sample}. The last PUs reported are $lastPU(i)$ and $lastPU(j)$ respectively.

applies: if $d_p < P1$, then proximity can be safely *not* detected as it must hold that $dist(i,j) > d_p + b$. The same holds for $P1 \leq d_p < P2$, since $dist(i,j) > d_p$. Finally, for $d_p >= P2$ proximity *can* be safely detected, since $dist(i,j) <= d_p + b$. The same argumentation holds for separation detection. In other terms, the error introduced by $d_{sample} := \frac{b}{4}$ is sufficiently small to safely decide about proximity in all conceivable situations. While being out of the scope of this paper, it can be shown that correct operation is guaranteed even for $d_{sample} := \frac{b}{3}$ preconditioned, however, the following two restrictions hold:

First, $prox(i,j)$ and $sep(i,j)$ are positively answered only alternately, i.e., if $prox(i,j)$ has been answered with *true*, further queries to $prox(i,j)$ are not answered until in turn $sep(i,j)$ has evaluated to *true*. The same holds for the other direction, i.e., after $sep(i,j)$ has been answered with *true*, $prox(i,j)$ must evaluate to *true* before any further processing of $sep(i,j)$. Second, it must hold that $d_s > d_p + b$, i.e., the separation distance has to be sufficiently larger than the proximity distance.

Finally, we would like to stress that for detecting proximity or separation, typically less PUs need to be transmitted than with worst case bound of $d_{sample} := \frac{b}{3}$. However, the actual value depends on the tracking strategy, the density of the targets as well as the frequency of queries.

4   Approach

In the following, a novel anonymization mechanism suitable for proximity and separation detection is presented. It can be classified as anonymization based on data obfuscation [BPB+04], whereas *anonymity* denotes "the state of being not identifiable within a set of subjects, the anonymity set" [PK01]. In dependence on the underlying trust model, the goal is to protect the targets' identity from being revealed by the LBS provider and the *location provider (LP)* respectively. The approach is based on pseudonymous communication.

4.1   Role and Trust Model

In the operation of an LBS participate different autonomous entities like persons, companies, or organizations, we refer to as *actors*. Each actor adopts one or several roles, which characterize the functions it fulfills from a technical point of view [Küp05]. For LBCSs, we distinguish the following roles. *Targets* are the tracked individuals. Based on their relative positions the *LBS provider* compiles location-based information. An intermediate LP is responsible for collecting, caching and managing position fixes of several targets and transferring them to the LBS providers. For this purpose, the *LP* operates an LS, which collects position data from the targets' MTs in the way described in the last section.

By a *trusted entity* we refer to an actor that is allowed to know a target's real position and identity. We assume secure communication between targets and trusted entities. Basically, our approach supports two different models of trust (see Figure 2).

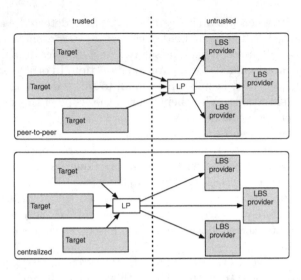

Fig. 2. Trust model: arrows denote the transmission of position data. Top: peer-to-peer approach, the targets are responsible for coordinate obfuscation and pseudonymous transmission of coordinates. Bottom: a trusted central LP collects and obfuscates coordinates and transmits them to LBS providers.

In the peer-to-peer scenario, the LBS provider and the LP are both non-trusted entities. A trusted relationship is only given between targets that belong to the respective community. The community itself is responsible for mutual authentication and authorization, key initiation, key distribution, member and pseudonym management and coordinate obfuscation[1]. In the second model, a centralized, trusted LP takes over these tasks for a community and serves different untrusted LBS providers.

While in both scenarios, the roles of LP and LBS provider can be realized by separate actors, the first one also permits an LBS provider to incorporate both roles, resulting in one LS per LBS provider.

At first glance, the first model may be preferable, as it only allows community members to have access to sensitive data. However, with a growing number of targets, scalability with regard to group and key management becomes a major problem. Furthermore, for larger communities, targets may want to have more detailed control about how other community members access their location information. For this purpose, in the centralized scenario, a target can deposit privacy policies at the trusted LP's repository.

4.2   Idea

In general, location data represents highly identifying information as it is related to a target's living or work place, leisure habits or other characteristic activities.

---

[1] Being outside the scope of this paper, please refer to [ZRM05] for a good reference on secure group communication and key establishment protocols.

To make matters worse, in LBCSs, multiple position fixes are collected that are associated with the same target pseudonym. In the following, we refer to such a collection as a *trace*. While single position fixes can be anonymized by relatively simple means (compare [GG03]), it is not that easy for traces. At large, it can be said that the more position fixes a trace contains, the more identifying it is for the respective target.

The objective of our method is to make a trace less identifying. To this end, we exploit a characteristic of LBCSs: as can be seen from the problem statement in Section 3, for detecting proximity and separation respectively only relative distances between targets are measured. Our idea is therefore to apply distance-preserving coordinate transformations to the position fixes of the targets of a community in an equal manner. This way, proximity and separation can be detected with unchanged quality, while the traces' global reference is removed together with possibly identifying characteristics of the targets.

4.3   Two-Step Obfuscation

The following describes how the transformations are parameterized (compare also Figure 3). Let

- $E = \{e_1, e_2, ..., e_n\}, 1 < i \leq n$ be a set of targets, which form a community,
- $p(e, t) : E \times \mathbb{R} \to \mathbb{R}^2$ the actual position of target $e \in E$ at time t,
- $s_G \in \mathbb{N}$ a secret key specific to E,
- $p^*(e, t, s_G) : E \times \mathbb{R} \times \mathbb{N} \to \mathbb{R}^2$ the obfuscated position of e at time t.

Our approach follows a two-step strategy: first, all coordinates are transformed by a time-independent global transformation, consisting of a rotation with angle α around $(j, k) \in \mathbb{R}^2$ followed by translation $(x_{global}, y_{global}) \in \mathbb{R}^2$.

In a second step, the local movement of targets is blurred by appending a time-dependent translation vector $v := (x_{local}, y_{local}) \in \mathbb{R}^2$. The motivation for the first step is to obfuscate the global reference of coordinates in order to avoid attacks based on known whereabouts of a target. By the second step, attacks based on knowledge about targets' mobility patterns or road patterns shall be avoided. Please refer to the next section for a detailed treatment of possible attacks of this kind.

The parameters α, j, k, x_{global} and y_{global} depend on s_G and are therefore secret within a community. The local obfuscation vector $v := (x_{local}, y_{local})$ is limited to length $|v| \leq r_{max\_local}$ and depends on s_G as well as the current time. As will be discussed in Section 5.3, one premise for the robustness of the approach is that the local transformation does not generate any PUs by itself, i.e., without the target having physically moved. With regard to our conclusions of Section 3, it should become clear now why $r_{max\_local} \leq d_{sample}$.

In the centralized scenario, the time is given by the LP. In the peer-to-peer scenario, we can assume that the clocks of the targets' MTs are synchronized. This is because we rely on GPS or a similar terminal-based positioning method. As GPS satellites have atomic clocks on board and the measured time is transmitted together with the positioning signals, a scalable method for time synchronization of the MTs is given.

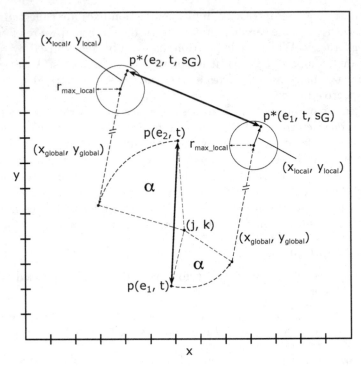

Fig. 3. Distance preserving obfuscation of two target positions $p(e_1, t)$ and $p(e_2, t)$

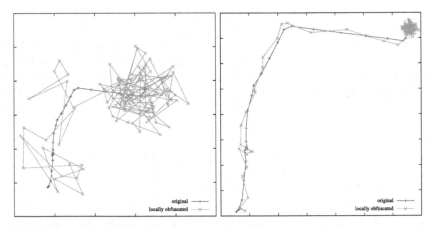

Fig. 4. A trace of coordinates (+) and its obfuscated version (x) with a bigger (left side) and smaller value (right side) for r_{max_local}. The global transformation has been omitted for sake of clarity.

Figure 4 shows a trace of coordinates that have been obfuscated by two different values for r_{max_local}. In the figure, the global transformation has been omitted for sake of clarity, i.e., it only shows the local, time-dependent translation, which aims to blur movement patterns.

5   Evaluation

In the following, a number of conceivable attacks on the proposed anonymity mechanism is discussed. The presented attacks are all executed *ex post*, i.e., their concern is to restore the mapping between a target's pseudonym and real identity from a database of previously collected trace data. They only differ in the way background information is employed to do so. We deliberately exclude *online* attacks, such as hijacking communication sessions or mapping network addresses to target identities as they are out of the scope of this paper. Instead, we presume the usage of appropriate counter-measures, such as cryptographic techniques or Mix Servers [Cha81]. Furthermore, our trust models implicitly exclude *insider* attacks due to malignance of targets or compromised MTs.

Dependent on the trust model, the trace database under attack can be hosted by the LBS Provider or the LP. Possible attackers include but are not limited to: the database host himself, e.g., in order to illegally sell private user data to third parties, malicious employees, e.g., in order to expose the privacy of a specific person, or external hackers, which have compromised the system.

5.1   The Known Whereabouts Attack

In the *Known Whereabouts Attack* (KWA), information about typical whereabouts of a person is used to restore the pseudonym-identity mapping. For instance, by knowing that person A lives at location L and/or works at location W, the pseudonym P of A is probably related with those traces, which bear most accumulations of L and W. The more whereabouts X of A are known, the more probable it is to find a unique trace containing all X, which yields the desired mapping from P to A.

In [GG03], the KWA is avoided by temporal and spatial cloaking of location data in order to achieve k-anonymity. However, this technique is only suited for protecting a single position fix of a target and cannot be applied for traces in general.

Another possible mechanism to avert the KWA is described in [BS03], where typical whereabouts of a target are simply excluded from the *application zone* of an LBS. The problem with this approach is that the respective LBS cannot be used most of the time, as by definition, typical whereabouts of a user are those where she spends most of her time.

Averting the KWA has been our main motivation for choosing coordinate transformations. It is not hard to see why the KWA cannot be conducted against coordinate-transformed traces: after applying transformations, they simply do not contain any known whereabouts of targets.

However, in the following, we would like to examine statistical attacks objecting to uncover the employed coordinate transformations. After successfully conducting one of them, an attacker may find the desired pseudonym-identity mapping, e.g., by the KWA.

5.2   The Campus Attack

While in the KWA, the trace database is searched for given locations, in the *Campus Attack* (CA), an attacker searches for locations common to a huge number of traces. The idea is that these locations are likely to represent a well-known or public area, such as a university campus. Based on one or more of such reference locations an attacker can establish a mapping between transformed and original data and thus uncover the coordinate transformation.

In the presented approach, a secret key is established for a group of targets to produce the coordinate transformation. Therefore, in general, locations common to traces of targets belonging to different groups do not map to the same original location. Thus, the effectiveness of the CA highly depends on the size of a community. For small or medium sized communities, such as the buddy list of a specific user, the CA seems useless. However, for large communities, like in a city-wide campus service allowing all students to track each other, the CA seems to be quite effective.

In the presumed trust model (section 4.1), there are two options. In the first one, mutual trust among the targets of a community is assumed. We think this option is not suited for large communities anyway, because maintaining a shared secret within so many confidants is hard. Instead, we suppose malicious targets disclosing the shared key to be a more critical threat than statistical attacks on the trace database. This can be seen in analogy to the problems associated with managing pre-shared keys in large WLANs.

However, for the second option, where the LP obfuscates the targets' locations on their behalf, which shows better scaling properties, the CA can be a serious threat for large groups. In this case, further means of protection have to be conceived. One possibility could be to establish an hierarchy of transformations within the group. Subgroups would each be associated with different transformation keys. While within a subgroup the targets' locations could be interrelated with unchanged accuracy, between subgroups only coarse-grained position-determination would be possible. However, devising these concepts is out of the scope of this paper and postponed to future work. Also, we do not have any quantitative data regarding critical groups sizes for conducting the CA. Doing simulations to that effect has been postponed to future work as well.

5.3   The Stationary Users Attack

While in the first step, a global and time-invariant transformation is used in order to avoid the KWA (see above), in the second step, a time-dependent transformation is used to protect traces against the *Mobility Pattern Attack* (MPA, see next section).

The objective of the *Stationary Users Attack* (SUA) is breaking the second transformation. It is based on the assumption that targets most of their time reside at a particular location, rather than being on the move. When several targets of one community show exactly the same mobility pattern, an attacker can assume that these targets are stationary in reality and that the observed behavior is solely due to the second transformation, which is applied for all targets synchronously. This way, the second transformation is already known to the attacker and thus the MPA much easier to conduct.

For avoiding the SUA, the second transformation is restricted to translations of length limited to r_{max_local}. If it holds that $r_{max\_local} \le d_{sample}$ (compare *minimum sampling distance*, section 3), it is guaranteed that stationary targets do not produce any PUs, which averts the SUA in the first place. Avoiding the SUA is our main motivation for limiting r_{max_local}.

5.4   The Mobility Pattern Attack

The MPA is probably the most interesting of the presented attacks and is therefore treated most extensively. It is based on the assumption that transformed target traces exhibit similar mobility patterns like the original ones. An attacker could, e.g., conduct a map-based attack, where she compares certain road patterns with the patterns of obfuscated traces in order to uncover the performed coordinate transformations. Another possibility is to search for patterns that are typical for a specific person. Suppose, it is known to an attacker that person A lives at location L, works at location W, has lunch at location F and uses particular travel paths at particular times. By searching the database for a trace that exhibits similar mobility patterns, the mapping from A to the corresponding pseudonym P could be uncovered.

In the following, the robustness of our approach against the MPA is examined by means of a simulation. First, our general method as well as type and amount of input data is summarized. After depicting how the simulation is parameterized, a short excursion on possible measures for comparing traces follows. Then, we describe and evaluate the obtained results. Finally, the role of the community key s_G is shortly discussed and it is sketched how s_G can be dynamically changed in order to improve trace anonymity.

Simulation. In general, we want to show that by our obfuscation method the shape of a trace looses resemblance to its original version so that it cannot be easily re-identified from a set of other traces that have been obfuscated. Our focus is to evaluate structural attacks, such as comparing collected traces with the road patterns of a city. That is, in our simulations the time-related aspects of traces, such as recurring events in a target's daily live, are not considered. Devising and simulating attack models that consider this type of background information is postponed to future work.

In order to simulate the attack, we have collected 69 GPS traces of students in and around the city of Munich, representing both pedestrian as well as vehicular movements. The timely duration of a trace varies between several minutes and five hours, whereby GPS position fixes occur in intervals of one second. The traces are obfuscated by the method presented in Section 4.3 according to the following parameters.

Simulation parameters. The local translation vector $v := (x_{local}, y_{local})$, which is dependent on the community key s_G as well as the time t, is generated by a pseudorandom function. Therefore, s_G, which serves as the seed value, is arbitrarily chosen and fixed for one simulation run. All traces are aligned in the time domain, so that every trace starts with $t := 0$. For every time step $t, 0 \leq t \leq t_{max}$, with t_{max} being the length of the longest trace, the local translation vector $v := (x_{local}, y_{local})$ is computed with the help of the random function. The length of v is chosen upon a uniform distribution with $0 < |v| \leq r_{max\_local}$. Furthermore, the direction of v is uniformly distributed between 0 and 2π. v is computed for each time step t and is then applied to all position fixes with time stamp t.

The parameters for the global transformation are arbitrarily chosen and fixed for one simulation run.

Trace similarity. Our interest is, how similar an obfuscated trace λ^* is to its original version λ and how many other obfuscated traces μ^* are more similar to λ than λ^* is to λ. We presume that, if a certain percentage of obfuscated traces μ^* is more similar to λ, then the structure of λ^* must be sufficiently blurred to provide a certain level of protection.

However, in order to obtain a similarity measure for comparing the structure of two traces the following considerations must be taken into account. Trace similarity is discussed, e.g., in [YAS03], where a shape-based similarity is described. [MdB02] presents raster-based spatial, temporal and spatial-temporal aggregation methods. Unfortunately, these and similar methods do not specify the way rotated traces have to be aligned for comparison. That is, the mechanisms only work for traces with conserved global reference. Thus, they cannot be used for our technique.

A possible solution are feature methods used in the field of similarity search in *computer aided design* (CAD) or molecular databases [MG95] [BMH92]. These algorithms are invariant to translations and rotations as they only deal with

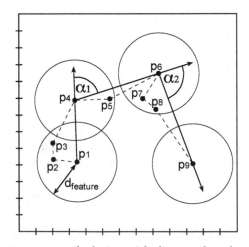

Fig. 5. Feature vector calculation with distance-based angular profile

relative changes within the tested object. Like in these approaches, we have used a feature-based similarity metric.

For each trace λ, a feature vector $F_\lambda = (\alpha_{\lambda 1}, ..., \alpha_{\lambda m}) \in \mathbb{R}^m$ is computed, which represents the distance-based angular profile of λ. Figure 5 illustrates this computation. Parameterized by a feature distance $d_{feature}$, the angle α is added to F_λ only if the distance between the current position p_c and the last considered position p_l is greater than $d_{feature}$. α corresponds to the difference between the last considered moving direction and the current moving direction.

We define the similarity between two feature vectors $F_\lambda = (\alpha_{\lambda 1}, ..., \alpha_{\lambda m})$ and $F_\mu = (\alpha_{\mu 1}, ..., \alpha_{\mu n})$ with $m \leq n$ to be the maximum of the Euclidean distances between F_λ and all possible candidate subsequences $(\alpha_{\mu i}, ..., \alpha_{\mu j}) \subseteq F_\mu$, $0 \leq i \leq j \leq n, j - i = m$. This represents a conservative metric with respect to the presented attack, because the worst match of a subset of a trace to another one is considered.

Simulation results. Each trace is compared to all others and each comparison is done 100 times. Each simulation run is conducted with a different group key s_G. We observed that changing the group sizes and thus the number of traces obfuscated by the same s_G has only negligible effects on the results. Figure 6 shows the results of the conducted simulations. The ordinate shows the percentage of obfuscated traces μ^* that are more similar to a given trace λ than λ^* is to λ. In other words, the ordinate corresponds to the relative size of the anonymity set

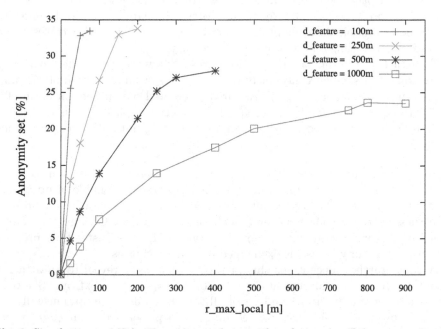

Fig. 6. Simulating an MPA: The ordinate denotes the relative size of the anonymity set related to the set of traces. The x-axis shows the maximum size of the local translation vector.

according to [PK01]. A value of 100% indicates maximum anonymity, whereas a value of 0% means that an obfuscated trace is unique in the set of traces. The x-axis shows the limit to the local translation, r_{max_local}. There are four curves depicted, each for a different value of $d_{feature}$, which parameterizes the calculation of the feature vector. In previous sections, we explained why it must hold that $r_{max\_local} < d_{sample}$. Therefore, the distance between two subsequent position fixes collected about a target can never be smaller than r_{max_local}, which in turn limits the feature calculation that can be conducted by an attacker to $r_{max\_local} < d_{feature}$. This is the reason why the curves stop at some point. Furthermore, the charts show that feature calculation with $d_{feature} = 1000m$ yields the best results from the point of view of an attacker for all possible values of r_{max_local}.

It becomes obvious that a higher r_{max_local} leads to an increase of the fraction of similar traces. With r_{max_local} set to $100m$, a possible borderline tolerance of $b = 300m$ for proximity and separation detection can be realized (compare Section 3). For that configuration, about 7.5% of all obfuscated traces μ^* are more similar to λ than λ^* is to λ. For $b = 1500m$ the fraction is almost 20%. If these values provide sufficient anonymity or not mainly depends on the number of traces in the database. That is, for supporting k-anonymity for a given k and a given fraction f of similar traces, the database must contain at least $k * f$ traces. Furthermore, the presented charts show average values. For guaranteeing that traces that a more characteristic than average cannot be distinguished from at least $k - 1$ other ones, even more traces would be necessary in the database. Finally, the presented results are specific to the simulated scenario. In order to obtain more reliable data, additional simulations, e.g., with GPS traces taken from targets traveling on highways, are necessary.

Nevertheless, the simulated scenario represents a worst case, where collected traces consist of samples continously taken with a spatial resolution of the minimum sampling distance d_{sample}. As already pointed out in Section 3, an efficient strategy for proximity and separation detection typically leads to a much lower number of collected position samples, which significantly enhances trace anonymity.

Role of community key. The longer a trace gets, the more identifying it is. Unfortunately, in our simulation, we only had traces available of up to five hours of recording. Thus, the results obtained are not authoritative for proving robustness for traces collected over a much longer time span. Changing a target's pseudonym every several hours is not an option for LBCSs. Instead, we propose that the community key s_G is exchanged on a regular basis.

Without further precautions this method could easily reveal to an attacker a mapping from the transformation based on one s_G to the next one. She only needs to observe that successive PUs of all targets suddenly jump unusually far apart. In order to avoid that, we recommend to preserve certain *guard times* between using different keys. During a guard time no PU may be transmitted by any community member.

6   Conclusion and Outlook

In this paper, we presented a novel anonymity technique suited for protecting the advanced LBS functions proximity and separation detection. These two functions are base mechanisms for realizing LBCSs. Our idea is to apply distance-preserving coordinate transformations to the positions of all targets of a community. This way, service quality remains unchanged while identifying characteristics of a target's trace can be removed.

We evaluated the approach by argument and by simulation and concluded that, despite some weaknesses for protecting very large groups, the technique is well-suited for withstanding a number of conceivable attacks, among them being map-based ones. Like in related approaches, it is difficult to give an absolute measure for how hard it is to break our mechanism, as it is highly dependent on the amount of background information an attacker has. While in this paper, one obvious attack scenario was simulated based on real data, doing this for other scenarios is still an open issue, which, however, cannot be in the scope of this work.

We also described how the quality of an LBCSs is (qualitatively) related to the protection level provided by our approach. Given this information, targets can trade off quality against privacy according to their individual convenience.

In further work, we are planning to devise efficient strategies for cluster detection as well as k-nearest-neighbor detection, which are based on the proximity and separation detection mechanisms protected by the presented approach. Furthermore, we investigate privacy mechanisms suited for protecting targets against the users of an LBCS. An interesting topic in this context is if white lying of targets about their position should be possible in order to reduce peer pressure. Otherwise, the only way to avoid being located by members of their community is an explicit veto, which can have negative social consequences in some situations.

References

[AEM+04]   A. Amir, A. Efrat, J. Myllymaki, L. Palaniappan, and K. Wampler. Buddy tracking - efficient proximity detection among mobile friends. In *INFO-COM*, 2004.

[BMH92]   Anne Badel, Jean Paul Mornon, and Serge Hazout. Searching for geometric molecular shape complementarity using bidimensional surface profiles. *Journal of Molecular Graphics*, 10(4):205–211, December 1992.

[BPB+04]   David E. Bakken, Rupa Parameswaran, Douglas M. Blough, Andy A. Franz, and Ty J. Palmer. Data obfuscation: anonymity and desensitization of usable data sets. *IEEE Security & Privacy*, pages 34–41, November/December 2004.

[BS03]   Alastair R. Beresford and Frank Stajano. Location privacy in pervasive computing. *IEEE Pervasive Computing*, 2(1):46–55, 2003.

[Cha81]   David L. Chaum. Untraceable electronic mail, return addresses, and digital pseudonyms. *Communications of the ACM*, 24(2):84–90, 1981.

[DK05]   Matt Duckham and Lars Kulik. A formal model of obfuscation and nego-
           tiation for location privacy. In *Pervasive*, pages 152–170, 2005.
[FJ04]   Keith B. Frikken and Mikhail J.AAtallah. Privacy preserving route plan-
           ning. In *WPES '04: Proceedings of the 2004 ACM workshop on Privacy in
           the electronic society*, pages 8–15, New York, NY, USA, 2004. ACM Press.
[GBG04]   Marco Gruteser, Jonathan Bredin, and Dirk Grunwald. Path privacy in
           location-aware computing. In *Proceedings of MobiSys 2004 Workshop on
           Context Awareness*, June 2004.
[GG03]   Marco Gruteser and Dirk Grunwald. Anonymous Usage of Location-Based
           Services Through Spatial and Temporal Cloaking. In *Proceedings of the
           First International Conference on Mobile Systems, Applications, and Ser-
           vices*, May 2003.
[GHT04]   Andreas Görlach, Andreas Heinemann, and Wesley W. Terpstra. Survey
           on location privacy in pervasive computing. In Philip Robinson, Harald
           Vogt, and Waleed Wagealla, editors, *Privacy, Security and Trust within
           the Context of Pervasive Computing (Workshop at Pervasive 2004)*, vol-
           ume 780 of *The Kluwer International Series in Engineering and Computer
           Science*, Vienna, Austria, April 2004. Springer-Verlag.
[KT05]   Axel Küpper and Georg Treu. From location to position management: User
           tracking for location-based services. In Paul Müller, Reinhard Gotzhein,
           and Jens B. Schmitt, editors, *Tagungsband der ITG/GI-Fachtagung Kom-
           munikation in Verteilten Systemen (KiVS 05)*, volume 61 of *Lecture
           Notes in Informatics (LNI)*, pages 81–88. Gesellschaft für Informatik (GI),
           Kaiserslautern, Germany, Februar 2005.
[Küp05]   A. Küpper. *Location–based Services — Fundamentals and Operation*. John
           Wiley & Sons, August 2005.
[LR02]   A. Leonhardi and K. Rothermel. Protocols for updating highly accurate
           location information. In A. Behcet, editor, *Geographic Location in the
           Internet.*, pages 111–141. Kluwer Academic Publishers, 2002.
[MdB02]   Nirvana Meratnia and Rolf A. de By. Aggregation and comparison of
           trajectories. In *GIS '02: Proceedings of the 10th ACM international sym-
           posium on Advances in geographic information systems*, pages 49–54, New
           York, NY, USA, 2002. ACM Press.
[MFD03]   Ginger Myles, Adrian Friday, and Nigel Davies. Preserving privacy in en-
           vironments with location-based applications. *IEEE Pervasive Computing*,
           2(1):56–64, 2003.
[MG95]   Rajiv Mehrotra and James E. Gary. Similar-shape retrieval in shape data
           management. *IEEE Computer*, 28(2):57 – 62, Sept. 1995.
[PK01]   A. Pfitzmann and M. Köhntopp. Anonymity, unobservability, and
           pseudonymity - a proposal for terminology. In H. Federrath, editor, *Pro-
           ceedings of the International Workshop on Design Issues in Anonymity
           and Unobservability, Berkeley, CA, USA, July 2000*, volume 2009 of *Lec-
           ture Notes in Computer Science*, pages 1–9. Springer, 2001.
[Swe02]   Latanya Sweeney. k-anonymity: a model for protecting privacy. *Interna-
           tional Journal on Uncertainty, Fuzziness and Knowledge-based Systems*,
           10(5):557–570, 2002.
[TK05]   Georg Treu and Axel Küpper. Efficient Proximity Detection for Location
           Based Services. In *Proceedings of the Joint 2nd Workshop on Positioning,
           Navigation and Communication 2005 (WPNC05) and 1st Ultra–Wideband
           Expert Talk (UET05)*, Hannover, Germany, March 2005.

[TKR05]   Georg Treu, Axel Küpper, and Peter Ruppel. Anonymization in proactive location based community services. In *Advances in Pervasive Computing. Adjunct Proceedings of the 3rd International Conference on Pervasive Computing, Munich, Germany*, number 191. Österreichische Computer Gesellschaft, Mai 2005.

[YAS03]   Yutaka Yanagisawa, Jun–ichi Akahani, and Tetsuji Satoh. Shape-based similarity query for trajectory of mobile objects. In *Mobile Data Management: 4th International Conference, MDM 2003 Melbourne, Australia, January 21-24, 2003. Proceedings*, Lecture Notes in Computer Science No. 2574, pages 63–77, 2003.

[ZRM05]   Xukai Zou, Byrav Ramamurthy, and Spyros S. Magliveras. *Secure Group Communications over Data Networks*. Springer Science+Business Media, Inc., 2005.

Towards Personalized Mobile Interruptibility Estimation

Nicky Kern and Bernt Schiele

Department of Computer Science,
TU Darmstadt, Germany
{kern, schiele}@mis.tu-darmstadt.de

Abstract. The automatic estimation of the user's current interruptibility is important to seamlessly adapt a device's behaviour to the user's situation. Different people differ in the way they rate their interruptibility. In this paper we investigate three options how to adapt an interruptibility estimation system to a particular user: by finding prototypical users, using experience sampling, or using knowledge of prototypical situations. We have experimentally tested all three approaches on a data set of 94 situations that have been annotated by 24 different users.

1 Introduction

To enable seamless interaction for mobile, context-aware devices, it is important to know how much attention the user has available for the system, i.e. how much the system would interrupt the user in his current situation.

We have shown in previous work [13, 14] that it is possible to estimate the user's interruptibility from data of body-worn sensors. It is important here to distinguish between interrupting the user and interrupting the environment. We make this explicit by dinstinguishing the *social interruptibility* and the *personal interruptibility*. We have shown in a user study that users do make use of this distinction, when given appropriate notification modalities.

A first contribution of this paper is to show that users rate their interruptibility very differently and that an automatic system for interruptibility estimation thus needs to adapt to its user. People rated each other's interruptibility correctly in only about 65% of the cases (for both personal and social interruptibility, using a comparable error measure as for the experiments below, see Section 3).

In this paper we concentrate on adapting an interruptibility estimation system to the user. For this we compare three different approaches to adapt the system to the user. Firstly by defining prototypical users, secondly by performing a (random) experience sampling, and thirdly by identifying prototypical situations and generalizing from them.

The first strategy aims to find users that rate different situations similarly and represent them as prototypical users in the system. The system would be pre-trained for each of the prototypical users. The user could then select the prototypical user which is closest to his own preferences, or the system could try to determine it automatically after a few user interactions.

M. Hazas, J. Krumm, and T. Strang (Eds.): LoCA 2006, LNCS 3987, pp. 134–150, 2006.

The second option is to adapt the system online during run-time. It would perform an experience sampling, i.e. regularly interrupt the user to ask how he would rate his current interruptibility. In order to avoid that the system becomes annoying to the user, the number of user interactions should be kept as small as possible. While it is possible to perform a random experience sampling, more sophisticated approaches might try to actively sample only unknown situations.

The third possibility is to identify situations that have prototypical interruptibility ratings and have the user annotate only those situations. The user would annotate a few situations before using the system. This would be similar to personalizing a speech recognizer by reading a defined passage of text to it.

This paper is structured as follows: we revise related work (Section 2) and introduce the interruptibility estimation algorithm (Section 3) and data set we collected (Section 4). As the first contribution we analyse how different people differ in their rating of each other's interruptibility (Section 4.1). Secondly, we discuss three options for adapting an interruptibility estimation system (Sections 5-7). As the third contribution we evaluate each of the three approaches and discuss their respective strengths and weaknesses (Section 8). We conclude the paper with a summary and outlook (Section 9).

2 Related Work

Human attention is a resource that has distinct and well-characterized limits and computer systems have to take these limitations into account (see for example Horvitz et al. [10]). Interruptions increase the load on human memory. Cutrell et al. [1] have shown that interruptions by instant messaging applications decrease human performance and have a negative effect on the memory required for resuming the original primary task. Czerwinski et al. [2] performed a week-long diary study of task interruption with ten subjects. Their subjects reported that there is a near one-to-one correspondence between tasks and interruptions. Hudson et al. [11] carried out an experience sampling study with 10 research managers. Some of them reported that, although they did not like being interrupted in their current task, they also did not want to miss the interruption, because they might miss an important issue. It is therefore important to correctly assess the importance of the interruption and the interruptibility of the user.

Estimating user attention and interruptibility has received attention for quite a while in very specialized settings, where the main task is bound to the computer and requires the entire user attention, e.g. in Horvitz et al. [8] for Space Shuttle monitoring and in Obermayer and Nugent [15] for military command control.

More recently, interruptibility estimation has been investigated in more standard office-type scenarios. Hudson et al. [12] collected 600 hours of audio and video data of 4 research managers. They used experience sampling to obtain 672 samples of the subjects' interruptibility on a scale from 1 to 5. Roughly 30% of this data was in the 'highly non-interruptible' class. They trained models on simulated features and obtained scores of up to 78% for a two-class problem ('highly non-interruptible' against the rest). In a follow-up study [3] they collected another 975 self-reports from 10 subjects. They investigate different user groups (managers, researchers, interns) and several sensor sets (full, laptop only, and a set without microphone for privacy reasons). They obtain comparable recognition results of 81-87% using real sensors.

Fogarty et al. [4] observed subjects during a programing task to investigate their interruptibility. They used the reaction time upon an interruption as a measure of interruptibility. Three levels of interruptibility emerged from their data: an 'interruptible' state (with a mean reaction time of 2.281 seconds and a standard deviation of 0.752 seconds), an 'engaged' state (mean: 6.917 seconds, standard deviation: 3.434 seconds), and a 'non-interruptible' state (mean: 43.065 seconds, standard deviation: 37.399 seconds). The statistical model for the two-class problem ('interruptible' against the remaining two) correctly classified 74.8% of the interruptible and 67.5% of the non-interruptible samples.

Estimated attention and interruptbility has been mainly used for e-mail and call handling. Horvitz et al. [9] present the Priorities system: they infer user attention from sounds in the office and from computer activity and estimate the user state in an application-centric way ("word-processor centric" vs. "e-mail centric"). They model the *net value* of an alert as a continuous variable. The system presents alerts differently depending on this value, by playing criticality specific sounds, automatically bringing the client to the front or opening messages automatically. In a follow-up system they allow users to define rules for their own interruptibility and importance of messages [7].

The MyVine system [5] uses speech detection, location, computer activity, and calendar entries to estimate interruptibility. It uses a unified telephone, instant messaging and e-mail communication system. Following a socially translucent approach, it presents peer 'contacts' grayed out depending on their level of interruptibility, and thus leave the choice of how to contact a particular person to the user.

Interruptibility estimation in mobile setting has received comparatively little attention. Sawhney et al. [16] address the issue of scalable, context-aware e-mail notifications for wearable computers. They use the importance of messages, the usage level of their device and (as the only "external" context) the likelihood of conversation. Kern et al. [13, 14] present a system for estimating the interruptibility of a user from real sensor or acceleration, audio, and location sensors.

Ho and Intille [6] use sensors to classify the user's activity in sitting, walking, and standing. They use this information to mediate interruptions. They found that users preferred to be interrupted when in transition from one activity to another. They did not aim at estimating the interruptibility explicitly.

The online adaption of an interruptibility estimation system has, to the authors' knowledge, not been investigated. All approaches listed above allow to train a system for a particular user, but do not allow to adapt it after training.

3   Interruptibility Estimation

As mentioned in the introduction, we distinguish between the interruptibility of the user (called *personal interruptibility*) and that of his environment (the *social interruptibility*). Figure 1(a) shows the two variables drawn along the axis of a two-dimensional space. We can use this space to describe the user's interruptibility for any given situation (see [14] for a more complete description).

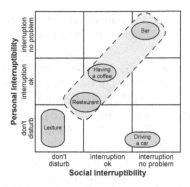

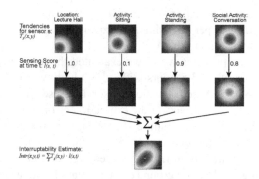

(a) The User's Social and Personal Interruptibility for Different Situations.

(b) Process of Automatic Interruptibility Estimation from Multiple Low-Level Contexts.

Fig. 1. Automatic Recognition of Interruptibility from Low-Level Contexts

An intuitive approach to estimate the user's interruptibility would be to recognize situations such as those depicted in Figure 1(a) and infer the interruptibility from them. However many situations do not give a precise enough hint about the user's interruptibility. For example the situations *Restaurant*, *Having A Coffee*, and *Bar* belong to a continuum that covers the diagonal of the space (see Figure 1(a)). Increasing the granularity of the situations would of course help, but would introduce so many special cases that the problem becomes intractable. Thus, we estimate the interruptibility directly from the output of low-level *context sensors*. A context sensor is an algorithm that gives information about a basic context, e.g. the user's physical activity (sitting, walking, etc.) or the auditory scene (in a restaurant, on the street, etc.).

The basic idea of our recognition approach is that for every low-level context sensor we can give a *tendency* where the interruptibility is likely to be. For example, for a *Lecture Hall* context sensor (e.g. based on audio) we know that the interruptibility is likely to be in the lower-left-hand corner of the space, because both the user and the environment should probably not be interrupted (see for example the top left tendency in Figure 1(b)). Since we can never know such low-level context for sure, different context sensors might be inconsistent or even contradicting. Treating context sensors as recognition sub-systems, we get a recognition score $l(s,t)$ for every context sensor s and reading at time step t. To incorporate all information available, we weigh the tendencies $T_s(x,y)$ with the recognition scores of the respective sensors $l(s,t)$ ((x,y) being the two directions in the interruptibility space). We then sum the weighted tendencies $Intr(x,y,t) = \sum_s T_s(x,y) \cdot l(s,t)$ and obtain a likelihood map over the interruptibility space, in which we search the maximum. Figure 1(b) shows an example of the procedure for four different context sensors.

We find low-level contexts automatically by applying a k-means clustering to the incoming sensor data. We use the distances to the cluster centers as 'likelihood' $l(s,t)$. We represent the tendencies as a two-dimensional grid of *bins*, where each bin has a fixed (scalar) value. We can thus compute the tendencies automatically: during training the values of $l(s,t)$ are known, and the $T_s(\hat{x},\hat{y})$ are to be estimated (where $(\hat{x},\hat{y})$ is the discrete two-dimensional bin-number). For every training example and bin $(\hat{x},\hat{y})$ we obtain a linear equation. Given a set of training examples we can solve this over-determined problem per bin using least-squares. To account for small variations in the data we blur the ground truth.

In previous work, we evaluated the approach experimentally [13]. We recorded a data set of 3.5 hours with 12 3D body-worn acceleration sensors, a microphone, and (WLAN-based) location sensor. Because we want to use this information for modality selection, we accept the estimation error if it is smaller than half the distance between the grid lines in Figure 1(a). We achieved a classification score of 97.2% for the social interruptibility and of 90.5% for the personal interruptibility.

In the experiments presented in this paper we use 50 low-level contexts. During training, we blur the ground truth annotation with a Gaussian with $\sigma=0.5$ (the interruptibility space uses the interval $[0; 3]$) and use a grid resolution of 6x6.

4   Data Acquisition

In this section, we introduce the data set we collected for this study and present baseline interruptibility recognition results (Section 4.2) using the algorithm presented in Section 3. We analyse how consistent users are in rating each others' interruptibility (Section 4.1).

To test the adaptation to a particular user we would ideally need sequences of data from multiple users with regular annotations. One approach to obtain such data would be to perform experience sampling. However, this incurs a high overhead in acquiring the data, since users need to be equipped with recording setups. Furthermore, experience sampling often produces little data and is hard to control and to compare between users. We therefore opted for a video-based approach, where we recorded videos of various situations and asked 24 users to annotate the situations in the videos. The user shown in the videos wore a recording setup that recorded data from body-worn acceleration, audio, and location sensors. We have thus obtained a set of real sensor data with annotations from 24 different users.

We collected two videos of 47 situations, resulting in a total of 94 situation videos. Each video is five seconds long. The videos all contain the same person (wearing a particular red backpack) to disambiguate which situation they actually show. We chose the situations to best possibly sample the interruptibility space. The situations varied between: looking at shop windows, sitting in a different restaurants (posh, student, Mc-Donalds), attending a lecture, studying in the university library, working in a computer lab, buying gum at a kiosk, etc.

Synchronized with the video we recorded sensor data from 12 3D body-worn acceleration sensors, audio, and (WLAN-based) location. As features we computed mean and variance on each channel of acceleration over windows of one second. For audio we computed 10 cepstral coefficients over windows of 30 ms and averaged those over one second. The location was sampled once per second. We thus obtained a feature vector every second. Out of the continuous stream of data we cut out 6 feature vectors for each video.

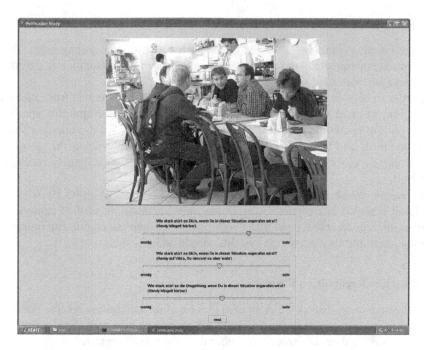

Fig. 2. Screenshot of the Annotation Application. This application was used by the 24 study participants to annotate all 94 different situations. On top a five second video was shown, which was annotated by the users using the three sliders below.

For this study we had 24 participants annotating the videos. They were all students either at the departement of computer science at ETH Zurich or at the psychology department of the University of Zurich. Half of the participants were female. The mean age was 24.6 year (stdev. 4.1 years). 23 out of the 24 participants reported to own a mobile phone.

Figure 2 shows a screenshot of the annotation application. On top the video was shown. For each video the participants had to provide a rating for the three questions below (in this paper we used only answers to questions 2 and 3). We used ratings on graphic rating scales (on a scale from *little (value 0) – much (value 1)*).

1. How much does it disturb **you**, if you receive a phone call in this situation? (Mobile phone rings audibly)
2. How much does it disturb **you**, if you receive a phone call in this situation? (Mobile phone vibrates, you notice it)
3. How much does it disturb **your environment**, if you receive a phone call in this situation? (Mobile phone rings audibly)

In summary, we collected data of 94 situations (two instances of 47 different situations). For each situation we have sensor data of 12 body-worn acceleration sensors, audio, and location sensors. We asked 24 different participants to annotate videos of those situations.

4.1   Consistency Between Users

As a first baseline result we computed the consistency of ratings among users. This is an important prerequisite: if the users ratings are consistent, an adaptation to the current user would not be needed.

In order to be able to compare the results with the results obtained from automatic recognition, we used a similar error measure: we divide the interruptibility space in a regular grid (of resolution 6x6, as for the other experiments). We use one user's rating as 'ground truth' and the other users as 'recognition'. We then evaluate the recognition performance using the same method that we use for automatic recognition results (see Section 3).

The results are shown in the third set of bars in Figure 3. With 65.5%/64.1% for social and personal interruptibility, users are quite inconsistent in their ratings. This confirms our argument that users differ significantly in their interruptibility ratings and that thus interruptibility estimation systems should adapt to their user [13].

4.2   Baseline Recognition Results

Using the data we collected, we computed two baseline recognition results. Firstly the recognition score on single users. Secondly we calculated how well the algorithm performs if it is trained on data from users other than the one being tested.

Single Person Recognition. To see how well we can recognize the interruptibility of a single user, we performed leave-one-out cross-validation: we trained the interruptibility estimation algorithm using data of 93 situations and tested on the last remaining situation. We thus tested each situation separately and averaged the results.

The first set of bars in Figure 3 shows the recognition score for single users (averaged over all users). We can classify the social interruptibility correctly in 78.3% of the time. The personal interruptibility performs nearly 10% better with 87.8%. We attribute this to the fact that the personal interruptibility in our setting is more subtle (due to the vibrating phone modality) and thus more consistent between situations. Both scores are about 10% lower than those we have obtained in previous work [13, 14]. This is probably due to the fact that the data in this study is much more varied and that there is considerably less training data available.

System trained on other users. Since we have data of multiple users available, we also test how well other users' annotations can be used for training. To test a user, we used the annotations of all other users to train the system. We averaged the annotations of the other users per situation, s.t. we obtained a single annotation per situation. We then tested the system using the annotations that user made on all situations. The results are depicted in the second set of bars in Figure 3 (averaged over all users). The results are with 65.8%/73.7% about 13-15% lower than for single user recognition. This can be explained by the fact that we did not use a single personal annotation. This again indicates that training on other users will not be sufficient.

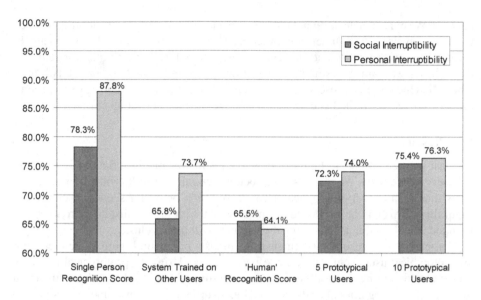

Fig. 3. Baseline Recognition Recognition Results and Recognition Score using Information from Prototypical Users. The first set of bars shows the recognition score of a single user's data. The second set the recognition scores of a system that is trained on other users' data. The consistency results between users is shown in the third set. The last two sets indicate the results with 5 and 10 prototypical users, respectively (the experiments are each repeated 10 times).

4.3 Discussion

The results of Sections 4.2 and 4.1 clearly show that it is necessary to train and adapt the system to individual users. The following Sections 5, 6, and 7 propose and analyze three different approaches to adapt to and learn from individual users in order to improve the system's ability to estimate a user's interruptibility.

5 Prototypical Users

In Section 4, we have shown that, in general, users are very dissimilar in the way they rate their interruptibility and thus systems need to adapt to their user. One possibility is to identify groups of users that are similar in the way they rate their interruptibility. Such a group could be represented by a single *prototypical user*. The user would have to pick the most similar prototypical user himself, or the system could estimate the most likely prototypical user from few user interactions.

In practice such a system would have predefined interruptibility estimation settings for each prototypical user. The user of the system would then have to find out, to which prototypical user his preferences are closest (e.g. by answering a series of questions) and choose this set of settings. Since the settings are determined in advance, no personal annotations are necessary.

Experimental Setup. To test, if we can identify users that are prototypical for others, we cluster the users' annotations and perform a cross-validated test within those clusters. We concatenate the annotations for social and personal interruptibility for each user, thus obtaining 188-dimensional vectors. These vectors are then clustered using k-means. Clusters with only one element are rejected and the clustering is restarted. For each cluster we train the estimation algorithm on N-1 users and test on the Nth user, where N is the number of users within that cluster. We then cross-validate over all combinations of users within that cluster, and average the results over all clusters.

5.1   Results

The last two sets of bars in Figure 3 show the results obtained for 5 and 10 prototypical users respectively. We obtain slightly better recognition results with 10 prototypical users than with only 5 prototypical users (2.3%/2.9% better for social/personal interruptibility). This can be explained by the fact that with fewer clusters more users are grouped in a cluster, thus increasing the variance within that cluster.

Compared to the results for a single user (first set of bars in Figure 3), neither 5 nor 10 prototypical users achieve the same performance. Using 10 prototypical users we obtain a recognition score for the social interruptibility that is only 2.9% less than that of single user recognition. For the personal interruptibility however, the results are not quite as good: the score using 10 prototypical users is 11.5% lower than that of single user recognition. We explain this by the fact that the personal interruptibility is more personal and generalizes less from user to user.

When comparing the recognition score using 10 prototypical users to the score where the system is trained on other users (second set of bars in Figure 3), we obtain a small increase in the recognition score of the personal interruptibility (2.6% increase to 76.3%). The recognition score of the social interruptibility profits increases considerably by 9.6% from 65.8% to 75.4%.

The comparison of 10 prototypical users with results of single users and of a system trained on other users leads to the conclusion that it is comparatively easy to find clusters in the social interruptibility that generalize from user to user. For the personal interruptibility it is much harder to find such clusters.

It is important to note that we have only very limited data available (we cluster 24 188-dimensional vectors), making it hard to draw any firm conclusion from the results. To test the approach more thoroughly substantially more user annotations would be required which in itself is an important limitation of the approach.

6   Random Experience Sampling

In Section 5 we presented an approach for adapting an interruptibility estimation system by generalizing from one user to another. A fundamentally different possibility is to ask the user to supply *personal annotations* of his interruptibility and use those to incrementally adapt the system. It is critical to keep the number of personal annotations as low as possible, so as to avoid to annoy the user. The strategy with which personal annotations are obtained determines to a large extent the number of required personal annotations.

There are three fundamentally different strategies for obtaining personal annotations: firstly by performing a random experience sampling, i.e. by randomly interrupting the user and asking him for his current interruptibility, secondly by actively sampling only 'unknown' situations, and lastly by asking for quality feedback on interruptions that would have occurred anyway.

Regularly interrupting the user might of course be annoying over time. It does however not make any assumptions about the situations a user might encounter and should thus work for any user with a sufficiently high number of personal annotations. Below, we show experimentally that this is indeed the case.

Actively sampling unknown situations allows to reduce the number of necessary personal annotations. It does however make assumptions about the situations a user is likely to encounter and might therefore not work for all users. We discuss such an approach in Section 7.

When using quality feedback, the user rates interruptions of the system. This could be done implicitly, e.g. by not rejecting a phone call, or explicitly by asking the user which modality would have been better suited. While this allows to reduce the number of personal annotations by only requiring negative annotations (i.e. when the system did not perform as desired), it might introduce a considerable bias, because the sampling is limited to times when the user is interrupted. Also the interpretation of positive samples, when the user did not correct the system, is not obvious. The user might have been satisfied with the interruption or might simply have forgotten to rate it. For these reasons we only consider the first two strategies in this paper.

Experimental Setup. We evaluate the approach using random experience sampling on the data described in Section 4. We start with a pre-initialized system (using the average of other users' annotations) and add personal annotations as they are entered into the system. The sequence in which situations are added plays of course a central role. To compensate for effects caused by the situation sequence we repeat the experiments with 50 different situation sequences.

For a given user we initialize the system using the averaged annotations of all other users (as in the *system trained on other user* result, second set of bars in Figure 3). One-by-one we replace those annotations by the personal annotation of the given user. After each situation is added we test the recognition performance on all remaining situations. In order to keep a minimal size of the test set we end the iteration after the addition of 85 out of the 94 situations.

6.1 Results

Figure 4 shows the result averaged over all users and all 50 repetitions of the experiment. The upper line indicates the recognition score for the personal interruptibility and the lower line that of the social interruptibility.

Most importantly, we can observe a (nearly) linear increase in recognition score with each added situation. The first recognition score (the left-most point of the lines) corresponds to the *system trained on other users* score as indicated in the second set of bars in Figure 3. We obtain here a score of 65.8% for the social interruptibility and 78.4% for the personal interruptibility. The last recognition score depicted in Figure 4 closely corresponds to the single user recognition score (see the first set of bars in Figure 3). It is slightly lower (about 2%) than the maximum score for the personal

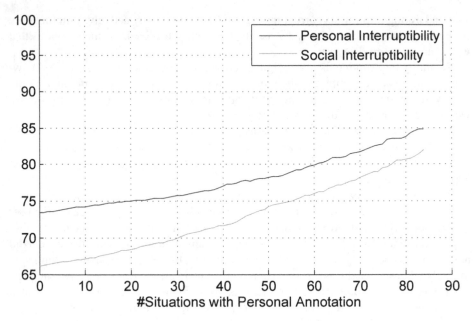

Fig. 4. Recognition Score using Random Experience Sampling. Users' annotations are incrementally used to adapt the system. Situations are selected in random order. The experiment is repeated 50 times.

interruptibility. We explain this by the fact that not all situations have been added to the training set. For the social interruptibility the recognition score is slightly (about 3%) higher than the score in Figure 3. This is an artefact of the random selection of situations.

7 Prototypical Situations

In this section we discuss an approach that tries to generalizing across situations. If two situations generally share the same interruptibility rating, it is sufficient to have a personal annotation for one of them. If such correspondences were known, the user could pre-train the system by annotating only a few *prototypical situations*, and the system could automatically generalize to other situations. This would be similar to speech recognizers, which can be pre-trained by reading a predefined passage of text.

In practice the user would annotate the prototypical situations before actually using the system. For each prototypical situation the system would store sensor data for a group of similar situations. When the system encounters a new situation during use, it would use the sensor data to find a similar situation out of this set. It can then use the annotation of the prototypical situation to adapt itself to that situation. Without the prototypical situation it would require a personal annotation, and thus a user interaction, the number of which should be kept minimal.

Active Experience Sampling. An important aspect of this approach is that it allows for *active experience sampling*: instead of randomly sampling the interruptibility of the user (as described in Section 6), the system could sample only those prototypical situations for which it has not obtained a personal annotation yet. For each newly encountered situation it would check, which of its stored situations is most similar. If the corresponding prototypical situation has been annotated by the user, that annotation can be used for the newly encountered situation as well. In consequence the number of personal annotations, and thus user interactions, would be limited to the number of prototypical situations.

Experimental Setup. To test how much we can profit from using prototypical situations, we have to perform two steps: firstly, we have to identify situations that have similar interruptibility ratings and secondly we have to test how the recognition score evolves with an increasing number of personal annotations.

For the first step, we have to find groups of situations that have similar interruptibility ratings, irrespective of the actual rating. We do this separately for the social and personal interruptibility. We base our approach on the paired t-test and use a variance measure similar to the t-test's significance. We compute this measure for each pair of situations of our data set. We use a threshold θ to decide whether two situations are similar or not. We then group situations: the situation with the largest number of 'similar' situations is selected as the first prototypical situation. We remove the prototypical situation and all similar situations from the set and iterate this procedure, until no situations are left.

For evaluating the impact on the recognition score, we compose a sequence of situations from the prototypical situations and incrementally add them to the training set, similar to the approach used in Section 6. Instead of changing only the annotation for the newly added situation we also change the annotation of all situations that belong to the same prototypical situation (unless we have a proper personal annotation for them). We initialize the system with the averaged annotation of all other users (as for the *system trained on other users* score depicted in Figure 3). After adding a new situation, we compute the recognition score on all remaining situations.

Specifically, from the groups of situations for social and personal interruptibility we compose two sequences of situations and merge them so that we have alternating situation samples. To compose a single sequence we randomly select a situation from the largest group of situations, then from the second largest group, etc. When we have selected a situation from all groups, we start over and iterate this procedure until no more situations are left. When two groups have the same size, we randomly select one of them.

For each personal annotation we add, we search for the closest situation (on the basis of the sensor data). We then change the annotation of that situation to the newly obtained personal annotation. We also seach all 'similar' situations, i.e. that belong to the same prototypical situation, and change their annotations to that of the newly obtained one (unless they have already been annotated by a matching personal annotation). Since we have only one set of sensor data for each situation we can find the exact situation the newly obtained personal annotations corresponds to. In a real system, we would have to employ a closeness measure on the basis of the sensor data.

7.1 Results

Figure 5 shows how the recognition score evolves with an increasing number of prototypical situations in the training set. The top line indicates the recognition score for the personal interruptibility and the bottom line that of the social interruptibility. The recognition score evolves from the score obtained from the baseline score of the system trained on the other users on the left to the maximal score that is obtained by training the system only on one user.

We can observe clearly that there is a sharp increase in recognition score within the first 20 situations. After that the recognition score increases only slightly (about 3%). Thus, the user would have to annotate only 20 prototypical situations (out of the 94 possible) to achieve a recognition score within 3% of the maximum recognition score.

For an active experience sampling, we only need to annotate as many situations as there are groups of situations. In Figure 5 we have 24 groups for the personal interruptibility and 32 for the social interruptibility. Since personal and social interruptibility are added to the training set in an alternating manner, we require about 40 personal annotations until all groups of the personal interruptibility have received at least one annotation and about 50 for the groups of the social interruptibility (the exact numbers vary slightly due to the randomization of the algorithm). As we can see from Figure 5 it is not even necessary to annotate all prototypical situations. Increasing the number of personal annotations from 20 to 40 increases the recognition score by only about 1-2%.

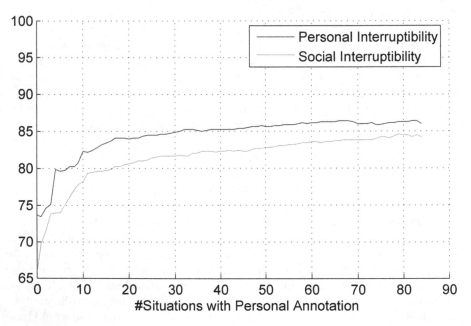

Fig. 5. Recognition Score using Prototypical Situations. Situations were grouped using a threshold $\theta = 0.8$. We thus obtained 24 groups of situations for the personal interruptibility and 32 for the social interruptibility. The experiment was repeated 50 times.

8   Discussion

The last three sections presented three variants of how an interruptibility estimation system can adapt to its user. The first approach identifies prototypical users and pre-trains the system using the settings from one of those prototypical users. The second approach uses random experience sampling to adapt itself gradually to the user. The last approach generalizes from prototypical situations and re-uses personal annotations by the user for all situations that are similar to a prototypical situation.

For the approach using prototypical users the system requires a predefined set of prototypes with corresponding interruptibility estimation settings. The user has to select the prototypical user whose settings are closest to his own preferences. The approach is advantageous, because it works without requiring the user to annotate a single situation himself. On the other hand, it is limited in the number of users for which it works.

Our experiments on prototypical users show that it is well possible to identify users that have similar settings for the social interruptibility. When using 10 prototypical users we can increase the recognition score by 9.6% to 75.4% from a system trained on other users. This is only 2.9% below the maximum score that can be obtained when training the system on a single user only. For the personal interruptibility, this is however not the case: compared to a system trained on other users we get only an increase of 2.4% in recognition score, which is 11.5% below the maximal recognition score. It is important to note here that we have a comparatively small data set available to find prototypical users (only 24 users), making it difficult to draw a firm conclusion from the results.

Using random experience sampling we regularly sample the user's interruptibility and incorporate such new personal annotations into the training set. This is very general, since we do not make any assumptions about the situations the user is likely to encounter. However, such a strategy requires many training examples.

We could show experimentally that the recognition score increases approximately linearly with an increasing number of personal annotations from the base score (system trained on the other users) to the maximum score (system trained on a single user only). To achieve a performance that is comparable to the prototypical users approach, we require 25 personal annotations for the personal interruptibility and 60 for the social interruptibility.

For the approach using prototypical situations, we identify situations that have similar interruptibility ratings and generalize from such a prototypical situation to a whole group of situations. The user would annotate a number of prototypical situations before using the system, similiar to personalizing a speech recognition system. While this approach adapts very quickly to the user, it does make assumptions about the situations he will encounter and is thus limited in its generality. Having groups of situations allows for active experience sampling, which combines the generality of the random experience sampling with the fast adaption of the prototypical situations approach.

Our experiments show that the approach indeed adapts very quickly to the user. To obtain a performance comparable to the prototypical users approach, it requires only 6 and 4 personal annotations for social and personal interruptibility, respectively. With 20 personal annotations we already obtain a recognition score that is only about 3% lower than the maximal score (recognition on a single user).

Using groups of prototypical situations allows to perform an active experience sampling, in which the user is only asked to annotate situations that are unknown to the system. We identified groups separately for the social and personal interruptibility and found 32 different groups for the social interruptibility and 24 for the personal interruptibility. For an active experience sampling, exactly one personal annotation is needed per group. Figure 5 shows that with 24 annotations we can achieve a recognition score that is only about 2% lower than the maximum recognition score.

The approaches using prototypical users or situations are both limited in their generality: if a particular user simply does not match the profiles of the prototypical users or does not encounter the situations that have been defined as prototypical, the system will not be able to adapt to that particular user. There are two possible solutions to this issue: firstly, to make the number of predefined users or situations sufficiently large. Secondly, to resort to random experience sampling as that does not make any assumption about the user or the situations he encounters.

The three approaches presented are of course not mutually exclusive, but should rather be combined for maximum efficiency. A system could be pre-initialized using prototypical users or with some personal annotations of prototypical situations and could then learn during run-time by acquiring additional personal annotations. To learn about the situations the user encounters a combination of active and random experience sampling, possibly in the form of quality feedback, seems to be suited best. This combines the fast learning of active experience sampling with the generality of random experience sampling.

9   Conclusion

The user's current interruptibility and attention are important ingredients for seamless user interaction with mobile, context-aware devices. We have shown in previous work that it is possible to estimate the interruptibility from body-worn sensors and that users differ considerably in their interruptibility ratings. In this paper we investigated how consistent users are in their interruptibility ratings, and discussed and evaluated three possibilities to adapt an interruptibility estimation system to a particular user.

For our experiments, we have collected a data set of annotations from 24 users on 94 different situations. We showed that users are only about 65% correct in their interruptibility ratings among each other. This low score shows that it is indeed necessary to adapt an interruptibility estimation system to its particular user.

We investigated and evaluated three possibilities to adapt an interruptibility estimation system to a particular user. Firstly by finding prototypical users, secondly using random experience sampling, and thirdly by generalizing from prototypical situations.

The approach using prototypical users provides a jump start for the social interruptibility, which is close to the maximum score that can be obtained. For the personal interruptibility it is harder to generalize from one user to another. The recognition score using 10 prototypical users is 11.5% below the maximal achievable score.

Performing a random experience sampling increases the recognition score nearly linearly with an increasing number of situations with personal annotations. While it is possible to reach the maximal recognition score, the approach is relatively slow and requires many user interactions. To achieve a performance that is comparable to that of the prototypical users approach, it requires 25 and 60 situations for personal and social interruptibility, respectively.

The approach using prototypical situations requires only very few personal annotations to achieve a high recognition score. With only 4 and 6 personal annotations for personal and social interruptibility respectively it obtains a recognition score comparable to the prototypical users approach. With 20 personal annotations it obtains a recognition score that is only about 3% lower than the maximum score. Using the knowledge of prototypical situations also allows for active experience sampling which interactively adapts to the user while minimizing the number of user interactions at the same time.

Many issues remain to be addressed: the approaches should be tested with sensor data from multiple users, ideally multiple users in a real-world setting. The approaches are of course not mutually exclusive. A combination of approaches might allow for a further increase in recognition score and adaptation speed.

Acknowledgements. This work has been supported by the European Commission funded project MOBVIS under grant number FP6-511051.

References

1. M. Cutrell, M Czerwinski, and E. Horvitz. Notification, disruption, and memory: Effects of messaging interruptions on memory and performance. In *Proc. of Interact*, pages 263–269, 2001.
2. M. Czerwinski, E. Horvitz, and S. Whilhite. A diary study of task switching and interruptions. In *Proc. CHI*, pages 175–182, Vienna, Austria, 2004.
3. J. Fogarty, S. E. Hudson, and J. Lai. Examining the robustness of sensor-based statistical models of human interruptability. In *Proc. ACM CHI*, pages 207–214, 2004.
4. J. Fogarty, A.J. Ko, H.H. Aung, E. Golden, K.P. Tang, and S.E. Hudson. Examining task engagement in sensor-based statistical models of human interruptibility. In *Proc. CHI*, 2005.
5. J. Fogarty, J. Lai, and J. Christensen. Presence versus availability: The design and evaluation of a context-aware communication client. *Intern. Journal of Human-Computer Studies (IJHCS)*, 61(3):299–317, September 2004.
6. Joyce Ho and Stephen S. Intille. Using context-aware computing to reduce the perceived burden of interruptions from mobile devices. In *CHI '05: Proceedings of the SIGCHI conference on Human factors in computing systems*, pages 909–918, New York, NY, USA, 2005. ACM Press.
7. Eric Horvitz, J. Apacible, M. Subramani, R. Sarin, P. Koch, J.J. Cadi, A. Narin, and Y. Rui. Experiences with the design, fielding, and evaluation of a real-time communications agent. Technical Report MSR-TR-2003-98, Microsoft Research, 2003.
8. Eric Horvitz and Matthew Barry. Display of information for time–critical decision making. In *Proc. 11th Conf. on Uncertainty in Artificial Intelligence*, pages 296–305. Morgan Kaufmann, 1995.
9. Eric Horvitz, Andy Jacobs, and David Hovel. Attention-sensitive alerting. In *Proc. of the 5th Annual Conference on Uncertainty in Artificial Intelligence*, pages 305–313, San Francisco, CA, 1999. Morgan Kaufmann Publishers.
10. Eric Horvitz, C.M. Kadie, T. Paek, and David Hovel. Models of attention in computing and communication: From principles to applications. *Communications of the ACM*, 46(3):52–59, March 2003.

11. J.M. Hudson, J. Christensen, W.A. Kellogg, and T. Erickson. 'I'd Be Overwhelmed, But It's Just One More Thing to Do': Availability and Interruption in Research Management. In *Proc. ACM CHI*, pages 97–104. ACM Press, 2002.

12. S. Hudson, J. Fogarty, C. Atkeson, D. Avrahami, J. Forlizzi, S. Kiesler, J. Lee, and J. Yang. Predicting human interruptibility with sensors: a wizard of oz feasibility study. In *Proc. ACM CHI*, pages 257–264. ACM Press, 2003.

13. N. Kern, S. Antifakos, B. Schiele, and A. Schwaninger. A model of human interruptability: Experimental evaluation and automatic estimation from wearable sensors. In *Proc. ISWC*, pages 158–165, Washington DC, USA, Nov 2004.

14. N. Kern and B. Schiele. Context–aware notfication for wearable computing. In *Proc. ISWC*, pages 223–230, White Plains, NY, USA, October 2003.

15. R. W. Obermayer and W. A. Nugent. Human–Computer Interaction (HCI) for alert warning and attention allocation systems for the multi–modal watchstation (MMWS). In *Proceedings of SPIE*, volume 4126, 2000.

16. Nitin Sawhney and Chris Schmandt. Nomadic radio: speech and audio interaction for contextual messaging in nomadic environments. *ACM Transactions on Computer-Human Interaction*, 7(3):353–383, 2000.

Unsupervised Discovery of Structure in Activity Data Using Multiple Eigenspaces

Tâm Huỳnh and Bernt Schiele

Computer Science Department,
TU Darmstadt, Germany
{tam, schiele}@mis.tu-darmstadt.de

Abstract. In this paper we propose a novel scheme for unsupervised detection of structure in activity data. Our method is based upon an algorithm that represents data in terms of multiple low-dimensional eigenspaces. We describe the algorithm and propose an extension that allows to handle multiple time scales. The validity of the approach is demonstrated on several data sets and using two types of acceleration features. Finally, we report on experiments that indicate that our approach can yield recognition rates comparable to other, supervised approaches.

1   Introduction

Activity recognition has gained a lot of interest in recent years due to its potential and usefulness for context-aware applications. Typically, the recognition of context such as activities is based on supervised learning techniques. These approaches therefore rely on labeled training data which has to be representative for the respective application scenario. Obtaining labeled data of sufficient quality however is often difficult and tedious. Therefore it is clearly desirable to reduce the amount of supervision to a minimum for various reasons. First, in order to scale to large amounts of data and large amounts of activity classes labeling simply becomes impractical and error-prone. Second, in order to adapt to different users and usage scenarios a context aware system should be able to support the adaption through unsupervised learning techniques. Last but not least, the burden of feedback and data annotation has to be kept to a minimum for different users and usage scenarios.

This paper proposes a novel scheme to discover structure in sensor data in order to model and recognize human activities using acceleration data. The proposed approach is neither limited to activity learning and recognition, nor to a particular type of sensor. Rather it can be applied more generally to many types of sensors and context information.

Interestingly, many different types of sensors have been proposed and used for activity recognition. The types of sensors range from simple sensors such as RFID tag readers [1], over relatively simple sensors such as tiny, wearable sensors [2], ball switches [3], and accelerometers [4] to more complex sensing methods such as audio processing[5] and computer vision [6, 7, 8]. Also the simultaneous use of

M. Hazas, J. Krumm, and T. Strang (Eds.): LoCA 2006, LNCS 3987, pp. 151–167, 2006.

several modalities has been proposed, e.g. [9, 4]. Besides sensing technology the type of algorithms also varies greatly. However, these approaches have in common that they require a significant amount of supervision and labeled training data. Consequently, a small number of approaches requiring far less supervision have been proposed. Two approaches are particularly relevant for this paper. The first is the work by Clarkson and Pentland [10, 11] which learn locations and scenes from audio and vision data in an unsupervised fashion. Their focus, however, is not activity recognition but the modeling of reoccurring locations and scenes such as supermarkets. The second approach introduced by Patterson et al. [12] uses an unsupervised learning scheme based on graphical models. Their focus however is on transportation modes (such as bus, car, walking) and the incorporation of commensense knowledge into the unsupervised learning scheme.

The main contributions of this paper are the following. First, an unsupervised learning scheme for the discovery of activities in sensor data is proposed using multiple eigenspaces. Second, the multiple eigenspace algorithm is extended e.g. to handle multiple time scales of sensor data. Third, an experimental comparison of two different feature representations for the discovery of activities at different time scales are evaluated. Fourth, the algorithm is evaluated on real-world data using body-worn sensors achieving comparable performance to fully supervised learning approaches.

2   Multiple Eigenspaces

Principal component analysis (PCA) is a standard technique in pattern recognition and machine learning to reduce the dimensionality of feature spaces. PCA finds the principal components (or eigenvectors) of a data distribution spanning a linear subspace of the feature space (often called eigenspace). PCA is an unsupervised technique in the sense that it finds the optimal linear subspace to represent the data without any annotation or user intervention. In many applications however, it is more appropriate to represent the inherent structure of a data-set not with a single but multiple eigenspaces [13]. This paper proposes and shows that the concept of multiple eigenspaces can be used to detect and represent structure such as individual activities in accelerometer data. This section first introduces the general concept of multiple eigenspaces (sec 2.1) and then describes an algorithm to extract multiple eigenspaces (sec 2.2–2.5). We then propose an extension to the algorithm that can handle multiple timescales (sec 2.6). Section 3 then gives an example illustrating the different stages of the algorithm.

2.1   Problem Description

Principle component analysis (PCA) allows to approximate a vector $\mathbf{x}_i$ of a set of data vectors $\mathcal{G} = \{\mathbf{x}_1, \mathbf{x}_2, ..., \mathbf{x}_m | \mathbf{x}_i \in \mathbb{R}^n\}$:

$$\hat{\mathbf{x}}_i = \mathbf{e}_0 + \sum_{k=1}^{p} y_k \mathbf{e}_k, \tag{1}$$

i.e., by a vector $\mathbf{e}_0 \in \mathbb{R}^n$ plus a linear combination of p (eigen-)vectors $\mathbf{e}_1, \ldots, \mathbf{e}_p$ ($p < n, \mathbf{e}_k \in \mathbb{R}^n$). Principal component analysis is optimal in the sense that the reconstruction error $\epsilon^2 = \sum_{i=1}^{m} \|\mathbf{x}_i - \hat{\mathbf{x}}_i\|$ is minimal. This is achieved by defining $\mathbf{e}_0$ as the mean of all $\mathbf{x}_i \in \mathcal{G}$ and $\mathbf{e}_1, \ldots, \mathbf{e}_p$ as the eigenvectors corresponding to the p largest eigenvalues of the covariance matrix of the vectors in $\mathcal{G}$. We call the linear subspace spanned by $\mathbf{e}_0, \mathbf{e}_1, \ldots, \mathbf{e}_p$ the *eigenspace* $\mathcal{E}(\mathcal{G})$ of $\mathcal{G}$ of dimension p. When $p = 0$ the eigenspace of $\mathcal{G}$ only consists of the mean.

If the vectors in $\mathcal{G}$ are sufficiently correlated p can be chosen to be much smaller than the dimension of the original vector space, while still maintaining a low reconstruction error ϵ^2. In such cases, $\mathcal{E}(\mathcal{G})$, together with the coefficients $y_1, \ldots, y_p$ (see eq. 1) of each $\mathbf{x}_i \in \mathcal{G}$, can serve as a low-dimensional representation of $\mathcal{G}$.

In many cases, however, a single linear eigenspace will be too general to capture the low-dimensional structure of the data. Consequently, the dimension of $\mathcal{E}(\mathcal{G})$ must be high in order to obtain acceptable reconstruction errors. Apart from the computational issues involved, this means that the eigenspace cannot serve as a good representation of the inherent structure of the data. In such cases, it would be more suitable to divide $\mathcal{G}$ into sufficiently correlated subsets $\mathcal{G}_j \subset \mathcal{G}$ and represent those subsets with eigenspaces $\mathcal{E}_j(\mathcal{G}_j)$. Each of those eigenspaces serves as a compact and low-dimensional model of the corresponding part of the data.

The problem to be solved is thus, given a set of data vectors $\mathcal{G}$, to find sets $\mathcal{G}_j \subset \mathcal{G}$, eigenspaces $\mathcal{E}_j(\mathcal{G}_j)$ and dimensions p_j, so that each $\mathbf{x}_i \in \mathcal{G}_j$ can be approximated to a predefined degree of accuracy by its projection

$$\hat{\mathbf{x}}_i = \mathbf{e}_{0j} + \sum_{k=1}^{p_j} y_{kj} \mathbf{e}_{kj}. \tag{2}$$

2.2 Overview of the Multiple Eigenspace Algorithm

Leonardis et al. [13] proposed an iterative procedure to solve the above problem by simultaneously finding subsets $\mathcal{G}_j \subset \mathcal{G}$, eigenspaces $\mathcal{E}_j(\mathcal{G}_j)$ and dimensions p_j. As a result the data in the input set $\mathcal{G}$ is divided into significantly correlated subsets of similar structure each represented by a separate eigenspace. As we will show in the experiments these multiple eigenspaces correspond to individual activities in accelerometer data and can be used for activity recognition.

The algorithm consists of three phases: initialization, eigenspace growing and eigenspace selection. During *initialization*, small subsets of data vectors are chosen from the input set $\mathcal{G}$, and their respective eigenspaces are calculated and initialized with dimension zero. During *eigenspace growing*, the initial sets are successively enlarged by adding data vectors and accepting or rejecting them based on reconstruction error. At the same time, the corresponding eigenspaces are recomputed and their dimension is adapted. As the growing process produces overlapping and thus redundant sets and eigenspaces, the final *eigenspace selection* phase applies an optimization procedure that finds a subset of eigenspaces that best represent the data with minimal redundancy. Importantly, the number of eigenspaces that are finally selected is determined automatically during eigenspace selection and does not have to be specified in advance. The following describes the three phases of the algorithm in more detail.

2.3   Initialization of the Multiple Eigenspace Algorithm

The input to the algorithm is a set $\mathcal{G} = \{\mathbf{x}_1, \mathbf{x}_2, ..., \mathbf{x}_m | \mathbf{x}_i \in \mathbb{R}^n\}$ containing data vectors which we will refer to as *segments* in the following. During initialization, a large number of small and redundant subsets $\mathcal{G}_j^0 \subset \mathcal{G}$ is generated, uniformly distributed across $\mathcal{G}$. In the extreme case, each segment in $\mathcal{G}$ can serve as an initial subset $\mathcal{G}_j^0$ (as in our examples). For each $\mathcal{G}_j^0$, the corresponding eigenspace $\mathcal{E}_j^0(\mathcal{G}_j^0)$ is calculated, and its dimension p_j^0 is set to zero, i.e., the eigenspace equals the mean of the segments contained in $\mathcal{G}_j^0$.

2.4   Eigenspace Growing

After the initial sets $\mathcal{G}_j^0$ have been constructed, they are iteratively enlarged and their corresponding eigenspaces are updated. In the following, $\mathcal{G}_j^t$ and $\mathcal{E}_j^t$ denote the set $\mathcal{G}_j$ and its eigenspace $\mathcal{E}_j(\mathcal{G}_j)$, respectively, at step t of the iteration. p_j^t denotes the dimension of $\mathcal{E}_j^t$ at step t.

The growing process is driven by two error measures, δ_i and ρ_j: δ_i is related to single segments and denotes the reconstruction error $||\mathbf{x}_i - \hat{\mathbf{x}}_i||$ of a segment $\mathbf{x}_i$ when projected onto an eigenspace. The second error measure, ρ_j, is related to eigenspaces and defined as the sum of the reconstruction errors of all segments contained in an eigenspace j. Both δ_i and ρ_j are associated with thresholds that cause the growing process to terminate once the errors get too large.

In step t of the iteration, the following procedure is applied to each set $\mathcal{G}_j^t$: Each segment not contained in $\mathcal{G}_j^t$ is projected onto $\mathcal{E}_j^t$. If a segment's reconstruction error δ_i is below a threshold, the segment is temporarily accepted into the set $\mathcal{G}_j^{t+1}$. If none of the segments are accepted, the growing for this set is terminated. Otherwise, the new eigenspace $\mathcal{E}_j^{t+1}$ and its reconstruction error ρ_j are calculated. If the error ρ_j is below a threshold, the new eigenspace is accepted. Else, the dimension p_j of $\mathcal{E}_j^{t+1}$ is increased by one, and ρ_j is recomputed. If the increase in dimension lowers the error ρ_j below the threshold, the new eigenspace is accepted. Otherwise, both $\mathcal{G}_j^{(t+1)}$ and $\mathcal{E}_j^{(t+1)}$ are reverted to their previous state, and growing is terminated.

2.5   Eigenspace Selection

The result of eigenspace growing is a set of eigenspaces $\mathcal{E}_j$ each representing a subset of the input data. However, those sets are redundant in the sense that the represented data subsets overlap in many cases. With respect to robustness of the final outcome this redundancy is an important property of the algorithm.

Thus, in this final step, a subset of the eigenspaces is selected that best represents the data with minimal overlap between the eigenspaces. This is achieved by solving an optimization problem based on the principle of minimum description length (MDL). The goal can be formulated as minimizing the overall description length $L(\mathcal{G})$ of the input $\mathcal{G}$ in terms of eigenspaces:

$$L(\mathcal{G}) = L(\mathcal{M}) + L(\mathcal{G}|\mathcal{M}). \tag{3}$$

Here, $L(\mathcal{M})$ denotes the encoding cost of the model, which in our case is the length of encoding of all eigenspaces, plus the length of encoding of the coefficients y_{kj} for all segments $\mathbf{x}_i \in \mathcal{G}$. $L(\mathcal{G}|\mathcal{M})$ are the costs of specifying the data given the model, which in our case equal the reconstruction errors resulting from the reduced dimension of the eigenspaces.

As noted by Leonardis et al. [13], minimizing the description length is equivalent to maximizing the savings $S(\mathcal{E}_j(\mathcal{G}_j))$ to encode the segments $\mathbf{x}_i \in \mathcal{G}_j$ in terms of the eigenspace $\mathcal{E}_j$ instead of encoding them individually. These savings can be expressed as

$$S(\mathcal{E}_j(\mathcal{G}_j)) = \underbrace{K_0|\mathcal{G}_j|}_{\text{individual encoding}} - \underbrace{(K_1 p_j + K_2 |\mathcal{G}_j| p_j + K_3 |\mathcal{G}_j| \rho_j)}_{\text{encoding with eigenspace}}. \tag{4}$$

In this equation, the constant K_0 is related to the cost of encoding a segment in $\mathcal{G}$ without an eigenspace, K_1 is related to the cost of describing an eigenvector, K_2 is related to the average cost of specifying a coefficient, and K_3 is related to the average cost of specifying the error. Using the savings $S(\mathcal{E}_j(\mathcal{G}_j))$, the optimization problem can be solved by maximizing an objective function of the form

$$F(\mathbf{h}) = \mathbf{h}^T \mathbf{C} \mathbf{h} = \mathbf{h}^T \begin{bmatrix} c_{11} & \cdots & c_{1r} \\ \vdots & \vdots & \vdots \\ c_{r1} & \cdots & c_{rr} \end{bmatrix} \mathbf{h}. \tag{5}$$

The vector $\mathbf{h} = [h_1, h_2, \ldots, h_r]^T$ represents a possible set of eigenspaces, h_j being 1 if the eigenspace j is included in the set, and 0 if not. The diagonal entries of the matrix $\mathbf{C}$ are defined as the savings obtained by the j-th eigenspace, i.e. $c_{jj} = S(\mathcal{E}_j(\mathcal{G}_j))$. The definition of the off-diagonal entries c_{jk} takes into account that two sets $\mathcal{G}_j$ and $\mathcal{G}_k$ might overlap:

$$c_{jk} = |\mathcal{G}_j \cap \mathcal{G}_k|(-K_0 + K_3 \rho_{jk})/2, \tag{6}$$

where $|\mathcal{G}_j \cap \mathcal{G}_k|$ denotes the number of segments shared by $\mathcal{G}_j$ and $\mathcal{G}_k$, and ρ_{jk} is the maximal error of the segments in $\mathcal{G}_j \cap \mathcal{G}_k$.

In Section 3 you can find a detailed example of the different phases of the multiple eigenspace algorithm. Next, we propose an extension that allows to analyze data on different timescales.

2.6 Multiple Timescales

The multiple eigenspace algorithm operates on a single scale, i.e., all input segments are of the same length. While this property may be acceptable in some domains, for activities it is not obvious which scale or length a data segment should have. Furthermore, there is probably no single 'best' segment size, as activities happen on different timescales. For these reasons, we extended the algorithm to include multiple scales and allow for different segment size.

The extended version of the algorithm accepts as input a signal and a list of n segment sizes. Initialization (sec 2.3) and eigenspace growing (sec 2.4) are then performed n times. Each time, the signal is divided into signals of a different size. This results in n sets of eigenspaces representing parts of the input at different scales. All of them compete to be included in the final description during a modifed version of the eigenspace selection step. We modified the eigenspace selection so that segments and reconstruction errors on different scales can be compared to each other. In the following we describe the modified selection step in more detail.

Modified Eigenspace Selection. In the selection step of the original approach, cost and savings were defined in terms of entire segments. Since in the modified algorithm, segments can be of different size, we need to redefine the savings in order to make them comparable across different segment sizes. We achieve this by defining the savings in terms of individual samples instead of segments. For a set $\mathcal{G}_j$ containing segments made up of l_i samples each, the savings $S(\mathcal{E}_j(\mathcal{G}_j))$ achieved by encoding the segments in terms of the eigenspace $\mathcal{E}_j$ can be expressed as

$$S(\mathcal{E}_j(\mathcal{G}_j)) = K_0|\mathcal{G}_j| - (K_1 p_j + K_2|\mathcal{G}_j|p_j + K_3|\mathcal{G}_j|\rho_j) \qquad (7)$$

$$= l_i|\mathcal{G}_j| - l_i p_j - K_2|\mathcal{G}_j|p_j - K_3|\mathcal{G}_j|\rho_j \qquad (8)$$

We thus replaced the constants K_0 (cost of describing a segment without an eigenspace) and K_1 (cost of encoding an eigenvector) by the variable segment length l_i. In the matrix $\mathbf{C}$ of the optimization function (see eq. 5) the diagonal terms now represent the adapted savings, $c_{jj} = S(\mathcal{E}_j(\mathcal{G}_j))$, and the off-diagonal entries c_{jk} are redefined as

$$c_{jk} = |\mathcal{G}_j \cap \mathcal{G}_k|(-1 + K_3\rho_{jk})/2 \qquad (9)$$

where $|\mathcal{G}_j \cap \mathcal{G}_k|$ describes the number samples contained in the intersection of the sets $\mathcal{G}_j$ and $\mathcal{G}_k$.

3   Example

Figures 1 and 2 illustrate the different phases of the multiple eigenspace algorithm for a single timescale. The top of Figure 1 shows an acceleration signal, recorded by an accelerometer attached to the wrist of a user while juggling 3, 4 and 5 balls, in that order. The signal was divided into segments of four seconds and transformed to the frequency domain before applying the algorithm.

Figure 2 illustrates the growing process: Initially, each set is made up of one segment. As the growing proceeds, one can observe three groups of sets forming along the three parts of the signal. Finally, during eigenspace selection (see sec. 2.5), one set of each of those groups gets selected.

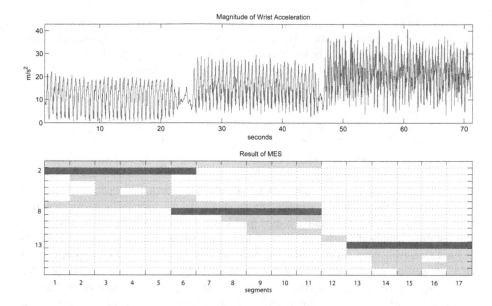

Fig. 1. Application of the multiple eigenspace algorithm to an acceleration signal. Top: Magnitude of wrist acceleration. Bottom: The result of eigenspace growing. The sets $\mathcal{G}_i$ are marked in gray, and those that were finally selected ($\mathcal{G}_2, \mathcal{G}_8$ and $\mathcal{G}_{13}$) are highlighted.

Fig. 2. Eigenspace growing and selection corresponding to the data in Figure 1. From left to right, different stages of the growing process are shown. The rightmost plot shows the result of the selection step.

The bottom plot of Figure 1 shows the result of the growing phase in gray, i.e. the sets $\mathcal{G}_j$. The horizontal axis represents the segments into which the signal was divided, and in each row, the segments belonging to one set $\mathcal{G}_j$ are marked (e.g., $\mathcal{G}_8$ consists of segments 6 to 11). Three sets were chosen during the final selection procedure, they are highlighted in the figure. Note that there are only a few sets of segments across the borders of the three juggling patterns, and the final sets match the three patterns closely.

Note that even though there are sets of segments across the borders of the three juggling patterns the final sets match the three patterns closely.

4   Initial Experiments

After describing the multiple eigenspace algorithm and giving an example in the previous sections, we now demonstrate the feasibility of our approach for analyzing sequences of activity data. First we briefly introduce the sensor platform and the data sets used for our experiments. Then, we discuss two possible methods of applying the algorithm: using raw acceleration data on multiple timescales and using FFT features on a single timescale. Finally we compare the two feature representations in terms of their classification performance.

4.1 Sensor Platform

Figure 3(a) shows the sensor platform used for the experiments. The main components are four inertial sensors connected to an IBM X40 laptop via a USB hub. The laptop, together with batteries and adapters, is situated in a small backpack carried by the user, and the inertial sensors are worn by the user, e.g. on wrist, hip, ankle or other parts of the body. The recording software runs on the laptop can be remote-controlled from a PDA. As inertial sensors, we initially used the model MT9-B by Xsens and later the model MTx, which features a larger measurement range and better on-board processing capabilities. Besides 3-D acceleration, the sensors output 3-D rate of turn and 3-D magnetic field data, as well as an absolute orientation estimate. In this work we only consider the acceleration signal, however. For annotation purposes, we also record audio data using a stereo microphone clipped to the shoulder strap of the backpack. Figure 3(b) shows the entire sensor platform worn by a user.

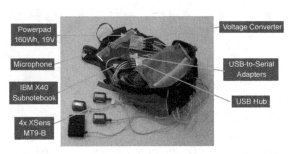

(a) The sensor platform used for the experiments.   (b) User with sensors on hip, thigh, wrist and ankle.

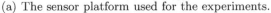

Fig. 3. Sensor Platform

4.2 Data Set

The sensor platform described above was used to record data of various activities, ranging in length from several seconds to about thirty minutes. During recordings, the inertial sensors were attached to wrist, hip, thigh and ankle of the experimenter. For the initial experiments, walking modes of different speeds were recorded separately. Subsequent recordings involve a mix of several activities, including different walking modes, climbing stairs and juggling different numbers of balls. The data set is available on the website of our group (www.mis.informatik.tu-darmstadt.de).

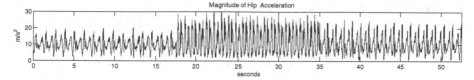

Fig. 4. Constructed dataset, consisting of three different walking modes concatenated (left third: walking, middle third: jogging, right third: walking fast). The signal corresponds to the magnitude of acceleration measured at the hip, sampled at 200 Hz.

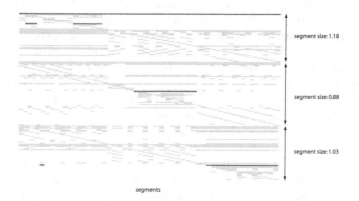

Fig. 5. Result of applying the adapted algorithm to the signal shown in Figure 4. Three different segment sizes between 0.88 and 1.18 seconds were used.

4.3   Experiments with Multiple Timescales

Figure 5 shows the result of applying the extended multiple eigenspace algorithm to the signal shown in Figure 4, using three different segment sizes that correspond to the periodicity of the three recorded activities. The signal consists of the acceleration magnitude measured at the hip, covering three different modes of walking (walking at normal pace, jogging and walking fast) and sampled at 200 Hz for about one minute. The vertical axis of Figure 5 covers the eigenspaces of all three segment sizes, and the horizontal axis corresponds to the length of the signal. The four eigenspaces chosen by the selection step of the algorithm are highlighted. The topmost covers the entire signal, while the remaining three each represent segments that correspond to the three walking modes, respectively. Each of those three eigenspaces is based on a different segment length.

We found that in order to obtain eigenspaces that represent activities well, the underlying segment lengths need to match the periodicity of the data closely. Thus, in order to get satisfying results, one has to carefully choose segment lengths e.g. based on the autocorrelation of the signal. This makes the approach rather inflexible. Furthermore, since we're interested in finding structure in an unsupervised fashion, we cannot assume that we know about the periodicity or other properties of the data in advance. To address these issues, we changed our features from raw signal data to frequency components, which we will discuss in the next section. Apart from that, we believe that the proposed extension of the multiple eigenspace algorithm to handle multiple time-scales is a general scheme that can be applied to any kind of data, and which allows simultaneous analysis of data at different timescales.

4.4   Experiments in Frequency Space

We conducted a series of experiments using FFT coefficients computed over the acceleration signal as features, with the goal of obtaining a representation of the data that does not require a priori knowledge about properties such as the periodicity of the signal. For these experiments we applied the multiple eigenspace algorithm on single timescales. We found that FFT features computed over a single scale can be used effectively to separate different activities using multiple eigenspaces. However, the choice of the segment length involves a tradeoff between short segments that capture basic activities but might yield unstable FFT results, and longer segments which yield more stable results but might be too long to allow discrimination between basic activities.

During the experiments, we found that segment sizes of around 4 seconds lead to good results when using FFT features. Figure 6 shows the result of applying the multiple eigenspace algorithm to the FFT coefficients computed over the signal shown in Figure 4. Figure 6(a) shows the spectrogram, the vertical axis corresponding to the first 35 FFT coefficients, the horizontal axis to the segments of the signal. For all three walking patterns, most of the energy is contained in the first three coefficients, however each activity has a distinct and consistent distribution of peaks in the rest of the spectrum. This structure is captured well by the eigenspaces, as can be seen from Figure 6(b). Three eigenspaces are selected, each of which corresponds to one walking pattern. Figure 6(c) shows one of the feature segments for the activity "walking at normal pace" and its reconstruction, which differs only slightly from the original.

These initial experiments led us to believe that using multiple eigenspaces on features in frequency space is a promising approach to detecting structure

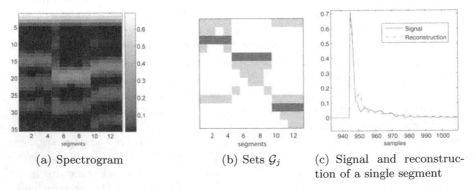

| (a) Spectrogram | (b) Sets $\mathcal{G}_j$ | (c) Signal and reconstruction of a single segment |

Fig. 6. Application of the multiple eigenspace algorithm to data of three different walking modes (see fig. 4). As features, FFT coefficients computed over windows of four seconds were used.

in more diverse sets of activities. Before discussing such experiments in Section 5, we will first report on some initial classification results in the next section.

4.5   Classification

The eigenspaces obtained from the algorithm can be used as classifiers for activities, based on the reconstruction error of unknown data segments. To classify a segment, it is projected onto each eigenspace and then assigned to the one that yields the lowest reconstruction error. When using a sliding window, we classify individual samples using segments that end at the sample. In the following we compare the classification performance of models based on signal- and FFT-features.

In Figure 7, two runs of the multiple eigenspace algorithm on the walking patterns, with subsequent classification, are compared side by side. Figure 7(a) shows the result when using the adapted version with multiple timescales on the plain acceleration signal. The bottom plot shows the reconstruction error of the signal for all five models (eigenspaces) that were selected. For each model, the reconstruction error was computed over a sliding window the size of the segment the model is based on, and shifted over the signal in steps of single samples. The error is smallest when the window is aligned to the segment positions at construction time of the models, and largest when shifted by 50%. This results in an oscillating reconstruction error with a period of the segment size of the eigenspace. Figure 7(c) shows a close-up view of the reconstruction errors in Figure 7(a). To avoid that the oscillating errors are reflected in an unstable classification result, we performed a smoothing by classifying each sample by the model with the lowest error over a window of preceding samples. This leads to the classification results of Figure 7(a). Walking normal, jogging and walking fast are assigned to models 1, 4 and 5 respectively. One can observe that model 2, which represents large parts of the signal as a result of the algorithm, is outperformed in terms of reconstruction error by other, more specialized models throughout the length of the signal.

Even though the classification results using plain acceleration data are acceptable, the sensitvity of the reconstruction error to the position of the sliding window reveals another drawback of using the raw signal as feature. In contrast, Figure 7(b) shows that in the frequency domain, similar (sample-based) classification results can be obtained without having to smooth out the error curve. The bottom plot of Figure 7(b) shows that for models based on FFT features, the curves of the reconstruction errors are smooth and stable within each of the three parts of the signal. This implies that this approach is insensitive to shifts between the sliding window and the segment boundaries at the time of model construction. Moreover, for each part of the signal, the errors are in distinct order. Altogether, these properties result in a more robust classification. As a consequence, we only consider FFT features in the remaining experiments.

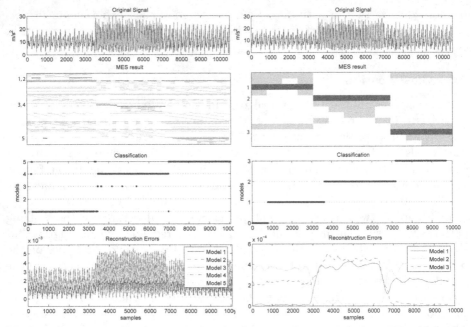

(a) Classification based on plain acceleration signal

(b) Classification based on FFT features

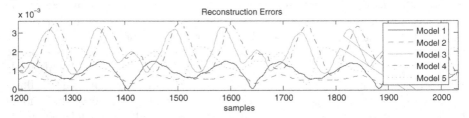

(c) Close-up view of the reconstruction errors shown at the bottom of Figure 7(a).

Fig. 7. Comparison of two different feature representations. Figures 7(a) and 7(b) show, from top to bottom: acceleration signal; result of applying the multiple eigenspace algorithm (the selected models are numbered); classification based on reconstruction error; reconstruction errors of the different models (i.e. eigenspaces).

5   Experiments with Mixed Activity Data

In this section, we show how our approach finds structure in real-world recordings that cover a number of different activities. The data was recorded using the sensor platform described in Section 4.1, and two inertial sensors were worn on wrist and hip of the user. We will first evaluate the recordings for hip and wrist individually, and then show how performance can be improved by combining the models of both recordings. The recordings lasted for about a quarter of an hour. As features we use absolute FFT coefficients, zero padded to twice the length,

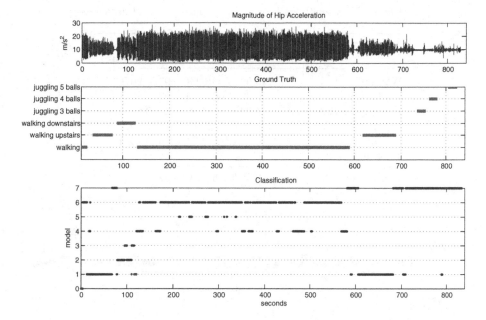

Fig. 8. Recording of approx. 14 min length, magnitude of **hip** acceleration. From top to bottom: raw signal, ground truth, and classification based on seven models constructed by the multiple eigenspace algorithm.

on a window over 4 seconds, as this combination had proven to yield the best results in the above experiments. The feature vectors were normalized to length 1 before being passed to the multiple eigenspace algorithm.

The recording shown in Figure 8 contains six different activities: walking, walking upstairs, walking downstairs, and juggling 3, 4 and 5 balls, respectively. The top of the figure shows the raw signal, which in this case is the magnitude of the acceleration occurring at the hip, sampled at 100 Hz. The middle plot shows manual annotations, i.e. ground truth for the data. Applying the multiple eigenspace algorithm to this data gave us 7 eigenspaces. With these eigenspaces we performed a classification of the training data based on reconstruction error, the same way as described in Section 4.5. The result is shown at the bottom of Figure 8. Samples that were not assigned to any model because of too large reconstruction errors appear in the row labeled with 0.

When comparing the ground truth to the model assignments, one can observe that the structure is visually similar. On closer inspection, one can see that the activity 'walking' is mainly represented by the models 4, 5 and 6. 'Walking upstairs' corresponds to model 1, and walking downstairs to models 2 and 3. The juggling sequences are all assigned to a single model (7), which is not surprising, since there is only very little (and thus nondiscriminative) hip movement during juggling.

In order to judge the quality of the model assignments, we manually chose for each activity the models that best represented them and computed recall

Table 1. Precision/Recall for different activities and data sets

Activity	Data Set		
	Hip	Wrist	Combined
Walking	0.99/0.98	0.93/0.97	0.99/0.97
Walking upstairs	0.80/1.00	0.49/1.00	0.84/1.00
Walking downstairs	1.00/0.93	0.95/0.45	0.98/0.93
Juggling 3 balls		0.76/1.00	0.82/1.00
Juggling 4 balls	0.32/1.00	0.04/1.00	0.84/1.00
Juggling 5 balls		0.60/1.00	0.60/1.00
Average over time	0.57/0.98	0.76/0.92	0.93/0.97

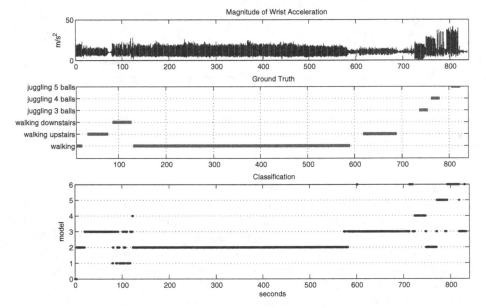

Fig. 9. Recording of approx. 14 min length, magnitude of **wrist** acceleration. From top to bottom: raw signal, ground truth, and classification based on six models constructed by the multiple eigenspace algorithm.

and precision values for each set of models representing an activity. The result for the data in Figure 8 is shown in the first column of Table 1. The models for walking (4, 5 and 6) reach precision and recall values close to 100% (0.99 and 0.98 respectively), followed by walking downstairs(1.0/0.93) and walking upstairs (0.80/1.0). As there is only one model (7) for the three juggling activities, the table contains only one entry for all three, which stands for the activity 'juggling'(0.32/1.0).

Figure 9 shows a second set of acceleration data, recorded at the wrist. The ground truth is the same as for Figure 8. Fewer models were selected this time, but they describe the data more precisely than the models for the hip recording

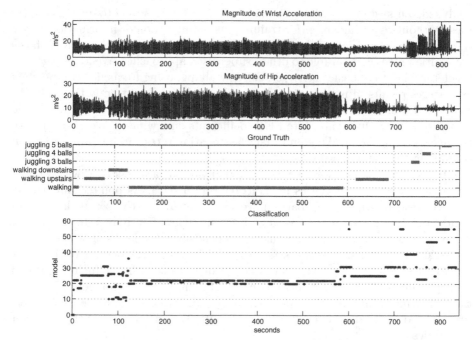

Fig. 10. Classification based on the combination of the models for hip (fig. 8) and wrist (fig. 9)

– there is a significant gain in the average precision over time (from 0.57 to 0.76) and only a slight reduction in recall (from 0.98 to 0.92). The increase in precision is due to the fact that the juggling patterns can be discriminated at the wrist.

In Figure 10, a combination of the models from the wrist and hip recordings is used for classification. Each model from the wrist recording was combined with each model from the hip recording to form a new model, which makes for 7*8 = 56 models (the 'not-assigned' cases were included as model 0). The result can be seen at the bottom of Figure 10. The overall precision and recall are now both over 90% (0.93/0.97). Compared to the hip recording this means a slight decrease in recall, but on the other hand, the three juggling patterns can now be separated. When comparing to the wrist recording, one can observe significant increases in the precision values for 'juggling 4 balls' (0.04 to 0.84) and 'walking upstairs'(0.49 to 0.84).

6   Conclusion

An important argument of this paper is that unsupervised techniques for activity recognition are highly desirable. To this end we haved proposed a novel approach to discover structure in sensor data of human activity in an unsupervised fashion. We demonstrated the feasibility of the approach by applying it to acceleration data recorded from body-worn sensors. For the set of activities analyzed, our system was able to build models that correspond to different activities, without requiring any prior training, user annotation or information about the number of activities involved. When used for classification, the system shows recognition rates comparable to other, supervised approaches. We found that for acceleration data of basic activities such as walking, using frequency components as features results in models that can represent the different activities well and that can be used for robust classification. For such activities we obtained the best results when using absolute FFT coefficients on a window over 4 seconds of the acceleration signal. We found that classification rates can be improved when combining the data of two sensors.

Clearly, the results presented in this paper are but a first step towards unsupervised discovery of activities in arbitrary sensor data. As pointed out before, however, the multiple eigenspace approach is general in the sense that it can handle different sensor modalities and different types of activities. In the future, we plan to incorporate data from more and possibly other kinds of sensors. Also, we plan to look at more diverse sets of activities over longer periods of time. For these cases, the extension of the multiple eigenspace algorithm to include data on multiple timescales will probably prove to be an important component. Based on the promising results in this paper we strongly believe that multiple eigenspaces can be used for unsupervised discovery of acitivities in a large variety of sensor modalities.

Acknowledgements. This work has been supported by the European Commission funded project MOBVIS under grant number FP6-511051. We would further like to thank Aleš Leonardis for stimulating discussions and for providing us with an implementation of the multiple eigenspace algorithm.

References

1. Philipose, M., Fishkin, K.P., Perkowitz, M., Patterson, D.J., Hahnel, D., Fox, D., Kautz, H.: Inferring Activities from Interactions with Objects. In: IEEE Pervasive Computing: Mobile and Ubiquitous Systems. Volume 3., IEEE (2004) 50–57
2. Bao, L., Intille, S.: Activity recognition from user-annotated acceleration data. In: Proc. Pervasive. Volume 3001 of Lecture Notes in Computer Science., Vienna, Austria, Springer (2004) 1–17
3. Laerhoven, K.V., Gellersen, H.W.: Spine versus porcupine: A study in distributed wearable activity recognition. In: ISWC. (2004) 142–149
4. Kern, N., Antifakos, S., Schiele, B., Schwaninger, A.: A model of human interruptability: Experimental evaluation and automatic estimation from wearable sensors. In: Proc. ISWC, Washington DC, USA (2004)
5. Choudhury, T., Pentland, A.: Sensing and modeling human networks using the sociometer. In: Proc. ISWC. (2003) 216–222
6. Davis, J., Bobick, A.: The representation and recognition of action using temporal templates. In: Proceedings Computer Vision and Pattern Recognition. (1997) 928–934
7. Jebara, T., Pentland, A.: Action reaction learning: Automatic visual analysis and synthesis of interactive behaviour. In: ICVS. (1999) 273–292

8. Shi, Y., Huang, Y., Minnen, D., Bobick, A.F., Essa, I.A.: Propagation networks for recognition of partially ordered sequential action. In: CVPR (2). (2004) 862–869

9. Lester, J., Choudhury, T., Kern, N., Borriello, G., Hannaford, B.: A hybrid discriminative/generative approach for modeling human activities. In: Proc. of the Nineteenth Intl. Joint Conf. on A.I.,, Edinburgh, Morgan-Kaufmann Publishers (2005)

10. Clarkson, B., Pentland, A.: Unsupervised clustering of ambulatory audio and video. In: Proc. ICASSP. (1999)

11. Clarkson, B.: Life Patterns: structure from wearable sensors. PhD thesis, Massachusetts Institute of Technology (2002)

12. Patterson, D.J., Liao, L., Fox, D., Kautz, H.: Inferring High-Level Behavior from Low-Level Sensors. In Dey, A., Schmidt, A., McCarthy, J.F., eds.: Proceedings of UBICOMP 2003: The Fifth International Conference on Ubiquitous Computing. Volume LNCS 2864., Springer-Verlag (2003) 73–89

13. Leonardis, A., Bischof, H., Maver, J.: Multiple eigenspaces. Pattern Recognition **35**(11) (2002) 2613–2627

Toward Scalable Activity Recognition for Sensor Networks

Christopher R. Wren and Emmanuel Munguia Tapia*

Mistubishi Electric Research Laboratories,
201 Broadway 8th Floor, Cambrige MA 02139, USA

Abstract. Sensor networks hold the promise of truly intelligent buildings: buildings that adapt to the behavior of their occupants to improve productivity, efficiency, safety, and security. To be practical, such a network must be economical to manufacture, install and maintain. Similarly, the methodology must be efficient and must scale well to very large spaces. Finally, be be widely acceptable, it must be inherently privacy-sensitive. We propose to address these requirements by employing networks of passive infrared (PIR) motion detectors. PIR sensors are inexpensive, reliable, and require very little bandwidth. They also protect privacy since they are neither capable of directly identifying individuals nor of capturing identifiable imagery or audio. However, with an appropriate analysis methodology, we show that they are capable of providing useful contextual information. The methodology we propose supports scalability by adopting a hierarchical framework that splits computation into localized, distributed tasks. To support our methodology we provide theoretical justification for the method that grounds it in the action recognition literature. We also present quantitative results on a dataset that we have recorded from a 400 square meter wing of our laboratory. Specifically, we report quantitative results that show better than 90% recognition performance for low-level activities such as walking, loitering, and turning. We also present experimental results for mid-level activities such as visiting and meeting.

1 Introduction

Buildings should be experts in the day to day activities of their inhabitants. This would make buildings safer by providing census data during emergencies. It would enhance security allowing the building to recognize daily patterns and flag unusual activity. It could improve efficiency by predicting demand for heating, lighting, and elevators. It could enrich human effort by providing presence and availability information, or supporting social networking applications. There is a tremendous potential benefit when buildings become experts in themselves, experts in the activities that occur within them.

---
* *Current address:* Massachusetts Institute of Technology; 1 Cambridge Center, 4FL; Cambridge, MA, 02142 USA; emunguiamit.edu.

M. Hazas, J. Krumm, and T. Strang (Eds.): LoCA 2006, LNCS 3987, pp. 168–185, 2006.

Sensor networks have been investigated for such tasks as environmental monitoring, and resource tracking[1, 2]. We present a sensor network and inference methodology that enables buildings to sense and interpret the context of the human occupants in a potentially economical, scalable, efficient, and privacy-sensitive manner. Our sensor network is composed of passive infrared motion detectors. These sensors only detect presence and movement of heat sources, so they preserve much of the privacy of the occupants.

The system estimates the physical topology of the network and uses that information to form *context neighborhoods* around each node. Loosely, a context neighborhood is the collection of nodes that have a semantically-grounded link to the central node. That is, nodes form a neighborhood if they are physically near to each other, and the constraints of the space allow people to move freely between their sensor range, so that their sensor readings are related to each other by the dynamics of the space. These neighborhoods are the basis for portable behavior recognition and system scalability and we will define the several specific kinds of neighborhood in this paper.

We choose the smallest neighborhoods to be large enough to accurately detect the atomic components of human behavior in a building. We do not require individuals to be tracked before behavior is recognized, this allows the system to be built with cheaper sensors, and eliminates much of the computational overhead associated with high-fidelity tracking. By accurately detecting low-level movement behaviors locally, we also greatly reduce the amount of data that must be communicated outside the neighborhoods. These features support scalability.

The neighborhoods are also defined small enough to be invariant to the larger context of a building. This means that the detectors should be portable from location to location. This fact reduces the overall cost by eliminating much of the on-site calibration and engineering cost. There is no need to accurately position the sensors, they only need to tile the space in a rough grid.

Scalability and re-usability benefits can be found by building larger neighborhoods as collections of smaller neighborhoods. In this paper we will present this hierarchical neighborhood architecture. The architecture makes sense both from a communication efficiency point of view[3] and from a behavioral context point of view. We will present our taxonomy of building occupant behaviors and discuss how those behaviors map onto our sensor hierarchy.

In Section 5, we support our claims with experimental results form our test facility. The current test facility is a 27 node network observing the hallways and walkways of a 400 square meter wing of our building. The map in Figure 1 depicts the test area. It is occupied by 16 administrators and executives and is a central hub of activity for all 90 employees at the site. This facility represents the first phase of a 250-node network that will eventually cover both floors of our 3500 square meter facility. All observations for evaluation include the real, spontaneous, potentially multi-actor behavior of the building occupants: never a scripted or otherwise contrived scenario.

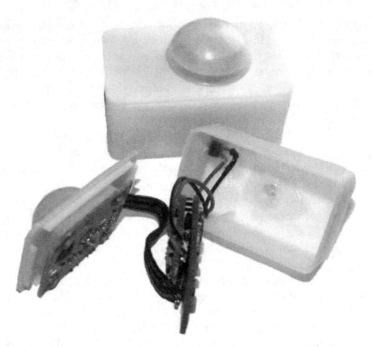

Fig. 1. The hardware implementation of the motion detector node

2   Related Work

Wilson and Atkeson [4] also utilize a network of motion detectors. Their system is targeted at the home, where they assume that only a few individuals will be present. This allows them to pursue a classic track-then-interpret methodology. More people means more ambiguity, and more ambiguity means exponentially more hypotheses that must be considered during tracking. Therefore, this approach is only applicable to low-census buildings, such as homes. Wilson and Atkeson also assume strategic placement of sensors. That level of specialization is not economical in large buildings, or where usage patterns change regularly. We assume that our network will be built into the lights, outlets, and vents, and that it will likely be installed by professional electricians and ventilation engineers, rather than behavioral psychologists or eldercare specialists.

There is a significant body of literature surrounding the interpretation of human behavior in video[5, 6, 7, 8, 9]. A common thread in all of this work is that tracking is the very first stage of processing. That limits the work to sensor modalities that can provide highly accurate tracking information in the absence of any high-level inference. In particular, the ambiguities inherent in using a motion detector network can be expected to introduce enough noise in the tracking results to render most of these approaches unusable.

There are a few works that have attempted to step outside this framework [10, 11]. These systems learn task-specific state models that allow the behaviors to

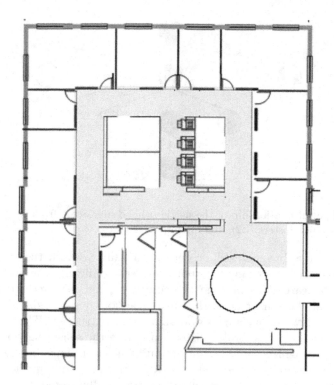

Fig. 2. The floor plan of the wing where experiment data was collected. In the very center is a collection of copiers and printers. Surrounding those are a set of cubicles. On the outside are offices. The areas observed by sensors (shaded) are hallways.

be recognized directly from the sensor data, without tracking. Our work follows this philosophy, and adapts it to the domain of sensor networks (see Figure 2).

3 Hierarchies of Neighborhoods

Bobick[12] presents a framework for thinking about the role of time and context in the interpretation of human behavior. He breaks behavior down into a tripartite hierarchy consisting of *movements, activities,* and *actions.* The most basic behaviors are called *movements* and have no link to the situational context and no temporal structure. Short sequences of movements may be combined with some temporal structure to form *activities.* And finally, activities may be interpreted within the larger context of the participants and the environment to recognize *actions.*

We borrow this framework, and map it onto our sensor network. Bobick defines movements to be behaviors without significant temporal structure, therefore we may recognize them with computationally light-weight models. They are also defined as not relying on the larger context, so we may detect them using only local information. Activities are defined as groups of movements, so they may

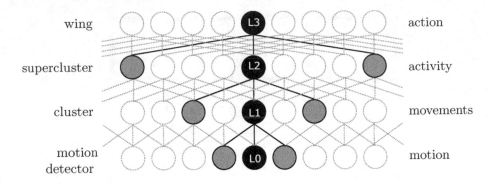

Fig. 3. The Spatial relationship of the neighborhood hierarchy, from sensors (L0), to clusters (L1), superclusters (L2), and finally wings (L3)

cover a larger area, but may still be detected locally, without the benefit of the global context. Activities may incorporate some significant temporal structure, so we must be careful to manage the computational resources those models may impose on the sensor network. Finally, actions require global context to recognize, and may have a complex grammar to their structure. Therefore actions may best be recognized centrally, instead of within the sensor network. That is, they are best recognized at the floor, or building level. Thus, we see that this context-based hierarchy maps well onto a spatial and computation hierarchy for the sensor network. This hierarchy is abstractly illustrated in Figure 3. The motion detectors are at the bottom of the hierarchy, providing the observations. Successive levels tap progressively wider areas of context. Black nodes are the cluster leader for that level, drawing information from the black and gray nodes one level down.

The rest of this section further explores this analytical decomposition. The next section, by contrast, will cover the implementation of the system.

3.1   Topology

We make the idea of locality concrete in the form of neighborhoods of sensor nodes. To create the neighborhoods, we need the physical topology of the network. The topology tells us both which nodes are the neighbors of each leader, and also the ordering of the neighbors around each leader. Note that this does *not* require manual calibration of the system. It has been shown that it is possible to recover the geometry of a sensor network from unconstrained motion[13]. We use a similar technique, where the unconstrained motion of building inhabitants is captured for a period of time and analyzed to find statistical evidence for causal links between the nodes. The topology is inferred directly from these links. Nodes that may be physically near each other, but are separated by a wall barring direct pedestrian traffic between them will not be linked in this topology, for example. That is right, since the behavior observed by those two nodes will be independent. Typically robust topologies can be estimated from just one day of data, but it depends on the character of the data captured.

Once the topology is known, then we can construct a neighborhood around each node. Each node is given a look up table that maps the IDs of its neighbor nodes into an ordered list. For convenience of the presentation we will say that each neighbor is given a label such as "Top". "Left", "Right", "Bottom", or "Center". Note that "Top" may be arbitrarily defined to some real-world direction, say West. The exact metric definition of these labels is not important. What is important is the local relationships between the nodes is consistent: for example that the "Top" node is both counter-clockwise from the "Right" node and antipodal to the "Bottom" node. This insensitivity to imprecise or poorly documented installation is an important feature of the system.

For clarity of presentation we also assume that all neighborhoods have exactly five nodes: the center node plus the top, left, right, and bottom nodes (C, T, L, R, B). The neighborhoods will be illustrated as idealized crosses, as in Figure 4. In practice it is straightforward to generalize to neighborhoods with different numbers of adjacent neighbors.

3.2   The Node

The lowest level of our hierarchy is the individual sensor node. The single motion detector is the *Level 0* neighborhood, a degenerate neighborhood with only a single member. Our sensor nodes are wireless motion detectors that detect motion over a small area. In our case, the coverage area of each sensor is about four square meters. The motion detectors are not very capable devices, for example: they cannot differentiate one person from a group of several people, or a person from an animal. However, they are a well-developed technology that is both inexpensive and robust.

Motion detectors generate binary events in response to change in the environment, and this is the basic unit of observation that we assume as input to the higher layers of processing. Any sensing technology can be filtered to generate such a stream of binary events, and so reasonably could be substituted at this level. In the rest of the text we will call these detections *motions* to differentiate them from the more interesting *movements* in Bobick's taxonomy.

3.3   The Cluster

The next level of the hierarchy is the sensor *cluster*, or *Level 1* neighborhood. Every sensor defines a cluster: that node, plus all the nodes in the immediate vicinity. The immediate vicinity is defined as the nodes that are one step away in any direction in the network topology. We assume that the space is tiled with sensors in a grid: with little or no overlap between sensor activation fields, but also with little or no gap between activation fields. If each sensor has a radius of two meters, and the space is tiled with sensors, then a typical cluster should consist of less than ten nodes and have a radius of approximately six meters.

The clusters are where real movement recognition occurs in our system. We define a set of possible movements that occupants of a building might exhibit in the small area: passing though, standing, turning, entering, leaving, joining,

Fig. 4. The neighborhood behaviors at Level 1. 1st line: canonical neighborhood layout, and the still behavior. 2nd: passing though movements. 3rd: turning movements. 4th: entering and exiting the space. 5th: some joining movements (splitting not shown).

and splitting. Some example movements are illustrated in Figure 4. In the illustrations time moves from dark to light, so the leftmost figure in the second row represents walking though, from bottom to top. We believe that these behaviors are so basic, and so local, that we should be able to define them, train detectors for them, and then use those detectors in novel environments. That is, so long as the sensors are installed in a similar configuration. the detectors for these movements should be invariant to the context that the cluster is immersed in, and thus can be built before installation, and reused across buildings.

The cluster leader collects the motion activations from Level 0, that is, from its neighbor nodes. The stream of motion activations are segmented into spans of contiguous time that contain motion. Within the spans, the leader computes a number of simple features, such as: the total number of activations, the sequence of neighbor activations, and which neighbors were activated first or last. These features, which will be discussed in more detail in Section 4, are fast to compute, and are designed to make the detectors invariant to orientation and velocity. Since movements do not have complex temporal structure, the detectors take the form of naïve Bayesian classifiers. The detectors are thus computationally efficient. This is important since they are consuming motion events that are possibly being generated several times a second.

Note that, if there are 100 sensors, then there will also be 100 clusters. Each node leads one cluster, even while it participates in the many clusters around it. All behaviors are defined as happening *at* the lead sensor in a cluster. It is therefore necessary to have clusters at each node, to detect the movement behaviors that happen under that node.

3.4   The Superclusters

The next level of the hierarchy, the *Level 2* neighborhood, is the *supercluster*. Superclusters are clusters of clusters. They consist of a lead cluster and all the clusters in the immediate vicinity. If sensors are a couple of meters across, and clusters are about six meters across, then superclusters are 10-15 meters across, depending on how *immediate vicinity* is defined.

The supercluster leader receives movement detections from the constituent clusters and uses this information to perform activity recognition. That is a supercluster might infer that a meeting has occurred when its sees a sequence of "enter enter enter", that is, several people entering a room in secession. At ten meters, the superclusters cover a span of hallway, or an intersection and it's local context, or other reusable elements of building structure. While they are large enough to begin to incorporate elements of building context, we assert that they still have sufficient locality to represent reusable components of behavior.

The Level 2 models must incorporate both spatial and temporal context to recognize activities in their field of view. The models take the form of dynamic belief networks. The results we present below include three activities: visits, chatting, and meeting. *Visiting* is an activity where a person approaches a locale, dwells in that locale for a short time, and then leaves. Examples include visiting fixed resources such as a printer or coffee pot, but also short visits to an individual's office. *Chatting* is an activity that involves two people joining in a hallway, presumably to have a short conversation. *Meeting* is the activity where several people converge on a location over a period of minutes, presumably to participate in a scheduled meeting.

While we claim that these models are reusable across buildings, they obviously are not as universal as the movement models. These models are appropriate to a corporate setting, and are likely portable to other collaborative environments. However, there are probably a large number of activities that could be observed at the supercluster level. Some of these activities will have more or less meaning depending on the context. Each class of application domain (factory, retail, office, home) would need a library of activities appropriate to that context.

3.5   The Multi-actor Problem

A major issue when observing multiple people is the data association problem: what observations belong to which person? Most systems approach this problem by assuming that individuals are accurately tracked within the space before any interpretation is attempted. In that case, all data is associated to a track first, and the track becomes the representation used by the recognition engine.

This approach assumes that the sensors used in the system will have sufficient fidelity and coverage to make tracking possible. That implies either ubiquitous camera coverage, or the presence of tracking and identification tags attached to individual users. In situations where this assumption is valid, the prior literature is already rich with solutions. However, we claim that these assumptions are not currently valid in most buildings. Further, we claim that economic, ethical, and privacy concerns surrounding ubiquitous cameras and microphones are likely to keep many, if not most spaces from implementing such systems.

Rather than trying to distinguish individuals at the very first stage of processing, we chose instead to first draw a distinction between independent individuals and co-acting individuals, Instead of assuming that we can track individual people, we assume that people within a certain distance of each other are not independent, that they are, together, engaged in some recognizable movement. Specifically, that distance in the radius of a Level 1 neighborhood. If two people meet in a particular neighborhood, then that is recognized as a single movement: joining.

At Level 2, we must begin to resolve the multi-actor problem. The radius of a Level 2 neighborhood could be ten meters, so it is unreasonable to assert that the movements of people 5-10 meters apart are significantly correlated. Such weakly correlated actors would cause an explosion in the variability of behavior, and therefore an explosion in the number and complexity of movement models that we would need to consider. Our solution at Level 2 is to recognize all possible interpretations of the observed activity. This allows us to capture recognizable activities that might occur in the presence of distracting motions due to other actors. The ambiguity generated by these non-exclusive detections is passed up to the next level, to be resolved using external context.

3.6 Architectural Spaces

We find that above Level 2, we begin to naturally refer to the neighborhoods with architectural terms: a lab, a wing, a floor, a building, a campus. We believe that behaviors at the floor- or wing-level naturally include the notion of individuals and places: person A left her office, visited the coffee machine, and returned. We posit therefore, that the next level of processing will necessarily include some form of stochastic parsing or chaining. This process will have much in common with tracking, except that it will be based not on the similarity of signal characteristics, but instead on the consistency of interpretations along the chain. Because this form of processing is very different from what we've described so far, and because it is well covered in the existing literature, for example see the work of Ivanov[14], we will not discuss it further in this work.

4   Implementation

This section will cover the implementation of the sensor network: both hardware implementation and analytic techniques.

4.1   The Node

The Level 0 detector is implemented in hardware, using passive infra-red (PIR) motion detectors. This is the same sensing technology used in most motion-activated lights and appliances on the market today. The sensors are inexpensive, approximately $30 per node in quantities of 500. They also require little power: they are able to run on a single nine volt battery for several months. Finally, what little they actually do, they do very reliably. We have used the widely available

KC7783R sensor package from Comedia Ltd. The nodes are approximately 2cm by 3cm by 5cm. A node is pictured in Figure 1.

As it comes from the factory, the KC7783R is only able to generate events once every few seconds. We modified the boards to reduce the recovery time so that events may be generated at about 1Hz. When an individual is within view of the sensor, the moving heat source changes the thermal signature measured by the device, and a rising voltage edge is generated. The sensor is noisy and sometimes generates both false positive and false negative signals. However it is insensitive to changes in visible lighting, and therefore has a distinct advantage over cameras.

The output of the node, at the Level 0, is simply a stream of binary events. When the motion is detected, a sensor-specific ID is broadcast over a wireless network. In our research prototype system, the packet is associated to a global time stamp and copied to a conventional LAN for central storage and analysis. However, we anticipate that in a production system, the nodes would communicate only locally, passing information directly between immediate neighbors to be analyzed locally.

4.2   The Cluster

The goal of a cluster is to process the binary motion activation events from its participant sensor nodes at level 0 and classify them into one of the 17 movements. The 17 movements to recognize are: entering, leaving, turning-top-right, turning-top-left, turning-bottom-right, turning-bottom-left, turning-right-bottom, turning-right-up, turning-left-bottom, turning-left-up, walking-up, walking-down, walking-right, walking-left, still, join, split. Note that the goal is not only to recognize if a person is "turning" but which direction (right vs. left and top vs bottom) the person is turning to with respect to an arbitrary reference point shared by all nodes. Furthermore, note that detecting movements at any point in the network only requires information from the local neighborhood or cluster (5 sensors in our case) of motion detectors.

Movement detection is accomplished in three, computationally light-weight steps: segmentation of motion events, feature extraction, and detection. The continuous stream of binary motion events is segmented using what we call idle segmentation. In idle segmentation, the leader node of the cluster starts collecting data as soon it receives a motion event from any of its neighbors and stops storing events after an idle time window of 3 seconds, containing no activations. The idle window corresponds to the average time it takes a person to walk away from a neighborhood at normal walking speed. Note that a conventional running window of fixed length could have been used to perform the segmentation of the motion events, however, idle segmentation was preferred for the lower number of false positives generated and less detections required by the system.

The features we extract are simple, yet powerful, so that they can be computed using the limited computational resources available at the sensor nodes. The first step in the feature computation is to use a look-up-table to convert the local motion event labels into the more portable top, bottom, left, right, and center labels that describe the local topological relationship between the nodes, as discussed in section 3.1. The first type of feature that is computed is temporal precedence. These features indicate the gross temporal relationship between the sensor activations. The mean value of all the timestamps associated with the motion events received from each sensor (T, B, L, R, C) is used to compute this feature. The total number of precedence features is $5 \times 5 = 25$. Another feature is the total number of motion events that comprise the segment. We also compute binary features that indicate if the center node or one of the neighbors was the first or the last sensor to be activated. Finally there are binary feature that indicate if a particular node was activated at all. For example, during an idealized example of the turning-bottom-left movement, The nodes B, C, L would be activated once each. The feature vector for that activity would be 30 elements with the following non-false values: $B, C, L, B \prec C, B \prec L, C \prec L, neighborsFirst,$ $neighborsLast,$ and $total = 3$. The notation B means "the Bottom sensor was activated." The notation $B \prec C$ means "the Bottom sensor was activated before the Center sensor."

Note that the feature vector is not a temporal sequence, it is just single vector that summarizes the entire observation sequence. In general, the features are designed to be invariant to the overall execution speed of the movement.

Once the features are extracted for a segment, detection is accomplished by using a naïve Bayesian classifier. The classifier takes the vector of 30 features and computes the likelihood for each of the 17 movements. Previous experimental testing has demonstrated that naïve Bayes networks are surprisingly good classifiers on some problem domains, despite their strict independence assumptions between attributes and the class and their computational simplicity. In fact, simple naïve networks have proven comparable to much more complex algorithms, such as the C4 decision tree algorithm [15, 16, 17]. The naïve Bayesian classifier was trained on 3 weeks of hand-labeled data were the number of training examples for each movement varies from 4–28. Examples of the 17 movement categories were hand labeled by watching 7.5Hz video from 20 ceiling mounted cameras. The examples were drawn from real data collected continuously over three weeks from the administrative wing. The confusion matrix and classification results are presented below,in Section 5.

4.3   Superclusters

At Level 2, the leader of a super cluster recognizes activities by segmenting and classifying the movement detection results from its neighbor leaders at Level 1. The activities that we recognize are chatting, meeting, and visiting. The recognition of these activities requires access to a broader spatial context as well as more detailed temporal models. The segmentation of level 1 events is performed using idle segmentation with an idle window of 10 seconds. It is important to notice that different idle window lengths could be used for different activities, however, good results were obtained using the 10s window.

Because the input events at this level are discrete movement labels generated relatively infrequently (once every several seconds), we can afford to recognize them with discrete output Hidden Markov Models (HMMs)[18]. HMMs are parametric models that contain a set of states and a model of how the process transitions through those states. Each state is associated with a distinct conditional probability distribution over the space of all possible observations. In our case, the observations are the discrete movement detections from level 1. We compute the optimal number of hidden states using a cross-validation procedure over the training data and the Baum-Welch algorithm assuming a uniform prior state distribution. Since our observation variable is discrete, the observation likelihood function is represented as a discrete set of probabilities:

$$b_i(\mathbf{f}_i) = Pr\,[\mathbf{f}_i]$$

where $\mathbf{f}_i$ is the vector of features at index i. The transitions are assumed to be first-order Markov, shaped by a transition probability matrix $\mathbf{A}$.

$$P(\mathbf{f}_i|\mathbf{F}, \lambda) = \sum_{q=1}^{N} b_q(\mathbf{f}_i) \left[\sum_{p=1}^{N} P(\mathbf{F}|Q = p, \lambda)\mathbf{a}_{pq} \right] \tag{1}$$

where a_{pq} is the element of $\mathbf{A}$ that specifies the probability of transitioning from state p to state q, Q is the current state, $\mathbf{F}$ is the collection of prior feature observations, and $b_q(\mathbf{f})$ is the probability of making the observation $\mathbf{f}$ while in state q. This model incorporates information about the temporal structure of a process in the transition matrix. It offers invariance to warping of the temporal signal. The observation process also allows it to tolerates noise in the signal.

We recognize the activities by creating one HMM for each activity to classify and computing the likelihood over the segmented data sequence using the forward-backward algorithm[19]. The final classification result is given by the activity label associated with the HMM that obtains the highest likelihood over the segment.

The training data for each activity model is usually obtained by observing and hand labeling video sequences of the different activities. However, given the simplicity and the ease of interpreting the features used at this level (simple movement events), it is possible to directly write down a set of hypothetical training examples using common sense. This is important because it means that new activities can be hand-defined on-the-fly by the end user of the system just by having a common sense understanding of the temporal relationships among the movement events. In our case, we created 20 training examples composed of five unique examples for each activity. For example, the 'meeting' activity was defined by these sequences of movements: "entering entering", "entering entering entering", "leaving leaving", and "leaving leaving leaving", among others. This allows us to identify meetings as events were at least two people consecutively enter or leave an office or space.

5   Experimental Results

The map in Figure 2 depicts the test area. Executives occupy the offices around
the outside edge of the space. Support staff occupy the cubicles in the center. At
the very middle there are printers and copiers. The open hallways to the lower
left and right provide access to the rest of the lab. The 16 occupants of the area
form a tightly collaborative group, so there are many person-to-person behaviors
that occur completely within this relatively small space. That is one reason the
area was chosen for this pilot study. The space is also visited often by the 70
employees when they seek the services of the area occupants. During the course
of the evaluation the occupants were notified of data gathering, but were never
instructed to behave in a particular way, nor were there any artificial constraints
placed on the number of people who could be moving at any given time. The
data contains observations of the honest, natural behavior of the occupants of
this busy space.

The Level 1 detectors were trained from a pool of hand-labeled examples in
the ground-truth video sequences. We expect these models to be portable to any
Level 1 neighborhood, so the examples were collected from different points in
the space. The models were trained and tested in a leave-one-out cross-validation
framework on the segmented data. Therefore, models were always trained and
tested on data from different parts of the experimental area. The leave-one-out
methodology was chosen to make the most efficient use of the limited quantity of
hand-labeled data, which was very time consuming to generate. The confusion
matrix is shown in Table 1. The cross-validation performance over the 221 labeled

Table 1. Confusion matrix for Movement detection experiments

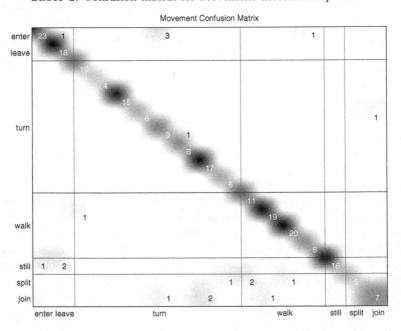

and segmented examples was 91%, with half the errors coming in the split and join movements. These movements show the most variability, and it is possible that they should be considered activities to be recognized at a higher level of processing. The rows of the table indicate the result of classifying all the examples of a known type, for example there are 28 "enter" events labeled in the test set. Numbers along the diagonal are correct: the known label on the row matches the classifier output on the column. Off-diagonal elements are errors: one enter event was incorrectly classified as a "leave" event, and three were incorrectly classified into one of the many "turn" classes.

A more realistic test of the performance of the movement detectors is run them on a long, unsegmented sequences of motion data and then compute spatial probability models that show where certain kinds of events occur. For this paper we ran the detectors on a 3 week long continuous stream of data, comprised of 3.84 million individual motion sensor activations. For example, Figure 5 depicts the spatial distribution of the walking movement. All of the figures in this section show just the walkways (shaded area) from Figure 2. The rectangles correspond to the coverage area of individual motion detectors. The walking movement is defined as walking though a neighborhood without stopping or turning. The figure shows regions of high probability (dark) along the hallways in the figure. That is, many more walking though detections were recorded along this path than elsewhere in the space. The hallway along the bottom of the map is a very high-traffic route connecting two wings of our building. Note also that at corners the walk probability is very, very low (white). This is due to the fact that it is not possible to walk at the locations: one must either turn or enter an office.

Similarly, Figure 5 shows the spatial distribution of turning movements over the space. Areas where turns are impossible, correctly show a very low probability (white) of witnessing a turning movement. Areas like corners and junctions, however, have a high probability (dark) of seeing a turning movement. These two figures, and similar plots for the other movement models, match our intuitions about the space very closely. This gives us confidence that the models

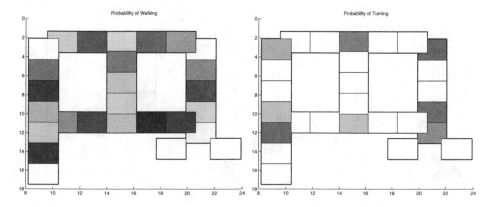

Fig. 5. Left: The spatial distribution of walking movements in the experimental area. **Right**: The spatial distribution of turning movements in the experimental area.

are generalizing well across large spans of time. These plots summarize three weeks of movement detection results.

It is very difficult to gather ground truth for 3.84 million sensor activations. Table 1 is intended to provide precise, quantitative detail on the performance of the classifiers: illustrating the nature of mistakes on a small, carefully analyzed section of data. On the other hand, the long sequence data is intended to qualitatively illustrate that the classifiers do work on large streams of data, and do produce sensible summaries of the building activity. These summaries are consistent with the building architecture in that they do not show nonsensical behaviors such as walking into walls They are also consistent with the intuitions of building occupants. For example, correctly highlighting the high-traffic corridor within the space.

The Level 2 detectors provided a similar challenge. While going to meetings may seem more common than we sometimes might like, they are, actually, rare enough that compiling even two examples per week is difficult, and very time consuming. Instead we manually generated models that described what we anticipate scheduled meetings to look like: a few people entering the same room over the course of several minutes. The inputs, the local movement detections, are reliable and abstract enough that this seems to work. The spatial distribution of meetings, shown in Figure 6, matches our intuitions about the way the space is used. Meetings are uncommon at most locations, but occur with higher probability inside the offices of the lab directors. The squares in Figure 6 do not correspond directly to doors. Some observations zones have multiple doors, and some have no doors. The real distribution of doors can be seen in Figure 2.

Figure 6 shows the spatial distribution of the visiting activity. Visiting is an activity where people approach a location, loiter there briefly, and then leave. This activity is common enough that we were able to train the activity models from real data. The result is a very clean probability map. The central spikes correspond to the printer and the copier. The high probability regions in the

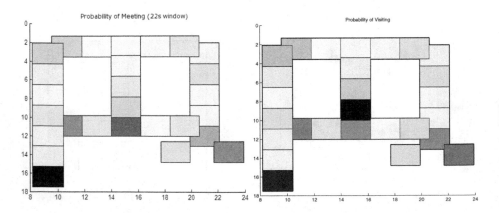

Fig. 6. Left: The spatial distribution of meeting activity in the experimental area. **Right**: The spatial distribution of visiting activity in the experimental area.

upper left correspond to the directors' offices, the office of human resources and several key administrators. The high probability node in the lower right is the office of the vice president of business development.

In almost all the plots we see spurious detections on the boundary nodes, at the extreme bottom, left and right, of the map. These boundary nodes represent places where the closed-world assumption is broken. The movement detectors fail because they are blind to motion that happens in what should be part of their local context. This is a strong argument for completely covering spaces with sensors. Ambiguities created by incomplete coverage are very hard to resolve through inference.

6   Applications

These results suggest that a number of context-sensitive applications may soon be not only possible, but practical. An inexpensive sensor network could hence building safety by tuning emergency response to an up-to-the-minute building census. It could enhance security while preserving privacy by providing more complete context information to monitoring systems without the invasiveness or cost of ubiquitous cameras. Current energy saving devices such as motion activated lights tend to be disabled by occupants because they are annoying. By understanding more of the local context, and the habits of the users, it might be possible to build systems that better match the expectations of the people in the building.

7   Summary

We have shown that a network of simple motion detectors can be used to recover useful information about the state of a building in an efficient, scalable, and privacy-friendly manner. It is possible to recognize both simple movements (walking, loitering, entering a room) and more complex activities (visiting and meeting). We see these low- and mid-level behavior detectors as the building blocks for high-level understanding of the context of a building. This recognition is accomplished by adopting a hierarchical framework for interpretation that is carefully tuned to the requirements for recognition of various the components of human activity. The movement detectors are intentionally simple to allow modest computational engines to evaluate them despite relatively high input data rates. The movement detectors locally summarize the data, lowering the data rate and making the more demanding activity recognition models tractable, allowing us to scale up the extent of our network. We have also presented a list of movements that appear to generalize well to novel contexts. We argue that these low-level detectors can provide a powerful tool, enabling the analysis of building activity without the need for significant adaptation to novel contexts. This scalable, reusable, efficient, privacy-friendly framework for behavior understanding in buildings enables an enormous field of applications for the future of responsive buildings.

Acknowledgments

We would like to thank the reviewers and our shepherd Jeffrey Hightower for helping to improve this document with their insightful and helpful comments. The sensor hardware used in this work includes a MITes board designed at the Massachusetts Institute of Technology House_n Group.

References

1. R. Szewczyk, E. Osterweil, J. Polastre, M. Hamilton, A. Mainwaring, D. Estrin, Habitat monitoring with sensor networks, Communications of the ACM 47 (6) (2004) 34–40.
2. B. Horling, R. Vincent, R. Mailler, J. Shen, R. Becker, K. Rawlins, V. Lesser, Distributed Sensor Network for Real Time Tracking, Proceedings of the 5th International Conference on Autonomous Agents (2001) 417–424.
   URL http://mas.cs.umass.edu/paper/199
3. W. Ye, J. Heidemann, D. Estrin, An energy-efficient mac protocol for wireless sensor networks, in: Proceedings 21st International Annual Joint Conference of the IEEE Computer and Communications Societies, New York, New York, USA, 2002.
4. D. H. Wilson, C. Atkeson, Simultaneous tracking & activity recognition (star) using many anonymous, binary sensors, in: The Third International Conference on Pervasive Computing, 2005, pp. 62–79.
5. C. Stauffer, E. Grimson, Learning patterns of activity using real-time tracking, IEEE Transactions on Pattern Recognition and Machine Intelligence 22 (8) (2000) 747–757.
6. N. Johnson, D. Hogg, Learning the distribution of object trajectories for event recognition, Image and Vision Computing 14 (8).
7. D. Minnen, I. Essa, T. Starner, Expectation grammars: Leveraging high-level expectations for activity recognition, in: Workshop on Event Mining, Event Detection, and Recognition in Video, held in Conjunction with Computer Vision and Pattern Recognition, Vol. 2, IEEE, 2003, p. 626.
8. R. Cutler, L. Davis, Real-time periodic motion detection, analysis and applications, in: Conference on Computer and Pattern Recognition, IEEE, Fort Collins, USA, 1999, pp. 326–331.
9. T. B. Moeslund, E. Granum, A survey of computer vision-based human motion capture, Computer Vision and Image Understanding 81 (2001) 231–268.
10. A. Wilson, A. Bobick, Realtime online adaptive gesture recognition, in: Proceedings of the International Conference on Pattern Recognition, Barcelona, Spain, 2000, pp. 111–6.
11. Y. Ivanov, B. Blumberg, A. Pentland, Em for perceptual coding and reinforcement learning tasks, in: 8th International Symposium on Intelligent Robotic Systems, Reading, UK, 2000, pp. 93–100.
12. A. F. Bobick, Movement, activity and action: the role of knowledge in the perception of motion, Philosophical Transactions: Biological Sciences 352 (1358) (1997) 1257–1265.
13. C. R. Wren, S. G. Rao, Self-configuring, lightweight sensor networks for ubiquitous computing, in: The Fifth International Conference on Ubiquitous Computing: Adjunct Proceedings, 2003, pp. 205–6, also MERL Technical Report TR2003-24.

14. Y. A. Ivanov, A. F. Bobick, Recognition of visual activities and interactions by stochastic parsing, Transactions on Pattern Analysis and Machine Intelligence 22 (8) (2000) 852–872.
15. P. Langley, W. Iba, K. Thompson, An analysis of bayesian classifiers, in: Proceedings of the Tenth National Conference on Artificial Intelligence, AAAI Press, San Jose, CA, 1992.
16. G. John, P. Langley, Estimating continuous distributions in bayesian classifiers, in: Proceedings of the Eleventh Conference on Uncertainty in Artificial Intelligence, San Mateo, CA, 1995.
17. P. Domingos, M. Pazzani, Beyond independence: Conditions for the optimality of a simple bayesian classifier, in: L. Saitta (Ed.), Proceedings of the Thirteenth International Conference on Machine Learning, Morgan Kauffman, 1996.
18. R. O. Duda, P. E. Hart, D. G. Stork, Pattern Classification, 2nd Edition, Wiley-Interscience, 2001.
19. L. R. Rabiner, A tutorial on hidden markov models and selected applications in speech recognition, Proceedings of IEEE 77 (2) (1989) 257–285.

Nomatic:
Location By, For, and Of Crowds

Donald J. Patterson, Xianghua Ding, and Nicholas Noack

University Of California at Irvine, USA
{djp3, dingx, nnoack}@ics.uci.edu

Abstract. In this paper we present a social and technical architecture which will enable the study of localization from the perspective of crowds. Our research agenda is to leverage new computing opportunities that arise when *many* people are simultaneously localizing themselves. By aggregating this and other types of context information we intend to develop a statistically powerful data set that can be used by urban planners, users and their software. This paper presents an end-to-end strategy, motivated with preliminary user studies, for lowering the social and technical barriers to sharing context information. The primary technology through which we motivate participation is an intelligent context-aware instant messaging client called Nomatic*Gaim. We investigate social barriers to participation with a small informal user study evaluating automatic privacy mechanisms which give people control over their context disclosure. We then analyze some preliminary data from an early deployment. Finally we show how leveraging these mass-collaborations could help to improve Nomatic*Gaim by allowing it to infer position to place mappings.

1 Introduction

A great deal of progress has been made in the pervasive computing community on the problem of localizing individuals. There are outdoor systems [1], indoor systems [2], and hybrid indoor-outdoor systems [3, 4, 5, 6]. There are infrastructure-based solutions [7] and wearable/mobile-based solutions [8]. There are IR [9], acoustic [10, 11], laser [12], single-point [13] and sensor fusion techniques [14, 15]. Hightower presents an excellent survey [16] with other examples and categorizations.

With such a wide array of techniques for empowering a user to digitally leverage their location, it is now justified to begin studying new computing opportunities that are enabled when *large numbers* of people begin using these technologies. Urban planners have implicitly begun studying these issues through the analysis of where cell-phones are carried and used [17, 18]. We view our work as complementary to theirs: crowd context can certainly be used for urban analysis. However, we wish to expand the types of analyses that can be done by providing statistically powerful data sets which can still be used by urban planners, but also by the crowds who generate the data, and the software that they

M. Hazas, J. Krumm, and T. Strang (Eds.): LoCA 2006, LNCS 3987, pp. 186–203, 2006.

use. A key component of our vision is to enable aggregations over place (as opposed to position [19]), activities and social situations.

To be specific, as a first order goal, we wish to develop methods of being able to answer location-aggregation questions such as "Where are UCI students right now?" One answer to such a question is to show positions on a map, but our different and novel approach is to answer in the form of a probability distribution over *places*: "90% of UCI students are *at home*." Different questions might be answered with distributions that can be interpreted as: "This weekend, 50% of the assisted living center residents went to a *store*", or "Right now, 10% of the sales force are in *developing nations*". Our future goals include being able to answer activity- and social status-aggregation questions that naturally spring to mind as well.

The risk versus benefit trade-off for a user who reveals context information changes in two ways when it is aggregated. The first change is that the privacy dynamic is altered. An observer trying to understand information about crowds does not need access to knowledge about a particular person. As a result, some of the risks of losing plausible deniability [20], and of being surveilled [21] are lowered. They certainly don't go away (see section 3 for example!) because in order to aggregate someone must have access to individual context information, but anonymity becomes more practical and sufficient statistics can be maintained without maintaining data on individual behavior. The second change is that motivation to reveal context information changes as well. Since no personal analysis of context is available to the user once their data is aggregated, the benefit of revealing that information is small. Therefore new ways of encouraging participation in the community from which aggregations are made must be developed.

The rest of our paper structures the social and technical architecture which we are developing to achieve our goal. The centerpiece of the architecture is our context-aware instant messaging client, Nomatic*Gaim, described in section 2. We argue that this application needs context-awareness immediately and, as a result, is sufficiently motivating for people to reveal context information. Nonetheless, this revelation is a *social* barrier that we do not take lightly. As a result, in section 3 we present the results of a small informal user study that we have conducted to help shape our design of privacy controls to further facilitate participation. Creating a well-designed IM client is a *technical* barrier that we investigate in a small deployment described in section 4. Encouraging results from these studies provides a suggestion that these barriers can be crossed, so in section 5 we show how remote data collection conducted by Nomatic*Gaim will support solving the position to place problem, and thus the aggregate query challenge posed above. Additionally, this particular solution can be used to further lower social and technical barriers to the use of Nomatic*Gaim and other location-aware systems.

2   Nomatic*Gaim

The prefix tag, "Nomatic*" refers to our system for collecting descriptions of context correlated with position. Nomatic has the particular characteristics of leveraging mass collaboration to get statistically powerful amounts of data which can then be used as data for data mining algorithms to solve challenging cultural and social context representation problems.

2.1   Our Use of Context

We use "context" as short hand for three types of data: a user's current place, a user's current activity, and a user's current social situation. While our approach could include other aspects of context as well, these three have immediate promise with regard to Instant Messaging (IM) usage.

- **Place:** Place is a way of describing a position in a semantic way. It is an inherently ambiguous and subjective label that depends on who is labeling a place, why they are labeling it and who they think is going to see the label. Unlike place, position is an exact location, that, while possibly difficult to gather, clearly describes where something is. It is usually described in a coordinate system such as latitude and longitude, but may also be described in other ways based on use and technology. Regardless of representation, position unambiguously maps where locations are (e.g., 31N -117W, 3 miles north of Exit 14 on highway I-5, etc.). Position to place is not a one-to-one mapping. Not only can a position have many place names, but a single place name may map to many positions (e.g., home, work, a Yoshinoya restaurant, an IKEA store). An excellent discussion of the issues surrounding position and place can be found in [19].
- **Activity:** Activity is also a subjective description of what a person is currently doing. Much of the same ambiguity that surrounds place also surrounds activity. A person may be walking, talking on a cell-phone, having a conversation, laughing, exercising, looking for the subway, all at the same time.
- **Social Situation:** This is the way in which a person would describe their current activity as it relates to other people. It includes situations such as "being alone", "being in a crowd", "in a meeting", "on a date", etc. Again, this is a highly subjective way of describing part of a person's context.

In fact, these three elements of context are closely tied together. To say that you are at a theater likely means that you are also watching a movie, and in a crowd of strangers. To say that you are flying to Sydney also implies that you are on a plane. So we do not suggest that these three types of context are independent, but rather they are different lenses through which we observe situations.

When necessary, some of the ambiguity of context can be eliminated by conforming to an ontology, hierarchical or otherwise. GIS systems, such as the U.S. Census bureau's [22], frequently impose such a structure on the description of places, so that each position has exactly one well characterized label, perhaps "light industrial", "park", or "shopping mall." Much work in the pervasive and ubiquitous computing community on activity recognition takes this tactic as well. Many algorithms are made tractable by the exclusive and unambiguous description of activities in progress (e.g., [23, 24]).

Nomatic, through its mass-collaborative nature, rejects the imposition of a strict ontology and supports the emergent creation of communal understandings of context that will arise through shared use. We allow users to arbitrarily tag locations in the style of de.li.cious [25], Flickr [26], and Etsy [27] so that Nomatic can grow and change with community use.

2.2 Instant Messaging Transformed

The first step in motivating crowds toward a mass-collaboration of context information disclosure is to provide an incentive for individuals to reveal it. We believe that a transformed IM client is just such an incentive.

The Human-Computer Interaction and Computer Supported Cooperative Work literature has thoroughly documented the value and use of "awareness technologies" to support and improve distributed group work [28, 29, 30, 31, 32, 33]. Ethnographic studies of IM have shown that the awareness associated with the online/offline status line of an IM client has substantial value in the maintenance of dyadic human relationships [34, 35, 36].

However, the computing context in which IM has been used has been rapidly changing. Until recently most users of IM were primarily using desktop computers. Computing has changed substantially in recent years such that laptops sales are outpacing desktop computer sales [37] and IM clients are now available on mobile phones. This means that the context provided by a label that says "online" vs. "offline" or "available" vs. "not available" is no longer sufficient to achieve the positive externalities mentioned in Nardi's work [36]. Some studies indicate that 13% of all IM dialog is simply related to negotiating availability [38]. Increasingly, individuals are always "online". The difference is that now a person might be "online" and only available for some kinds of IM messages. She may be driving, giving a presentation, using the same hardware to make a phone call, or incur fees to receive IM messages. "Online", no longer means that a user can gracefully accept all interruptions.

To adapt to this new reality, we have developed a context-aware, open-source[1], cross-platform[2], and cross-protocol[3] instant messaging client called Nomatic*Gaim. It is the merger of two existing projects, Gaim [39] and Place Lab [6], with the Nomatic mass-collaboration context collection system. Unlike previous IM clients, this one reports more nuanced context information in the status line (see figure 1). When a user sets their context information, their position is simultaneously queried from the Place Lab system. These two pieces of information are then alternately reported on the awareness status line where the "available" label was previously. (Figures 2–3 shows other clients displaying Nomatic*Gaim status).

---

[1] Nomatic*Gaim is licensed under a combination of GPL, and other redistributable licenses.

[2] It compiles and runs on Windows, Linux and Mac OS platforms.

[3] MSN Messenger, Yahoo! Messenger, AIM/AOL/iChat, Jabber/Google, and others.

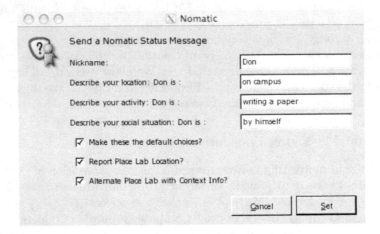

Fig. 1. Nomatic*Gaim's context entry dialog for manual context entry

Fig. 2. Apple iChat client displaying status created by Nomatic*Gaim

Fig. 3. Yahoo! Messenger client displaying status created by Nomatic*Gaim

At the same time as the current context information is reported to a user's buddies, the Nomatic*Gaim client also anonymizes the (context,position) pair and sends it to the Nomatic Mass-Collaboration Database (NMCDB) where a database entry is made matching the position with the manual context information. In this way the user is provided immediate benefit while a database of position to place name mappings and, more generally, position to context mappings is being developed.

As exciting as this new way of using IM is, there are some clear concerns about privacy that need to be addressed. Lack of appropriate controls over context disclosure may make users uncomfortable about adopting Nomatic*Gaim's awareness model. In order to understand user attitudes and to develop models for automatically managing privacy, we conducted a small Wizard-Of-Oz pilot study to direct our efforts.

3 Privacy Pilot Study

We made the hypothesis that a user would be motivated to use Nomatic*Gaim's context disclosure system if they had appropriate control over the method in which the information was released. To evaluate this, we conducted a small pilot study prototyping various IM privacy configuration management strategies. For this study, we focused on what benefits users can achieve from location disclosure through IM, what concerns this entails, and what factors affect their disclosure attitudes. Although this study is small and informal, we hope it will iteratively guide more formal user studies in the future.

Previous work has exposed some of the underlying privacy issues associated with location disclosure. The private nature of location information and users' unwillingness to disclose it has caused some research efforts to fail [9, 40, 41]. Some have found that automated location disclosure is not very well accepted by users, and concluded that automatic features lacked value [42]. Others have determined that people first choose whether or not to reveal location, and if so, then specify their location in the most useful terms for a given relationship [43]. Still others have supported this idea that relationship dominates disclosure decisions [44].

Part of why we believe we may be able to succeed where others have not is because we suspect that the underlying technology has a significant effect on how people choose to reveal context information. Most previous work has focused on SMS[4] communication, but IM represents a different mode of communication, and affords different information practices (i.e. different degrees of synchronicity, central vs. ambient attention demands, "pulling" vs. "pushing" modes of operation, etc.). The employment of different communication media for location disclosure may change the balance between benefits and costs, affecting a user's sense of control, and thus their attitudes.

The issue of privacy in our IM client is partially mitigated by controls built into the IM protocols themselves which allow users to control access to their online/offline status, and therefore Nomatic*Gaim status, to people whom they

---

[4] Short Message Service: text messages sent to cell-phones.

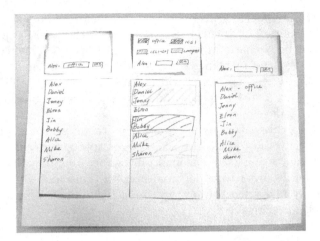

Fig. 4. Three customized paper prototypes of potential future Nomatic*Gaim interfaces used in the pilot study. The left interface is manual. The right interface is completely automated. The center interface gives the most control to the user in disclosing their current place.

have previously approved. The discussion of context disclosure is therefore made within the boundaries of preexisting privacy mechanisms. (see [45] for more details on IM privacy by protocol).

3.1   Methodology

Our study consisted of two parts, a paper-prototyping/Wizard-Of-Oz study and a scenario-based questionnaire evaluating potential location-aware IM usage models for a laptop computer. The paper prototypes demonstrate possible functionality that differs from the existing Nomatic*Gaim client.

The study was conducted on the UCI campus in November 2005. Restricting ourselves to students within our research group who were not working on Nomatic, we screened potential participants to ensure they used IM daily and were mobile laptop users. We recruited five students (3 male-2 female, 4 graduate-1 undergraduate) who received a short application form that collected information to customize the subsequent scenarios.

During each one-hour session, we introduced three paper prototypes, presented several scenarios that required users to interact with the prototypes, and then conducted a semi-structured interview with the participants to understand their experiences.

Privacy Interface Options. The three paper prototypes were designed to give the users a spectrum of automation over location disclosure. In the first one, the system doesn't do any automated disclosure, but users can manually enter and disclose their current place to their entire buddy list. In the second one, the system automatically detects a variety of place names that describe the user's position. The user is then able to drag place names over groups of individuals to reveal their place. The third one automatically chooses and reveals a place name to all the people in the buddy list. As with the scenarios, the interfaces were customized for each participant. An example is shown in figure 4.

3.2   Discussion

Our screening interviews reflected a wide variety of practices and environments involved with IM usage. One unexpected situation involved IM usage during church services. Opinions of showing location information also varied during the study. One participant began their session by saying that location disclosure is not something they wanted and didn't have any value to them. However, she later expressed several times that she had changed her mind, and agreed that this feature could be very convenient and useful.

Benefits. Through the study, the following four benefits emerged as recurring themes:

- **Facilitating Activity Coordination:** Nomatic*Gaim has the potential to let others know where you are and vice versa. This appeared to be useful for pre-defined, but flexible activity coordination (e.g, impromptu office meetings, coffee shop meetings and project meetings before a class). Our interviews demonstrated that these would be the highest value scenarios for the participants as they were useful, convenient and efficient.
- **To Facilitate Socially Appropriate IM Interactions:** Most participants agreed that location information is a good indicator of a user's social context. Providing location information through IM can inform and signal others how to interact more appropriately. Seeing an IM buddy at a meeting location was interpreted as a signal that their buddy was waiting for them. Additionally, "Meeting Room", "Church", and "Classroom" locations all indicate strong expectations over interruptibility. It also signals different expectations for different people. For example, one participant emphasized that the "Church" label means he doesn't mind people from the same church contacting him (before the service starts), but not others. The observation was also made that for people who are familiar with each other's schedule, place information reveals what types of activities they are engaged in and provides cues for interruptibility.
- **Emotional Benefits:** One participant mentioned that his parents call him all the time, just wanting to know where he is. Another participant stated that "There are probably 2-3 people I'd like to disclose [my location] to all the time", and another, "I guess I also care what my parents know, because they are most likely to give me crap over the telephone, or to worry (i.e. I'd like them to know I am home after a plane flight)" These statements suggest that location information revealed through IM could enhance social connections. Unlike phone calls and SMS, IM costs less in terms of time and attention and may achieve better benefits as a result. Two participants mentioned that this feature could save time by reducing the frequency of check-up calls from parents. As one participant suggested, it provides "background" awareness of her remote friends.

- **Increased Opportunities for Socializing:** Location information can lead to opportunistic social interactions. One participant mentioned that when she sees her friend is in New York, she will start a conversation by "Hey, what are you doing in NY?" Another participant suggested that "Home" means he is available for his friends. Yet another participant mentioned that if she sees her friends at "Home", she will "feel more comfortable to reach them, without any worries". In our coffee shop scenarios, participants expressed their willingness to disclose their location information if they are alone, "so [friends] nearby can join me".

Information Leakage. Besides benefits, the scenarios and interview questions also expose some tensions and concerns involved. Some participants were concerned that location disclosure might cause information leakage over scope and time, and lead to undesirable consequences.

Our participants demonstrated an unwillingness to disclose some location information to conceptual groups of people in their buddy list. As one participant put it, "a couple [people] I'd actually want to hide information from, I'm protective of my face time." In a home scenario, one participant said "office mates don't need to know [where I am] for sure". Some locations are especially sensitive to some people such as "bars" to parents, or "home" to boss, although as a result of current IM practice, participants also mentioned that these people were currently not in their buddy list.

One participant was afraid of information leakage over time, either choosing to disclose or choosing not to disclose location can be informative "in ways you don't like." The example given is "parents asking 'why I didn't display 'Home' all weekend?' Even if it doesn't show where I actually am." Another participant also pointed out choosing not to disclose location may cause social pressure. A third mentioned that people might learn her rhythms, and could predict her locations in an undesired way. System security was also raised as a concern.

High Level of Acceptance. Our pilot study showed a high level of acceptance of location disclosure through IM and the corresponding automatic features. All participants answered "yes" when asked whether they would use this feature if it were available. At the same time, two participants also mentioned that they would adopt it only when it became very popular suggesting that achieving critical mass will be an important social barrier to adoption. Nothing about the proposed system requires multiple users to participate.

The high level of acceptance exceeded our original expectations, and is contrasted with findings from previous location disclosure systems. We speculate several reasons why this might be:

- **More Benefits:** IM makes location exchange very easy, which is significant for activity coordination. Secondly, although existing IM clients support quick and informal conversations, they suffer from a lack of social context which location disclosure helps to mitigate.
- **Lower Attention Cost:** One major feature of IM is its presence awareness. It works like an ambient display [46], operating in the background, utilizing

peripheral attention, and supports easy movement between background and foreground operation. This feature significantly lowers the attention cost on the information receivers, and makes it less annoying and interruptive.

 – **Sufficient Level of Control:** In contrast with cell-phones and PDAs, laptops are less intimate. People typically do not bring them everywhere they go. This eliminates some of the threats to a person's privacy. Secondly, the buddy list provides a natural and controllable boundary in terms of the scope of information leakage. Finally, the awareness metaphor associated with IM status disclosure is simple to conceptualize.

3.3   Future Design Directions

 – **Temporality:** Several participants distinguished between regular and one time events, and suggested different ways of automating each. For scheduled and regular activities, automatic features have the potential to reduce tedious manual specification. Also, with regular activities, participants seem to have less privacy concerns. In contrast, for one time events, manual disclosure is acceptable or even preferred.

 – **Spatiality:** In some places, such as work, our participants showed their willingness to use automatic features to reveal location information. It had high value, and little privacy risk. In contrast, "home", or "coffee shop" were more private.

 – **People Aspect:** People want to disclose their location to groups of people in different ways. Furthermore people categorize their acquaintances differently. This suggests a flexible buddy organizing mechanism is an important requirement for automatic location disclosure design.

 – **Activity Aspect:** Our study showed that for the same location, different social situations altered attitudes towards location disclosure. For example, while waiting at a coffee shop, almost everybody indicated they would "definitely" choose to disclose location. However, after they start socializing, nobody wanted to disclose location anymore. When the socializing is over, if they remained alone, they all chose to disclose location again. This suggests the need to provide a very easy mechanism to quickly start and stop location disclosure.

 – **Information Aspect:** People are less concerned about disclosing more generalized location information to their buddy list. For most participants, generalized information doesn't convey too much information, and yet is useful enough for relevant people. Detailed information such as room numbers were only appropriate for certain people. This suggests using generalized information as default settings.

 – **Easy Control:** Our participants made it clear that control had to be "dead easy" – "No more than one click to override."

3.4   Summary of Pilot Study

The size and informality of our study makes it impossible to make conclusive statements about privacy in IM. We did observe generally positive attitudes towards location disclosure from our well-informed and computer literate user sample. They also emphasized that automatic privacy mechanisms need to be flexible in regard to recognizing what times and places were valid to make default disclosures and to provide very clear feedback and control about what information was being revealed. We also got hints that made us suspect that critical mass, rather than privacy will be the determining factor in wide adoption of this feature.

4   Preliminary Nomatic*Gaim Deployment

In parallel with our work on privacy automation we tested an initial version of our system to evaluate technical barriers that would impact the effectiveness and system design of Nomatic*Gaim. We used an instrumented version of our client running on Windows and Macintosh laptops that collected statistics about how our users used physical space and IM. We had one professor and two graduate students use our client over the course of one week each. At the end of the usage period we collected and analyzed the resulting logs.

4.1   Collected Statistics

The first set of statistics that we collected related to protocol usage and supported our decision to use a multi-protocol approach. Figure 5 shows the number of buddies on each persons IM list separated according to protocol. These numbers are in line with similar research into IM usage that determined that an average buddy list has 22 people [35]. Figure 6 shows a similar analysis based on number of messages per protocol.

The second set of statistics that we collected was related to Wi-Fi Access Point (AP) localization. This is the underlying technology present in Place Lab which in turn is used by Nomatic*Gaim to determine a user's position. This is

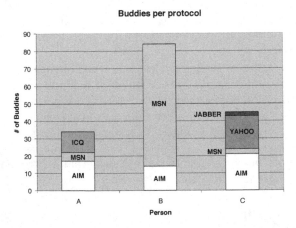

Fig. 5. Number of buddies per IM protocol in pilot deployment

% Messages per protocol

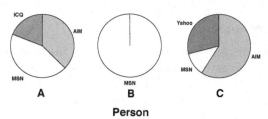

Person

Fig. 6. Number of IM messages per protocol in pilot deployment

Unique Access Points Found

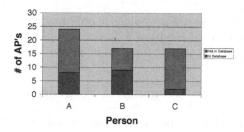

Person

Fig. 7. Unique access points found by each user. Light gray reflects APs that were not in the database.

a beacon-based technology that compares the currently observed APs to a local database of AP locations. By triangulating a position among the observed APs, a user can passively ascertain his location with moderate accuracy.

We looked at how many unique APs our users encountered and what percentage of them were not represented in the Place Lab data base (see figure 7). Over the course of the week there was no period of time in which a laptop was used outside the range of an AP. This was despite the fact that one of the users in our study made a cross-country plane trip during the study period.

4.2   Discussion

- **AP Coverage.** The number of APs in the database was surprisingly low. There were always APs visible, but their location was frequently not known. Whenever this was the case, Place Lab was unable to find a latitude/longitude for the user. However, the set of AP signatures did suggest a particular location, just one that was unable to be placed in a coordinate system.
- **Accuracy.** The literature cites resolution accuracy that is very high under ideal situations, sometimes under 10m [6, 47]. Although we didn't formally analyze accuracy, our anecdotal experience suggested that we achieved approximately 30m accuracy in practice.
- **Mobility.** Consistent with the results of a study into the mobility of CMU students [48], we found that most laptop usage was in a few regular

repeated areas. Only during the cross-country travel episode did we see many locations per user.

4.3   Future Directions

These results suggest a few important features for the Nomatic system. First, bootstrapping and auto-extension of APs must be easy and integral to the system. A system like Microsoft Live Local [49] that accepts unknown APs and attempts to localize them based on co-location with known APs will be essential for the success of this system.

Additionally it would be convenient to have an interface that allowed the user to act as a manual GPS. Such an interface would allow them to pick a position on a map that is their actual position and then update the relevant databases to reflect the APs in sight.

Finally the mapping of position to place should not fail just because absolute position is not known. A graceful segue between known unique positions and absolute positions is critical while AP localization is in the bootstrapping stage.

5   Closing the Loop: Leveraging Aggregates

So far we have discussed a preliminary system, based on an IM client that will collect and reveal context information about a user, in a manner with which they are comfortable. We have argued that IM is a compelling application that provides immediate gratification to the user. It is less clear how a user would benefit from providing their context information to the NMCDB and why they wouldn't forgo that aspect of the system while they displayed the same information to their buddies.

Motivating the mass-collaboration aspect comes from the powerful ability for a Nomatic*Gaim client to use statistical inference from the data that has been submitted to the NMCDB. This inference can determine the best place label for the given position, L^*, based on the data collected so far at all nearby positions, x, and the currently observed location, z:

$$L^* = \underset{L \in Places}{\operatorname{argmax}} \int_x P(L \,|\, Data(x)) P(x \,|\, z)$$

Since $P(x \mid z)$ is essentially a neighbor function, we can generalize position to be either a latitude and longitude pair, or a set of APs, and thus support bootstrapping. In the latitude/longitude case, the notion of a neighborhood is physical. In the AP case the notion of a neighborhood is "all locations that have a non-empty intersection of APs". We can assume that the greater the overlap the closer the locations.

We can further differentiate between the data that the user has personally collected and data that the rest of the community has collected and assume the two are independent:

$$L^* = \underset{L \in Places}{\operatorname{argmax}} \int_x P(L \,|\, Data_{user}(x), Data_{\neg user}(x)) P(x \,|\, z) \tag{1}$$

$$L^* = \operatorname*{argmax}_{L \in Places} \int_x P(L \mid Data_{user}(x)) P(L \mid Data_{\neg user}(x)) P(x \mid z) \qquad (2)$$

We now consider the case of a user who has never used Nomatic*Gaim before. This user arrives at a new location and opens their laptop. Place Lab localizes the user's position. Nomatic*Gaim gets the position and sends it to the NMCDB. The NMCDB responds with the optimal place label for the given location, L^*, calculated according to equation 2. Since $Data_{user}(x) = \emptyset$, $P(L \mid Data_{user}(x))$ is uniform and uninformative.

After a user has entered information into the database on their own, their particular labelings of space are non-empty and begin to contribute toward the understanding of place for their IM client.

We can now incorporate the design guidelines that we have uncovered to create a better user experience. Rather than having the NMCDB respond with, L^*, it can respond with the list of highest rated place labels, ($L^* = L_0, L_1, L_2...$) and the associated probabilities, ($P(L_0 \mid \hat{z}), P(L_1 \mid \hat{z}), P(L_2 \mid \hat{z})...$). Nomatic*Gaim can now take one of four options under the assumption that $\alpha > \beta > \gamma$:

- If $P(L_0 \mid \hat{z}) > \alpha$ then Nomatic*Gaim will automatically set the place context for the user
- If $P(L_0 \mid \hat{z}) > \beta$ then Nomatic*Gaim will automatically set the place context for the user and ask for the user to confirm the setting.
- If $P(L_0 \mid \hat{z}) > \gamma$ then Nomatic*Gaim will open the context dialog with the list of locations, $L_0...L_n$, ordered according to their associated probabilities in a drop down box for user selection.
- Otherwise, Nomatic*Gaim will open the dialog box for the user and allow him to manually set the current location place.

The final user experience is compelling. If a user is willing to collaborate with NMCDB, when they arrive at a brand-new location and open their laptop, Nomatic*Gaim will take one of the proposed U/I options. If this new location has a common name that all previous people have used to label that location, the user's place (not position) status will be set for them automatically. They will never have to touch their IM client and a semantic understanding of their current location will be displayed. If the user doesn't like the common place labeling, and they correct it manually, the next time they arrive at the same location, their customized place label will automatically be used. The user never again has to touch their status when in that location. If for reasons of privacy or ambiguity a location has multiple place names, the user's current place will be confirmed before it is set for the user. The sensitivity to the automatic processes can be set by altering α, β, and γ.

6   Conclusions

In this paper we have presented a social and technical architecture for collecting large amounts of context information from users in real-time.

Through the use of several small user studies we have identified social and technical barriers to the adoption of our context-aware instant messaging client, Nomatic*Gaim. Our privacy study was surprisingly positive given related work in the field. We attribute this apparent willingness of people to participate in context disclosure to the unique features of IM that are different from SMS messaging. Our early deployment study supported our client design decisions of being cross-protocol and identified the need for techniques that work in the absence of absolute knowledge of position.

While previous work and technological trends suggest that the context awareness provided by Nomatic*Gaim has immediate benefits for a user and their buddies. It is crucial to the overall vision of Nomatic that users also reveal their context information to the NMCDB. To this end Nomatic*Gaim also leverages data submitted to the NMCDB to improve it's U/I, as an example of statistical inference over the data from crowds, but also to encourage continued mass-collaboration from the individual user.

Ultimately by leveraging this architecture, we are able to provide information that will assist urban planners, people and software to answer novel new queries that aggregate over the semantic contexts of crowds of people. This information can be used by people for aggregate social analysis, or by machines to create more social interfaces.

Acknowledgments

Thanks to all the folks who helped us out with this paper: Kah Liu, Matt Nguyen, Mike Moore, Grace Chen, Amanda Williams, Paul Dourish.

References

1. Hatch, R., Sharpe, T., Galyean, P.: Starfire: A global high accuracy differential gps system. Technical report, NavCom Technologies (2006)
2. Bahl, P., Padmanabhan, V.N.: RADAR: An In-Building RF-Based User Location and Tracking System. In: INFOCOM (2). (2000) 775–784
3. Griswold, W.G., Boyer, R., Brown, S.W., Truong, T.M.: A Component Architecture for an Extensible, Highly Integrated Context-Aware Computing Infrastructure. In: Proc. of the 25th International Conf. on Software Engineering, IEEE Computer Society (2003) 363–372
4. Griswold, W.G., Shanahan, P., Brown, S.W., Boyer, R., Ratto, M., Shapiro, R.B., Truong, T.M.: ActiveCampus - Experiments in Community-Oriented Ubiquitous Computing. Technical Report CS2003-0750, UC San Diego (2003)
5. Schilit, B., LaMarca, A., Borriello, G., Griswold, W., McDonald, D., Lazowska, E., Balachandran, A., Hong, J., Iverson, V.: Challenge: Ubiquitous Location-Aware Computing and the Place Lab Initiative. In: Proc. of WMASH 2003: The First ACM International Workshop on Wireless Mobile Applications and Services on WLAN. (2003)
6. LaMarca, A., Chawathe, Y., Consolvo, S., Hightower, J., Smith, I.E., Scott, J., Sohn, T., Howard, J., Hughes, J., Potter, F., Tabert, J., Powledge, P., Borriello, G., Schilit, B.N.: Place lab: Device positioning using radio beacons in the wild. [50] 116–133

7. Krumm, J., Williams, L., Smith, G.: SmartMoveX on a Graph – An Inexpensive Active Badge Tracker. In Borriello, G., Holmquist, L.E., eds.: Proc. of UBICOMP 2002. Volume LNCS 2498., Springer-Verlag (2002) 299–307

8. Krumm, J., Cermak, G., Horvitz, E.: RightSPOT: A Novel Sense of Location for Smart Personal Object. In Dey, A., Schmidt, A., McCarthy, J.F., eds.: Proc. of UBICOMP 2003. Volume LNCS 2864., Springer-Verlag (2003)

9. Want, R., Hopper, A., Falcão, V., Gibbons, J.: The active badge location system. ACM Transactions on Information Systems 10(1) (1992) 91–102

10. Lopes, C.V., Haghighat, A., Mandal, A., Givargis, T., Baldi, P.: Localization of off-the-shelf mobile devices using audible sound: Architectures, protocols and performance assessment. Mobile Computing and Communications Review **to appear** (2006)

11. Scott, J., Dragovic, B.: Audio location: Accurate low-cost location sensing. [50] 1–18

12. Fox, D., Burgard, W., Thrun, S.: Markov localization for mobile robots in dynamic environments. Journal of Artificial Intelligence Research 11 (1999)

13. Wilson, D.H., Atkeson, C.G.: Simultaneous tracking and activity recognition (star) using many anonymous, binary sensors. [50] 62–79

14. Hightower, J., Brumitt, B., Borriello, G.: The Location Stack: A Layered Model for Location in Ubiquitous Computing. In: Proc. of the Fourth IEEE Workshop on Mobile Computing Systems and Applications, IEEE Computer Society (2002)

15. Liao, L., Fox, D., Hightower, J., Kautz, H., Schulz, D.: Voronoi Tracking: Location Estimation using Sparse and Noisy Sensor Data. In: Proceedings of the IEEE/RSJ International Conference on Intelligent Robots and Systems (IROS), IEEE/RSJ (2003) 723–728

16. Hightower, J., Borriello, G.: A Survey and Taxonomy of Location Systems for Ubiquitous Computing (2001)

17. Polak, E., Society, W.: Amsterdam realtime (2002)

18. Ratti, C., Pulselli, R.M., Williams, S., Frenchman, D.: Mobile landscape: using location data from cell-phones for urban analysis. Environment and Planning B **to appear** (2006)

19. Hightower, J.: From position to place. In: Proceedings of The 2003 Workshop on Location-Aware Computing. (2003) 10–12 part of the 2003 Ubiquitous Computing Conference.

20. Smith, I.E., Consolvo, S., LaMarca, A., Hightower, J., Scott, J., Sohn, T., Hughes, J., Iachello, G., Abowd, G.D.: Social disclosure of place: From location technology to communication practices. [50] 134–151

21. Mann, S.: "sousveillance": inverse surveillance in multimedia imaging. In: MULTIMEDIA '04: Proceedings of the 12th annual ACM international conference on Multimedia, New York, NY, USA, ACM Press (2004) 620–627

22. Bureau, U.C.: Census 2000 TIGER/Line Data. http://www.esri.com/data/download/census2000-tigerline/ (2000)

23. Patterson, D.J., Fox, D., Kautz, H.A., Philipose, M.: Fine-grained activity recognition by aggregating abstract object usage. [51] 44–51

24. Bao, L., Intille, S.S.: Activity recognition from user-annotated acceleration data. In Ferscha, A., Mattern, F., eds.: Pervasive. Volume 3001 of Lecture Notes in Computer Science., Springer (2004) 1–17

25. (Del.icio.us social bookmarking website: http://del.icio.us/)

26. (Flickr photo sharing and tagging website :http://www.flickr.com/)

27. (Etsy handmade goods website:http://www.etsy.com/)

28. Heath, C., Luff, P.: Disembodied conduct: Communication through video in a multi-media office environment. In: CHI '91: Proceedings of the SIGCHI conference on Human factors in computing systems, New York, NY, USA, ACM Press (1991) 99–103

29. Dourish, P., Bellotti, V.: Awareness and coordination in shared workspaces. In: CSCW '92: Proceedings of the 1992 ACM conference on Computer-supported cooperative work, New York, NY, USA, ACM Press (1992) 107–114

30. Dourish, P., Bly, S.: Portholes: supporting awareness in a distributed work group. In: CHI '92: Proceedings of the SIGCHI conference on Human factors in computing systems, New York, NY, USA, ACM Press (1992) 541–547

31. Gutwin, C., Greenberg, S.: Effects of awareness support on groupware usability. In: CHI '98: Proceedings of the SIGCHI conference on Human factors in computing systems, New York, NY, USA, ACM Press/Addison-Wesley Publishing Co. (1998) 511–518

32. Milewski, A.E., Smith, T.M.: Providing presence cues to telephone users. In: CSCW '00: Proceedings of the 2000 ACM conference on Computer supported cooperative work, New York, NY, USA, ACM Press (2000) 89–96

33. Tang, J.C., Yankelovich, N., Begole, J., Kleek, M.V., Li, F., Bhalodia, J.: Connexus to awarenex: extending awareness to mobile users. In: CHI '01: Proceedings of the SIGCHI conference on Human factors in computing systems, New York, NY, USA, ACM Press (2001) 221–228

34. Nardi, B.A., Whittaker, S., Bradner, E.: Interaction and outeraction: instant messaging in action. In: CSCW '00: Proceedings of the 2000 ACM conference on Computer supported cooperative work, New York, NY, USA, ACM Press (2000) 79–88

35. Nardi, B.A., Whittaker, S., Schwarz, H.: Networkers and their activity in intensional networks. Computer Supported Cooperative Work 11(1-2) (2002) 205–242

36. Nardi, B.A.: Beyond bandwidth: Dimensions of connection in interpersonal communication. Computer Supported Cooperative Work 14(2) (2005) 91–130

37. Steve Alexander: Sales of Laptops Zip Ahead of Desktops (unknown) http://www.wirelessnewsfactor.com/perl/story/21861.html.

38. Handel, M., Herbsleb, J.D.: What is chat doing in the workplace? In: CSCW '02: Proceedings of the 2002 ACM conference on Computer supported cooperative work, New York, NY, USA, ACM Press (2002) 1–10

39. Gaim website (2006)

40. Spreitzer, M., Theimer, M.: Providing location information in a ubiquitous computing environment (panel session). In: SOSP '93: Proceedings of the fourteenth ACM symposium on Operating systems principles, New York, NY, USA, ACM Press (1993) 270–283

41. Hudson, S.E., Smith, I.: Techniques for addressing fundamental privacy and disruption tradeoffs in awareness support systems. In: CSCW '96: Proceedings of the 1996 ACM conference on Computer supported cooperative work, New York, NY, USA, ACM Press (1996) 248–257

42. Iachello, G., Smith, I.E., Consolvo, S., Abowd, G.D., Hughes, J., Howard, J., Potter, F., Scott, J., Sohn, T., Hightower, J., LaMarca, A.: Control, deception, and communication: Evaluating the deployment of a location-enhanced messaging service. [52] 213–231

43. Consolvo, S., Smith, I.E., Matthews, T., LaMarca, A., Tabert, J., Powledge, P.: Location disclosure to social relations: why, when, & what people want to share. In: CHI '05: Proceedings of the SIGCHI conference on Human factors in computing systems, New York, NY, USA, ACM Press (2005) 81–90

44. Lederer, S., Mankoff, J., Dey, A.K.: Who wants to know what when? privacy preference determinants in ubiquitous computing. In: CHI '03: CHI '03 extended abstracts on Human factors in computing systems, New York, NY, USA, ACM Press (2003) 724–725
45. Patil, S., Kobsa, A.: The challenges in preserving privacy in awareness systems. Technical report, Institute for Sofware Research, University of California at Irvine (2003) http://www.isr.uci.edu/tech_reports/UCI-ISR-03-3.pdf.
46. Wisneski, C., Ishii, H., Dahley, A., Gorbet, M.G., Brave, S., Ullmer, B., Yarin, P.: Ambient displays: Turning architectural space into an interface between people and digital information. In Streitz, N.A., Konomi, S., Burkhardt, H.J., eds.: CoBuild. Volume 1370 of Lecture Notes in Computer Science., Springer (1998) 22–32
47. Letchner, J., Fox, D., LaMarca, A.: Large-scale localization from wireless signal strength. In Veloso, M.M., Kambhampati, S., eds.: Proceedings of The Twentieth National Conference on Artificial Intelligence and the Seventeenth Innovative Applications of Artificial Intelligence Conference, AAAI Press AAAI Press / The MIT Press (2005) 15–20
48. Shaffer, J., Siewiorek, D.P., Smailagic, A.: Analysis of movement and mobility of wireless network users. [51] 60–69
49. (Microsoft live local:http://local.live.com/)
50. Gellersen, H.W., Want, R., Schmidt, A., eds.: Pervasive Computing, Third International Conference, PERVASIVE 2005. In Gellersen, H.W., Want, R., Schmidt, A., eds.: Pervasive. Volume 3468 of Lecture Notes in Computer Science., Springer (2005)
51. Mase, K., Rhodes, B., eds.: Ninth IEEE International Symposium on Wearable Computers. In Mase, K., Rhodes, B., eds.: ISWC, IEEE Computer Society (2005)
52. Beigl, M., Intille, S.S., Rekimoto, J., Tokuda, H., eds.: UbiComp 2005: Ubiquitous Computing, 7th International Conference, UbiComp 2005. In Beigl, M., Intille, S.S., Rekimoto, J., Tokuda, H., eds.: Ubicomp. Volume 3660 of Lecture Notes in Computer Science., Springer (2005)

An Unsupervised Learning Paradigm for Peer-to-Peer Labeling and Naming of Locations and Contexts

John A. Flanagan

Nokia Research Center,
P.O. Box 407,
FIN-00045 NOKIA GROUP,
Finland
adrian.flanagan@nokia.com

Abstract. Several approaches to context awareness have been proposed ranging from unsupervised learning to ontologies. Independent of the type of context awareness used a consistent approach to naming contexts is required. A novel paradigm for labeling contexts is described based on close range wireless connections between devices and a very simple, unsupervised learning algorithm. It is shown by simulation analysis that it is possible to achieve a labeling of different contexts which allows context related information to be communicated in a consistent manner between devices. As the learning is unsupervised no user input is required for it to work. Furthermore this approach requires no extra infrastructure or resources to manage the names assigned to the contexts.

1 Introduction

One of the basic requirements for two agents to communicate is the existence of a standard communication protocol. This is true whether two computers are connected over an IP (Internet Protocol) network or two people are talking face to face in a common language. We use these two simple communication examples to illustrate two very radical approaches to generating communication protocols. In the case of a computer network the communication protocol is defined and agreed on beforehand by interested parties. Prior to connection to the network each computer is then programmed to transmit and receive information based on the protocol. On the other hand for a child learning to talk English the parent does not explain that a "dog" is a four legged, hairy animal with a wet nose before the child has even seen a dog. Rather when the child sees a dog the parent tells the child its a "dog". Later the parent may talk about the "dog" and the child understands what the parent is referring to. We also note that in this case the labeling of the dog occurs when the parent and the child are both in the presence of a dog. Furthermore the mechanism by which the parent or child can distinguish between a dog and for example a cat is not important. The important point is they are both able to distinguish a dog and they essentially agree to call it by the same label.

M. Hazas, J. Krumm, and T. Strang (Eds.): LoCA 2006, LNCS 3987, pp. 204–221, 2006.

In the case of location awareness or the more general case of context awareness [1] it is also very important to label locations or contexts in a standardized manner. By having standard names for locations or contexts it is possible to communicate, infer and reason about the contexts and locations. In a similar manner to defining a communication protocol for networked computers it is possible to define a protocol for labeling contexts based for example on an ontology [2]. In this work we set out to show how an alternative method to labeling contexts in a mobile environment can be achieved based on an unsupervised learning mechanism. A parallel can be drawn between our method and the example of the parent and child using a common label for a dog. Like the parent and child example the method is based on a set of agents in close physical proximity in a location or context that each agent can distinguish. How each agent distinguishes the location or context is not important. However, if there exists a means of communicating label information with each other they are able to arrive at a standardized name for each of the distinguished locations or contexts. As it turns out this method is very suitable for implementation in mobile devices.

Apart from ever increasing computational and memory resources, typical mobile devices are also equipped with short range wireless connections such as Bluetooth. Hence devices in close physical proximity can connect to each other and exchange information in peer-to-peer, ad-hoc type networks. Persson et al [3] and Eagle [4] have studied such short range connections that allow for the exchange of personal details in social network applications. Moloney [5] has studied the implications of using a distributed recommendation system to improve security with short range connections. Given the world-wide wireless phone subscriber base is predicted to increase to 3 billion in the next few years it would seem that the opportunity for devices to form, short-range, peer-to-peer connections will also increase significantly. Hence if a mobile device is context aware then with its computational and short-range wireless communication ability the method we describe could be implemented in current mobile devices. In what follows however we are only able to describe and analyze a simulation of the method.

In section 2 we overview the ontology and unsupervised learning approach to context awareness in a mobile environment. While each approach has its advantages and disadvantages it is clear that being able to name identified contexts in a consistent manner between different mobile devices would be of huge benefit. In the case of an unsupervised learning approach to context awareness it is even essential. Context reasoning would be greatly enhanced through knowledge sharing as would service propagation between devices, given a consistent naming of contexts. One simple example of service propagation is illustrated in section 2 where each agent has different means of identifying a context. In section 3 we describe a very simple means of labeling contexts using an unsupervised learning algorithm. The algorithm is based on devices in close proximity, establishing a wireless (e.g. Bluetooth) connection and exchanging information on the names or labels they have for the context in which they find themselves. In section 4 a simulation of an implementation of the context labeling algorithm is described. The simulation is based on an abstraction of the real-world problem where agents are allowed to move in simulation space between different contexts and exchange context labels when in close proximity. Different aspects of the context labeling algorithm are illustrated. The model and methods used in the simulation are not intended to prove that the approach to labeling of contexts as presented here will work in the real-world. In section 5 we discuss some of the shortcomings of the model and simulation with respect to the real-world. Section 6 contains concluding remarks.

2   Context Awareness

2.1   Approaches to Context Awareness

It is possible to identify two essentially different approaches to context awareness. The first most widely studied approach is based on an ontology [2]. An ontology can be described as an explicit formal specification of how to represent objects, concepts and other entities that are assumed to exist in some area of interest. Typically the different entities and their interpretation can be labeled in a human understandable form and in a form that can be manipulated by software in a computer. The resulting ontology is governed by a set of logical statements about the represented knowledge. The process of *inference* is then used to derive consequences from the knowledge encapsulated in the ontology. Another important characteristic of an ontology is that the agents which subscribe to the ontology can communicate to each other knowledge represented in the ontology. The agents can in turn use this communicated knowledge for inference within the ontology in a logically consistent manner. This ability to communicate once again stems from the ability to represent the knowledge in a machine and even human readable form. The ontology approach to context awareness and pervasive computing has been widely studied for example by Chen et al [6] and Wang et al [7]. In the case of context aware mobile devices it has been analyzed by Korpipää and Mäntyjärvi [8].

The advantages of using an ontology for context awareness are obvious from the description which include well defined objects and entities in a consistent framework allowing consistent communication of information between agents. The disadvantages of using an ontology for context awareness in a mobile environment are discussed in [9]. With respect to labeling contexts consider the case where there are two groups of agents which subscribe to two different ontologies. In order to enable cross communication between the two groups there needs to be a translator or mapping between the ontologies. Given that each ontology may be constantly evolving this would mean the mapping should also be constantly evolving.

In another approach to context awareness Flanagan et al [10], [11] use unsupervised learning to extract clusters from measured data . Each of the extracted clusters is assumed to represent a user context. The main advantage to this approach is that the learned contexts are personal to the user and there is no need for user input. Furthermore the learning is computationally relatively light and can run on a mobile device. On the other hand a major drawback of this unsupervised learning approach is that for a group of devices the learned contexts and their representation is completely dependent on each user's history. This means there is no formal means to name the learned contexts in a consistent manner across devices, making it impossible to communicate context information between devices in a standard manner.

It is possible to look beyond the means of recognizing context and just consider the case of different agents with different capabilities for recognizing contexts. For example in the location recognition case, one user could have a GPS system on their mobile device while another may not and identify locations based on the nearest Wireless Local Area Network (WLAN) connection point. If these two users are standing beside each other in the same location then they should probably have the same label for the location.

In what follows a method that allows labeling of contexts across devices is described. An obvious application of the method is to a situation where each one of a group of devices has an unsupervised learning approach to context awareness. As it turns out the method is independent of the approach to context awareness and the capabilities of the agent. The basic assumption of the method is that each device or agent has some means of identifying different contexts. In the more general case it can provide a means of labeling contexts that would allow a context aware device using an ontology to communicate context information with an unsupervised learning based context aware device and vice-versa. It would also allow two sets of agents committed to two different ontologies to communicate with each other by learning the mapping between the two ontologies. As the method is learning based it is very flexible and can adapt to changes in contexts.

2.2   Example Scenario

In this section we describe a very simple user scenario where the ability to name contexts in a consistent manner between devices with different definitions of the same context allows for the propagation of services between the devices.

Consider Mary waiting at the bus stop. On her mobile device there is a service which allows her to buy the bus ticket before entering the bus at a reduced price. Mary's device has a GPS receiver which provides location information. Based on this location information her context aware mobile device infers that Mary is at the bus stop and starts the ticketing service allowing her to quickly purchase a bus ticket. Hence Mary is not required to manually find the ticketing service and start it. Now assume the context aware application on Mary's device has labeled or named the bus stop context 'XYZ' based on the GPS coordinates. John is a friend of Mary who also uses the same bus stop but his mobile device does not have GPS. Despite not being GPS enabled John's device can identify the bus stop close to his home based on a combination of three factors, the Cell ID from the GSM network, the time at which he typically takes the bus and accelerometers on his device which means it can determine when he walks the 10 minutes from his home to the bus stop. This approach to recognizing the bus

	Mary	John
Bus stop context definition	GPS: 60°17'N, 24°53'E	Cell ID: 32 LAC: 102 Country Code: 19 Time: Morning, 7:30 Activity: 10 minutes walk from home.
Bus stop label	'XYZ'	'XYZ'

Fig. 1. Even though Mary and John have different criteria for recognizing the same context if the contexts are labeled in the same manner then it is possible for their devices to communicate information related to the contexts. The GSM network provides basic location information in the form of the Cell ID, Location Area Code (LAC) and Country Code.

stop is less accurate than GPS but sufficient. By whatever means the context aware application on John's device has labeled the bus stop context with the same label 'XYZ'.

Assume that John's device is unaware of the ticketing service. John and Mary meet in the cafe and both have their Bluetooth switched on allowing their devices to connect. Comparing their publicly available information John's device detects that Mary's device also has a context 'XYZ'. It also detects that Mary's device has associated the ticketing service with this 'XYZ' label. John's device then receives details from Mary's device on accessing the service available at context 'XYZ'. The next time John is at the bus stop his device detects the context and alerts him to the fact that the ticketing service is available. Figure 1 shows a summary of this example. From this example scenario we see:

1. Each device can be context aware but not necessarily use the same criteria or features to define the same context.
2. If the devices have a consistent means of naming contexts which is independent of how the context awareness is carried out then they can share information about different contexts without necessarily being in those contexts.

3   An Algorithm for Unsupervised Labeling of Contexts

To describe the algorithm we consider P agents each one capable of distinguishing between M contexts denoted by $C_j, j = 1, \ldots, M$. There is no requirement for the agents to recognize the contexts in the same manner or using the same criteria. The set of recognized contexts is denoted by

$$\mathcal{C} = \{C_1, C_2, \ldots, C_M\} \ . \tag{1}$$

For each context C_j and each agent i there is a list of names $\{\psi_{ij}^k, \ k = 1, \ldots, n_{ij}\}$ associated with the context which the agent can use to label that context. The list of names is denoted by

$$\mathcal{L}_{ij} = \{\psi_{ij}^1, \psi_{ij}^2, \ldots, \psi_{ij}^{n_{ij}}\} \ . \tag{2}$$

The use of the labels is discussed in more detail in what follows. Associated with $\mathcal{L}_{ij}$ is a set of weights Ω_{ij} where

$$\Omega_{ij} = \left(\omega_{ij}^1, \omega_{ij}^2, \ldots, \omega_{ij}^{n_{ij}}\right) , \tag{3}$$

with $w_{ij}^k \in [0,1]$ a scalar and directly associated with ψ_{ij}^k. In all cases $n_{ij} \geq 1, \forall i,j$ which means each agent has at least one name for each context at all times. Initially the ω_{ij}^k and ψ_{ij}^k can be chosen randomly. We now define the *primary name* or *label* that agent i uses for C_j. Denote by S_{ij} the name that agent i assigns to each recognizable context C_j. At any given time

$$S_{ij} = \psi_{ij}^v , \tag{4}$$

with v defined as the index of the weight with maximum value,

$$\omega_{ij}^v > \omega_{ij}^k, \quad \forall\, k \neq v . \tag{5}$$

In other words the primary name S_{ij} an agent i uses for context C_j is given by the name ψ_{ij}^v in the list $\mathcal{L}_{ij}$ for which the associated weight ω_{ij}^v is maximum.

Each agent is capable of forming short range, wireless, connections over which they can exchange information with other agents. When an agent finds itself in context C_j with other agents they exchange the names. The technical details of exchanging the name information between the agents is not discussed here but assumed to be possible. Each agent updates its own list $\mathcal{L}_{ij}$ and Ω_{ij} as a function of the names of the other agents to which it is connected. The update is carried out as follows:

– In the first case there are μ agents $m_1, m_2, \ldots, m_\mu$ within range of each other and able to make a connection. It is assumed that all agents are in context C_j. The names $S_{m_i j}$ of the agents are compared to see which one occurs most often amongst the agents $m_1, m_2, \ldots, m_\mu$. Denote by S the most common name then $\forall\, k \in \{m_1, \ldots, m_\mu\}$,

1. If $S \notin \mathcal{L}_{kj}$ then add $\psi_{kj}^{n_{kj}+1} = S$ to $\mathcal{L}_{kj}$ and add an associated weight of

$$\omega_{kj}^{n_{kj}+1} = \gamma \tag{6}$$

to Ω_{kj}, with $\gamma \in [0,1]$, $\gamma \ll 1$ can be either a predefined constant value or a random number.

2. If $S \in \mathcal{L}_{kj}$ and $\psi_{kj}^r = S$ update ω_{kj}^r as follows,

$$\omega_{kj}^r = \omega_{kj}^r + \alpha\bigl(1.0 - \omega_{kj}^r\bigr) . \tag{7}$$

3. $\forall r = 1, \ldots, n_{kj}$ if $\psi_{kj}^r \neq S$ then

$$\omega_{kj}^r = \omega_{kj}^r + \alpha\bigl(0.0 - \omega_{kj}^r\bigr) . \tag{8}$$

4. $\forall r = 1, \ldots, n_{kj}$ and $\rho \ll 1$ a threshold, if

$$\omega_{kj}^r < \rho , \tag{9}$$

then ψ_{kj}^r is deleted from $\mathcal{L}_{kj}$ and ω_{kj}^r is deleted from Ω_{kj}.

– In the second case where there are only 2 agents p, q within range of each other and make a connection then the weights ω_{pj}^s associated with $S_{pj} = \psi_{pj}^r$ and ω_{qj}^s associated with $S_{qj} = \psi_{qj}^s$ are compared. Assuming $\omega_{pj}^r > \omega_{qj}^s$ then $S = S_{pj}$ and the same updates as in Eqs. (6), (7), (8),above are applied.

In brief, for a set of agents physically close enough to each other to make a connection and assumed to be in the same context, the most common name used by the agents to describe this context is found. The weight associated with this name for each agent is increased towards 1 (i.e. Eq. (6), (7)) and any other names the agent associates with the context are decreased towards 0 (i.e. Eq. (8)). Based on Eq. (4) and Eq. (5) it is clear that the most common name for a context is reinforced amongst the agents. A consequence of the above updates is that the value of n_{ij} can both increase and decrease.

Despite the simple means of exchanging and updating context name information the agents with their movements and interactions create a complex dynamic system. The main aim of this work is to determine whether agents working within this paradigm can arrive at a consistent means of naming each recognizable context. The behavior of this system is analyzed through simulation in the next section.

4   Simulation

In this section we describe two types of simulation, the first type is based on small scale simulations with few agents and contexts. In the second type based on large scale simulations we vary the number of agents over several orders of magnitude to examine the scalability of the proposed method.

The basic unit of time in the simulations is a simulation step. In order to simplify and speed up the implementation of the simulation, at each step the states of the agents are updated. For small scale simulations we are concerned about the evolution of the naming of contexts rather than the absolute convergence time. In the large scale simulations the agents are also updated at each simulation step but the convergence time is measured in terms of the number of times an agent visits a context which is independent of the simulation step. The relationship between the simulation step, the application of the name update algorithm in the simulation and a real-world application of the algorithm are discussed further in section 5.

4.1   Small Scale Simulation

Simulation Setup. The initialization of the simulation is carried out by setting $n_{ij} = 1$ with $\omega_{ij}^1 \ll 1$ and ψ_{ij}^1 a random 3 letter word for each agent i and context j. This means the simulation probably starts from the worst possible scenario where none of the agents have a label for any context in common with any other agent. The parameter γ of Eq. (6) is chosen randomly in the range $[0, 0.1]$.

The user interface to the simulation is shown in Fig. 2 (a). The outer rectangle represents the area within which the agents can move. In this area are 6 centers denoted by a '+' at position $(\gamma_{1i}, \gamma_{2i})$. The position (x_{1j}, x_{2j}) of each agent j is represented by a small black 'o'. This simulation does not have any input context data and the agents do not carry out any context recognition. Rather the context recognized by the agent, for the purposes of the simulation, is based on a distance measure. Hence, each agent j identifies the context C_v it is in based on a distance measure where v is defined as follows,

$$(\gamma_{1v} - x_{1j})^2 + (\gamma_{2v} - x_{2j})^2 < (\gamma_{1k} - x_{1j})^2 + (\gamma_{2k} - x_{2j})^2, \ \forall \ k \neq v \ . \quad (10)$$

Thus an agent's 'recognized context' is given by the context center to which the agent's position is closest. It should be emphasized that while the contexts in this simulation are based on position and distance, we are only using the distance measure as a convenience and we assume the contexts we are dealing with can range from low level contexts such as the 'location' to higher level contexts. For example, being in the same location such as 'home' in the 'morning' and 'evening' could be considered two different contexts and of a higher level than the location context alone. Thus in this simulation using a distance measure is a convenient way to present and differentiate between contexts. The 6 distinct polygons, outlined in gray, based on this distance measure, represent the areas associated with each context. Adjacent to each o is the name S_{ij}, defined in Eq. (4), Eq. (5), the agent assigns to the context j that it is currently in.

The agents are moved between different contexts in a random manner. Initially each agent is assigned a random *target* context C_i independent of the agents initial position. At each time step the position of agent j is changed as,

$$x_{kj} = x_{kj} + 0.01 * (\gamma_{ki} - x_{kj}) \ , \quad k = 1, 2 \quad (11)$$

and hence is moved towards the target context center $(\gamma_{1i}, \gamma_{2i})$. When agent k reaches the context center and

$$((\gamma_{1k} - x_{1j})^2 + (\gamma_{2k} - x_{2j})^2)^{0.5} < 0.25 \ , \quad (12)$$

denoted by the gray circles centered on the context center, the agent remains inside this circle for a number of simulation steps chosen randomly in the range $30 - 80$. At the end of this period another context center is randomly chosen and the process is repeated over. The choice of context centers for different agents and the periods they spend in the context center circles are chosen randomly and are not correlated in anyway.

When the agents are inside the context center circles they are considered to be in range long enough to allow connections to be made with other agents also in the context center circle. When the connections are made the agents exchange context names and update the context lists as described in section 3. Figure 2 (b) shows the state of the agents after several 1000 simulation steps. From this figure we see agents $3, 7, 15$ are in context C_5 with agents $3, 15$ in the context center circle. The names $S_{3,5}$, $S_{7,5}$ and $S_{15,5}$ the 3 agents have for context C_5 are all 'fbb'. On the other hand for agents $1, 6, 9$ all in context C_1 both S_{11}, S_{91} have the same name 'pis' for C_1 while agent 6 has a name S_{61} given by 'nrv'. In the next section the simulation is analyzed in more detail to show how the naming of the contexts among the agents evolves.

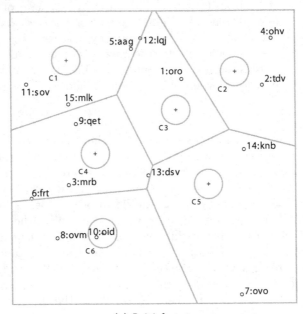

(a) Initial state

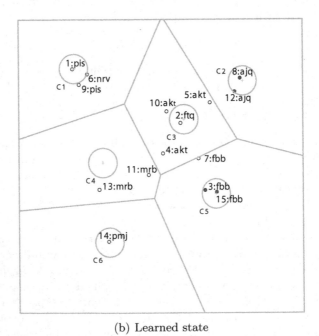

(b) Learned state

Fig. 2. User interface to the small scale simulator

Simulation Analysis Simulation 1. We first consider a single simulation with 15 agents and 6 contexts. The simulation setup is the same as described above with $\alpha = 0.01$ and $\rho = 0.005$. The aim of this analysis is to determine if the agents can arrive at a situation of *'full-communication'* where we define full communication as follows.

Definition 1 (Full-Communication). *A set of P agents have full communication when for every context C_j there is a single label S_j for which*

$$S_{ij} = S_j, \quad \forall\, i = 1, \ldots, P, \quad \forall\, j = 1, \ldots, M \;, \tag{13}$$

where we have defined S_{ij} in Eq. (4), (5). This definition means that at any location/context each agent can communicate with every other agent any information it has related to the context C_j. Figure 3 illustrates this result for each of the 6 contexts. In order to understand the illustration consider Fig. 3(d). On the vertical axis is shown all of the names used by the agents to name context C_4, hence there are 15 different names, since each agent is randomly assigned a name for each context at the start of the simulation. On the horizontal axis is the number of simulation steps and the plots show at each step the names S_{i4} used by all the agents for C_4. While it is difficult to follow the lines the most important point is that for simulation step > 3000 there is one name 'mrb' that is used by the agents for C_4. Between steps $[\approx 2000 - 3000]$ there are two names 'mrb', 'ghl' used by the agents for C_4. In this case, using only the names S_{i4} it is clear that some agents may not be able to communicate with all of the other agents information related to C_4.

Note when comparing the plots for the different contexts in Fig. 3 it seems that the final name for each context typically converges to the first or second name on the vertical axis. This is due to the way the simulation data is collected and processed and is not due to any bias in the simulation itself. The data on the name used by the agents for a context was only recorded when the agents were in that context. Hence the plot for the names at the top of the vertical axis sometimes only start after several hundred steps. This also allows us to conclude that typically the final unique name used to label a context by all the agents is quite often the name used by the agents found in the context at the beginning of the simulation.

Considering the results for each of the 6 contexts it is clear that the number of steps taken to reach a unique name for the contexts varies quite considerably from less than 2000 steps for context C_6 to almost 8000 steps for context C_3. So far we have stated that an agent can communicate with every other agent, information related to a context C_j, when $S_{ij} = S_{kj}, \forall i, k$. However this is quite a stringent condition and does not recognize the fact that each agent has a list of names $\mathcal{L}_{ij}$ associated with C_j.

Simulation 2. Instead of restricting the name for communicating information to other agents to just S_{ij} as defined in Eq. (4), Eq. (5) we allow each agent to use more than one name for each context which it can use to communicate

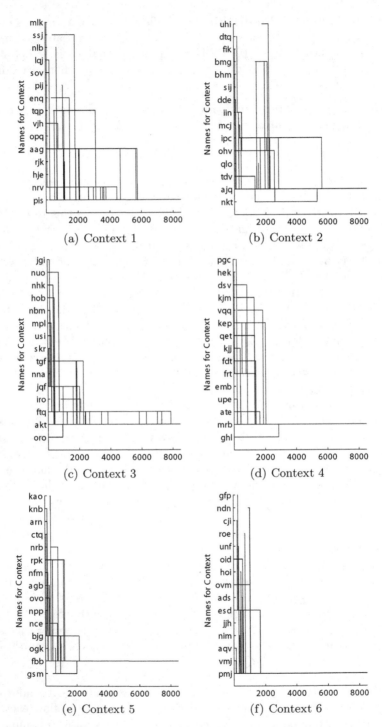

Fig. 3. Context name evolution v's number of simulation steps

with other agents. As an example, we allow each agent to have a maximum of 3 names for each context and S_{ij} is defined as a set of 3 names as follows,

$$S_{ij} = \{\psi_{ij}^{v_1}, \psi_{ij}^{v_2}, \psi_{ij}^{v_3}\} , \tag{14}$$

with

$$\omega_{ij}^{v_1}, \omega_{ij}^{v_2}, \omega_{ij}^{v_3} > \omega_{ij}^k, \quad \forall k \neq v_1, v_2, v_3 . \tag{15}$$

This means that the set of names S_{ij} corresponds to the labels from $\mathcal{L}_{ij}$ whose associated weights $\{\omega_{ij}^{v_1}, \omega_{ij}^{v_2}, \omega_{ij}^{v_3}\}$ are the 3 biggest weights in Ω_{ij}. In the next simulation we examine the time taken for an agent to be able to communicate with other agents based on this generalization of S_{ij}. The simulation scenario is the same as that in **Simulation 1** with 15 agents and 6 contexts. Figure 4 shows for each context, 3 plots of the number of agents able to communicate with more than 9, more than 12 and 15 (i.e. full-communication) of the other agents based on the generalized context name against the number of simulation steps. In contexts $5, 6$ the number of steps for all agents to be able to communicate with all other agents is less than 1250. On the other hand for context 2 it takes almost 4000 simulation steps before full agent communication is reached. However after 2000 simulation steps 12 of the agents are able to communicate with at least 12 of the other agents. This type of result is observed quite often where there are $2 - 3$ agents without a common label for a context for an extended number of simulation steps. This is followed by abrupt changes in the number of agents able to fully-communicate when these agents finally learn a commonly used name for a context. The reason for this is related to the fact that some agents, by chance, do not go to a certain context for a large number of time steps. Overall from Fig. 4 it is clear that using the more generalized definition of S_{ij} means the agents arrive at full-communication quicker (i.e. ≈ 4000 steps in Fig. 4), as against the more restricted case demonstrated in simulation 1 and Fig. 3.

The Choice of Simulation Parameters. In the simulations carried out there has been a certain choice of parameters. Most of the reasons for choosing the values of certain parameters are related to a visualization of the simulation. For example in Eq. (11) a value of 0.01 is used as a gain parameter which restricts the changes in positions of the agents to quite small values and is easier to follow on the screen. It also implies however that the number of simulation steps to travel between contexts and achieve full-communication is measured in 1000's of steps. This choice of 0.01 also affects the choice of $30 - 80$ steps that the agents spend in each context which in turn affects the parameter $\alpha = 0.01$ in Eq. (6), Eq. (7) and $\rho = 0.005$ in Eq. (9). Note that it is better that $\rho < \alpha$. The absolute values of these parameters is not important but what is more important is their relative values. In conclusion the choice of parameters does not greatly affect the simulation results rather its presentation.

4.2   Large Scale Simulation

In this section we examine the affect of varying the number of agents and contexts over a much larger range compared to that in the small scale simulations

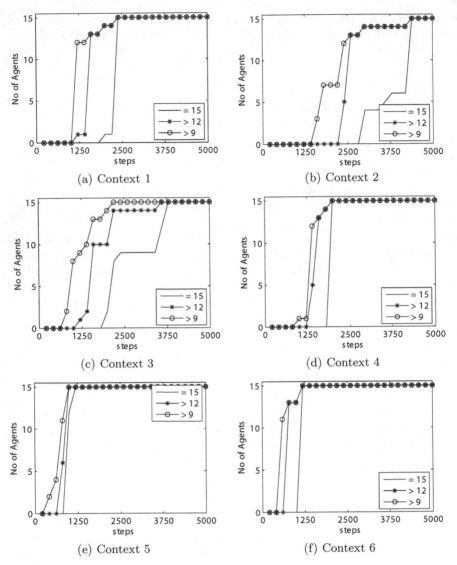

Fig. 4. Context labeling and the agents' ability to communicate based on the definition of S_{ij} in Eq. (14), Eq. (15)

of the previous section. The implementation of the labeling algorithm remains the same, however, for practical reasons some small changes have been made. As there is no visualization of the agents moving between contexts each agent is simply assigned to a context for a number of simulation steps. The number of simulation steps the agent remains in the context is chosen randomly in the range $2 - 10$. Once assigned to a context the agent starts to communicate name information and update name parameters as described in section 3. The parameter α of Eq. (7), (8) used in the update of the weights ω_{ij}^{k} is set to 0.1. In the case of the small scale simulations the convergence results were presented in terms of simulation steps which allows the relative speeds of convergence to be compared. In the following simulations we use a different measure of convergence time. The convergence time is measured as the average number of visits the agents make to a context. We define a convergence time R_j for each context j as

$$R_j = \frac{1}{P} \sum_{i=1}^{P} V_{ij} , \tag{16}$$

where once again P is the total number of agents in the simulation. V_{ij} is the total number of times agent i has visited context j at the first time when all agents have the same name $S_j = S_{ij} \; \forall \; i$ for context j. The definition of S_{ij} in Eq. (4), (5) is used. Hence R_j is a measure of the average number of visits agents make to context j until the state is reached where every agent has the same name for that context. The average convergence time over all contexts for a simulation, denoted by R, is defined as

$$R = \frac{1}{M} \sum_{j=1}^{M} R_j , \tag{17}$$

where once again M is the total number of contexts in the simulation. Figure 5 shows R plotted against $\log_{10}(P)$ of different numbers of agents P in the range $[10, 10000]$. Each line plot represents $R \; v's \; \log_{10}(P)$ for the same number of contexts. The 5 line plots respectively illustrate the results for $M = 5, 10, 20, 50, 100$. In fact each simulation with a given number of agents and contexts was repeated 5 times and the value of R that is plotted is the average taken over the 5 simulations. Based on this result the curves exhibit some interesting behavior and each curve could be considered as consisting of two parts.

If $M \ll P$ or there are significantly more agents than contexts the curves seem quite linear. It also appears that independent of the number of contexts the curves have a similar slope. For $M \geq P$ a curve's characteristic changes and R increases dramatically as the number of agents decreases below the number of contexts. Not plotted here is the value of $R \approx 93$ for $P = 10$ and $M = 100$. So for example in the case of $M = 20$ contexts and $P = 10$ agents then $R = 14.94$. Keeping 20 contexts and increasing the number of agents to 100 causes R to drop to 5.2. Increasing the number of agents from $100 - 10000$ gives an approximately straight line with $R = 7.23$ for $P = 1000$ and $R = 8.99$ for $P = 10000$. In this case the value of R increases by a factor of less than 2 while the number of agents increases by a factor of 100. This result would indicate that the characteristics of R are more dependent on the ratio P/M rather than the absolute values of M or P.

Intuitively the result of the simulation seems reasonable. One of the basic assumptions of the algorithm is that agents find themselves in contexts along with other agents. It is only by sharing information on labels that the names used by agents for a context can converge to the same name. In the case where $P < M$ and where there is equi-probability of an agent being in a context at any time

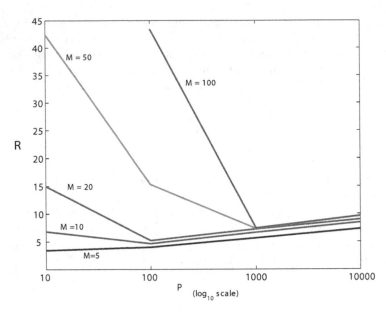

Fig. 5. A plot of the average convergence time R (Eq. (17)) versus $\log_{10}(P)$ with P. Each of the 5 lines is a plot for a different number of contexts M.

it is likely that an agent will find itself alone in a context. Hence agents have to visit contexts more often before eventually occupying the same context as other agents. On the other hand for $M > P$ the chances of several agents occupying the same context at the same time increases. This in turn facilitates the exchange of information and hence should speed up the convergence. Increasing the absolute number of agents should however act to increase the value of R. From a practical point of view it is reassuring that these results indicate the increase of R is linear with the logarithm of P for $M < P$. At least if R was directly proportional to P the method for labeling contexts described here would probably not be feasible in any sort of real-world application.

5   Modeling, Simulation and the Real-World

In this work we have raised the issue of naming and labeling locations and in the more general case contexts in a mobile environment. It is clear that this issue needs to be addressed in order to allow for the communication of location or context information in real-world applications. We have presented a basic model consisting of agents moving between contexts in a random fashion and communicating in an ad-hoc, peer-to-peer fashion. Based on this model we proposed a method using a general unsupervised learning algorithm which we claim would allow the agents to arrive at a consistent naming of the contexts. Simulating this simple model in an essentially perfect-world we have shown that the proposed labeling method does work in a reasonable manner. This is not to say that the model presented corresponds to the real-world, as it clearly does not, or that the proposed naming method would work in a real-world model or in the real-world itself. In the same way that we expect the model should be adapted to more closely reflect real-world characteristics we do not consider the naming method as fixed and it can also be adapted to handle the increased complexity of the real-world.

In the simulation the updating of the agents has happened at every simulation step. In a real-world application the question is how much time, for example minutes or seconds, does a simulation step correspond to? In fact a simulation step would probably not need to be reproduced in a real-world application. Rather the application would be event driven. For example when an agent establishes a new connection the exchange of information and name updates would occur only once. Consecutive repetitions of the updates in Eq. (7), (8) as happens in the simulation would be achieved in the real-world in a single repetition by increasing the value of α. Once again the most important factor in determining the context names is the relative value of the weights ω_{ij}^k rather than their absolute value. Of course agents would need to check periodically to see which agents are in their immediate vicinity.

The model does not take into account how real-world contexts may not be so well defined, even in the case of location. For example as explained in [12] when standing in exactly the same position at the boundary between two GSM network cells the location as defined by the Cell ID can fluctuate depending on environmental conditions. This could result in a group of agents physically beside each other but fluctuating between being in the same and different locations or Cell IDs. How does the naming method react in this situation, would it converge? The definitive answer would be found by modeling and simulating the situation. Our conjecture is that each agent would end up with the same name associated with each of the two Cell IDs.

Earlier we referred to high and low-level contexts which in terms of of location could be interpreted as a problem of resolution. GPS has a much higher resolution than Cell ID so a group of agents with GPS would be better able to distinguish different locations. In the case of a mixed group of agents some with GPS enabled devices and others only with Cell ID capability what would happen, which names would the labels for the contexts converge to? Intuitively all agents would probably end up with several names for the same location whether determined by GPS or Cell ID. This assumes of course that the name method is not changed. One option would be to introduce some form of hierarchical structure into the list of names associated with a given location or context which in turn would have an affect on the means of communicating name information between agents.

In conclusion the model, simulation and naming method described here serve primarily as an initial investigation of how unsupervised methods can be used in the naming and labeling of locations or contexts. This study raises as many, if not more, questions than it answers. Future work will concentrate on bringing the model and simulation closer to the real-world and adapting the unsupervised learning method to cope with the extra complexities that this entails.

6 Conclusion

The mobile device is set to become the pervasive device of the future. With the range of technologies available it will become an increasingly complex device to use and benefit from. Context awareness is one means of helping users to benefit from that which the device has to offer. Unsupervised learning of contexts has many advantages but has no means of communicating context related information between devices because it has no defined way of naming the learned contexts. The method we have proposed allows names to be assigned to contexts in a consistent manner across devices allowing for the communication of context related information. It also allows for communication between devices using approaches to context awareness, other than unsupervised learning, such as ontologies.

The one enabling technology required to achieve this is the ability for devices to make short range wireless connections, using for example Bluetooth. The assumption in this case is that devices in close proximity, what ever the means of defining the context, are in the same context. Simulations of the context naming paradigm indicate its feasibility for use in a mobile environment, requiring small memory and computational resources. The final proof of concept will be tested with real devices and users.

Acknowledgements

This work has been performed in the framework of the IST project IST-2004-511607 MobiLife, which is partly funded by the European Union. The author would like to acknowledge the contributions of his colleagues, although the views expressed are those of the author and do not necessarily represent the project.

The author would like to thank to Henk Muller for his guidance during the revision stage of this paper.

References

1. Dey, A.: Understanding and using context. Personal and Ubiquitous Computing **5** (2001) 4–7
2. Staab, S.: Handbook on Ontologies. Springer (2004)
3. Persson, P., Blom, J., Jung, Y.: Digidress: A field trial of an expressive social proximity application. In Beigl, M., ed.: 7th Intl' Conf. on Ubiquitous Computing (UbiComp), Berlin Heidelberg, Springer-Verlag (2005) 195–211 LNCS 3660.
4. Eagle, N., Pentland, A.: Social serendipity: Mobilizing social software. IEEE Pervasive Computing **4** (2005) 28–34
5. Moloney, S.: Simulation of a distributed recommendation system for pervasive networks. In: ACM Symposium on Applied Computing, Santa Fe, New Mexico, USA (2005) 1577–1581
6. Chen, H., Finin, T., Joshi, A.: An ontology for context-aware pervasive computing environments. Knowledge Engineering Review **18** (2004) 197–207 Special Issue on Ontologies for Distributed Systems.

7. Wang, X., Zhang, D.Q., Gu, T., Pung, H.K.: Ontology-based context modeling and reasoning using OWL. In: Workshop on Context Modeling and Reasoning at IEEE International Conference on Pervasive Computing and Communication (PerCom'04), Orlando, Florida, US (2004)
8. Korpipää, P., Mäntyjärvi, J.: An ontology for a mobile device sensor-based context awareness. In: Proc. Context03. LNAI no. 2680, Springer-Verlag (2003) 451–459
9. Flanagan, J.: Context awareness in a mobile device: Ontologies versus unsupervised/supervised learning. In T. Honkela, V. Könönen M. Pöllä, O.S., ed.: Intl' and Interdisciplinary Conf. on Adpative Knowledge Representation and Reasoning, (AKKR05), Espoo, Finland, Otamedia Oy (2005) 167–170
10. Flanagan, J.A.: Unsupervised clustering of context data and learning user requirements for a mobile device. In Dey, A., ed.: Fifth International and Interdisciplinary Conference on Modeling and Using Context (CONTEXT-05), Berlin Heidelberg, Springer-Verlag LNAI 3554 (2005) 155–168
11. Flanagan, J.A., Mäntyjärvi, J., Himberg, J.: Unsupervised clustering of symbol strings and context recognition. In: IEEE Intl' Conf. on Data Mining (ICDM02), Maebashi City, Japan (2002) 171–178
12. Battestini, A., Flanagan, J.: Analysis and cluster based modelling and recognition of context in a mobile environment. In Roth-Berghofer, T., Schulz, S., Leake, D., eds.: Proc. of the 2nd Intl' Workshop on Modeling and Retrieval of Context (MRC), ISSN 1613-0073 (2005) 85–96 online CEUR-WS.org//Vol-146//.

Building Common Ground for Face to Face Interactions by Sharing Mobile Device Context

Vassilis Kostakos, Eamonn O'Neill, and Anuroop Shahi

Department of Computer Science,
University of Bath,
Bath BA2 7AY, UK
{vk, eamon}@cs.bath.ac.uk, anu.shahi@gmail.com

Abstract. We describe an application used to share context and build common ground between nearby users. Our application runs on mobile devices and allows users securely to exchange the contents of their address books. This exchange reveals only which entries are common to the two users. We explore the use of our application using both Bluetooth and NFC as an underlying technology. Finally, we present the results of a small user study we have conducted.

1 Introduction

A frequent activity amongst people who meet for the first time is the establishment, and subsequent refinement, of common ground [3]. When we meet someone we do not know, we often try to establish whom and what we have in common. This shared knowledge, referred to as common ground, is used to frame our communication. In this paper we describe a mobile application that facilitates the process of sharing and establishing common ground between people within physical proximity.

A number of similar systems have previously been developed, but we feel they are overambitious in their design; they try to replace, rather than assist, the human ability to communicate with other humans within physical proximity. Our system does not aim to strengthen the social bonds within communities, nor to provide its users with new friends; these are things that still need to be done by humans. Our aim is to assist users in building common ground by means of identifying shared context. There are of course many different elements of common ground or shared context. For our purposes in this paper, the shared context is already stored in users' address books: whom they know. Using our application, two users can identify their common address book entries.

In this paper we explore the implementation of our system with two proximity-based technologies: Bluetooth and Near Field Communication (NFC)[1]. Because of their differences, these two technologies offer distinct social affordances to users, and allow for different uses of our application. Specifically, Bluetooth systems can act as a first point of contact, while with NFC this is not the case. We also present our

---

[1] See http://www.nfc-forum.org

M. Hazas, J. Krumm, and T. Strang (Eds.): LoCA 2006, LNCS 3987, pp. 222–238, 2006.

findings from a small user study. Our results point to the perceived utility of our application, and highlight the differences in the underlying technologies as a crucial factor in shaping users' experience and use.

In Section 2 we present related work in this area, and in Section 3 we describe the motivation and theoretical background which informed the development of our system. In Section 4 we describe two different versions of our system, based on Bluetooth and NFC respectively. Here we describe the implementation process, and highlight the technical implications of our theoretical motivation. Finally, in Section 5 we discuss the results of a small user study we carried out to compare the two systems, and the feedback we obtained from users.

2 Related Work

A number of systems have been developed that aim to socially engage and connect their users. Most common are online web portals such as Friendster.com and Match.com. Such systems typically allow users to upload their profile and search for others with similar profiles or specific criteria. These portals are only available online, and are thus suitable for computer-mediated communication rather than face-to-face, co-located interactions.

An interesting category of systems is based on the notion of familiar strangers [12]. One such example is Jabberwocky [15]. This application continuously scans the environment for other Bluetooth devices, and gradually builds a visual map of the familiar strangers that the user encounters. Although Jabberwocky mainly shows graphical information about nearby devices, users can gradually get a feel for the environment around them, and the people next to them. The Telelogs application [6] takes a further step in allowing for interactions between familiar strangers. This system allows profiles in the form of auditory blogs to be shared between familiar strangers. If two people encounter each other more than once, they obtain access to each other's most recent voice blog entry. This information allows strangers to gradually get to know each other. The information delivered with this system depends on the sender or broadcaster of the Telelogs. Crucially, this means that the information could potentially be irrelevant to the recipients. Additionally, users need to record new audio blogs daily in order to keep their profile up to date.

An interesting application which makes use of implicit user input is ContextContacts [16]. This application allows for presence and context cues to be shared between users over the network. ContextContacts is used between people who already know each other. Information such as location, time spent there, state of the phone (ringer, vibrator), and number of friends or strangers nearby is shared via servers over the network. This application acts very much like instant messaging applications, and is aimed at enhancing the communication between friends across distances.

A system which tries to bridge the gap between online services and local interactions is BlueAware [8]. This system runs on mobile devices and scans every 5 minutes for nearby Bluetooth devices. When it detects a new device, it sends the device's BTID to an online server. The server carries out a comparison between the two users' profiles. If there is a match, the server sends both users an alert, along with the photo of the other user, their commonalities, as well as contact information. An issue with this system is the need for establishing communication links with an online server and service. Also, the recipients of an introductory message are not informed whether or not the other user has been made aware of the receiving message, or if in fact the other person is still in their vicinity. This system, however, remains an interesting adaptation of online dating services to local situations.

The need for an online third party is overcome with Nokia's Sensor[2] system. This system allows users to broadcast their profile locally using Bluetooth. Users can actively search for Sensor-enabled phones around them, and can view others' profiles as well as engage in text-based conversation. With Sensor, users engage in direct and live interactions, but the problems of the broadcast model associated with Telelogs apply here. Also, Sensor relies on explicit input for providing an up to date profile of its user. Despite its commercialisation, Sensor does not appear to have successfully penetrated the market.

A similar system is Bluedating [2], which works by storing dating profiles on users' mobile devices and then uses Bluetooth to discover and transfer profiles found on nearby devices. All matching is performed on the mobile device therefore avoiding the need for a central matching service. Similar to Nokia Sensor, this system relies on users' explicit input for updating their profile. Additionally, the broadcast nature of this system leaves room for potential abuse by users. Finally, the system does not guarantee that both users will be aware of the matching.

Many interesting systems have been developed to date, but we feel that most of them fall short of their own expectations. A number of factors contribute to the apparent difficulty in socially engaging friends or strangers via the use of technology. These factors include:

- the complexity of the technology involved, which can act as a barrier rather than an enabler
- the sometimes irrelevant information being broadcast by users
- the potential for abuse
- the outdated information presented in users' profiles
- the possibly inconsistent levels of awareness between the users
- the social awkwardness of being introduced to a nearby person via a non-human entity.

These are issues which we have attempted to address in the design of our application. We now proceed to describe the motivation and background to our application.

3   Motivation and Background

3.1   Building Common Ground

Part of the work of getting to know someone is in determining and constructing shared knowledge, assumptions and beliefs. Stalnaker [18] coined the term common ground to include shared or mutual knowledge, assumptions and beliefs, while Clark [3] presents an extensive body of work on the construction of common ground in language use. However, Clark [4] identifies language use, and its reliance on common

---

[2] See http://www.nokia.com/sensor

ground, as just one example of the more general notion of a joint activity. Other examples of joint activities are playing music together, working on a shared drawing, dancing, playing games, and using technology together. Successful collaborative activities both depend on and contribute to the construction of common ground.

Clark and Marshall [5] proposed that "very often mutual knowledge is established by a combination of physical or linguistic copresence and mutual knowledge based on community membership" (p.41). Later, Clark [4] refined this proposal to two main types of evidence used in constructing common ground:

(i) evidence of common membership of cultural communities;
(ii) joint perceptual experiences and joint actions.

Evidence of common membership of cultural communities and associated assumptions (such as universality of particular knowledge within the community) leads to communal common ground, while joint perceptual experiences, joint actions and associated assumptions (such as rationality and shared inductive standards) leads to personal common ground. Personal common ground is specific common ground established amongst people who share a joint experience. However, their assumptions of rationality and shared inductive standards depend ultimately on their previously established communal common ground.

Our premise is that effectively to facilitate co-located social interaction, it is best to assist, rather than to replace, human capabilities. This is a well established HCI principle [e.g. 7]. Our fine-tuned human communication capabilities can only be hindered if we introduce cumbersome devices and mechanisms aimed at carrying out communication on behalf of humans. This is evident in the numerous systems already developed. Fundamentally, we still need to establish eye contact, body language and verbal communication [9, 13]. Technology, we maintain, should be focused on assisting where the advantages over "manual" mode are clear.

In this respect, the construction of common ground is an aspect of social interaction that may lend itself to technological assistance. The most important basis for the construction of common ground, *evidence of common membership* of cultural communities, is often difficult to establish. Every day, we implicitly and explicitly provide such evidence to others through our appearance, the ways we dress, our language and accent, and in many other ways. Yet there are no such commonly used indicators for one critical aspect of our membership of cultural communities: whom we know. Often, this evidential basis for communal common ground is built up serendipitously and we may take moments or years to discover that we have a friend in common.

3.2 Locally Sharing Address Book Information

Our application uses Bluetooth, NFC and mobile device address books as a means of locally sharing context for a number of reasons. Increasingly, through our use of mobile devices such as smartphones, we carry around with us a large body of evidence of our membership of cultural communities, in a form that is accessible by us and potentially by others. A contacts or address book on a mobile device stores details about the people we know and often includes implicit and explicit information about which cultural communities we share with them. The information stored in address books describes our family, friends, colleagues and institutions that have been meaningful enough to us that we have stored them.

Our use of mobile device address book data seeks to provide the first of Clark's [4] evidential bases of common ground: *common membership of cultural communities.* Our use of Bluetooth and NFC as the data sharing technologies seeks to provide the second: *copresent joint actions and joint perceptual experiences.* In Figure 1 we show how our system relates to the identification of communal common ground, and the generation of personal common ground.

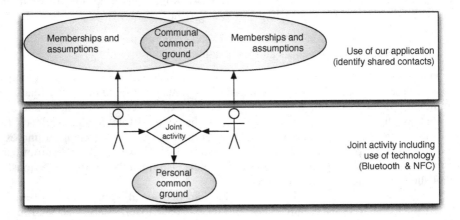

Fig. 1. Our application helps users identify their communal common ground (top half) by helping them identify whom they know in common. The copresent use of the enabling technology (Bluetooth and NFC) supports the creation of personal common ground (bottom half).

Both Bluetooth and NFC rely on physical copresence for communication – they are proximity-based, rather than location-based, communication channels – and both rely on enabling actions performed by the users. However, both the physical range of communication and the joint enabling actions are very different between Bluetooth and NFC. These differences and their influences on the utility, usability and acceptability of our application is an exciting research issue raised by this work.

There are other advantages to our choice of mobile device address books. Particularly in the case of mobile phones, address books are used extensively and frequently. Hence, address books are typically well maintained by users. By drawing on address book information, we are making use of implicit user input, reducing the burden of having explicitly to enter and update information specifically for our application. Thus, we overcome the problem of outdated profiles that seems to deter the use of similar systems.

Also, the information stored in address books (i.e. telephone numbers and email addresses) is effectively unique in identifying a person or entity. This feature lends itself to comparison and matching. Furthermore, our encryption scheme is based on this uniqueness.

Because users share common information only with others who are physically local, this is a convenient way of addressing the problems associated with a broadcast model (swamping users with irrelevant information).

Finally, we felt that this application could potentially be controversial; after all, advertising and broadcasting one's own address book is not commonplace. We are interested in developing such provocative applications as a vehicle for probing and better understanding users' attitudes towards social technology and pervasive computing.

3.3 Security and Privacy Concerns

From the outset of this research, we were aware of potential privacy concerns. In our system, we decided to address two main privacy concerns in relation to exchanging address books:

- Can others gain access to all of my address book entries?
- Even though I have a contact in common with another user, I may want to hide this fact.

The first concern relates to the fact that our application transmits the whole address during an exchange process. This raises the issue of how much of this information can be read by the receiving party. We address this concern by employing a one-way hash function using an SHA-1 algorithm (as defined in FIPS PUB 180-1)[3]. This generates a digest for each entry in the address book, which cannot (easily) be reverse engineered to retrieve the original piece of information. An exchange, therefore, involves generating digests for each entry in the address book (name, phone, email) and transmitting every digest. On the receiving end, the device generates digests for each of its local entries, and compares the local digests to the received digests. Since local digests can be traced back to their source, the receiving party can associate local information with received digests.

The result is that if both Alice and Bob have Peter's phone number, Alice will be shown only her local information about Peter (e.g. "Peter (Husband)"), which may be different to what Bob sees (e.g. "Peter (Coach)"). This encryption scheme, therefore, can reveal the common entries (such as a phone number) with another user, while displaying to each user only the information that user already had about the entry.

Another concern relates to the fact that a user may wish to hide their relationship with certain individuals. Sharing "too much" context could lead to potentially awkward, or even harmful situations. We addressed this issue by drawing on the information classification presented in [14]. Based on this work, users can classify entries in the address book as belonging to the public or private sphere.

In our system, private entries are completely hidden from all operations of our system. This means that private entries are neither transmitted nor used locally to check for matches with received digests. On the other hand, public entries are always used in the exchange process. By default, new entries are private.

---

[3] For the SHA-1 standard, see http://www.itl.nist.gov/fipspubs/fip180-1.htm

3.4 Technological Affordances

There are a number of technologies that could be used for carrying out the digest exchange. Such technologies include SMS, MMS, Infrared, HTTP/Web, GPRS, WiFi, Bluetooth and NFC. We decided to implement our application using Bluetooth and NFC for a number of reasons.

First, both Bluetooth and NFC are proximity-based technologies; thus, communication taking place with these technologies has to be between nearby users. This was an important feature, as we were interested in supporting the construction of common ground between users having copresent interactions. Additionally, both of these technologies support true peer-to-peer interactions, as opposed to server-based interactions. This aligns the technological interactions provided by our system more closely to the copresent interactions of users.

Despite their similarity in being proximity-based technologies, Bluetooth and NFC support very different social interactions. Bluetooth, on the one hand, allows for interacting with someone across the room or train carriage. Depending on the class of the Bluetooth device, this can be up to 10, 100 or 250 metres. On the other hand, NFC requires that the two devices are physically within 2 cm of each other. This difference in range plays a crucial role in the affordances of the technologies, and the interactions they can support. This is a dimension we were interested in exploring, and these differences were observed in our study.

With Bluetooth, two people can use our application without having established prior physical communication (in the form of eye contact, body language, or verbal communication). On the other hand, the use of NFC requires that the users and devices enter each other's "intimate zones" [10]. For this to take place, users will almost certainly have established some form of previous physical communication. Thus, although Bluetooth and NFC are both proximity-based peer-to-peer technologies, their affordances in relation to our application are very different. With Bluetooth, our system may be used without prior physical communication. In this case, communication will be between strangers. With NFC, our system almost certainly will not be the first point of contact. In this case, communication will be between people who have already communicated at least to the extent of allowing intrusion into their intimate zones.

Also, the different ranges of Bluetooth and NFC create two different models of interaction between the users. Using Bluetooth, users need verbally to negotiate and coordinate their efforts to exchange data. With NFC, users have the cue of physically touching their phones. This tangible interaction is an explicit action which synchronises both the data exchange between devices and the coordination process between the users.

3.5 Interaction Design

In addition to the restrictions imposed by technology, the interface of our system enforces certain rules in the underlying social interaction model. These rules are consistent between both the Bluetooth and NFC versions of our system. These are:

- An exchange is always two-way.
- No exchange can take place without explicit input from both users.
- The received digests are discarded after the comparison.

The first feature is used to ensure reciprocity in the social interactions. Reciprocity has been shown to have a positive effect on human-human and human-computer interaction [e.g. 17]. By requiring both users to exchange address book digests, we ensure the presence of reciprocity.

The requirement for explicit user input is used to ensure that both parties are aware of the exchange taking place. This avoids the problems inherent in systems like BlueAware where users may not be aware of the interaction taking place. Additionally, it also avoids unwanted interactions and potential privacy breaches. In the case of Bluetooth, this could be a potential threat of unwittingly broadcasting information. In the case of NFC, this could accidentally happen in situations such as in a crowded bus, where people stand close to each other and have their phones in their pockets.

Finally, by discarding the received digests, our application reflects the ephemeral nature of social interaction. This is a concern which has been shown to be of importance to users [1]. Obviously, this restriction can easily be lifted, as one could develop a similar system that actually records the received digests. These could potentially be used for future reference — for example, being alerted that the contact you just added exists in a previously received digest. Additionally, by collecting a large number of digests, one could start building up a model of the social network represented in the digests. Despite these potential uses however, we felt that the perceived ephemeral nature of social interaction is a key aspect, and so we opted to preserve it in the current version of our application. Not recording the digests also avoids potential problems of received digests becoming outdated. As noted in Section 2, our use of implicit input in the form of address book entries addresses the problem of keeping information up to date. But this is undermined if digests are kept by a receiving user since updates made in the sender's address book after the synchronisation will not be reflected in the digest.

4 The Address Book Application

Our system runs on mobile devices with J2ME, such as phones and PDAs, and allows users to encrypt and exchange address book information. This includes names, phone numbers, and email addresses stored in users' mobile devices. For our prototype, these were stored directly in our application instead of tapping into the phone's native address book. Accessing the phone's native address book was not possible across all the devices for which we were developing, but is becoming increasingly achievable as J2ME is upgraded and phones are changed. Before a data exchange takes place, our system performs a one-way encryption (digest) of every entry in the address book. This ensures that the two-way exchange can reveal only information that is common to the users. Additionally, users have the option of identifying certain entries as "Private" (as opposed to "Public") thereby withdrawing them from the exchange process.

The functionality of our system is shown in Figure 2. We developed two versions of our system - one using Bluetooth (on a Nokia 6680) and one using NFC (on a Nokia 3220 with NFC shell). Unfortunately a phone with both Bluetooth and NFC

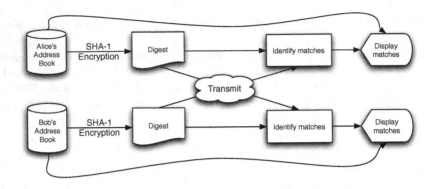

Fig. 2. Alice and Bob exchange digests of their address books. They then compare the received digests with their local digests to identify matches. Alice is then shown her local information linked to the matches, and so is Bob. The displayed information is not necessarily identical.

is not yet available. The interface functionality was the same across both systems, but each device rendered the interface components differently. This is a feature of J2ME over which we had no control.

4.1   The Encryption Scheme

We utilised the SHA-1 algorithm for generating the digests. Our implementation was based on Sam Ruby's port of SHA-1 to J2ME[4]. Our encryption scheme works as follows. Each device generates digests of all its address book entries. These digests are locally concatenated into one long string which is exchanged with the other device. Each device then generates a digest for each local entry, and searches for it in the received digest. If the local digest is found in the received digest, this means that the local entry also exists on the remote device. At the end of this process, the device displays a summary of the matched entries.

One obvious problem with this scheme is that string matching needs to be exact. For instance, a telephone number such as +1 123 1234567 would not match the number 123 1234567. This is because the digests of each number would be different. This issue can be addressed by a filter which turns phone numbers into a uniform format before encryption. The same problem applies to names. For instance, "Dr. Alice" would not match "Alice". This, however, is not such a problem with email addresses, as they tend to be recorded without variations.

A brute-force attack could decrypt the transmitted digests. This is because the full strength of the encryption algorithm is not utilised, as the input strings are actually smaller than the generated digests. Prior to encryption, each string is appended with padding bits, as described in the SHA-1 standard. The number of combinations that would have to be tried are in the range of 35^(length-of-data). Thus, a digest of a 10 digit number would require approximately 2.75e+15 comparisons. Effectively, critical information should not be shared using our application (either by not including it in the address book, or by marking it as Private).

---

4 See http://www.intertwingly.net/blog/2004/07/18/Base64-of-SHA1-for-J2ME

4.2 The Bluetooth Implementation

The Bluetooth and NFC versions of our application have the same hashing and matching functionality. Their differences lie in the communication protocol, and the required user actions to initiate the communication. Our Bluetooth application (Figure 3) runs as a multi-threaded application. It can serve and respond to Exchange requests from nearby peers, together with performing exchange requests on behalf of the user. Our application exposes a proprietary Bluetooth service for carrying out the address book exchange. Note that private entries are indicated with an exclamation mark.

To perform an exchange over Bluetooth, the user first selects the "Exchange" option causing the application to perform a Bluetooth inquiry scan that discovers all Bluetooth devices situated within close proximity to the user. Once discovered, all devices are listed by their Bluetooth defined names. The user can then select the desired device name to initiate the exchange process. This name identifies who the user

Fig. 3. Using Bluetooth, a user needs to activate the exchange mechanism (photos 1 to 4). The other user is alerted to the request for exchange (photo 5). If the user agrees, the phones carry out a two-way exchange of digests. Upon successful completion of the exchange, the phones present the common entries (photo 6).

will interact with. This name is customisable by the owner of the device, and sample names include "John's phone" and "Nokia 6680".

Once a connection has been established, the application determines whether the proprietary service is available on the target device; if so, an exchange is attempted causing an alert message to appear on the remote device. Essentially, this message acts as a prompt allowing a user to participate in an exchange with the requesting device; if the user accepts, a mutual exchange of the address books is performed over Bluetooth based RFCOMM channels. Upon a successful exchange, both devices display the matches.

4.3 The NFC Implementation

Near Field Communication (NFC) is an RFID based communication protocol targeted at mobile devices. A number of companies are members of the NFC Forum, and NFC-enabled devices are beginning to emerge in the market. NFC allows for communication between devices and tags with a range of approximately 2-3 cm. Envisioned applications for this technology include mobile ticketing, physical hyperlinking, secure purchasing, and service discovery.

The initial concept behind NFC was for devices to establish a trusted connection due to the physical limitation of the protocol's range. This connection would then be used to negotiate a long-range protocol, such as Bluetooth or WiFi. Thus, it was envisioned that two users could physically touch their laptops to establish a trusted WiFi connection (via an NFC negotiation), or touch two phones to establish a trusted Bluetooth connection (again via an NFC negotiation). The other proposed use of NFC was for users to touch their phones on a tag in order to receive information about an artefact or service associated with the tag. Our use of NFC for peer to peer device communication is quite different to the intended uses of NFC, and in this sense is novel.

We developed our application on a Nokia 3320 NFC-enabled phone. Development was done using the Nokia J2ME NFC SDK. Additionally we used the Nokia UI API Extension For Nokia 3220 Lights to employ the lights and vibrator of the phone as a means of user feedback. The hashing and matching functionality is identical to that used with the Bluetooth system.

The first obstacle we had to overcome with NFC was that users could not easily use their phone's keypad while touching another phone. This meant that our system could not ask for user input while an NFC communication was taking place. Additionally, we found that users could not easily read the phone's screen while touching another phone; this meant that we had to use the phone's lights and vibrator to notify users of the progress and status of the exchange.

A minor problem was the fact that when the battery level dropped below approximately 20 percent, the operating system did not allow for connections to the NFC hardware. This caused inexplicable behaviour by our software, as exceptions were raised for no apparent reason.

Another problem we faced was that, currently, NFC does not allow for a direct communication channel between devices. Existing phones have an NFC reader which can also emulate a tag. Therefore, two-way communications are made slow because to switch from receiving to sending data, a device must alter its hardware configuration from acting as a reader to emulating a tag, and wait for the partner device to read the information. This means that, effectively, two-way protocol exchanges are slowed.

One way of carrying out the two-way digest exchange would be to have two inter-face options: "Send information" and "Receive information". This would make the NFC exchanges themselves very fast, but would require extra user input as well as physically separating and retouching the phones.

Our solution was to have only one interface option — "Exchange". Both users had to select "Exchange", and then touch the devices. At this stage, both devices would be attempting to send as well as receive information. What happens in practice is that, apparently randomly, one of the two devices succeeds in transmitting the data first. At this stage, the devices have to rediscover each other (whilst still touching) and carry out the second part of the exchange.

In short, the use of our NFC system is as follows: both users issue the exchange command. At this stage the phone lights glow orange to indicate the discovery stage. The users then touch their phones for 5-7 seconds, during which time the phone lights blink red to indicate communication. Finally, the users are notified by a vibration and green blinking lights that the exchange was successful. Any matches then appear on the phones' displays.

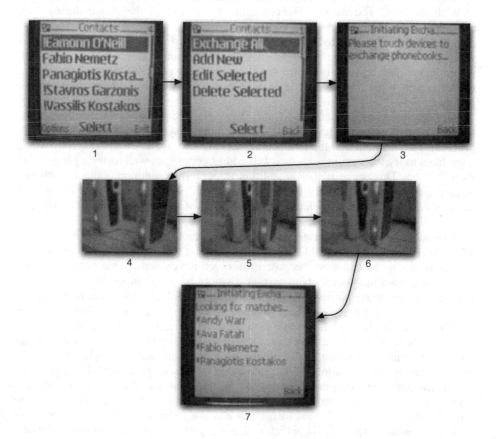

Fig. 4. Using NFC, both users need to activate the exchange mechanism (photos 1 to 3). The users place the phones next to each other, and wait for the exchange to take place (photos 4 to 6). The phones then display the common entries (photo 7).

5   Results of a User Study

We have so far carried out a limited user evaluation of our application with five participants. Our study was a probe aimed at getting some initial reactions and feedback from users. Specifically, we were interested in observing instances of joint activities, which in turn could lead to the establishment and construction of common ground.

Each trial involved one participant and one of the authors, and all participants used both the Bluetooth and NFC systems. The participants were undergraduate students at our university, aged 18-24, and they did not receive any financial compensations. All participants previously owned mobile phones for more than one year.

We gave each user a phone and explained to them how the system works. For training purposes, we asked them to enter some names, numbers and emails into our application. This helped users get acquainted with the phone itself as well as our application. We then carried out the exchange of digests. We repeated the same process with the second system. We observed users during the trials, and all users were asked open-ended questions about the systems and their impressions and attitudes.

With the NFC system we observed limited usability of the phone during NFC communication. This observation confirmed our predictions during the design process. Additionally, we had to explain to the participants that the purpose of our system was *not* to exchange phone numbers. All our participants commented that the NFC technology would be very useful for simply exchanging phone numbers. This appears to be a user requirement which currently is not effectively addressed by mobile phones.

All participants mentioned that identifying common contacts is something they often do with new acquaintances. They claimed that our system could help them in this process. Two claimed that the trial setting was not very realistic, and that they would have liked to try the system with their full address books, as well as trying it out with their friends. This suggests that in addition to exploring common contacts with new acquaintances, users would try to do the same with people they already know well. This reflects our observation that without this kind of technological aid we may take years to discover that we have a friend in common.

Participants appeared to prefer the NFC application for face to face interactions. When asked to elaborate on this, they claimed that it was easier to carry out the exchange using the NFC system because it involved fewer steps. One participant preferred the Bluetooth system, claiming that it would be useful in getting to know new people. However, one participant claimed that she would be very reluctant to respond to Bluetooth exchange requests from someone unknown. She claimed that with Bluetooth everyone could "see" her, while with NFC only friends could "see" her.

Our trials highlighted the importance of the underlying technology in establishing common ground. In Section 3.1 we identified joint experiences as a primary basis for the construction of common ground. Our observations suggest that NFC provides a much stronger joint experience because of the physical act of touching the phones. This is symmetric between users, and they receive the same feedback from the phones. With Bluetooth, the joint experience is not so strong; Bluetooth technology imposes a request-reply model, which makes the experience asymmetrical. Furthermore, there is little or no physical interaction using Bluetooth.

From our discussions with participants, we conclude that both systems can be useful in certain situations, their usefulness relating to the affordances and limitations of the two technologies. The choice of Bluetooth or NFC for exchanging address books depends on the type of experience that a user wants. Bluetooth will be preferred in situations where the user wants to meet or "discover" someone new. Another potential benefit of Bluetooth is that it does not give away strong physical cues, so users seeking to remain "hidden" will prefer Bluetooth. NFC may be preferred if the users are having a face to face conversation and are close enough to touch their phones. Additionally, the joint physical experience and ease of interaction when using NFC makes it preferable to use when the users are very proximate and have already established the common ground necessary to permit intrusion into one's intimate zone of very close proximity.

Crucially, however, the technology itself has an effect on the joint action experienced by users. NFC provides a much more engaging physical experience, which is reinforced by the symmetry of users' physical actions. This fosters the establishment of common ground. Conversely, Bluetooth's weak and asymmetrical physical user actions contribute less to the construction of common ground. In Table 1 we provide a summary of the lessons learned from the evaluation of our system.

Table 1. Lessons learned from our evaluation of the address book application

Bluetooth	NFC
• Could be useful for getting to meet strangers	• Limited usability when using the phone
• Users reluctant to respond to requests from unknowns	• Participants initially thought the system would exchange numbers
• Does not give away physical location of user	• Preferred for face to face interaction
• Weak joint experience	• Strong joint experience
• Request - reply model	• Symmetric model

6   Conclusions and Ongoing Work

In this paper we describe a system that enables the sharing of context between users in physical proximity. Drawing on our survey of existing systems, we identified a number of problems which we addressed in our design. We utilise users' address books as the source of context. Using our application, two users are made aware of the common entries in their address books. This informs the users of part of their shared context and reveals a critical aspect of their communal common ground. We have implemented our system with two proximity-based technologies: Bluetooth and NFC.

Our user study suggested a preference for NFC over Bluetooth for interactions with friends. This is due to a combination of the affordances of each technology. NFC offers synchronous reciprocity – making the same interface actions at the same time, simultaneously reaching out to each other, getting the same kind of feedback at the same time. NFC also requires that the users feel comfortable with coming into each other's intimate zones of very close proximity. Bluetooth interaction is less synchronous and less reciprocal and requires no intimate proximity or tangible interaction. With Bluetooth you may not even be able to see or hear the other user.

Conversely, our user study suggested a preference for Bluetooth over NFC for interactions with strangers. In this case, the very same affordances of the technologies make Bluetooth more appropriate than NFC to supporting the social processes involved. Strangers typically do not appreciate our intrusion into their intimate zones.

Interesting distinctions appeared in relation to our theoretical motivations of supporting the construction of common ground through evidence of shared community membership and joint actions and experiences. The mutual identification of common contacts was intended to provide users with evidence of shared community membership. This is effective in the face to face situation (required by NFC and possible with Bluetooth) partly because the users are likely already to have some established communal common ground that has brought them together in the first place. It is also effective in a face to face situation because the users enjoy mutual knowledge that the contacts are common to both users. In other words, each user not only knows that he shares contacts with the other, copresent user. In addition, he knows that the other user knows that they share these contacts, and so on *ad infinitum*. This mutual knowledge is the cornerstone of common ground [4, 11, 18].

In contrast, it can be less effective with Bluetooth when the users are not face to face, since the users may be completely unknown to each other and therefore lack previously established communal common ground. It is also less effective when users are not face to face since they may not know with whom they have established a Bluetooth connection. In this case, each user simply knows that he has common contacts with someone in reasonably close proximity. He has no knowledge of which nearby people actually have the common contacts. In turn, there can be no mutual knowledge, so a key component of common ground is missing.

Our system has taken into account issues raised by previous "social software" applications. Our user study has suggested some user preferences for one technology or the other depending on the situation and user desires, and indicates that users may find our system useful, although an extensive evaluation study is required to make any more definitive statements. We are currently planning such a study. We are interested in exploring the use of our system in a more realistic environment, where users are shown actual matches from their own address books. This would allow us to assess the impact of actual common ground between two users of our system.

Another dimension we wish to explore is a comparison of the use of our system between friends versus new acquaintances versus strangers. We are interested in identifying situations were two friends or two strangers will feel comfortable enough to carry out a phonebook match. Such an evaluation will have to take place in the field, in a setting such as a cafeteria or restaurant. We also wish to explore further the impact of the two different technologies on the use of our application, and gain a better understanding of the strengths and weaknesses of both Bluetooth and NFC in relation to face to face and proximate communication and interaction.

Finally, the address book application can be augmented to handle additional types of information. For instance, by including company or university names, our system would indicate that the two users know people from the same organisation. Furthermore, our matching system can be adapted to handle different types of data which can also serve as indicators of common context. For example, we can utilise schedule and calendar data to identify common free slots between users. Another example would be to identify common preferences, common Internet bookmarks or music that both users listen to.

Acknowledgements

The authors' research is funded by the UK Engineering and Physical Sciences Research Council grant EP/C547683/1 (Cityware: urban design and pervasive systems). We thank Vodafone Group R&D and Nokia Insight & Foresight for their support of this work. We also thank Stavros Garzonis, Andy Warr, Kharsim Al Mosawi, Tim Kindberg and Danaë Stanton Fraser.

References

1. Adams, A. and Sasse, M. A. (1999). Privacy Issues in Ubiquitous Multimedia Environments: Wake Sleeping Dogs, or Let Them Lie? In proceedings of INTERACT 1999, pp. 214-221.
2. Beale, R. (2005). "Supporting social interaction with the smartphone – designing pervasive systems", IEEE Pervasive Computing, 4(2): 35-41.
3. Clark, H.H. (1992). Arenas of language use, Chicago, University of Chicago Press.
4. Clark, H.H. (1996). Using language, Cambridge, Cambridge University Press.
5. Clark, H.H. and Marshall, C.R. (1981). Definite reference and mutual knowledge. In A.K. Joshi, B.L. Webber and I.A. Sag (eds) Elements of discourse understanding, Cambridge, Cambridge University Press, pp. 10-63.
6. Davis B. and Karahalis, K. (2005). Telelogs: a social communication space for urban environments. In proceedings of the 7th interantional Conference on Human Computer interaction with Mobile Devices & Services (MobileHCI '05), pp. 231-234.
7. Dix, A., Finlay, J., Abowd, G. D. and Beale, R. (2003). Human-computer interaction. 3rd Edition, London, Prentice Hall Europe.
8. Eagle, N. and Pentland, A. (2005). Reality mining: sensing complex social systems. Journal of Personal and Ubiquitous Computing, December 2005, pp. 1-14.
9. Grayson, D. M. and Monk, A. F. (2003). Are you looking at me? Eye contact and desktop video conferencing. ACM TOCHI, 10(3): 221-243.
10. Hall, E. T. (1969). The hidden dimension. Man's use of space in public and private. Bodley Head, London.
11. Lewis, D.K. (1969). Convention: a philosophical study, Cambridge, MA, Harvard University Press.
12. Milgram, S. (1977). The individual in a social world: essays and experiments. Reading, Mass.: Addison-Wesley Pub. Co.
13. Nardi, B. (2005). Beyond bandwidth: Dimension of connection in interpersonal interaction. The Journal of Computer-supported Cooperative Work, 14: 91-130.
14. O'Neill, E., Woodgate, D. and Kostakos, V. (2004) Easing the wait in the Emergency Room: building a theory of public information systems. In proceedings of the ACM Designing Interactive Systems (DIS '04), Boston, MA., pp. 17-25.
15. Paulos, E. and Goodman, E. (2004). The familiar stranger: anxiety, comfort, and play in public spaces. In proceedings of CHI '04, pp. 223-230.
16. Raento, M., Oulasvirta, A., Petit, R., Toivonen, H. (2005). ContextPhone - A prototyping platform for context-aware mobile applications. IEEE Pervasive Computing 4(2): 51-59.

17. Salvador, T., Barile, S., and Sherry, J. (2004). Ubiquitous computing design principles: supporting human-human and human-computer transactions. In Extended Abstracts of CHI '04, pp. 1497-1500.
18. Stalnaker, R.C. (1978). Assertions. In P. Cole (ed.) Syntax and Semantics 9: pragmatics, New York, Academic Press, pp. 315-32.

Evaluating Performance in Continuous Context Recognition Using Event-Driven Error Characterisation

Jamie A. Ward[1], Paul Lukowicz[2], and Gerhard Tröster[1]

[1] Swiss Federal Institute of Technology (ETH),
Wearable Computing Lab,
8092 Zürich, CH
[2] Institute for computer Systems and Netorks,
UMIT- University for Health Sciences, Medical Informatics and Technology,
Hall i. Tirol, Austria

Abstract. Evaluating the performance of a continuous activity recognition system can be a challenging problem. To-date there is no widely accepted standard for dealing with this, and in general methods and measures are adapted from related fields such as speech and vision. Much of the problem stems from the often imprecise and ambiguous nature of the real-world events that an activity recognition system has to deal with. A recognised event might have variable duration, or be shifted in time from the corresponding real-world event. Equally it might be broken up into smaller pieces, or joined together to form larger events. Most evaluation attempts tend to smooth over these issues, using "fuzzy" boundaries, or some other parameter based error decision, so as to make possible the use of standard performance measures (such as insertions and deletions.) However, we argue that reducing the various facets of a activity system into limited error categories - that were originally intended for different problem domains - can be overly restrictive. In this paper we attempt to identify and characterise the errors typical to continuous activity recognition, and develop a method for quantifying them in an unambiguous manner.

By way of an initial investigation, we apply the method to an example taken from previous work, and discuss the advantages that this provides over two of the most commonly used methods.

1 Introduction

As research interest into recognition of user activities, and more generally user activity, continues to grow, so too does the demand for standard methods of evaluating and comparing performance of the different approaches. There are two main criteria involved in the development of such methods. One is in establishing open datasets to be used as a benchmark, of which to-date work is only just beginning.[1] The second criteria, and the one which is the focus of this

---

[1] For example, see the dedicated workshop on this topic at Pervasive '04 [8].

M. Hazas, J. Krumm, and T. Strang (Eds.): LoCA 2006, LNCS 3987, pp. 239–255, 2006.

paper, is the issue of appropriate performance measures. While working on different recognition problems [23, 12, 16] and looking at related publications (such as [18, 11, 21, 2]) we have found that existing evaluation measures, mostly taken from related fields such as automatic speech recognition (ASR), information retrieval (IR), and vision related fields such as optical character recognition (OCR), often fail to adequately reflect the specific problems of the activity recognition task, in particular with the non segmented, continuous case.

The performance evaluation of a continuous activity recognition system can be viewed as a problem of how to measure the similarity of two time series; the similarity of a prediction sequence to its corresponding ground truth. In the topic of activity recognition, these time series are made up of discrete events, each representing a particular activity which the system is designed to recognise. As such events are based on real world activities, or concern changes to a user's environment, it is often the case that they are of variable duration and have ambiguous start and stop times. This can lead to events being detected some time before or after they actually occur. It can also lead to single events being fragmented into multiple smaller events of the same class; or, alternatively, the merging of several real events into a single detected event.

Dealing with such traits poses a problem for satisfactory performance evaluation. Using existing methods of evaluation, designers have the choice of making a direct timewise (frame-by-frame) comparison of the ground and prediction sequences, thereby loosing information on the nature of events; or of performing a comparison of the events, at the expense of loosing information on the timing. In the later case, the definitions of the event errors - insertion, deletion, etc. - is further complicated by how to treat events which are fragmented or merged. Often the designer is forced to make a decision as to whether fragmented or merged events are undesirable or not, whether to ignore them or to count them as full inserted or deleted events.

1.1   Paper Contributions and Organisation

Our repeated encounters with such cases prompted us to investigate the problem of finding suitable evaluation measures in continuous activity recognition. In this paper we propose an alternative strategy for evaluation which combines the strengths of several existing methods without throwing away critical information that might be judged important by application developers wishing to use such activity recognition systems.

The paper is divided into four main parts. In section 2 we motivate the work by highlighting the problems of existing measures when used on a typical activity recognition example, as obtained from an earlier published work. In section 3 we provide a detailed analysis of these problems. Section 4 introduces our proposed categorisation and error scoring methods to combat these problems. Finally, in closing, we apply our methods to the original motivational examples, and use them to fuel the discussion on how they might be used in practice.

2   Motivation

As a motivation for this work, consider Figure1. Plot (a) is an example of output
from a multi-class, continuous activity recognition task which was carried out on
a mock assembly scenario in the wood workshop of our lab [23]. The plot shows
hand-labelled ground truth for five activities which we attempted to recognise
in this experiment: use of a grinder, file, screwdriver, vice and drawer. The time
where no relevant activity was performed is recorded as *NULL*. Plotted above
the ground truth are the recognition system's predictions. This data is output
on a timewise frame by frame basis, with each frame being one second in length.

For most of the non-*NULL* activities, these prediction sequences seem to visually correlate well with the ground truth. There are few insertions and only
one completely deleted activity. Contrast this result with the middle(b) and
bottom(c) plots of Figure 1. A casual visual assessment might report, due to the
abundance of insertions in (b) and the heavily fragmented output of (c), that
this data is much poorer than that of (a).

2.1   Frame Based Analysis

When evaluating such data quantitatively, a standard practise is to make a frame
by frame comparison of the ground truth with the predictions. Counts of correct
and incorrect matches can then be tallied for each class and entered into a confusion matrix [6]. From here a number of standard performance measures can be
calculated, the most common of these being accuracy (the overall correct rate).

However, when this analysis is performed on the examples, as shown in the
tables to the right of Figure 1, a somewhat unsatisfying result is obtained: they
all have identical accuracy. This result seems contrary to what observation tells
us. Furthermore, the confusion matrices for examples (a) and (b), simplified to
the summation of positive classes vs. *NULL*, are very similar and tell us nothing
about, for example, the prevalence of insertion errors in (b).

These results are not wrong - the numbers of frame errors in all three examples are in fact equal. What the visual analysis shows, and the frame analysis
does not show, is that every positive frame forms part of an *event* - a contiguous
sequence of same class frames. When judged from an event perspective, then the
distribution of frame errors becomes more important. Many of the false positives in (a), for example, are joined to otherwise correctly classified sequences;
however, in (b) they tend to form part of *event insertions* - an arguably more
serious misclassification.

2.2   Event Analysis

Researchers in the fields of optical character recognition (OCR) [5, 13] and automatic speech recognition (ASR) both commonly employ counts of insertion
(I_e), deletion (D_e) and substitution (S_e) event errors to measure performance.
These give indicators of the discrete event performance of a system, and seem a
natural choice for evaluating a discrete sequence of activity events.

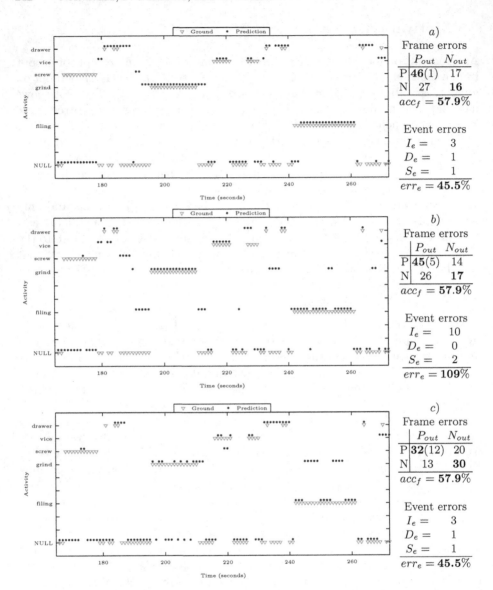

Fig. 1. Examples $(a - c)$ from multi-class continuous activity problem. The tables give performance information using standard methods: *Frame errors* using binary confusion matrices of positive (P) vs. *NULL* (N) frames, where rows denote the ground truth and columns the output predictions. Positive substitutions are entered in brackets alongside True Positives (TP) in these matrices. Accuracy is calculated as: $acc_f = \frac{TP+TN-subst.}{T_f}$, with the total frames in each example being $T_f = 106$. *Event errors* are given as insertion (I_e), deletion (D_e) and substitution (S_e) counts. The *event error rate* is $err_e = \frac{I_e+D_e+S_e}{T_e}$, with total number of positive events, $T_e = 11$.

When these scores are calculated for each of the examples (see the lower tables of Figure 1), the differences between examples (a) and (b) become much clearer. Example (a) shows a relatively low insertion count in comparison with the very high number of insertions in example (b). However, if we look at example (c) - again a very different output from (a) - we are once again disappointed: the deletion, substitution and insertion counts of (c) are identical to those of (a).

There are two main problems underlying these results, neither of which are highlighted by any of the commonly used evaluation methods. The first problem is that many of the events are fragmented: several smaller segments, although correctly classified, only sparsely cover parts of the ground truth. Some of these segments are separated by small fragments of *NULL* (frame deletions); while others, such as the 'filing' event, are fragmented by insertions of another class (frame substitutions).

The second problem is that events can be merged together, (i.e.) two or more events of the same class can be recognised as a single large event. In the examples given here, this happens on only two occasions (the 'drawer' events of (a) and (c)). In each case, this error only affects two closely occurring events. For purposes of evaluation, the fact that these two separate events have been merged is simply ignored. They are both treated as correct. Alternatively, it might be decided that such a merging, reducing two or more events to one, is also a deletion of all merged events except the first.

In both of these cases, fragmenting and merging, it is clear that there are several ways one might choose to score the results, and here lies the problem: there is no standard definition for such errors. The existing designations of D_e, I_e and S_e, were developed for fields such as OCR which enjoy well-defined, discrete events. In continuous activity recognition, as highlighted by these examples, this is not always the case.

3   Problem Specification

In order to develop more appropriate evaluation metrics, the problems illustrated in the previous section should first be formulated in a more systematic way. This section begins with a definition of the performance evaluation task. From this definition we discuss specific characteristics of performance which are common to continuous context recognition.

3.1   Definition of Performance Evaluation

In the most general classification problem we have n classes $(c_1, c_2, \cdots c_n)$ without a designated class for *NULL*. The ground truth consists of a number of m distinct events $(e_1, e_2, \cdots e_m)$, each mapping to one of the n classes. We assume the system to be time discrete with the smallest considered time unit being a frame. In most cases, a frame would correspond to the length of the sensor sampling window.

An ideal classifier would be one where every ground truth event, e_i, has a start time, stop time and label matching an event in the prediction sequence. Correspondingly, all constituent frames would also match.

Unfortunately such perfect alignment is rare. A typical recognition system deletes, inserts, and substitutes data. In addition even for correctly correlated data the start and stop frames might be shifted in the recognised sequence. The problem of evaluating such imperfect classification is equivalent to that of finding an appropriate similarity metric for the comparison of two time series. As we see it, this problem can be tackled on three levels:

1. *Frame by frame.* For each pair of corresponding time frames f (from the ground truth) and $\bar{f}$ (from the recognition system output) we perform a simple comparison of the class labels.
2. *Event-based.* Determine how many of the m ground truth events ($e_1, e_2, \cdots e_m$) are accurately reflected in the $\bar{m}$ events $\bar{e}_1, \bar{e}_2 \cdots \bar{e}_{\bar{m}}$ produced by the recognition system. The difficulty of event based evaluation stems from the fact that neither the number of events nor their start and end points are necessarily identical in the ground truth and the recogniser output.
3. *Hybrid frame and event based.* A frame by frame comparison which takes into account the events to which individual frames are a part. Thus frame errors that merely cause the start and end points of events to be shifted are treated differently from frame errors that contribute to the deletion and insertion of events. This type of evaluation only makes sense if some prior event analysis has been carried out.

3.2   General Considerations

Given two time series there can be no such thing as an optimal measure of similarity which holds for all applications. As a consequence there is no optimal, problem independent performance evaluation. Different application domains are subject to different performance criteria. In speech recognition, for example, it is more important that the system recognises what words have been spoken, and in which order, rather than how long it took to utter them. Consequently, methods which emphasise correct ordering of symbols over their specific duration are used to evaluate these systems. An input to a real-time system, on the other hand, would need to be extremely time sensitive. As such an evaluation metric which emphasises timing errors and delays, i.e. based on a direct timewise comparison, would be more appropriate.

For every domain, a specific metric must be chosen that characterises and highlights the type of error(s) most critical to that domain. This means that evaluation methods that are successful in one domain need not necessarily be so in another. Applying methods to a different domain only makes sense if both domains have the same type of dominant error types and similar relevance is assigned to equivalent errors.

3.3   Evaluation Requirements of Continuous Activity Recognition

The study of activity recognition encompasses a wide range of problems, including standard modes of locomotion (walking, standing, running, etc.) [18, 15, 11, 21], tracking of specific procedures (e.g. assembly tasks [17]), and the detection of changes in environmental conditions[2, 15]. While each of these problems have their own characteristic and relevant error types, there are a number of things that most continuous activity recognition tasks have in common:

Large variability in event length. In many activity recognition tasks, event length can vary by an order of magnitude or more. A wood workshop assembly example includes such activities as sawing which can take minutes, as well as taking or putting away tools which take just a few seconds. Similarly, when recognising modes of locomotion, there can be instances of long uninterrupted walks, as well as instances of a user making only a few steps. A direct frame by frame evaluation can be misleading in such cases.

Fragmented events. Long lasting events are often interrupted by the occurrence of short events. Thus a long sawing sequence might include one or two interruptions or an instance of the user changing the saw. A long walk might include a few short stops. Since the recognition system must be able to spot such situations, it is also prone to false fragmentation. As an example, a slight irregularity in the sawing motion might be falsely interpreted as an interruption, or a short instance of an entirely different activity. In addition to inserting a new event, fragmentation also breaks up one long event in the ground truth, producing several events in the recogniser output.

Event merging. Trying to avoid false fragmentation can lead to a system that tends to overlook genuinely fragmented outputs. Thus two events of the same class separated by a short event of another class might be merged into a single long event of the first class. This in a sense is a 'double deletion' since it deletes the short event in the middle, and causes the two events of the outer class to become one.

Lack of well defined NULL class. Many activity recognition tasks aim to spot a small set of interesting activities/situations while regarding the rest as instances of a 'garbage' or NULL class. This NULL class has the same function as the pauses in speech, or spaces in character recognition. The problem is that many activity recognition tasks have a NULL class which is complex and difficult to model. In the assembly task, for example, any motion made between the specific tool activities falls into this class. This includes everything from scratching one's head to unpacking a chocolate bar. As a consequence the NULL class model tends to be 'greedy', so that any unusual segment in an event (e.g. strange motion while sawing) tends to create a NULL event, thus contributing to the fragmentation problem.

Fuzzy event boundaries. When collecting large, real life data sets it is often impossible to perfectly time ground truth labels by hand. The definition of start and stop times of an event are often arbitrary and by nature imprecise. This is particularly so for domains such as activity recognition, where even the event is often difficult to define - e.g. at which point does a walking event end and a running event begin? This leads to timing errors in the recognition, even if the system can be said to work perfectly. Similarly, in tasks where interesting events are separated by a greedy *NULL*, the lack of a well defined *NULL* model will inevitably result in some incursion into the boundaries of the correct events.

The importance of these different issues is dependent on the specific application for which the system is being evaluated. However, we believe that for most activity recognition tasks, one or more of these issues is important, and that they should be taken into account when evaluating these systems.

4   Error Characterisation and Representation

Following from the above observations we now present a characterisation of the critical error types in continuous activity recognition. Specifically we propose an approach which (1) includes event mergers and fragmentation as errors in their own right; and (2) provides information about event timing errors. This section presents both the definition of the proposed errors, and a precise method on how to score them. We then show how this information can be tabulated for presentation of a system's results. Additionally we show how the methods can be tailored for dealing with activity recognition systems that treat *NULL* as a special case.

Our evaluation method is based on partitioning the signal stream into what we call *segments*. As an example, Figure 3 shows a three class recognition problem broken up into 14 segments (denoted by the vertical dotted lines). A segment is a variable-duration, contiguous sequence of frames, during which neither prediction nor the ground truth label changes. That is, each boundary of a segment is defined by either the boundary of a ground truth, or of a prediction event.

From the point of view of performance evaluation such a segment definition has two advantages. The first is that there are no ambiguities in comparison: each segment can either have the prediction and the ground truth fully agree, or fully disagree. The second advantage is that from an analysis of these segments, an exhaustive definition of the event and timing errors appropriate to activity recognition can be derived. This strategy has three main steps:

1. Create the segment sequence and note each segment as matching or non matching. A *match* being when both the ground truth segment and its corresponding prediction segment have the same class label.
2. Use segment match information to score events and event timing errors. Prediction and ground truth events are scored separately. The left flowchart of Figure 2 shows the algorithm to do this for ground truth events, with possible outputs of fragmenting F, deletion D, underfill U, correct, and *no label* (a single matching segment event to which none of the other designations apply). Prediction events are scored using the same algorithm, but with the alternate outputs of: merge (M), insertion(I) and overfill (O).

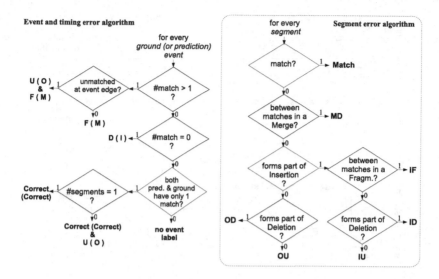

Fig. 2. (Left) flowchart of algorithm for assigning error labels to each ground truth event, and to each prediction event: for processing ground truth events, use F,D and U, for fragmenting, deletion and underfill; for processing prediction events, use bracketed labels (M), (I) and (O), referring to merge, insertion and overfill errors respectively; *correct* or *no label* can be assigned to both. #*segments* refers to the number of segments that make up an event, #*match* refers to the number of matching segments in that event, with a *match* defined as a segment where ground truth and prediction agree. (Right, boxed) flowchart of algorithm for assigning error pair labels to a segment based on its constituent event error designations.

3. Score the segment errors. The flowchart to the right of Figure 2 shows how this is done. Each (non matching) segment is assigned an error pair based on the ground and prediction events to which it forms part.

The example of Figure 3 shows three analyses of a 3-class (A,B,C) recognition example: one for counting event errors, one for counting event timing errors, and the third for counting segment errors. In each of the analyses, the same example prediction sequence is shown (with I,M or O assigned for each incorrect event or segment) against a possible ground truth (with D,F or U assigned to each incorrect event or segment). These error categories, and how to score them, are described in greater detail in the following sections.

4.1   Event Analysis

There are four types of event error, each falling into one of two divisions depending on whether they are part of the ground truth or prediction sequence. A *positive* error in the prediction sequence, can be defined as either:

Insertion - a prediction event that contains no matching segment(s), or
Merge - a prediction event that contains more then one matching segment.

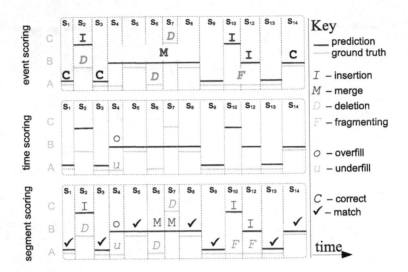

Fig. 3. Some possible error combinations for three class (A, B, C) example: upper diagram shows event errors, middle diagram shows event timing errors, and lower diagram shows segment error pairs. The dotted vertical lines show how the sequence is broken up into segments $s_{1..14}$. Event error labelling is shown in boldface (**C,I,D,M,F**), and is distinct from the segment labelling in that it applies to an entire event rather than just one segment.

A *negative* error, the failure to detect all or part of an event in the ground truth, is defined as either:

Deletion - a ground truth event that contains no matching segment(s), or
Fragmentation - a ground truth event that contains more than one match.

Correct is only assigned to where both prediction and the corresponding ground truth events are free from *all* the above categories. The example of Figure 3 shows 3 such correct event scores (s_1, s_3 and s_14). There are some cases where a single-segment, matched event is not assigned any designation (for example, see the merged ground events s_5 and s_8 in Figure 3). On an event analysis, these cannot be said to be correct - but neither can they be called errors. Instead, we treat these cases only as segment level matches.

Positive and negative errors are related: an insertion in the prediction sequence, for example, can result in the deletion or fragmentation of an event in the ground truth. This relationship is not always one-to-one however: a fragmentation might be caused by more than one insertion, possible of different classes. For this reason, the two scorings - positive and negative - are kept separate at event level.

Event timing. Often an event might be judged correct (or merged, or fragmented) but fail to align completely with its boundaries. The prediction event might spill over the ground truth boundaries; or it might fall short of them. For these cases, we introduce two *event timing* error categories which can be applied to an event in addition to a correct, merge[2], or fragmenting score:

Underfill - *ground truth* event not completely covered by prediction.
Overfill - *prediction* event which spills over its ground truth boundary.

The algorithm for assigning both event errors and event timing errors is shown to the left of Figure 2.

Event error and timing error representation. Counts of the four types of event error - insertion, deletion, merge and fragmentation - can be summed up for each class and presented in a simple table, one entry for each error type and each class. Similarly, counts of the timing event errors - overfill and underfill - can also be summed up and presented, in a separate table, alongside the specific time lengths (or number of frames) associated with them.

4.2   Segment Analysis

One aspect of performance which event based scoring does not capture is the absolute time duration (in terms of frames or seconds) for each type of error. Additionally, subtle information such as the cause-effect relationship between prediction and ground truth errors is not captured. It can be shown that the following pairings are possible:

1. An event is deleted by insertions, merging, or overfilling of another class
2. An event is underfilled by either an overfill or an insertion of another class
3. An event is fragmented by insertion(s) of another class.

Rarely do event level comparisons allow a one-to-one relation between the prediction and ground truth. One deletion, for example, might be the result of a combination of an overfill plus several different insertions. Segments do allow such a relation. By definition, every segment forms part of exactly one prediction event and one ground truth event. The specific combination of event and timing errors for each ground truth and prediction can therefore be used to define the segment error type, as detailed in Figure2(right). In total, there are six possible error types for non-matching segments based on the event combinations: *insertion-deletion*(ID), *overfill-deletion*(OD), *merge-deletion*(MD), *insertion-underfill*(IU), *overfill-underfill*(OU) and *insertion-fragmentation*(IF).

These pairings are codified and presented in Table 1, which we name the Segment Error Table (SET). Prediction errors (insertion, overfill and merge) form the rows, while ground truth errors (deletion, underfill and fragmentation) make up the columns of this table.

Analysis of segments provides an unambiguous assessment of errors. In the simplest analysis, segment counts of the six different error types, ID, IU, IF, OD, OU, and MD are made and filled into the table. Additional information on the absolute time length, or frame counts, of these segments can also be included. Such a combined segment and frame count SET provides a representation of error that combines the temporal resolution of frame by frame evaluation with the descriptive power of event level evaluation.

---

[2] Segment s_4 of Figure 3 shows one such example of this.

Table 1. Possible segment error designations: rows represent prediction segment errors, columns ground truth errors; ID=*insertion-deletion*, OD=*overfill-deletion*, MD=*merge-deletion*, IU=*insertion-underfill*, OU=*overfill-underfill* and IF=*insertion-fragmentation*

	Deletion	Underfill	Fragmentation
Insertion	ID	IU	IF
Overfill	OD	OU	
Merge	MD		

NULL as a special case. We can expand the table thus described to handle *NULL* as separate from the other classes - a separation required for most activity recognition tasks. This is achieved by the addition of rows and columns denoting the six error combinations with respect to *NULL*, as shown to the left of Table 2[3]. The SET to the top left corner of the expanded table now only contains information regarding substitution errors between non-*NULL* positive classes. The top right section of the table then gives a breakdown of false positive errors, while the bottom section gives information about false negative errors.

Table 2. Segment Error Table with *NULL*(N) as special case: full table (left) and reduced version (right)

Full table (left):

	D	U	F	D_N	U_N	F_N
I	ID	IU	IF	ID_N	IU_N	IF_N
O	OD	OU		OD_N	OU_N	
M	MD			MD_N		
I_N	$I_N D$	$I_N U$	$I_N F$			
O_N	$O_N D$	$O_N U$				
M_N	$M_N D$					

Reduced version (right):

	D	U	F	N
I	ID	IU	IF	I
O	OD	OU		O
M	MD			M
N	D	U	F	

In many continuous recognition scenarios we are not interested in whether a ground segment labelled *NULL* has been completely deleted, fragmented or underfilled; likewise we are not interested whether a positive class deletion was caused by an insertion or an overfilling of *NULL*. In such situations, the error designations can be combined to produce a reduced table, as shown to the right of Table 2. For convenience, we drop the 'N' suffix and the dual error designation from the errors involving *NULL*, referring to them directly as I, O, M, D, U and F. The remaining *substitution* errors retain the dual OU, IU, etc. designators.

5   Discussion

5.1   Application of Method to Worked Example

We now apply the described error characterisations to our examples from Section 2, and give examples of how the event, timing and SET representations might look.

---

[3] Similarly, such an expansion can also be carried out for every class in a system, leading to an enhanced SET with greater detail on the relations between different classes (i.e. similar to the confusion matrix).

Event and timing results. Treating *NULL* again as a special case, we present counts of the non-null class insertions, deletions, merge and fragmentation for the examples of Figure 1. Comparing the insertion and deletion counts of the earlier event analysis of Section 2 with those of , we can draw much the same conclusions. Notably however, the new method allows us to see clearly the additional merge and fragmentation errors which prevail in example (*c*) . The poorer timing performance of (*a*), with many overfilled events in comparison with the other examples, is also now evident.

The information regarding class substitution errors, however, has been lost in this representation - they are dissolved into pairs, such as insertion/deletion. The lack of a one-to-one relationship between prediction and ground truth errors makes such a joint 'substitution event' measure difficult to define at the event level. Therefore we defer to the segment analysis to provide this information.

Table 3. Event errors (for Positive, non-*NULL* classes only), I'=Insertion, D'= Deletion, M=Merge and F=Fragmentation; and event timing errors, Overfill and Underfill. Number of timing event errors are given together with the corresponding frame counts

a)

#events		#timing(#frames)	
I'	4		
D'	2		
M	1	Overfill	8 (18)
F	0	Underfill	4 (6)

b)

#events		#timing(#frames)	
I'	12		
D'	2		
M	0	Overfill	1 (1)
F	1	Underfill	3 (11)

c)

#events		#timing(#frames)	
I'	4		
D'	2		
M	1	Overfill	4 (6)
F	3	Underfill	4 (12)

Segment (and frame-by-frame) results. The segment and frame errors for the examples are presented in Table 4. The major difference which becomes apparent is the higher proportion of segments forming part of timing errors (Underfilling by *NULL*, U and Overfill onto *NULL*, O) in (*a*), versus the higher proportion forming event errors in (*b*) and (*c*) . Note that examples *b*, and in particular (*c*), contain fragmenting errors whereas (*a*) does not. Of merger errors, there are only two instances - in (*a*) and (*c*) - each of which involves only a single merge of two 'drawer' events.

Again, the information provided by the new method is clearly more detailed than that of the basic frame-by-frame analysis.

Table 4. SETs for positive classes (P) vs. *NULL* for the examples in Figure 1, with counts of segment errors and corresponding number of frames

a)

#segments (#frames)	D	U	F	N
I	1(1)			5(7)
O				8(18)
M				1(2)
N	1(11)	4(6)		

b)

#segments (#frames)	D	U	F	N
I	2(3)		1(2)	9(25)
O				1(1)
M				
N	1(2)	3(11)	1(1)	

c)

#segments (#frames)	D	U	F	N
I	1(1)		3(11)	(3)
O				4(6)
M				1(4)
N	1(1)	4(12)	1(7)	

5.2 Significance and Limitations

As shown above our scheme has three advantages over standard performance evaluation methods used in activity recognition:

1. It introduces the notion of segments as the largest continuous time slices in which no ambiguities occur in scoring the correctness of the predictions
2. Based on this notion it leads to an *unambiguous*, objective characterization of event level error.
3. It makes explicit different sources of error (timing, fragmentation merges) which are ignored in conventional evaluation methods, although they are wide spread in activity recognition systems.

The main limitation of the method concerns events with a large time shift between ground truth and the prediction. A prediction that is shifted by so much, that it has no overlap with the corresponding ground truth will be scored as an insertion and the corresponding ground truth event as a deletion.

The above advantages and limitations clearly follow from the algorithm described in this paper. As the algorithm is fully deterministic and an exact method rather then a heuristic, there is no further need of an empirical validation. There can also be little doubts concerning the benefits of having an objective,*unambiguous* method for scoring events. Even if it were to turn out that in most cases the scores produced by our method are very similar to what people have arrived at to date, having a consistent, objective scoring method is an undisputed methodological advantage.

What certainly does require further investigation are the benefits of the additional error information. They are obviously dependent on the application in which the recognition system is to be used. For a safety critical system, such as an accident avoidance system in an industrial setting, timing may be regarded as critical, and the minimization of overfill and underfill of recognized activities would clearly be desirable. On the other hand, for a system interested only in which activities are carried out, such errors would be less critical. Imagine, for example, a system monitoring the sequence of events as a mechanic repairs part of an aircraft engine. What is important then is that the number of insertions and deletions is kept low - that the system does not miss out any activities, and that it gets the sequence correct. If further information on the count of specific activities is required (how many bolts have been removed from the engine), then errors such as fragmenting and merge errors must also be kept to a minimum.

For a conclusive proof of the value of the information provided by our method an elaborate empirical study is needed. Such a study would need to consider a wide range of applications and preferably look at previously published activity recognition experiments and re-score their results using the above method.

For a meaningful study access to data from different groups would be required and the associated effort would beyond the scope of this paper. This is clearly a limitation and means that no authoritative statement can be made about the value of the additional error information. Nonetheless such benefits are very plausible. Considering the undisputed benefit of an objective scoring method we believe that this paper consist a valuable contribution to the community.

5.3   Work in Related Fields

Some of the problem domains closest to continuous activity recognition are perhaps line detection in 2D Graphics [22] and video analysis [7, 10]. Consider the case of a 2D line: the ground truth indicates a single line, but the recognition system might return a sequence of shorter lines. Further, these might overlap with the ground line, or be slightly offset from it. Different approaches have been suggested to tackle this problem of fragmentation. One suggestion is to redefine the error measures to incorporate fragmented events as some lower weighted correct event[22].

Some decision function based on a measure of closeness might also be used; perhaps utilising fuzzy error margins (as suggested at TRECVID '03[20]). However this approach, as with weighting, requires the introduction of further parameters which only serve to further complicate the evaluation process. In addition, all of these approaches aim to "cover up" the problem rather than finding a way of presenting it as a result in itself.

In extreme cases, particularly in the vision domain, the problem of finding a suitable measure is sidestepped altogether in favour of showing typical example images (as commented by Hoover et al. [9] and by Müller [19]). This is an approach which has - out of necessity for lack of a standard measure - been used by researchers publishing in the activity domain. The trouble is that although valid for establishing the feasibility of a method with a small number of samples, it does not scale up well to comparative studies with large databases.

Time series matching methods. More generally, the performance evaluation problem can be viewed as the matching of two time series - the prediction output with a trusted ground truth. Time-series similarity methods are used in an extremely wide variety of domains - astronomy, finance, chemistry, robotics, etc., to mention only a few. Even more vast is the number of performance measures that are introduced for every specific application (Keogh & Kassetty[14] give an extensive overview). Some of the more common similarity measures are generally based on dynamic time warping (DTW)[3], or methods using longest common subsequences (LCS)[1]. Another useful method, as introduced by Perng et al.[4] utilises 'landmarks' in the data, applying several different transformations (shifting, time warping, etc.) to approximate a more human perception of similarity. Though useful in measuring similarity, these methods do not provide a clear means of measuring phenomena such as event fragmenting and merging.

Rather than selecting some measure of "similarity", or parametrized boundary decision to fit existing error designations, we aim to characterise and present the errors as they are - in a quantifiable way which corresponds closely to that of the human observer.

6   Conclusion

In this paper we present a non-ambiguous scoring of event errors in a continuous activity recognition system. Observing the lack of a one-to-one relationship between events in the ground truth and those in the prediction sequence, we target errors in these two sequences separately: specifically, we define positive errors as *insertion (I)* and *merge (M)* events by the prediction sequence; and negative errors as *deleted (D)* and *fragmented (D)* events in the ground truth. Complementary to these, we introduce timing event categories which score whether a prediction event overfills its ground truth, or a ground event is underfilled by its prediction.

We introduce a timewise method of comparison based on the idea of segments - a segment being a contiguous section of time where neither ground truth nor prediction changes. This allows the representation of an unambiguous one-to-one relation between ground and prediction segments, which we have shown to produce a maximum of six possible error combinations, each assigned depending on the nature of the events to which each segment forms part: ID, IU, IF, OD, OU, and MD. These error pairings can be represented in the so-called *Segment Error Table (SET)*, with scoring on the number of segments, and their corresponding time durations (or number of frames).

The paper has presented a detailed description of the evaluation algorithm and demonstrated how the above mentioned properties follow from this algorithm. As the algorithm is deterministic and exact, no empirical study is needed to prove those properties. With respect to the usefulness of the additional information provided by our method only a simple illustrative example and a plausibility argument were given. As a consequence the main motivation behind this paper is to make the community aware of the existence and the properties of the method. We hope that this will lead to other groups adopting this method and/or to a wider discussion about appropriate evaluation standards. In the end we would like to see the emergence and adoption of a generally accepted, objective and informative evaluation method based on our ideas.

References

1. R. Agrawal, K.-I. Lin, H. S. Sawhney, and K. Shim. Fast similarity search in the presence of noise, scaling, and translation in time-series databases. In *21st Int'l Conf. on Very Large Data Bases*, pages 490–501, Zurich, CH, 1995. MKaufmann.
2. L. Bao and S. Intille. Activity recognition from user-annotated acceleration data. In *Pervasive, LNCS 3001*, 2004.
3. D. Berndt and J. Clifford. Using dynamic time warping to find patterns in time series. In *Proc. KDD Workshop*, pages 359–370, Seattle, WA, 1994.
4. C-S.Perng, H.Wang, S.R.Zhang, and D.S.Parker. Landmarks: a new model for similarity-based pattern querying in time series databases. In *ICDE*, 2000.
5. A.F. Clark and C.Clark. Performance characterization in computer vision a tutorial. In *http://www.peipa.essex.ac.uk/benchmark/*, Essex, UK, 1999.
6. R. Duda, P. Hart, and D. Stork. *Pattern Classification, 2nd Edition*. Wiley, 2001.
7. S. Eickeler and G. Rigoll. A novel error measure for the evaluation of video indexing systems. In *Int'l. Conf. on Acous., Speech & Sig. Proc.*, Jun 2000.
8. H.Junker, J.A.Ward, P.Lukowicz, and G.Tröster. *Benchmarks and a Data Base for Context Recognition*. ISBN 3-9522686-2-3, 2004.
9. A. Hoover, G. Jean-Baptiste, X. Jiang, P. Flynn, H. Bunke, D. Goldof, K. Bowyer, D. Eggert, A. Fitzgibbon, and R. Fisher. An experimental comparison of range image segmentation algorithms. *IEEE Trans. PAMI*, 18(7):673–689, 1996.

10. W. Hsu, L. Kennedy, C.-W. Huang, S.-F. Chang, C.-Y. Lin, and G. Iyengar. News video story segmentation using fusion of multi-level multi-modal features in trecvid 2003. In *ICASSP*, May 2004.

11. A. Ali J.K. Aggarwal. Segmentation and recognition of continuous human activity. In *IEEE Workshop on detection and recognition of Events in Video*, pages 28–35, Vancouver, Canada, 2001.

12. H. Junker, P. Lukowicz, and G. Tröster. Continuous recognition of arm activities with body-worn inertial sensors. In *Proc. IEEE Int'l Symp. on Wearable Comp.*, pages 188–189, 2004.

13. T. Kanungo, G. A. Marton, and O. Bulbul. Paired model evaluation of ocr algorithms. Technical report, Center for Automation Research, Uni.Maryland, 1998.

14. E. Keogh and S. Kasetty. On the need for time series data mining benchmarks: a survey and empirical demonstration. In *8th int'l. conf. on knowledge discovery and data mining*, pages 102–111, NY, USA, 2002. ACM.

15. N. Kern, H. Junker, P. Lukowicz, B. Schiele, and G. Tröster. Wearable sensing to annotate meeting recordings. *Personal and Ubiquitous Computing*, 2003.

16. K. Kunze, P. Lukowicz, H. Junker, and G. Troester. Where am i: Recognizing on-body positions of wearable sensors. In *LoCA*, volume 1, May 2005.

17. M. Lampe, M. Strassner, and E. Fleisch. A ubiquitous computing environment for aircraft maintenance. In *ACM symp. on Applied comp.*, pages 1586–1592, 2004.

18. J. Lester, T. Choudhury, N. Kern, G. Borriello, and B. Hannaford. A hybrid discriminative/generative approach for modeling human activities. In *IJCAI*, 2005.

19. H. Müller, W. Müller, D. McG. Squire, S. Marchand-Maillet, and T. Pun. Performance evaluation in content-based image retrieval: Overview and proposals. Technical report, Uni. Geneve, Switzerland, 1999.

20. NIST. *Proc. of TREC Video Retrieval Evaluation Conference (TRECVID)*. 2003.

21. V. Pavlovic and J. Rehg. Impact of dynamic model learning on classification of human motion. In *Comp. Vision and Pattern Rec. (CVPR)*, pages 788–795, 2000.

22. I.T. Phillips and A.K. Chhabra. Empirical performance evaluation of graphics recognition systems. *IEEE Trans. PAMI*, 21:9:849–870, 1999.

23. P.Lukowicz, J.A.Ward, H. Junker, G. Tröster, A.Atrash, and T.Starner. Recognizing workshop activity using body worn microphones and accelerometers. In *Pervasive, LNCS*, 2004.

Location-Based Context Retrieval and Filtering

Carsten Pils[1], Ioanna Roussaki[2], and Maria Strimpakou[2]

[1] Telecommunications Software & Systems Group (TSSG),
Waterford Institute of Technology, Ireland
cpils@tssg.org
[2] School of Electrical and Computer Engineering,
National Technical University of Athens, Greece
{nanario, mstrim}@telecom.ntua.gr

Abstract. Context-based applications are supposed to decrease human-machine interactions. To this end, they must interpret the meaning of context data. Ontologies are a commonly accepted approach of specifying data semantics and are thus considered a precondition for the implementation of context-based systems. Yet, experiences gained from the European project Daidalos evoke concerns that this approach has its flaws when the application domain can hardly be delimited. These concerns are raised by the human limitation in dealing with complex specifications.

This paper proposes a relaxation of the situation: Humans strength is the understating of natural languages, computers, however, possess superior pattern matching power. Therefore, it is suggested to enrich or even replace semantic specifications of context data items by free-text descriptions. For instance, rather than using an Ontology specification to describe an Italian restaurant the restaurant can simply be described by its menu card.

To facilitate this methodology, context documents are introduced and a novel information retrieval approach is elucidated, evaluated, and analysed with the help of Bose-Einstein statistics. It is demonstrated that the new approach clearly outperforms conventional information retrieval engines and is an excellent addition to context Ontologies.

1 Introduction

Though computers are strong in processing data, they are unable to understand its meaning. For the development of pervasive and context-based applications, this limitation is a major drawback. Researchers attempt to tackle this problem by applying Ontologies which are basically standards specifying the meaning of context data. As long as the application domain is manageable, this approach appears to be quite powerful [1, 2, 3, 4, 5]. Yet, for context-based frameworks facilitating various business scenarios, it exhibits serious problems. Lately, Noy expressed similar concerns with respect to the Semantic Web [6].

Readability. Whilst context information is supposed to be consumed by machines, humans will still have to deal with it. They may read information returned by applications or feed it into the system. By nature, standards and this

M. Hazas, J. Krumm, and T. Strang (Eds.): LoCA 2006, LNCS 3987, pp. 256–273, 2006.

encompasses also Ontologies are dull reading. Even worse, strict standardisation of semantics is typically based on classification schemes, thus making it even hard to find relevant information.

Costs. Consequently, Ontologies are to complicated to be understood by non professionals. For small businesses like shops or restaurants it may therefore be prohibitively expensive to adopt them. Yet, the success of large scale context-based frameworks strongly depends on these context sources.

Disorder. As humans are still involved in the process of semantic tagging, there is a significant error probability. Typically the probability $\pi(\iota_i)$ that humans misinterpret information is proportional to its penetration, i.e. its usage frequency. Thus, $\pi(\iota_i)$ is Pareto distributed. Remarkably, the described system $\mathcal{S}$ of semantic specifications exhibits entropy $\mathcal{H}$:

$$\mathcal{H}(\mathcal{S}) = -\sum_{i=0}^{n} \pi(\iota_i) \cdot \log(\pi(\iota_i))$$

Here n is the number of data types in the system at a given instant of time. As time passes by, new sensors are developed and context evolves towards consisting of any conceivable information. Consequently, both n and the system entropy are approaching infinity. According to the second law of thermodynamics, the entropy of such systems tends to increase [7]. That is, the more structured the Ontology model is, the more effort is required to increase the structure or even maintain the status quo. Means for decreasing entropy are for example user training and the operation of maintenance services.

In essence the supposed advantage of Ontologies, the ability to teach machines meaning, is its weakness. The approach appears too static to suit large scale context systems. Therefore, to alleviate its drawbacks the structure must be relaxed: While humans are superior in using natural language, computers have stronger processing capabilities for pattern matching. Enrichment of semantics by free-text descriptions combined with Information Retrieval (IR) techniques helps both humans and computers to understand the meaning of context data.

1.1   Application Scenarios

The proposed approach focuses on the retrieval of static location context and exploits its hierarchical structure to yield improved retrieval performance. Yet its application is not limited to location context, it can be applied to any hierarchical structured information space.

Location context is associated with a graph structure which is implied by the included-in relation. For example, a city has included-in relationships with its suburbs, streets, and buildings. On the premise that the context entities are not only described by an Ontology but also by textual descriptions, the proposed retrieval engine retrieves context information in a user friendly way. For example, when the user is looking for an Italian restaurant in Waterford city which serves Spaghetti Bolognese he just has to submit the query (`Waterford city Italian restaurant Spaghetti Bolognese`). Given that the context entity of Waterford city and the Italian restaurants have textual descriptions, the user will receive a list of all matching context entities. The webpage of Waterford and menu cards are sufficient to describe the context entities in this simple scenario. Like restaurants any other place of interest can be searched like cinemas, shops, and museums. Descriptive look-up of context entities can also be used to describe the vicinity of a place of interest. When the address is unknown the user can describe well-known nearby context entities like churches, bridges, and shops. The search engine looks-up the context space for such an area and returns a list of addresses. Context searching can also be applied to museums where context entities representing paintings, statues, styles, and artists have textual descriptions. Similarly, devices and rooms can be described to help users to find their way around. Like location-based context, Ontologies and service directories also have hierarchical structures which are implied by classification schemes. The proposed retrieval algorithm can be used to search specifications and descriptions by taking classifications into account. Thus the engine helps developers to find Ontology specifications or suitable services (and their specifications).

In the next section a basic context model and its implementation is described. A brief overview of related work can be found in section 3. The actual context retrieval approach is presented in section 4. Finally, the approach is evaluated in section 5 and discussed in section 6.

2   Location Models and Context Databases

According to A. Dey, context is basically information which is relevant for human-computer interactions [8]. Apparently, this definition is weak and cannot be used as a requirement specification of context databases. Fortunately there is a common understanding that a large domain of context information, especially for mobile devices, is related to location. Therefore context databases must meet the requirements of two use-cases: Entity queries and location queries.

Entity queries are requests for known context information. The look-up for a friend's phone number is an example of this kind of query. Here it is presupposed that the requestor possesses a unique identification of his friend and consequently for his context. Hence retrieving the friend's context is straightforward.

Location queries comprise location information. The restaurant finder, an application which searches nearby restaurants, is a prominent example of this use-case. Other examples are navigation queries where the context system is supposed to find shortest routes.

2.1   Daidalos Location Model

Typically context databases like that of Daidalos are optimised for these use-cases [9][10]. To support location queries they implement location models which

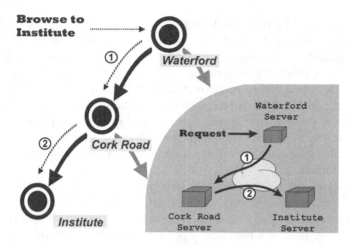

Fig. 1. Example location model

describe the geographic interrelations of context entities. In [11] Bauer *et al.* give a concise overview of location models and identify three classes: Geometric, symbolic, and hybrid models. Geometric models simply associate information with coordinates. These models, however, lack any means for describing semantic interrelations between objects like street junctions or houses located at a street. Symbolic models solve this problem by applying graph models. In these models entities like rooms and streets are modelled by vertices, their interrelations are described by edges. Finally, hybrid models are a combination of geometric and symbolic models. In terms of expressiveness hybrid models are the most powerful ones. Thus, Daidalos' context database also implements a hybrid model: $G = (V, E)$ is graph with vertices V and edges E. Vertices are associated with attributes that describe their details. Among those attributes are identifiers, names, coordinates, textual descriptions, and ontology specifications. Vertices may represent entities like devices, rooms, buildings, or regions. Edges, however, represent relations between these entities. One type of edge, vertex relation respectively, is of particular importance: the including edge. Including edges are directed edges and describe inclusion relations between vertices. For example a city has an inclusion relation with a building and the building has inclusion relations with its rooms. The vertex which represents the including entity (e.g. the building) is called the parent of the inclusion relations while the vertices representing the included entities (e.g. rooms) are called children. It is assumed that a parent vertex has multiple children, yet a child vertex has only one parent. To distinguish including edges the subset I of E is introduced. Figure 1 shows an example location model. It is a description of the *Waterford Institute of Technology* located at the *Cork Road* in *Waterford*.

2.2   Distributed Context Database

Including edges imply a spatial hierarchy. This implication can be utilised to efficiently distribute location information among database servers. Context data of location-domains like for example buildings or cities can be stored on dedicated servers. Figure 1 shows also a server deployment that corresponds to the model view. The advantage of such a hierarchy is that it supports easy look-up of vertices being associated with locations. When a position query is passed to a local client, the client either retrieves a matching vertex from its local storage or it passes the query to its parent server. Upward passing of a query continues until a server is reached that covers the searched area. Finally, that server may pass the query to a child server covering sub-location-domains. Efficient query passing requires that each server has a root location-domain-vertex describing the covered domain.

Figure 1 shows the routing requests of coordinates pointing to the *Waterford Institute of Technology*. Initially, the request is send to the *Waterford* vertex, from here it is past via the *Cork Road* vertex to the *Institute's one*. Apparently, moving along an inclusion hierarchy's path corresponds to zooming in and out of context details.

In the Daidalos context database, lookups of vertices and edges are also straightforward: Each vertex and edge is required to have an identifier attribute encapsulating a Uniform Resource Locator (URL) which references the responsible database server. Since users and mobile devices are represented by vertices, retrieving their context is simple. Only the identifier of the entity must be passed to the local database client. Following the client just extracts the URL of the responsible server from the identifier and contacts the server to retrieve the information.

3   Related Work

Context databases are not the only systems that are optimised for location queries. Actually, Geographic Information Systems (GIS) and Geographic Information Retrieval (GIR) systems are designed for similar use cases. GIS are designed to query information about geographic structures. They aim at data management related to the physical world (e.g. geography and astronomy), parts of living organisms, engineering design and conceptual information spaces (e.g. electromagnetic fields) [12]. In contrast to context databases, these systems are focused on geographic structure rather than the objects themselves. The application domain of GIR systems differs considerably from both context databases and GIS. They are basically plain information retrieval systems that filter documents based on geographic constraints [13]. With respect to the proposed free-text context retrieval approach, the GIR methodology appears to be genuinely interesting. Yet, they are not designed to retrieve location context and thus to take document relationships into account, e.g. they are unable to determine that a document describing a city is related to documents describing the city's streets. In [16] Jones *et al.* propose describing location context by text documents. Their retrieval algorithm filters only addresses and coordinates, however geographic relationships are ignored. A more detailed discussion of their approach can be found in section 4.3. Context-based retrieval is also a research area of

Information Retrieval. But rather than location context these approaches take the user context like the browse history into account. For example, when a user has most recently visited a webpage of a travel agent and submits the query term *Java* these systems retrieve webpages about the island rather than the programming language [14]. A similar approach for web-based collaborations can be found in [15].

4   Context Document Retrieval

Information Retrieval (IR) is one of the first research fields in applied computer science. IR systems are not restricted to documents retrieval. They can also process audio, photographic, and movie data. Internet search-engines like Google or Yahoo are popular examples of IR systems [17]. In general, IR systems analyse the occurrence of query terms in documents and the overall document collection. Based on this analysis systems select and rank potentially relevant documents. The ranking is based on similarity values that are calculated with the help of two probabilities, namely P_1 and P_2. $P_1(\mathtt{t}, \mathtt{tf})$ is the probability that a randomly selected document contains a term $\mathtt{tf}$ times, $P_2(\mathtt{t}, \mathtt{tf})$ is the probability that a matching document contains a term $\mathtt{tf}$ times. The similarity function (score function respectively) *Sim* between a document D and a query Q is calculated as follows:

$$Sim(D, Q) = \sum_{t \in Q} - \log(P_1(\mathtt{t}, \mathtt{tf})) \cdot (1 - P_2(\mathtt{t}, \mathtt{tf}))$$

There are many approaches to calculate P_1 and P_2 (see [18] and [19]). All of them are making the assumption that terms having little information value are randomly distributed on the whole set of documents. However, terms having a high information value are concentrated in relevant documents. In [19] Amati *et al.* calculate P_1 with the help of the Bose-Einstein statistic: It is assumed that a term $\mathtt{t}$ occurs F times in a collection comprising N documents. Given that term $\mathtt{t}$ has been observed $\mathtt{tf}_k$ times in a document k, P_1 is given by expression:

$$P_1(\mathtt{t}, \mathtt{tf}_k) = \frac{\binom{N-1+(F-\mathtt{tf}_k)-1}{F-\mathtt{tf}_k}}{\binom{N+F-1}{F}} \tag{1}$$

Probability P_2 is given by the conditional probability of having one more term $\mathtt{t}$ in a document, given that $\mathtt{tf}$ have already been observed:

$$P_2(\mathtt{t}, \mathtt{tf}) \approx \frac{\mathtt{tf} + 1}{\mathtt{tf} + 2} \tag{2}$$

Apparently, the probability of observing scores of terms in a large document is higher than observing them in a small one. On this account, IR systems implement a document length normalisation. That is, the observed term frequency $\mathtt{tf}$ is normalised with respect to the document length:

$$\mathtt{tfn} = \mathtt{tf} \cdot \frac{avg_l}{l(D)},$$

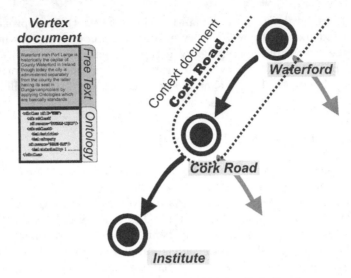

Fig. 2. Context-document of the Cork Road

where t fn is the normalised term frequency, avg_l is the average document length in the collection, and $l(D)$ is the length of the evaluated document D.

4.1 Context-Document

Unlike document collections such as paper abstracts, context data is not independent. Actually context is described by a graph model that specifies semantic relations. Thus, the question is: What is a document in terms of context?

As stated in section 2 a vertex comprises a set of attributes. Among these attributes are textual descriptions that describe the semantics of vertices. Such a textual description could for example be a chapter of a guide book (to describe a city entity), a restaurant menu card, a device manual, or just a street name. The text document and any other semantic description like for example Ontology specifications are part of a vertex's context-document. In the remainder, documents containing data collected from just a single vertex are called vertex-documents.

Vertex-documents describe only the semantics of a single vertex. Yet, they do not contain any information about a vertex's collocation in a graph. Consider for example, a vertex representing an Italian restaurant. The vertex-document may contain the keyword "Italian restaurant" and the menu card; but it may not contain its address, the name of the suburb, or the information that it is situated in a recreation area. To describe the full context of the restaurant its context-document must be extended by the vertex-documents of all parent vertices: Let $D(\mathfrak{v})$ be the vertex-document of vertex $\mathfrak{v}$. $\mathfrak{P}(\mathfrak{v})$ is the path from $\mathfrak{v}$ to the root of the tree that is implied by I. With the help of the concatenation operator $+$ the context-document $\mathfrak{C}(\mathfrak{v})$ of vertex $\mathfrak{v}$ is composed as follows:

$$\mathfrak{C}(\mathfrak{v}) = \sum_{\acute{\mathfrak{v}} \in \mathfrak{P}(\mathfrak{v})} D(\acute{\mathfrak{v}}) \tag{3}$$

Figure 2 shows the context-document of the vertex *Cork Road* and a sample vertex-document. Some IR approaches like query expansion make assumptions about the collocation of terms in a document [20]. Dependencies between vertices are inversely proportional decreasing with distance. Thus, vertex-documents of adjacent vertices must be stored in successive sections of the context-document.

Implicitly, it has been assumed that any parent vertex is part of the context. Yet, in some cases this assumption is not tenable. For example, a temperature sensor in a fridge has relevance within the fridge's context, but it is irrelevant within the context of the room or the building. A user standing in the room where the fridge is situated querying a temperature sensor is certainly interested in the room temperature, but not in the one of the fridge. When the user wants to know the actual state of the fridge, he will specify the context of the fridge explicitly in his query. Thus, context-documents of vertices whose relevance is restricted to a certain context do not comprise the vertex-documents of all parent vertices. $\bar{\mathfrak{v}}$ is the bounding vertex of vertex $\mathfrak{v}$. The context-document $\mathfrak{C}(\mathfrak{v})$ is given by:

$$\mathfrak{C}(\mathfrak{v}) = \sum_{\acute{\mathfrak{v}} \in \mathfrak{P}(\mathfrak{v}) \setminus \mathfrak{P}(\bar{\mathfrak{v}})} D(\acute{\mathfrak{v}}) + D(\bar{\mathfrak{v}}) \tag{4}$$

It is expected that vertices having a constrained context are not unusual. Apart from fridges, vehicles and buildings are typical candidates for bounding vertices.

4.2   Properties of Context-Documents

Equations 3 and 4 specify a transformation of a graph-based location model into a context-document collection. Preconditioned that all vertices $\mathfrak{v} \in V$ are covered by the set of including edges I, the following three observations can be made:

PROPOSITION 1
The number of vertices, $|V|$, equals the context-document collection's size.

The proof of Proposition 1 is trivial. It is a direct conclusion from equations 3 and 4. The second proposition refers to the duplication of vertex-documents. Vertex-documents which correspond to vertices having a low level in the inclusion hierarchy, i.e. vertices that have many direct and indirect children, are included in many context-documents. Thus the weight of terms which are characteristic for those documents decreases.

DEFINITION 1 (CHARACTERISTIC TERM)
A term is a characteristic term of a vertex-document when it frequently occurs in that document, but infrequently occurs in any other child or parent vertex-document.

PROPOSITION 2
In the Bose-Einstein information retrieval model, the term weight of a characteristic term decreases with the hierarchy level of its corresponding vertex: The lower the level, the lower the term weight.

Proof. It is shown that the context-document composition changes the probabilities P_1. Let t be a characteristic term of the vertex-document $D(v)$ of vertex v. t occurs F times in the whole document collection and f times in document $D(v)$. Given that v has n direct and indirect child vertices then there are at least $F + f \cdot (n - 1)$ occurrences of term t in the context-document collection. P_1 is associated with the initial collection, $\acute{P}_1$ is associated with composed context-document collection. The following inequality holds (see also equation 1):

$$\acute{P}_1(t, tf) = \frac{\binom{N-1+(F\cdot x - tf)-1}{F\cdot x - tf}}{\binom{N+F\cdot x-1}{F\cdot x}} \geq P_1(t, tf) = \frac{\binom{N-1+(F-tf)-1}{F-tf}}{\binom{N+F-1}{F}}$$

where $F \cdot x = f \cdot (n - 1) + F$ and thus $x \geq 1$. tf is the term frequency of t in document $D(v)$. By factorising the inequality one obtains:

$$\frac{(N + F \cdot x - tf - 2)! \cdot (F \cdot x)! \cdot (N - 1)!}{(F \cdot x - tf)! \cdot (N - 2)!(N + F \cdot x - 1)!} \geq \frac{(N + F - tf - 2)! \cdot F! \cdot (N - 1)!}{(F - tf)! \cdot (N - 2)!(N + F - 1)!}$$

$$\Leftrightarrow (N - 1) \cdot \frac{\prod_{i=1}^{tf}(F \cdot x - i + 1)}{\prod_{i=1}^{tf}(N + F \cdot x - i - 1)} \geq (N - 1) \cdot \frac{\prod_{i=1}^{tf}(F - i + 1)}{\prod_{i=1}^{tf}(N + F - i - 1)}$$

Since all products are positive, following simplification can be made:

$$\prod_{i=1}^{tf}(F \cdot x - i + 1) \cdot (N + F - i - 1) \geq \prod_{i=1}^{tf}(F - i + 1) \cdot (N + F \cdot x - i - 1)$$

When each product meets the inequality the whole inequality is met. Note that the inequality is hold when $F = 0$. Assuming that $F > 0$ one gets:

$$(F \cdot x - i + 1) \cdot (N + F - i - 1) \geq (F - i + 1) \cdot (N + F \cdot x - i - 1)$$
$$\Leftrightarrow (x - 1) \cdot (N - 2) \geq 0$$

Since $x \geq 1$ and $N \ggg 2$, the inequality is true. It follows that $\acute{P}_1(t, tf)$ increases with n and thus $\log(\acute{P}_1(t, tf))$ decreases. $\acute{P}_2(t, tf)$ is independent of the hierarchy level. Consequently, $Sim(D(v), t)$ decreases in n.   □

Proposition 2 describes a very desirable property. When a user queries ("Cork Road" Waterford Ireland) he will expect that Ireland has less weight than Waterford or "Cork Road". Due to the weighting of the query terms the vertex representing the *Cork Road* will yield a higher score than those representing *Waterford* or *Ireland*. But does the context-document composition still preserve the term characteristic? That is, can a parent vertex still be distinguished from its children by the help of its characteristic terms?

DEFINITION 2 (DISCRIMINATORY TERM)
A discriminatory term is a characteristic term which occurs only in the characterised vertex-document, but in none of the other child or parent documents.

PROPOSITION 3 (CHARACTERISTIC TERM PRESERVATION)
$\mathfrak{C}(\mathfrak{v})$ *and* $\mathfrak{C}(\acute{\mathfrak{v}})$ *are two context-documents matching a term* $\acute{t}$. *In the Bose-Einstein information retrieval model following properties hold:*

1. *If* $\acute{t}$ *is a discriminatory term of the vertex-document* $D(\acute{\mathfrak{v}})$ *and vertex* $\acute{\mathfrak{v}}$ *is a parent of* $\mathfrak{v}$ *then inequality* $Sim(\mathfrak{C}(\acute{\mathfrak{v}}), \acute{t}) \geq Sim(\mathfrak{C}(\mathfrak{v}), \acute{t})$ *holds.*
2. *Context-document composition does not preserve the term characteristic, i.e. characteristic terms are not preserved.*

Proof. Let $\acute{tf}$ be the term frequency of term $\acute{t}$ with respect to the context-document $\mathfrak{C}(\acute{\mathfrak{v}})$. $\acute{tf} + tf$, $tf \geq 0$ is its frequency with respect to context-document $\mathfrak{C}(\mathfrak{v})$:

$$Sim(\mathfrak{C}(\acute{\mathfrak{v}}), \acute{t}) \geq Sim(\mathfrak{C}(\mathfrak{v}), \acute{t})$$

$$\Leftrightarrow -\log\left(P_1\left(\acute{t}, \acute{tf} \cdot \frac{avg_l}{l(\mathfrak{C}(\acute{\mathfrak{v}}))}\right)\right) \cdot \left(1 - P_2\left(\acute{t}, \acute{tf} \cdot \frac{avg_l}{l(\mathfrak{C}(\acute{\mathfrak{v}}))}\right)\right) \geq$$

$$-\log\left(P_1\left(\acute{t}, (tf + \acute{tf}) \cdot \frac{avg_l}{l(\mathfrak{C}(\mathfrak{v}))}\right)\right) \cdot \left(1 - P_2\left(\acute{t}, (tf + \acute{tf}) \cdot \frac{avg_l}{l(\mathfrak{C}(\mathfrak{v}))}\right)\right)$$

Since the context of $\mathfrak{v}$ is a specialisation of $\acute{\mathfrak{v}}$ context, $l(\mathfrak{C}(\mathfrak{v})) \geq \mathfrak{C}(\acute{\mathfrak{v}})$. Therefore, $\frac{(tf+\acute{tf})}{l(\mathfrak{C}(\mathfrak{v}))} \leq \frac{\acute{tf}}{l(\mathfrak{C}(\acute{\mathfrak{v}}))}$ is valid when $tf = 0$, i.e. $\acute{t}$ is discriminatory. However, the truth-value is unknown when $\acute{tf} > 0$, i.e. t is a characteristic term. $\qquad\square$

As a consequence of proposition 3 conventional search engines do not suit context-document collections.

4.3   Retrieval Algorithm

Jones *et al.* suggest in [16] the creation of context-documents and the use of IR to retrieve them. But rather than exploiting the hierarchic nature of context, they assume self-contained documents that simply contain location information. This approach has a similar problem as the *characteristic term preservation* problem. In [21] they require that location information must yield higher scores than other terms. However, conventional IR algorithms are ignorant of location terms and do not assign higher relevance ratings. Therefore, they propose to assign predefined weights to these terms. Obviously, this approach has the disadvantage that the retrieval engine must be pre-configured to yield optimal performance. Rather than adopting this pre-configuration approach for composed context-documents, it is proposed to allow the data to speak for itself.

As already mentioned in section 2.2 moving along a context path corresponds to zooming in and out of context details. For a context retrieval engine, selecting documents is not only about ranking them it is rather about selecting the level of detail. Hence, a context retrieval engine must meet the following requirements:

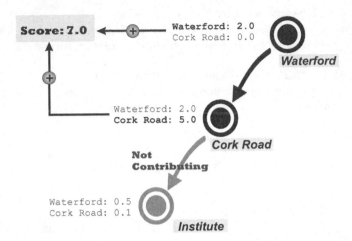

Fig. 3. Example of the context retrieval algorithm. Query terms are `Waterford` and `Cork Road`.

- One document per path: Multiple levels of details of a single context (i.e. context path) are expected to confuse the user. Therefore, the result-set should not contain a parent and any of its child vertices.
- Conservative selection: Zooming into irrelevant details is confusing for the user. When in doubt the algorithm should select a vertex which is associated with a less detailed view, i.e. it should zoom out rather than zoom in.

The retrieval algorithm is drafted in Figure 3. It is subdivided into two steps: Scoring and Filtering.

Scoring. Rather than scoring the composed context-documents, only the vertex-documents are scored. The score of the composed context-document is finally calculated from the vertex-document scores:

1. Calculate the term scores for each vertex-document.
2. Remove the documents from the result-set that do not match the query.
3. For each term and for each context path determine the maximum term scores.
4. The score value of the composed context-document is the sum of all its maximum term scores.

Figure 3 shows the score calculation for the context-documents *Cork Road* and *Waterford Institute*. The *Waterford* vertex yields the maximum score for the term *Waterford* and the *Cork Road* vertex yields the maximum score for the term *Cork Road*. These scores are summed-up and yield the scores of the context-documents *Cork Road* and *Waterford Institute of Technology*.

Filtering. The scoring algorithm identifies relevant context-documents. Still it does not select the level of detail and thus it might be that more than one vertex per context-document is returned. The solution to this problem is quite simple and is based on the observation that characteristic terms specify a level of detail: After the scoring step, the context retrieval engine removes all vertices that do not contribute to the term score of its context-document. Moreover, it removes all context-documents that are included in context-documents yielding a higher rating.

Figure 3 shows the filtering step. The vertex-document of the *Waterford Institute of Technology* does not contain any of the maximum term scores and thus it does not contribute to its context-document score. Consequently, the vertex is removed from the result-set. The *Waterford* vertex is also removed from the set as its context-document score is less than that of the *Cork Road*'s document. Finally, only the *Cork Road* vertex is returned. By Scoring of the individual vertex-documents, the algorithm preserves the term characteristics. The filtering step gives characteristic terms referring to a more detailed context-document a higher relevance than those referring to a less detailed view. Moreover, the filtering step implements the required conservative selection.

4.4   Result-Set Filtering

The described retrieval algorithm retrieves and filters context-documents with respect to the relevance of query terms. However, relevance with respect to location is not considered. Yet, location plays a decisive role in context-based systems. To take location constraints into account, the context retrieval engine must apply an additional filtering step to the result-set. To this end, it must just match the location information of the retrieved vertices with the location constraints of the query.

Apart from explicitly specified query terms context retrieval engines could also take implicitly captured information into account. That is, the user context could be exploited for further filtering operations. Finkelstein *et al.* [14] and Haveliwala [22] implement context-based search engines for web-browser. To this end, they capture the content of the current web-page or the browser history to improve queries. The basic idea of their approaches is that a user who has recently browsed tourist information will probably be interested in information about the island rather than the programming language when searching for Java. Similarly, a user's location context or activity context could be taken into account when retrieving context data. Lately, Chen proposed a *recommender system* based approach for a restaurant finder in [23]. It is expected that other information filtering approaches could also be adopted for context-based frameworks.[1]

4.5   Distributed Context Search Engine

Scalability is a major requirement of large scale context databases like the one developed by the Daidalos project [10]. Section 2.2 describes how Daidalos stores context information in a scalable way. Scalable storage is, however, useless when the retrieval algorithm does not scale. IR systems transform documents into vectors. Here, each vector component refers to a document term and its frequency.

---

[1] See [24] for an overview of information filtering systems.

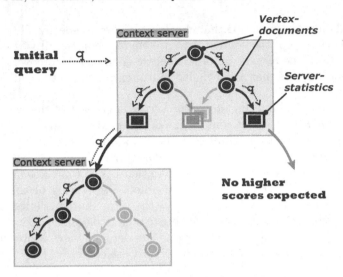

Fig. 4. Distributed query processing

The vectors are stored in an indexing database, based on this database document matching and ranking are straightforward. Context database servers are supposed to have the same setup. As long as all vertex-documents are stored in a single context database, matching and ranking is still simple. Yet, this approach does not suit a distributed context database.

Distributed Retrieval. Ideally, a query would propagate down the hierarchical structure and be processed in parallel. In fact, such a parallel processing approach can easily be implemented: Since the context retrieval algorithm's scoring step requires fetching of term scores, the query is propagated down the hierarchy; on its way collecting all the required statistics. Furthermore, the individual database servers filter vertex-documents that do not match the query's location constraints, thus reducing the amount of data exchanged between context database servers. Finally, the statistics are forwarded to the requesting database server, i.e. the server which received the query first. Here, the local context retrieval engine processes the statistics and retrieves the vertices. The described retrieval approach has the advantage that queries are processed in parallel. Yet, its performance can still be improved: Queries are passed down the hierarchy, irrespective of whether child vertices are relevant or not. Thus, lowering the retrieval performance and eventually overloading leaf servers. Basically, this problem corresponds to the database selection problem of IR. Yu *et al.* describe the problem in [25] and give a concise overview of potential solutions. Among these are quantitative solutions which are based on statistic information about the databases to select from. The principles of this solution can be applied to the actual context retrieval problem. The distributed context retrieval approach is drafted in Figure 4. Context database servers are required to store statistics about sub-trees in vectors, i.e. statistics about child server content. These vectors contain the maximum term scores of all vertex-documents stored on the corresponding servers. Thus, before the query is passed down to a child database server, the local retrieval engine firstly analyses whether the server is expected to contain content that is more relevant to the query than the vertex-documents already inspected.

5 Evaluation

The evaluation of an IR system is the process of assessing how well a system meets the information needs of its users — a measure which can hardly be obtained by statistical models. Therefore, the performance of IR systems is evaluated by laboratory tests: Such tests comprise test collections, test queries, and relevance judgments obtained from independent experts [26]. The Text REtrieval Conference (TREC), organised by the American National Institute of Standards and Technology (NIST), is probably the most well-known laboratory experiment [27]. Unfortunately, due to the fact that the context retrieval approach is novel there are no suitable test collections available.

5.1 Test Collection and Metrics

There is no alternative to the creation of a test collection. To get a representative set of documents already existing ones have been used; the collection is published on the Internet [28]. Basically, the test collection comprises models of Waterford and Athens city. Following information sources have been used: maps of Waterford and Athens, wikipedia.org, web-pages retrieved by Google, and the guidebooks: "The Rough Guide to Ireland" and "The City of Athens"[2].

Three query-sets have been created: streets, addresses, and sightseeing. The *streets* query-sets contains just street name queries. It is context independent in the sense that all information required to retrieve relevant documents is contained in vertex-documents. However, the query-set *addresses* (Waterford collection only) is partially context dependent, i.e. vertices cannot be found without knowledge of their context. (BP station "Cork Road") is an example of such a query. The vertex-document of the *BP station* has been created from the BP web-page and does not contain any information specific to the filling station at *Cork Road*. Finally, the collection *sightseeing* contains only context dependent queries. The overall test collection comprises 290 documents and 340 queries.

The context-retrieval engine has been compared with Terrier, a conventional IR engine developed by the Glasgow University [29, 30]. To demonstrate the power of the scoring algorithm, the engine has also been compared with a context search engine that scores composed context-documents. Based on the tests the metrics *precision* and *recall* have been calculated. *Precision* is measured as the proportion of documents retrieved which are relevant, whereas *recall* is the proportion of the available relevant documents that have been retrieved [31].

---

[2] http://www.cityofathens.gr, http://www.greece-athens.com

Table 1. Evaluation results: precision and recall (* context dependent)

Waterford collection						
	Streets		Addresses*		Sightseeing*	
Engine	Prec.	Rec.	Prec.	Rec.	Prec.	Rec.
naive retriever	0.66	0.71	0.94	0.98	0.88	0.92
Terrier	0.73	0.96	0.71	0.79	0.14	0.15
context-retriever	0.87	0.96	0.93	0.98	0.88	0.92
Athens collection						
	Streets		Addresses		Sightseeing*	
Engine	Prec.	Rec.	Prec.	Rec.	Prec.	Rec.
naive retriever	0.47	0.47	0.82	0.95	0.74	0.78
Terrier	0.71	0.95	0.83	0.96	0.25	0.31
context-retriever	0.81	1.00	0.86	0.97	0.90	0.99

Precision and *recall* do not take relevance rankings into account. But on the one hand *precision* and *recall* are popular metrics and on the other hand it is expected that relevance rankings are of minor importance in context-based retrieval: With context-aware applications the user is often mobile and frequently involved in other tasks. When a retrieved document is brought to his attention this is an intrusion in his activities. Rhodes and Maes [32] have observed that in context-based environments *precision* is generally more important than *recall*. It is therefore concluded that document ranking is also of minor importance.

5.2 Results

Table 1 shows the experiments' results. The three retrieval engines are the naive-retriever which is a conventional IR engine that is enhanced by result-set filtering, Terrier, and the context-retriever as described in section 4.3. In contrast to the context-retriever and naive-retriever Terrier has been applied to the vertex-document collection rather than to composed context-documents. Otherwise its precision would have been considerably low. The experiments show that the context-retriever clearly outperforms the other engines. Particularly, when the queries are strongly context dependent the context-retriever is superior. Here, Terrier's performance is extremely poor as it lacks any means to analyse documents in their context, i.e. it is unable to analyse the document hierarchy - admittedly an unfair comparison. But also in case that the queries are context independent, the context-retriever's result-set filtering algorithm yields superior noise reduction, i.e. yields higher precision. It easily filters out irrelevant documents having similar context as relevent ones when the documents share a hierarchy path. For example, when querying a street name, Terrier returns the street entity and all restaurants located at this street as the restaurants' menu cards (which are used to describe the restaurants) contain address information. However, the context-retriever is able to analyse the relationships between the street and the restaurants. Thus it filters the restaurant entities out. Though the naive-retriever performs quite well on context dependent query-sets, it fails when queries are context independent. A close analysis of the log-files showed that this failure is caused by the engine's inability to weigh up document length against term frequencies. That is, the engine fails to filter out leaf-vertex noise. Actually, this has been predicted by proposition 3. Leaf-vertex noise is caused by child nodes containing their parents' characteristic terms; a phenomenon that is due to the manner the collection has been created. The authors of the documents did not expect them to be placed in their location context. That is, they considered their documents to be self-contained and added context information.

Even though the performance of the context-retriever is excellent, it cannot guarantee the retrieval of relevant documents. The retrieval results can therefore hardly be processed by context reasoning systems; a problem which will be addressed by future research.

6   Discussion

It is very difficult to design a consistent context Ontology. Noy who discussed this problem with respect to the Semantic Web believes that consistency is even impossible [6]. He suggests using Ontology editors to mend the imminent chaos. The proposed context retrieval approach has similar objectives. Yet, it is more than a support tool for Ontology implementation and usage; it partially replaces Ontologies by plain text documents where strict specifications are not required. Small businesses like restaurants can simply describe their business by textual descriptions like menu cards — and still they are adequately represented in the context model. Users and applications can retrieve them by submitting free-text query terms. However, the results are only human readable, applications can hardly reason with free-text semantic descriptions. It is an interesting field of future research to investigate means allowing even applications to understand free-text semantics. A further area of research will be the refinement of the approach. In particular, the search engine will be extended to facilitate the retrieval of highly dynamic context objects like for example users and cars. Such objects have tight time-constraints and therefore the engine must be able to process real-time information.

References

1. Gu, T., Pung, H., Zhang, D.Q.: Toward an OSGI-based Infrastructure for Context-Aware Applications. IEEE Pervasive Computing **3** (2004) 66–74
2. Wang, X., Dong, J.S., Chin, C., Hettiarachchi, S., Zhang, D.: Semantic Space: An Infrastructure for Smart Spaces. IEEE Pervasive Computing **3** (2004) 32–39
3. Christopoulou, E., Kameas, A.: GAS Ontology: An ontology for collaboration among ubiquitous computing. International Journal of Human-Computer Studies: Special issue on Protege **62** (2005) 664–685
4. Preuveneers, J., Bergh, D.W., Georges, A., Rigole, P., Clerckx, T., Berbers, Y., Coninx, K., Jonckers, V., Bosschere, K.: Towards an extensible context ontology for Ambient Intelligence. In: 2nd European Symposium on Ambient Intelligence

(EUSAI 2004). Volume 3295 of LNCS., Eindhoven, Nederlands, Springer-Verlag, Germany (2004) 148–159

5. Khedr, M., Karmouch, A.: ACAI: Agent-based context-aware infrastructure for spontaneous applications. Journal of Network and Computer Applications **28** (2005) 19–44

6. Noy, N.: Order from chaos. ACM Queue **3** (2005) http://www.acmqueue.org.

7. Guiasu, S.: Information theory with applications. McGraw-Hill Inc., UK (1977)

8. Dey, A.K.: Understanding and using context. Personal and Ubiquitous Computing Journal **5** (2001) 4–7

9. Daidalos Consortium: Designing Advanced network Interfaces for the Delivery and Administration of Location independent, Optimised personal Services (DAIDA-LOS). http://www.ist-daidalos.org (2005)

10. Strimpakou, M., Roussaki, I., Pils, C., Angermann, M., Robertson, P., Anagnostou, M.: Context modelling and management in ambient-aware pervasive environments. In: Location- and Context-Awareness: First International Workshop (LoCA 2005). Volume 3479 of LNCS., Munich, Springer-Verlag, Germany (2005) 2–15

11. Bauer, M., Becker, C., Rothermel, K.: Location models from the perspective of context-aware applications and mobile ad hoc networks. Personal and Ubiquitous Computing **6** (2002) 322–328

12. Shekhar, S., Chawla, S., Ravada, S., Fetterer, A., Liu, X., Lu, C.: Spatial databases — Accomplishments and research needs. IEEE Transactions on Knowledge and Data Engineering **11** (1999) 45–55

13. Larson, R.R., Frontiera, P.: Spatial ranking methods for Geographic Information Retrieval (GIR) in digital libraries. In Heery, R., Lyon, L., eds.: 8th European Conference of Research and Advanced Technology for Digital Libraries (ECDL 2004). Volume 3232 of Lecture Notes in Computer Science (LNCS)., Bath, UK, Springer-Verlag Berlin, Germany (2004) 45–56

14. Finkelstein, L., Gabrilovich, E., Matias, Y., Rivlin, E., Solan, Z., Wolfman, G., Ruppin, E.: Placing search in context: The concept revisited. ACM Transactions on Information Systems **20** (2002) 116–131

15. Kammanahalli, H., Gopalan, S., Sridhar, V., Ramamritham, K.: Context aware retrieval in web-based collaborations. In: Third IEEE International Conference on Pervasive Computing and Communications Workshops (PERCOMW'05): Workshop on Context Modeling and Reasoning (CoMoRea'04), IEEE computer society press (2004) 8–12

16. Jones, G.J.F., Brown, P.J.: Context-aware retrieval for ubiquitous computing environments. In Crestani, F., Dunlop, M.D., Mizzaro, S., eds.: Mobile HCI Workshop on Mobile and Ubiquitous Information Access. Volume 2954 of Lecture Notes in Computer Science., Udine, Italy (2003) 227–243

17. Lesk, M.: The seven ages of information retrieval. In: Proceedings of the conference for the 50th anniversery of As we May Think, International Federation of Library Associations and Institutions (1995) http://www.ifla.org/VI/5/op/udtop5/udt-op5.pdf.

18. Jones, K.S., Walker, S., Robertson, S.E.: A probabilistic model of information retrieval: development and comparative experiments - part 2. Information Processing and Management **36** (2000) 809–840

19. Amati, G., Van Rijsbergen, J.C.: Probabilistic models of information retrieval based on measuring the divergence from randomness. ACM Transactions on Information Systems (TOIS) **20** (2002) 357–389

20. Carpineto, C., de Mori, R., Romano, G., Bigi, B.: An information-theoretic approach to automaitc query expansion. ACM Transactions on Information Systems **19** (2001) 1–27

21. Brown, J.P., Jones, G.J.: Exploiting contextual change in context-aware retrieval. In: Proceedings of the 17th ACM Symposium on Applied Computing (SAC 2002), Madrid, ACM press (2002) 650–656
22. Haveliwala, T.H.: Topic-sensitive pagerank: A context-sensitive ranking algorithm for web search. IEEE Transactions on Knowledge and Data Engineering **15** (2003) 784–796
23. Chen, A.: Context-aware collaborative filtering system: Predicting the user's preference in the ubiquitous computing environment. In: Location- and Context-Awareness: First International Workshop (LoCA 2005). Volume 3479 of LNCS., Munich, Springer-Verlag, Germany (2005) 244–253
24. Hanani, U., Shapira, B., Shoval, P.: Information filtering: Overview of issues, research and systems. User Modeling and User-Adapted Interaction **11** (2001) 203–259
25. Yu, C., Liu, K.L., Meng, W., Wu, Z., Rishe, N.: A methodology to retrieve text documents from multiple databases. IEEE Transactions on Knowledge and Data Engineering **14** (2002) 1347–1361
26. Voorhees, E.: The philosophy of information retrieval evaluation. In Peters, C., Barschler, M., Gonzalo, J., Kluck, M., eds.: Evaluation of Cross-Language Information Retrieval Systems. Second Workshop of the Cross-Language Evaluation Forum, CLEFF 2001. Volume 2406 of Lecture Notes in Computer Science (LNCS)., Darmstad, Germany, Springer Verlag, Berlin (2001) 355–370
27. National Institute of Standards and Technology: Text REtrieval Conference (TREC). http://trec.nist.gov (2005)
28. Pils, C.: Homepage. http://www.pils.it (2005)
29. University of Glasgow, Informtion Retrieval Group: TERabyte RetrIEveR (Terrier). http://ir.dcs.gla.ac.uk/terrier (2005)
30. Ounis, I., Amati, G., V., P., He, B., Macdonald, C., Johnson: Terrier Information Retrieval Platform. In: Proceedings of the 27th European Conference on IR Research (ECIR 2005). Volume 3408 of Lecture Notes in Computer Science (LNCS)., Springer-Verlag Berlin, Germany (2005) 517–519
31. Rijsbergen, C.: 7. Evaluation. In: Information Retrieval. 2 edn. Butterworths (1979) 112–139
32. Rhodes, B.J., Maes, P.: Just-in-time information retrieval agents. IBM Systems Journal **39** (2000) 685–704

Scripting Your Home

Mirko Knoll[1], Torben Weis[1], Andreas Ulbrich[2], and Alexander Brändle[3]

[1] Universität Stuttgart, Universitätsstrasse 38, Stuttgart
{knoll, weis}@informatik.uni-stuttgart.de
[2] Technische Universität Berlin, Einsteinufer 17, 10587 Berlin
ulbi@ivs.tu-berlin.de
[3] Microsoft Research Cambridge
alexbr@microsoft.com

Abstract. Our homes and lives are as individual as ourselves. Many aspects, such as technical equipment, furniture, and usage patterns in these surroundings differ. Thus, personalization of applications that operate in such environments is required. The challenge for tools and programming paradigms is to provide a powerful but yet easy-to-use platform. In this paper we illustrate how our visual scripting language puts these requirements for programming ubiquitous computing environments into action.

1 Introduction

Ubiquitous computing and its application in the smart home have been in the focus of research for some time [1][2][3]. New kinds of applications create demand for specialized software engineering tools. Thus, system support [4] for pervasive applications, specialized middleware [5][6], and end-user tools [7][8][9][10] have been investigated. However, these tools address either professional developers or end-users. Our target audience, advanced computer users and hobby programmers, reside between both extremes, though the tools available are not suited for them. Devices are very heterogeneous due to the variation of capabilities of devices, e.g. some devices react on hard-wired commands, some on infrared signals as well as some devices have powerful CPUs and a large amount of memory where as others only have the computing power of a calculator. This makes it hard for the developers to integrate different classes of devices into a single application. Furthermore, applications integrating several devices are inherently distributed. These facts among others make the development process tedious, long winded and to complex for our target audience. On the other hand, developers could apply end-user tools such as SiteView [7] or iCap [8]. These tools allow a simpler development process as they abstract from heterogeneity. Thus, they are suited for end-users but not for professional developers as the simplification takes place at the expense of expressiveness. We believe that there is a gap between the high-end programming frameworks and end-user tools. Therefore, with VRDK we present a toolkit that is easier to use and at the same time more expressive than end-user tools.

The next section discusses related programming models for pervasive computing. Then, we demonstrate VRDK's functionality followed by a more detailed

M. Hazas, J. Krumm, and T. Strang (Eds.): LoCA 2006, LNCS 3987, pp. 274–288, 2006.

presentation of its main concepts. In the following sections we highlight the tool architecture and describe our experience with the tool. The paper closes with conclusions and outlook.

2   Programming Models

Programming pervasive applications is very complex and still subject to ongoing research. This is due to several facts like the use of many heterogeneous devices, the distributed execution of programs, or the mobility of devices. Thus, the related work consists of many different approaches, which we discuss in the following sections.

2.1   General Purpose Programming Languages

Many end-user applications provide means for scripting with a general purpose programming language. However, only few end-users are able to use this feature. These languages map everything to stateful objects and messages which are exchanged between these objects. This is the swiss army knife approach to all kinds of programming tasks. For computer scientists this is a great achievement of object-orientation. For non-computer scientists this abstraction results in a steep learning curve. Ideally, important concepts such as context and persons should become first-level concepts of the language.

Todays programming languages often use a text-based notation. However, text-based languages are easier to read than to write. Writing a program implies that you know the syntax and keywords by heart. Tools will tell you about your mistakes only *after* you made (i.e. typed) them. Ideally, a tool could tell you *before-hand* which options you have. We conclude that general programming languages are very powerful tools, but too difficult for the intended audience.

2.2   End-User Programming Tools

In contrast to general purpose programming languages, end-user programming tools are designed to be used intuitively. This way even computer illiterates should be able to develop simple applications.

Programming by demonstration. A simple way of telling the computer what to do, is to demonstrate one's intentions to it. We distinguish between two methods, the input via a physical demonstration, e.g., in front of a camera and the input by recording a macro.

Physical. In [7] the authors present SiteView, a rule-based toolkit that bases on tangibles as a means to interact with the environment. Applications are built by adding rules to the situation the user is actually in. Therefore, she arranges tangibles, which are foam cards, representing objects in the environment, on a floorplan. Those are equipped with RFID tags and will be recognized by computer cameras and tag readers. Thus, a user can create a rule, e.g. one that switches on the lights and turns up the heat when it is raining in the morning.

The difficulty is that users have to learn how to arrange the tangibles on the floorplan so that the computer understands the situation as intended by the developer. Furthermore, special hardware is needed for building and recognizing the tangibles. Other systems like iCap [8] (developed from SATIN [11]) and a CAPpella [9] share a similar set of functions but feature different input methods e.g. creating rules by demonstration. However, these tools do not support negation of conditions, for instance it is not possible to specify the condition "if no one is in the room".

Macro. Office applications usually feature a macro recorder. The user starts the recorder, performs a sequence of actions, and the recorder saves this sequence as a macro. Afterwards, the user can replay the macro whenever needed. Applied to ubiquitous systems, the user would just have to perform a sequence of actions in the real world and instruct the computer to repeat them. It sounds interesting to apply this idea to pervasive systems since it does not require any programming in the classical sense. The problem here is that macro recorders cannot distinguish between events and actions. Imagine a user who leaves his house, locks the door, and turns on the alarm system. Here, leaving the house *and* locking the door build a composed event that should lead to an action: the activation of the alarm system. But the computer could as well assume that it should lock the door when someone leaves the house.

Furthermore, the limitations of the real world may force the user to perform the action before she performs the triggering event. For example, the user wants the computer to stop playing music when she leaves the house. For obvious reasons, the user must first turn off the music and then leave the house. The software must be clever enough to understand that leaving the house is the triggering event and stopping the music the desired action (although they occurred in reverse order).

Storyboards. Topiary [10] is a rapid-prototyping tool for location-based applications developed by GUIR Berkeley. It builds on a storyboard-based approach. A storyboard consists of a set of *screens* and *events* that trigger a transition from one screen to another. In Topiary the user can define location-related events, for example "Alice is near Bob". This event can cause the "My friends" screen to appear on the PDA of Bob. Storyboards in general are useful for prototyping. However, their expressive power is limited. Furthermore, Topiary is limited to location-related events and it can only influence screens on a PDA or monitor. It is not possible to react to other events such as "DVD playback started" and the user cannot control arbitrary devices.

Jigsaw. In [12] an editor for applications in ubiquitous domestic environments is presented. It allows the user to connect components using a jigsaw puzzle-style approach. Devices available in a room present themselves as a jigsaw piece on a graphical editor. By combining several pieces on the screen the user connects the output of one piece with the input of another. For example, pieces for motion detector, camera, and PDA can be combined to construct a simplistic surveillance system. The motion detector triggers the camera and the camera shows its picture on the PDA. The drawback of this approach is that it has only a linear control flow and no means for mathematics. Essential control structures like branches and loops cannot be mapped to this programming model.

2.3   Domain-Specific Programming Languages

This area comprises languages that are specialized for a single application domain. Thus, they are very powerful and yet easy to use even by non-professional developers. However, the specialization for a single domain prevents these languages from being used in other domains as they would not be applicable there.

Scientific Programming. Physicists use special programming tools such as LabView or SoftWire to evaluate the sensor data they collect during experiments and to control their equipment. These tools rely on the basic idea of wiring components. A component can represent a real device or a piece of software. Each component features input and output connectors which can be connected. This works quite well for applications that are concerned with continuous flow of pseudo analog data, i.e. if programmers have to deal with raw sensor data or audio/video streams. In our scenario end-user programmers are more interested in discrete high-level events such as "Alice entered the room" or "DVD playback started". For this purpose these tools do not provide the optimal level of abstraction.

Toy Robots. Programmable toy robots such as Lego Mindstorms are extremely popular. The Lego robots ship with a simple graphical programming language that can even be mastered by children. In this programming model the robot is treated as a set of sensors and actuators. Sensors are the sources of events. The user can program a workflow that is executed when such an event occurs. Throughout this workflow the actuators (i.e., motor, lamp, etc.) can be controlled. The Lego Mindstorms approach is a graphical language that combines sensors and actuators as first-level concepts with flow concepts (branch, loop, etc.) found in general purpose programming languages. This approach has fewer restrictions than storyboards, jigsaw puzzles, or macro recording since it is closer to general purpose languages. Due to its specialization for its target application domain (i.e., robotics) it is still easy to learn and use.

VRDK. With VRDK we present a high-level graphical language to develop pervasive applications. Thus, we provide a counterpart to languages like VisualBasic in the domain of desktop applications. Our tool is more powerful than end-user programming tools since we support all major programming constructs. This makes VRDK as potent as any other programming language. However, we managed to integrate concepts as context and persons into the language as well. This makes our tool suitable for developing pervasive applications while keeping the complexity on a moderate level. Scientific Programming and the toy robots address the same audience as we do, but concentrate on another application domain. This is why we think that we can fill the gap between professional and end-user development tools. In the following sections we will describe our tool in more detail and fortify our allegations.

3   The Tool at a Glance

VRDK is an easy to learn graphical tool that enables users to script their e-home. Its capabilities reach from easy automation tasks to more complex control applications. As VRDK is a TabletPC application, it can be used with a pen. It does not require keyboard input. The user can create scripts either via drag&drop or by handwriting commands directly on the screen. In this section we provide a quick walkthrough that demonstrates the simplicity of software development (see Figure 1) when using VRDK.

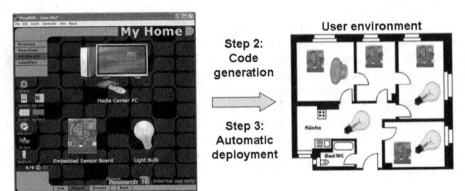

Fig. 1. Development process

In our example, we want to accomplish two tasks utilizing the basic features of VRDK. First, we want to put the living room in cinema mode when DVD playback starts. Once the playback stops or is paused, we want to switch the room back to normal. Second, we want the light to turn on when somebody moves into the living room.

A VRDK script consists of a set of *processes* and a set of *hardware*. For each of these concepts, our tool provides a dedicated screen. Using the buttons in the upper left corner the user can switch between these screens. The user starts by dragging in the required hardware from the tool bar on the left, i.e. the Media Center PC, an intelligent light bulb, and an embedded sensor board with motion detector. This is shown in Figure 1 Step 1.

The user then switches to the process screen. He creates a new process and drags in the required commands. Figure 2 shows how the user adds a wait command to the process. He can achieve this either via drag&drop or via hand-writing. The first thing our application has to do is to wait for DVD playback to start. The user can simply click on the matching event in the wait command dialog. Then, the user drags in some commands to switch off the light in cinema mode and to set the volume to a decent level. Finally, our application has to wait until playback stops and turn the light on again. Our second task is to turn on the light when someone enters the room. Therefore, the user adds a second

Fig. 2. Waiting for DVD playback to start

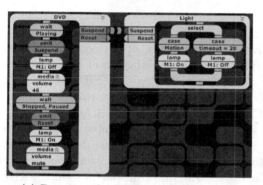

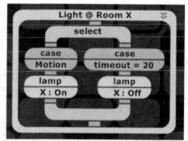

(a) Processes for DVD and light control   (b) Location-dependent processes

Fig. 3. Example applications

process to the script. The process waits either for a movement or a certain time to elapse. Upon movement the light is turned on, upon timeout it is turned off. Figure 3(a) shows the complete example. Step 2-4 in Figure 1 complete the development process. The code generator transforms the script into executable code and automatically deploys it on the participating devices: the application runs distributed in the environment of the user.

The drawback of this intermediate solution is that both processes interfere. During DVD playback we don't want the light to be turned on when someone moves in the room. To demonstrate interprocess communication in VRDK we want to achieve this by suspending the Light process during DVD playback. Therefore the DVD process emits a Suspend signal during DVD playback and a Reset signal after playback. These signals are connected to receivers in the Light process. The user can connect emitters and receivers simply by drawing a line from emitter to receiver. The belt indicates that emitter and receiver are connected. VRDK shows the connection only when the pen or mouse hovers over the emitter or receiver to avoid too many lines crossing each others. The next section discusses the programming model behind VRDK and its relation to other end-user programming approaches.

4   A Programming Model for E-Home Scripting

Every programming model has its pros and cons. On one hand, extremely special-ized ones are comparatively easy to learn but limited to a small set of scenarios. On the other hand, generic solutions are powerful but hard to learn. The aim of our tool is to find a balance between both extremes. Our target audience are technically interested users who do not necessarily master a general purpose programming language. If someone is able to program a Lego robot, she should be able to use our tool, too. The tool builds on the following concepts: compo-nents, events, commands, mathematical expressions, workflows, and context. In the following sections we motivate and discuss these concepts in more detail.

4.1   Components

Ubiquitous applications usually involve a large range of devices and services. Currently, our tool supports Smartphones, PDAs, Media Center PCs, Browser, Media Player, Microsoft Agents, Embedded Sensor Boards (ESB) [13], RC5 re-mote controls (for HiFi and TV equipment) and several toy robots including Lego Mindstorms and an enhanced RoboSapiens. These devices and services are represented by components which are dragged from the toolbar on the editor window (see Figure 1). To the user it does not matter how these devices are con-trolled and which networking protocols they provide as this is encapsulated in the component. Thus, our tool offers full distribution transparency since VRDK automatically disseminates the program on the proper devices.

With each component a set of commands and events are introduced. For example, a component for controlling a Media Center PC introduces commands, e.g. to start playback or adjust the volume. Additionally, this component emits an event when it starts the DVD playback.

4.2   Events

Events are central to ubiquitous applications [14][15]. Typically, applications spend most of their time waiting for an event in the real world. End-users do not care about raw sensor data and its routing, aggregation, and interpretation. They are interested in high-level events such as "Alice enters the room" or "DVD playback stopped". Components emit these events. Often applications have to wait for composite events [16], for example "Everybody left the house and the door is locked".

Our tool takes this into consideration and features a very powerful but easy to use wait command (see Figure 2). With a special dialog, the user can select the events the application should wait for. Additionally, the user can specify a timeout or time of day. Furthermore, advanced users can constrain events with expressions, for example "`LivingRoom.People` > 3". In this case, the wait command is satisfied when more than three people are in the living room.

4.3   Commands

Unlike object-oriented languages, VRDK does not break down everything into objects and methods. If a component offers some functionality, it introduces a new command. A command provides means to create side-effects, i.e. to control the components. Each command features a graphical representation for the GUI and a dialog to configure the command. For example, the media player component offers a command for controlling audio/video playback. Thus, the user can program audio playback using drag&drop and a file dialog to select the audio file. Commands are conceptually comparable to calling methods of a component, however a VRDK command is more coarse grained than a method of an object-oriented language. For example, our MediaPlayer plug-in features only one command to control media playback, although the component features a multitude of methods. Otherwise the user interface would not scale up, because all commands are listed in the icon-bar on the left side of the screen.

4.4   Workflow

We already discussed that VRDK allows the programmer to wait for events and to control components with commands. Workflows orchestrate events and commands. VRDK supports the full range of workflow elements: processes, branches (if/then/else), loops and select.

A VRDK program consists of one or multiple processes each containing a workflow that is executed in an infinite loop. The workflow determines for which events the application waits and which commands are executed if an event occurs. Figure 3(a) shows how the workflow constructs are displayed in the editor. Branches and loops are self explanatory. The select statement waits for any of several alternative events.

Users can even program inter-process communication using asynchronous events. Hence processes can suspend and reset other processes. This is realized by sending signals with the `emit` command which can be connected to one or multiple `receivers`. The workflow on the receiver side can wait for a signal using the standard `wait` command.

4.5   Context

Context is a very important concept in pervasive applications. Thus, we made it a first-level entity of our programming language. In traditional programming languages we bind functionality to dedicated computers. If the user wants to use an application, she must interact with the computer executing this application. In pervasive applications functionality is bound to context, i.e. a certain location, situation, or person. Following the ideas of [17] VRDK allows you to define tasks (i.e. processes in VRDK terms) and attach these processes to some context. Currently, VRDK allows you to bind processes to *locations, physical mobile objects*, and *situations*. The user just opens the properties dialog of a process and selects from a list of possible anchors, e.g. "kitchen", "living room", "Alice", "Bob", "meeting". These anchors are derived at design time from the meta-model of our context-server, e.g. if the meta-model knows about "kitchens", VRDK applications can bind functionality to kitchens. In addition to locations and physical objects, the context-server knows about situations, e.g. "meetings" or "dinner". If the meta-model knows about "meetings" and that persons participate in meetings, an application can bind itself to meetings and ask the context-server for the meeting room and all persons participating in this meetings. For evaluation purposes we are using a light version of the Nexus context-server [18]. All communication with the context-server is encapsulated in a plug-in which allows us to replace the context-server without major changes to VRDK itself. At runtime VRDK applications send subscriptions to the context-server, e.g. to track the position of a person or to become notified about started meetings. The context-server sends events back to the application. Furthermore, VRDK sends queries to the context-server to retrieve location data and to find devices such as beamers or media players. The following sections discuss how VRDK applications can use context information.

Location. VRDK developers can bind functionality to a location (e.g. a special room) or a type of location (e.g. all rooms, all doors). Therefore, VRDK requires a *location model* [19][20][15] to learn about the environment in which the application executes. The context-server uses maps and 3D-models about the environment, which have been entered manually in the database of the context-server. In the future we plan to enable the user to draw his/her own floorplan as this will greatly simplify the process of creating location models for use by the context-server. Through the plug-in the context-server then tells VRDK which location types exist (rooms, floors, houses) and which instances exist (room 1.432, Joe's bedroom). Processes can then be bound to these location types and instances. If such a process refers to a device, e.g. a media player, VRDK will query the location model for devices at the specified location. Figure 3(b) provides an example that binds functionality to every room and starts one light-control process for each of them. This process waits for a motion event and turns on the light. If there is no motion for a certain time, it turns off the light. VRDK will find out that in our example the process requires one motion sensor and one controllable lamp per room. Rooms that do not feature the required components are ignored. We are currently investigating debug mechanisms that explain the developer *why* some location has been ignored.

Situations. If the context-server can detect situations (i.e. "family having dinner", or "Alice meets Bob"), you can bind functionality to situations. Once such a situation is detected, a corresponding process is started. When the situation ends, the processes receives a stop signal. For example, you could implement a process that turns off a TV and bind it to "family having dinner". Thus, when the context-server detects an ongoing dinner and a nearby TV, the process is executed and turns off the TV. Implementing this example in VRDK is a one minute job. However, detecting situations is beyond the scope of our work. We expect the context-server to provide this information, i.e. to send an event when a situation is detected and to answer queries regarding the location and the participating persons.

Physical Objects. For "follow-me" applications it is important to bind functionality to physical objects. This does of course require that sensors can track the position of these objects and submit this information to the context-server. Thus, you could for example bind a process to every employee to track when she entered or left the building.

5   Tool Architecture

In this section we discuss the user interface of our tool. Furthermore, we illustrate the script execution of VRDK. VRDK has been designed as an open and extensible platform for e-home scripting. Therefore, it realizes a framework-based approach that builds on the concept of plug-ins.

5.1   Plug-Ins

Since VRDK is written in C# and .NET, VRDK plug-ins must reside in a .NET DLL. Currently, VRDK can control Microsoft Media Center, Smartphones, PDAs, Browsers, Media Player, MS Agents, several robots (including Lego Mindstorm and RoboSapiens), and Embedded Sensors Boards. Furthermore, VRDK features a plug-in wizard that further simplifies plug-in development. An average plug-in consists of 500 lines of C# code, where more than half is generated by the wizard.

A plug-in can add new components, commands, and events to VRDK. All components appear in the icon-bar on the left side of the screen (see Figure 1). Once the user drags a component on the hardware view (Figure 1 Step 1) or location model (Figure 1 Step 4), the associated commands, and events become available in the editor. In doing so, the user has those commands at hand that make sense for his current scenario. Following the above example, the media player component added a `media` command to the icon bar.

As detailed in the following section, VRDK supports a built-in interpreter and code generation framework. If a plug-in adds new components, commands, and events, it must provide callbacks for the interpreter and extensions for the code generator. Although plug-ins must be implemented in .NET, that does not imply that the supported devices must be .NET compatible. Only the design-time support in VRDK is .NET specific. The runtime can use any possible technology. This way, the tool is not limited to a fixed set of devices and can easily be extended.

5.2   User Interface

VRDK can be used in mouse mode and in ink mode. In mouse mode the user drags commands from the icon-bar on the left side of the screen on the editor. While the user is dragging a command, the editor provides immediate visual feedback. In Figure 4(a) the user drags the icon of the wait command on the process. This causes the process box to expand vertically. This way, the user can see where the wait command would be inserted if she drops it now. Once the command has been dropped, the user can open a properties dialog to configure the command.

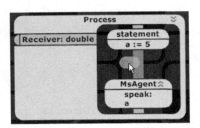   

(a) Mouse mode   (b) Auto-size for ink input

Fig. 4. Input methods

Ink mode requires a TabletPC and is therefore optional. In ink mode the user can write in the diagram as shown in Figure 4(b). In our first attempt the user could write across the diagram. Once finished, VRDK runs the text recognition and analyzes where the user put the ink. VRDK used this geometry information to decide where the recognized command should be inserted in the diagram. Our user experiments have shown that this is not very useful. First, the ink is hard to read when written across a colored diagram. Second, the immediate feedback is missing, i.e. the user is writing a command such as `wait Receiver` and afterwards VRDK decides where in the diagram the text belongs. The result was often not the intended one. In our second approach, we exploit the expanding diagram feature as discussed above. When the user starts writing, VRDK decides where in the diagram the recognized text will be inserted. The diagram expands and inserts a half-transparent white background as shown in Figure 4(b). This way the user knows from the very beginning where the recognized text will be inserted. Furthermore, the ink is better readable due to the higher contrast. As the user keeps on writing, the half-transparent background and the diagram continuously expand to make room for the handwriting.

VRDK can be used without a keyboard, which is especially useful for Tablet-PCs. As it turned out, entering mathematical formulas with ink still results in unacceptable recognition rates. Therefore, we added a pocket calculator style interface for entering formulas (see Figure 5). Another advantage of this dialog is that you do not have to learn any syntax. All possible operators and identifiers are listed in the dialog. The user just clicks on them.

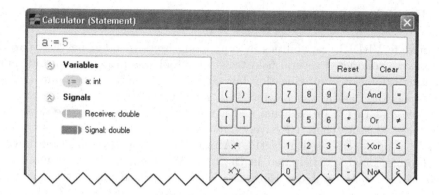

Fig. 5. Writing statements using the calculator

5.3   Script Execution: Interpreter

The interpreter can be started by clicking on the Run button at the bottom of the screen. Clicking on the screen again immediately stops the script and turns off all involved devices. This way, users can quickly and conveniently experiment with scripts.

The VRDK interpreter is able to execute the workflow (via the state machines) and evaluate mathematical expression. Furthermore, all event handling is done by the interpreter. Whenever the interpreter comes across a command or event that has been introduced by a plug-in, it asks the plug-in to execute the command. This way, the interpreter can be easily extended with plug-ins.

The interpreter uses a centralized approach, i.e. all application-logic is executed on a PC. Therefore some devices have to be accessed remotely. To the interpreter this does not matter since all communication with the component or service is managed by the plug-in that introduced the component.

5.4   Script Execution: Code Generation

VRDK features a code generation framework. The concrete code generator is realized with a plug-in, too. Currently, we support C# and C. New plug-ins could support different target languages.

The key advantage of code generation is that we can avoid centralized script execution. If several programmable devices are involved, VRDK can distribute the script across the devices. In the case of distributed code generation, we rely on a middleware that can transport messages between the devices. In our current settings we are using a publish/subscribe middleware [21] that is available for .NET and .NET compact framework. Efficiently distributing the script across the involved devices is very demanding and is subject to ongoing research. In general, our code generator framework supports two modes. One is a master-slave mode where one device takes over the roll of the coordinator. This is useful if a powerful device such as a PC is available. The other mode is completely decentralized and is applicable if all devices are restricted with respect to CPU, RAM, and energy.

6   Experience

To validate VRDK's capabilities in supporting users to build pervasive applications, we conducted several field tests. Our tool was presented on four non-scientific exhibitions, an education fair, and Europe's largest tech fair. On the latter one, our booth was located at a large Home Entertainment exhibitor to likewise attract a professional and a non-scientific audience. We developed challenges to study how effectively the users were able to create scripts in VRDK using a pen-based TabletPC. Around 500 people ranging from novices to IT-professionals participated in the task. We spent about 5 minutes with each user in a tutorial on using the VRDK interface and describing their task.

The first task was to write a simple control program that only contained a series of commands. The users could rely on set of predefined functions. The concept of dragging commands from the icon-bar on the editor proved to be useful especially at the beginning. However, the testers soon got accustomed with the user interface and the preferred ink support over the drag&drop input for writing commands. Therefore they solved the task much faster than originally expected.

The next task built on the first one but included the necessity for loops and mathematical formulas. Therefore, the concept of events and the ability to wait for events were briefly explained. After the tutorial everybody could apply those concepts. Loops and events were easily integrated into the programs, but devising mathematical formulas turned out to be difficult for half of the testees lacked basic mathematical knowledge. Once they knew which formula to enter they had no problem using the pen to enter it in VRDK. Nevertheless, the overall result for this task has been poorer than expected.

The VRDK user interface appeared to have a shallow learning curve. The participants did not need much assistance and their speed increased as they were given some hints and got familiar with the pen. Interestingly, nobody ever asked for a keyboard. Though many testers had difficulties with mathematical formulas at the beginning, the overall feedback reported was that the system was easy to use.

7   Conclusions and Future Work

With VRDK we presented a tool that enables users to script all kind of e-home devices ranging from a MediaCenter PC over PDAs and SmartPhones to toy robots and embedded sensor boards. While abstracting from heterogeneity the tool keeps simple tasks simple and makes complex tasks possible. The graphical editor can entirely be used via the mouse or (preferably) a pen while a keyboard input is not required.

VRDK achieves its high level of abstraction of heterogeneity through a centralized programming approach. Thus, users can add various devices without having to learn how to develop for these devices. With the static location model, the user can specify which devices are available and where they are located. By attaching processes to a set of locations, the user can easily automate tasks that are bound to every room, every floor, or any other kind of location.

We regard the achievements of VRDK as similar to what Visual Basic did for desktop applications. Its simple GUI but powerful engine made it far more popular among our target audience than other complex languages like C++. Our tool features an easy-to-use user interface and is optimized for developing pervasive applications. Still, it is as potent as any other complex language as it supports most of their concepts.

In the future we want to add macro recording to VRDK. That means the user performs a sequence of actions in the real world. VRDK records these actions and creates a script that can replay these actions. Furthermore, we want to integrate GUI support in VRDK. We intend to use XAML (the GUI markup language of Vista's graphic engine Avalon) to specify the appearance of dialogs. Using VRDK, the user will be able to add behavior to the GUI dialogs. Finally, we are working on a VRDK version for Set-Top boxes. Due to its graphical language, VRDK can be used on a low resolution TV. The remaining challenge is to perform basic programming tasks with entertainment controls, such as the MediaCenter PC remote control.

References

1. Kidd, C., Orr, R., Abowd, G., Atkeson, C., Essa, I., MacIntyre, B., Mynatt, E., Starner, T., Newstetter, W.: The Aware Home: A Living Laboratory for Ubiquitous Computing Research. In: Second International Workshop on Cooperative Buildings. (1999)
2. Roman, M., Campbell, R.: GAIA: Enabling Active Spaces. In: 9th ACM SIGOPS European Workshop. (2000) 229–234
3. Addlesee, M., Curwen, R., Hodges, S., Newman, J., Steggles, P., Ward, A., Hopper, A.: Implementing a Sentient Computing System. IEEE Computer Magazine **34** (2001) 50–56
4. Grimm, R., Davis, J., Lemar, E., Macbeth, A., Swanson, S., Anderson, T., Bershad, B., Borriello, G., Gribble, S., Wetherall, D.: System Support for Pervasive Applications. ACM Transactions on Computer Systems **22** (2004) 421–486
5. Becker, C., Schiele, G., Gubbels, H., Rothermel, K.: BASE - A Micro-broker-based Middleware for Pervasive Computing. In: 1st IEEE International Conference on Pervasive Computing and Communication. (2003) 443–451
6. Becker, C., Handte, M., Schiele, G., Rothermel, K.: PCOM - A Component System for Pervasive Computing. In: Second IEEE International Conference on Pervasive Computing and Communications (PerCom'04). (2004)
7. Beckmann, C., Dey, A.: SiteView: Tangibly Programming Active Environments with Predictive Visualization. Technical Report IRB-TR-03-019, Intel Berkeley Research (2003)
8. Sohn, T., Dey, A.: iCAP: An Informal Tool for Interactive Prototyping of Context-Aware Applications. In: CHI '03 Extended Abstracts on Human Factors in Computing Systems, New York, NY, USA, ACM Press (2003) 974–975

9. Dey, A., Hamid, R., Beckmann, C., Li, I., Hsu, D.: a CAPpella: Programming by Demonstration of Context-Aware Applications. In: CHI '04: Proceedings of the SIGCHI Conference on Human Factors in Computing Systems, New York, NY, USA, ACM Press (2004) 33–40

10. Li, Y., Jong, J., Landay, J.: Topiary: A Tool for Prototyping Location-enhanced Applications. In: Proceedings of the 17th Annual ACM Symposium on User Interface Software and Technology, ACM Press (2004) 217 – 226

11. Hong, J.I., Landay, J.A.: SATIN: A Toolkit for Informal Ink-based Applications. In: UIST '00: Proceedings of the 13th Annual ACM Symposium on User Interface Software and Technology, New York, NY, USA, ACM Press (2000) 63–72

12. Humble, J., Crabtree, A., Hemmings, T., Akesson, K., Koleva, B., Rodden, T., Hansson, P.: Playing with the Bits User-configuration of Ubiquitous Domestic Environments. In: UbiComp2003. (2003)

13. Scatterweb: The Embedded Sensor Board (2005) http://www.scatterweb.de/ESB.

14. Grimm, R., Anderson, T., Bershad, B., Wetherall, D.: A System Architecture for Pervasive Computing. In: 9th ACM SIGOPS European Workshop. (2000) 177–182

15. Johanson, B., Fox, A., Winograd, T.: The Interactive Workspaces Project: Experiences with Ubiquitous Computing Rooms. IEEE Pervasive Computing 1 (2002) 67–74

16. Pietzuch, P.R., Shand, B., Beacon, J.: Composite Event Detection as a Generic Middleware Extension. IEEE Network (2004) 44–55

17. Banavar, G., Beck, J., Gluzberg, E., Munson, J., Sussman, J., Zukowski, D.: Challenges: An Application Model for Pervasive Computing. In: MobiCom '00: Proceedings of the 6th Annual International Conference on Mobile Computing and Networking, New York, NY, USA, ACM Press (2000) 266–274

18. Grossmann, M., Bauer, M., Hönle, N., Käppeler, U.P., Nicklas, D., Schwarz, T.: Efficiently Managing Context Information for Large-scale Scenarios. In: Proceedings of the 3rd IEEE Conference on Pervasive Computing and Communications (PerCom2005), IEEE Computer Society (2005)

19. Becker, C., Dürr, F.: On Location Models for Ubiquitous Computing. Personal and Ubiquitous Computing 9 (2005) 20–31

20. Brumitt, B., S., S.: Topological World Modeling using Semantic Spaces. In: Workshop on Location Modeling for Ubiquitous Computing. (2001)

21. Ulbrich, A., Mühl, G., Weis, T., Geihs, K.: Programming Abstractions for Content-based Publish/Subscribe in Object-oriented Languages. In: Confederated International Conferences CoopIS, DOA, and ODBASE 2004. Volume 3291 of Lecture Notes in Computer Science (LNCS)., Larnaca, Cyprus, Springer (2004) 1538–1557

Author Index

Lecture Notes in Computer Science

For information about Vols. 1–3858

please contact your bookseller or Springer

Vol. 3907: F. Rothlauf, J. Branke, S. Cagnoni, E. Costa, C. Cotta, R. Drechsler, E. Lutton, P. Machado, J.H. Moore, J. Romero, G.D. Smith, G. Squillero, H. Takagi (Eds.), Applications of Evolutionary Computing. XXIV, 813 pages. 2006.

Vol. 3906: J. Gottlieb, G.R. Raidl (Eds.), Evolutionary Computation in Combinatorial Optimization. XI, 293 pages. 2006.

Vol. 3905: P. Collet, M. Tomassini, M. Ebner, S. Gustafson, A. Ekárt (Eds.), Genetic Programming. XI, 361 pages. 2006.

Vol. 3904: M. Baldoni, U. Endriss, A. Omicini, P. Torroni (Eds.), Declarative Agent Languages and Technologies III. XII, 245 pages. 2006. (Sublibrary LNAI).

Vol. 3903: K. Chen, R. Deng, X. Lai, J. Zhou (Eds.), Information Security Practice and Experience. XIV, 392 pages. 2006.

Vol. 3901: P.M. Hill (Ed.), Logic Based Program Synthesis and Transformation. X, 179 pages. 2006.

Vol. 3900: F. Toni, P. Torroni (Eds.), Computational Logic in Multi-Agent Systems. XVII, 427 pages. 2006. (Sublibrary LNAI).

Vol. 3899: S. Frintrop, VOCUS: A Visual Attention System for Object Detection and Goal-Directed Search. XIV, 216 pages. 2006. (Sublibrary LNAI).

Vol. 3898: K. Tuyls, P.J. 't Hoen, K. Verbeeck, S. Sen (Eds.), Learning and Adaption in Multi-Agent Systems. X, 217 pages. 2006. (Sublibrary LNAI).

Vol. 3897: B. Preneel, S. Tavares (Eds.), Selected Areas in Cryptography. XI, 371 pages. 2006.

Vol. 3896: Y. Ioannidis, M.H. Scholl, J.W. Schmidt, F. Matthes, M. Hatzopoulos, K. Boehm, A. Kemper, T. Grust, C. Boehm (Eds.), Advances in Database Technology - EDBT 2006. XIV, 1208 pages. 2006.

Vol. 3895: O. Goldreich, A.L. Rosenberg, A.L. Selman (Eds.), Theoretical Computer Science. XII, 399 pages. 2006.

Vol. 3894: W. Grass, B. Sick, K. Waldschmidt (Eds.), Architecture of Computing Systems - ARCS 2006. XII, 496 pages. 2006.

Vol. 3893: L. Atzori, D.D. Giusto, R. Leonardi, F. Pereira (Eds.), Visual Content Processing and Representation. IX, 224 pages. 2006.

Vol. 3891: J.S. Sichman, L. Antunes (Eds.), Multi-Agent-Based Simulation VI. X, 191 pages. 2006. (Sublibrary LNAI).

Vol. 3890: S.G. Thompson, R. Ghanea-Hercock (Eds.), Defence Applications of Multi-Agent Systems. XII, 141 pages. 2006. (Sublibrary LNAI).

Vol. 3889: J. Rosca, D. Erdogmus, J.C. Príncipe, S. Haykin (Eds.), Independent Component Analysis and Blind Signal Separation. XXI, 980 pages. 2006.

Vol. 3888: D. Draheim, G. Weber (Eds.), Trends in Enterprise Application Architecture. IX, 145 pages. 2006.

Vol. 3887: J.R. Correa, A. Hevia, M. Kiwi (Eds.), LATIN 2006: Theoretical Informatics. XVI, 814 pages. 2006.

Vol. 3886: E.G. Bremer, J. Hakenberg, E.-H.(S.) Han, D. Berrar, W. Dubitzky (Eds.), Knowledge Discovery in Life Science Literature. XIV, 147 pages. 2006. (Sublibrary LNBI).

Vol. 3885: V. Torra, Y. Narukawa, A. Valls, J. Domingo-Ferrer (Eds.), Modeling Decisions for Artificial Intelligence. XII, 374 pages. 2006. (Sublibrary LNAI).

Vol. 3884: B. Durand, W. Thomas (Eds.), STACS 2006. XIV, 714 pages. 2006.

Vol. 3882: M.L. Lee, K.-L. Tan, V. Wuwongse (Eds.), Database Systems for Advanced Applications. XIX, 923 pages. 2006.

Vol. 3881: S. Gibet, N. Courty, J.-F. Kamp (Eds.), Gesture in Human-Computer Interaction and Simulation. XIII, 344 pages. 2006. (Sublibrary LNAI).

Vol. 3880: A. Rashid, M. Aksit (Eds.), Transactions on Aspect-Oriented Software Development I. IX, 335 pages. 2006.

Vol. 3879: T. Erlebach, G. Persinao (Eds.), Approximation and Online Algorithms. X, 349 pages. 2006.

Vol. 3878: A. Gelbukh (Ed.), Computational Linguistics and Intelligent Text Processing. XVII, 589 pages. 2006.

Vol. 3877: M. Detyniecki, J.M. Jose, A. Nürnberger, C. J. '. van Rijsbergen (Eds.), Adaptive Multimedia Retrieval: User, Context, and Feedback. XI, 279 pages. 2006.

Vol. 3876: S. Halevi, T. Rabin (Eds.), Theory of Cryptography. XI, 617 pages. 2006.

Vol. 3875: S. Ur, E. Bin, Y. Wolfsthal (Eds.), Hardware and Software, Verification and Testing. X, 265 pages. 2006.

Vol. 3874: R. Missaoui, J. Schmidt (Eds.), Formal Concept Analysis. X, 309 pages. 2006. (Sublibrary LNAI).

Vol. 3873: L. Maicher, J. Park (Eds.), Charting the Topic Maps Research and Applications Landscape. VIII, 281 pages. 2006. (Sublibrary LNAI).

Vol. 3872: H. Bunke, A. L. Spitz (Eds.), Document Analysis Systems VII. XIII, 630 pages. 2006.

Vol. 3871: E.-G. Talbi, P. Liardet, P. Collet, E. Lutton, M. Schoenauer (Eds.), Artificial Evolution. XI, 310 pages. 2006.

Vol. 3870: S. Spaccapietra, P. Atzeni, W.W. Chu, T. Catarci, K.P. Sycara (Eds.), Journal on Data Semantics V. XIII, 237 pages. 2006.

Vol. 3869: S. Renals, S. Bengio (Eds.), Machine Learning for Multimodal Interaction. XIII, 490 pages. 2006.

Vol. 3868: K. Römer, H. Karl, F. Mattern (Eds.), Wireless Sensor Networks. XI, 342 pages. 2006.

Vol. 3866: T. Dimitrakos, F. Martinelli, P.Y.A. Ryan, S. Schneider (Eds.), Formal Aspects in Security and Trust. X, 259 pages. 2006.

Vol. 3865: W. Shen, K.-M. Chao, Z. Lin, J.-P.A. Barthès, A. James (Eds.), Computer Supported Cooperative Work in Design II. XII, 659 pages. 2006.

Vol. 3863: M. Kohlhase (Ed.), Mathematical Knowledge Management. XI, 405 pages. 2006. (Sublibrary LNAI).

Vol. 3862: R.H. Bordini, M. Dastani, J. Dix, A.E.F. Seghrouchni (Eds.), Programming Multi-Agent Systems. XIV, 267 pages. 2006. (Sublibrary LNAI).

Vol. 3861: J. Dix, S.J. Hegner (Eds.), Foundations of Information and Knowledge Systems. X, 331 pages. 2006.

Vol. 3860: D. Pointcheval (Ed.), Topics in Cryptology – CT-RSA 2006. XI, 365 pages. 2006.